# BUSES UNDER FIRE

## NORTHERN IRELAND'S BUSES IN THE TROUBLES

2558

558 EZ

**This book is dedicated to my father, Inspector Jim Collins, and to all the men and women who kept the wheels turning through three decades of the 'Troubles'.**

Michael Collins was born in 1949 and comes from a transport background. His grandfather joined Belfast Corporation as a tram conductor before World War I and retired as an inspector in 1947. In the same year his father joined the NIRTB as a driver, became a conductor and later an inspector under the UTA and Ulsterbus.

In 1967, whilst a student, Michael's father arranged for him to join the newly formed Ulsterbus as a conductor attached to Smithfield depot in Belfast. Michael returned to this holiday job each summer until 1972. He graduated from Queen's University Belfast in that year with a BA in Geography and Political Science and a post-graduate Diploma in Business Administration, later upgraded to an MBA.

On graduation he was offered the post of Personal Assistant to Werner Heubeck, Ulsterbus's charismatic Managing Director. After two years in this job, he moved to a management post in the Health Service before eventually taking up a lecturing position in business and management at the College of Business Studies in Belfast.

Since his Ulsterbus days, he has retained his interest in transport and currently is both a committee member of the Irish Transport Trust, an organisation involved in bus preservation, and chairman of the Downpatrick and County Down Railway, a railway preservation project.

Michael has recently retired from his post as a Principal Lecturer at the Belfast Institute of Further and Higher Education. He is married with four children and lives in Strangford, Co Down.

This is his second book.

Michael Collins

6 5 4 3 2 1

© Michael Collins and Colourpoint Books 2006

Designed by Colourpoint Books,
Newtownards
Printed by ColourBooks Ltd

ISBN 1 904242 34 0

**Colourpoint Books**
Colourpoint House
Jubilee Business Park
21 Jubilee Road
NEWTOWNARDS
County Down
Northern Ireland
BT23 4YH
Tel: 028 9182 0505
Fax: 028 9182 1900
E-mail: info@colourpoint.co.uk
Web site: www.colourpoint.co.uk

Unless otherwise credited, the pictures used in this book are from the author's collection.

**Cover pictures:**

*Front (main picture):  A Belfast Corporation Daimler Fleetline on fire.*
**Alain Le Garsmeur/CORBIS**

**Rear:** *Not much remains of Citybus (Metro) Volvo B7TL double-decker No 2927 (HCZ 9927) at Enfield Street, Belfast on 5 August 2005. The plume of white smoke drifting to the left of the picture is coming from the diesel tank.*
**Paul Savage**

**Title page:** *A fireman tackles the blazing Citybus Daimler Fleetline/ MH Cars No 2558 on the Cliftonville Road on 11 October 1977.*
**Belfast Telegraph**

# CONTENTS

Introduction .................................................................. 5

Historical summary ........................................................ 6

Operating in adversity ................................................... 18

Management's problems .................................................. 61

The Trades Union perspective ........................................ 100

Personal recollections ................................................... 107

The Laganside memorial ................................................ 161

And in conclusion, the legacy . . . ................................... 164

The toll of destruction .................................................. 165

The end of the road....................................................... 180

Bibliography ................................................................ 181

Index .......................................................................... 182

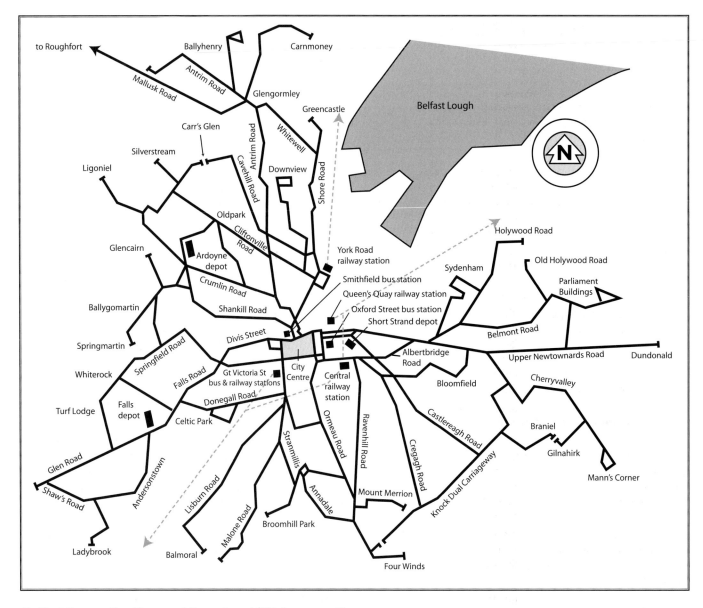

*Belfast Corporation Transport Department/Citybus operating area*

# INTRODUCTION

*I always remember an incident with a policeman. I said to him, "You get danger money, and you get there whenever a riot has already started, whenever you are called into action." I asked him, "Whenever you first go to that riot, what's the first thing you see?" He said, "There's a bus burning." I said, "The bus drivers get it first. The police and the army come next. It's always the bus drivers who are on the front line."*

Denis O'Neill, Citybus driver

In the various episodes of civil unrest that have taken place in Ireland during the twentieth century, public transport has often found itself in the front line. This was the case, for example, during the 1916 Easter Rising when the Dublin tramway system was disrupted and a number of trams destroyed. In one incident, a group of IRA men travelling from Harold's Cross to the seat of the rising at the General Post Office in Sackville (O'Connell) Street, commandeered their tram, but according to some accounts, insisted on paying their fares!

Again, during the Irish Civil War, in the early 1920s, the 'Irregulars' as part of their campaign against the forces of the new Irish Free State targeted the railways, destroying infrastructure, locomotives and rolling stock in various parts of the country. For example, on the Great Southern and Western Railway alone, over 200 signal cabins were destroyed and, occasionally, railway staff trying to effect repairs came under fire.

In Northern Ireland, during the sectarian troubles of the 1920s, there were occasions when crews and passengers had to lie on the floor of their trams when passing streets linking interface communities, to avoid the risk of injury or death from sniper fire. On 24 November 1921, the IRA bombed a shipyard tram in Corporation Street in Belfast killing one man and wounding several others. This attack took place the day following one when there had been 14 deaths, ten of them Catholic. Two days later another shipyard tram was bombed in Royal Avenue, killing a further two men. Trams were also attacked in retaliation for the forcible expulsion of Catholics from the shipyard.

During the IRA's border campaign of 1956–62, the railway network as well as buses were regarded as 'legitimate' economic targets and a number of UTA vehicles were damaged or destroyed.

However, none of the above compares with the level of destruction caused during the current period of civil unrest in the Province. This began in the mid-1960s and, at the time of writing, has not completely ceased. During nearly four decades of the current 'Troubles', bus workers have been injured, or even killed, and hundreds of buses to the value of millions of pounds, as well as depots and other facilities, have been damaged or destroyed. If all the vehicles destroyed between 1964 and 1998 could be lined up nose to tail, they would stretch a distance of around nine miles – in other words, from the City Hall in Belfast to beyond Lisburn or, in London terms, from Westminster to Croydon.

The managers and staff of Ulsterbus, the Belfast Corporation Transport Department, and later Citybus, have had to try to provide transport services to the public of Northern Ireland in conditions not experienced anywhere else in the United Kingdom, with the possible exception of brief periods during the Second World War in British cities subjected to sustained air attack.

The aim of this book is to chart these events, from the loss of the first trolleybus, fleet number 174, in October 1964, to the signing of the Belfast (or Good Friday) Agreement, which marked the end of the main period of civil unrest. To give a complete picture, brief references will be made to the losses of the 1956 IRA campaign, and to those that have taken place since the Good Friday Agreement in 1998.

The book also includes some personal recollections from operating staff and bus company managers of civil disturbance-related events in which they were involved. I must, at this point, thank Ruth Graham for giving permission to use interviews collected as part of the *Routes* project. My thanks must also go to Howard Cunningham, Will Hughes, Irvine Millar and Billy Montgomery of the Irish Transport Trust and Frank Clegg, Jonathan Gardiner and John Montgomery of Translink, for the tremendous work they carried out in identifying the dates when and the locations where so many of the buses were destroyed. If you have any further information/corrections which would help complete the lists then please contact me via the publishers.

Unfortunately, good quality photographs of buses under fire have proved hard to obtain, probably as a result of their destruction during those difficult times, so please accept my apologies now if the pictures reproduced aren't quite of the quality you've come to expect from Colourpoint.

*Michael Collins*
*Strangford*
*May 2006*

# HISTORICAL SUMMARY

In this section, a brief account of the key political developments of the period will be given. Although the main period covered by this book is between 1964 and 1998, a survey of the IRA's 1956–1962 border campaign is included, as well as a brief roundup of the main events since the signing of the 1998 Belfast (or Good Friday) Agreement.

## The IRA's border campaign

Between 1956 and 1962, the IRA mounted an unsuccessful campaign on the northern side of the border. It was given the name *Operation Harvest* and was launched by the IRA's central command in Dublin, to head off the possibility of being upstaged by a breakaway northern group calling itself Saor Uladh (Free Ulster). Saor Uladh had launched an unsuccessful raid on Rosslea police station in November 1955 and attacked six border Customs posts in 1956.

The IRA campaign was designed to achieve ". . . an independent, united, democratic Irish Republic" and the IRA vowed to fight ". . . until the invader is driven from our soil and victory is ours." The IRA did not intend to try and outgun the police and army, but to create support in Ireland for its cause, draw the Republic of Ireland in behind its efforts and so persuade the British to withdraw of their own accord.

*Operation Harvest* commenced at midnight on 11 December 1956. It was to be limited to Northern Ireland although Belfast was not to be touched. Volunteers could shoot at members of the auxiliary police force, the hated 'B' Specials, but not at full time members of the Royal Ulster Constabulary. However, in practice this distinction was ignored. 'Flying Columns' were to be brought into Northern Ireland from all over the Republic for active service. The main tactic was to be that of groups infiltrating the North from over the border and returning to the Republic after their attacks. They would mainly carry out their raids close to the border.

The initial assault was on the BBC's transmitter in Londonderry, which was destroyed; Magherafelt courthouse was burned down; the Territorial Army building in Enniskillen was destroyed and a 'B' Special hut in Newry was set on fire. Mines were also placed on bridges around Lough Erne, but did not cause permanent damage. An attack on the Torr Head radar station was thwarted when the IRA volunteers were arrested before they could blow it up.

The Northern Ireland government, based at Stormont, just outside Belfast, countered by spiking minor border roads and augmenting police numbers with a full call-up of 'B' Specials. In the Irish Republic, President DeValera's government introduced internment in 1957 and this was quickly followed by similar action by the Stormont government.

In spite of the fact that the great majority of Catholics in Northern Ireland remained indifferent to the campaign, it staggered on until early in 1962. IRA targets included railway infrastructure, bus depots, police stations, Territorial Army training centres and Customs posts.

However, by 1958 nearly all the leading activists were interned, in gaol or had been killed. By 1960, all the internees in the Republic had been released and in 1961, the last internee was released in the North.

On 26 February 1962, the IRA called off the campaign. During the period of the campaign, 12 militant republicans and six police officers had been killed, 32 members of the security forces injured, over 200 people gaoled and many hundreds more interned. Economic damage was estimated at £700,000 as well additional security costs to the two governments of £850,000 for the period.

## 1964 The Divis Street riots

After the failure of the 1950s campaign, the IRA, under a new leadership, gave up violence as a means of achieving its political agenda and turned to political methods, adopting a Marxist philosophy. Its objective now was to achieve a 32 county socialist republic by uniting both main communities in Northern Ireland. However, this approach did not cut much ice with the majority of Nationalists who, taking their lead from the Catholic Church, were fervently anti-communist. Needless to say, the Unionist community was not much drawn to it either!

On the mainstream political front, relations between the two Irish governments began to improve. Captain Terence O'Neill, Northern Ireland's Prime Minister, nicknamed 'The Cautious Crusader', invited the Irish Republic's Taoiseach (Prime Minister) Sean Lemass to Stormont. This was followed by a trip by O'Neill to Dublin. However, O'Neill's attempts to improve relations both with Dublin and with the nationalist minority in Northern Ireland started to run aground on the intransigence of certain right-wing unionists, a key figure being the Rev Ian Paisley.

In 1964, a Westminster general election was called. Interest in Northern Ireland was concentrated on the

*Belfast Corporation Guy BTX trolleybus No 174 at Divis Street on the night of 1/2 October 1964.*

constituency of West Belfast, which straddled the nationalist Falls and unionist Shankill Roads. There were four candidates – Republican, Republican Labour, Northern Ireland Labour and Unionist. The Unionist Party feared a Labour victory in London as the Labour Party leader, Harold Wilson, had promised to act to end discrimination against Catholics if he became Prime Minister. Wilson was hoping the Northern Ireland Labour candidate would attract enough Protestants to split the Unionist vote and allow the Republican Labour candidate to win.

At this point Ian Paisley learned that an Irish tricolour was on display in the window of the Republican Party's election headquarters in Divis Street in Catholic West Belfast. Displaying the Irish Tricolour was contrary to the Stormont government's Flags and Emblems Act. On 29 September, Paisley threatened to take a group of his supporters into this nationalist area to remove the flag if the authorities did not act.

Using powers vested in them under the Flags and Emblems Act, the police removed the flag but clashed with local people in the process. Another tricolour appeared in the window on 1 October. The police smashed their way into the premises and removed it too. This act was followed by several days of vicious rioting in which, amongst other damage, a trolleybus was destroyed. The police deployed armoured cars and water cannon and the rioters bricks, bottles and petrol bombs. It was a miracle no one was killed. Other ugly incidents

occurred in Dungannon, Enniskillen and Coleraine. However, overall the violence was limited and ended after a few days.

At the election, the Unionist candidate, Jim Kilfedder was returned for West Belfast.

# 1966 The First Sparks

The year began with some worrying portents. At the start of February, the IRA denied responsibility for a Molotov cocktail attack on a police Land Rover in Andersonstown, in nationalist West Belfast. Other sporadic incidents were to follow over the next weeks and months, including an attack on the Unionist Party's HQ in Glengall Street. In March, in a spectacular night-time attack, Nelson's Pillar in the heart of Dublin city centre was blown up.

The IRA denied involvement in all of these incidents. Although the authorities were convinced that freelance republican groups, unhappy with the IRA's new Marxist political approach, were carrying out the attacks, no one claimed responsibility for them. The fact that the IRA bogeyman was starting to worry some people was reflected in the fact that the *Belfast Telegraph* ran a series entitled 'The mind of the IRA'. At the end of the month, on the other side of the sectarian divide, came an announcement that an Ulster Volunteer Force unit had re-formed in County Tyrone.

Also in February, a major row broke out in the Unionist camp. The ruling Unionist majority on the Belfast Corporation chose the name 'Carson' for a major new bridge being built over the river Lagan. The name selected was in memory of Lord Edward Carson, a founder of the Northern state. It was planned that the Queen would visit Belfast in July and open the new bridge during her visit. However, after the vote in the City Hall, the Governor of Northern Ireland, Lord Erskine, contacted the Town Clerk, expressing concern that the name 'Carson' might cause community division and suggested that the name 'Queen Elizabeth II Bridge' be used instead to " . . . avoid embarrassment to the Queen". This was accepted, but with poor grace on the part of some Unionists.

Other Unionists were angered by the Governor's action, the Orange Order, for example, denouncing the 'Queen Elizabeth' name. The Rev Ian Paisley went further. He organised rallies and brought over Sir Edward Carson's son to review the newly formed Ulster Protestant Volunteers. In March, Carson announced that with the backing of Paisley's Ulster Constitution Defence Committee, he would run against the official Unionist candidate in North Belfast in the 1966 general election. However, great pressure was brought to bear on Carson and Paisley by the Unionist Party machine and Carson backed down. This was seen at the time as a setback for Paisley's political ambitions.

The row amongst Unionists over the name of the bridge was not confined to the City Hall, but spilled over into the Stormont parliament as well. Nationalist politicians added petrol to the flames by letting it be known that they had informed the Governor, before he made his request to the City Hall, that they would be prepared to back the 'Queen Elizabeth' name for the new bridge.

A further complication that year was that it was the fiftieth anniversary of the 1916 Easter Rising in Dublin. Republican ceremonies and celebrations were being organised for Nationalist areas. A large parade was planned to march from Divis Street to Andersonstown. Paisley threatened a counter march. Although the nationalist march would go ahead without any problems, to try to avoid trouble elsewhere, Prime Minister O'Neill mobilised 10,500 'B' Specials, sent helicopters to the border, armed the RUC border checks with armoured cars and machine-guns and stopped trains from Dublin from entering Northern Ireland for 24 hours.

Also in April, the Stormont government issued a warning to 'IRA insurgents' and referred to a 'four-man committee' headed by the prime minister, which had been investigating 'the IRA threat' and went on to say that government forces were in a state of instant readiness. The statement went on to quote from a Minister of Home Affairs' statement the previous December in which he had said that information received by the government indicated that the IRA were planning a renewal of subversive activities against Northern Ireland. This 'warning' can only have added to Unionist paranoia.

In June, Paisley led a protest against the Presbyterian Church's 'Romanising' tendencies. Part of the march passed close to the Nationalist Markets area. Local people tried to block Paisley's march but the police forced it through. The locals threw missiles at the marchers and rioted in the area. Paisley's march proceeded to the Presbyterian Church's headquarters in Belfast city centre where insults were hurled at the Presbyterian Moderator and his guests, who included the Governor of Northern Ireland and his wife. Later, the police fought a battle with rioters in the Markets area into the night. Because of these incidents, Paisley was gaoled on 20 July. The following weekend, having blocked an attempt by Paisley's supporters to march down the Shankill, into the city centre, the police ended up fighting rioting Protestants with baton charges and water cannon.

A more ominous development for the future was linked to the fact that 1966 was also the fiftieth anniversary of the Battle of the Somme where many Protestant members of the original Ulster Volunteer Force had met their deaths. Militant loyalists in Belfast decided to resurrect the UVF and then embarked on a campaign of assassination of Catholics whom they claimed to be republicans.

Because of his attempts to build bridges with the nationalist community in the North and the Irish government in the South, pressure was mounting from the right on Terence O'Neill to leave office. Although one of the most vociferous in this campaign was Ian Paisley, many senior members of O'Neill's own party were also of the same view. Paisley and his followers, shouting, "O'Neill must go!" dogged the Prime Minister at every public appearance. The police even uncovered a UVF plot to assassinate the Prime Minister.

## 1967–68 The Civil Rights Campaign

In 1967, the Northern Ireland Civil Rights Association (NICRA) was formed. Its main tactic, based on that of the civil rights campaign in the USA, was to use street demonstrations to lobby for civil rights in Northern Ireland, changes that would impact more directly on the Catholic population than the Protestant. The Civil Rights movement owed much to the emergence of a Catholic middle class, largely the result of the 1947 Education Act.

In September, Cathal Goulding, chief of the IRA, felt that the IRA's position needed to be re-stated. He said that the movement had no plans for a military campaign ". . . in the near or distant future." He went on to state that the IRA's objective was to follow a political route based on socialism. But the Stormont government did not believe Goulding's protestations. They branded the NICRA as a front for the IRA and banned its marches. The Minister of Home Affairs, William Craig, said that ". . . the NICRA, despite its high-sounding name, is essentially a Republican, Nationalist organisation." He went on to say, in reference to a march he had banned in Derry planned for 5 October, that, "If they (the NICRA) want to hold meetings, it would be proper for them to have them in their own quarter" (ie, not in the city centre.)

The 5 October Civil Rights march went ahead in Derry, in defiance of Craig's ban. It led to clashes between the police and the marchers with 29 arrests and 100 needing hospital treatment. The RUC used heavy-handed tactics to break up the march and much of this was shown on television. It is reckoned now that this relatively new phenomenon of television news coverage helped destabilise Northern Ireland. Sectarian tensions were well and truly re-awakened and London became very worried. The Prime Minister, Harold Wilson, called for a report on the weekend's disturbances. He was not happy with how Stormont was dealing with the civil rights issue in the Province, but, as he was engaged in trying to resolve the problem of Rhodesia's Unilateral Declaration of Independence, Northern Ireland was put on the back burner.

On Tuesday 8 October 1968, the Queen's University Students' Union organised a march from the Union building to the city centre. The march was to be non-violent and non-sectarian. There were about 3000 demonstrators, Protestant and Catholic, and included a number of the university's academic staff. The march was re-directed by the police to avoid a meeting held by Ian Paisley and his followers across the students' route. However, some loyalist demonstrators got to the City Hall before the march and instead of removing them, the police stopped the legal march a few hundred yards away from the City Hall.

The students held a peaceful three-hour sit down protest before returning to a mass meeting at the University where they formed the 'Peoples' Democracy'. The PD announced a programme to campaign for 'one man, one vote', fair electoral boundaries, houses on need, jobs on merit and repeal of the Stormont government's Special Powers Act. The PD was an important addition to the civil rights movement now sweeping Northern Ireland.

The Civil Rights Association expanded rapidly, setting up branches all across the Province, particularly in towns with significant Catholic populations. Programmes of civil disobedience and marches followed and, in October, O'Neill and two of his key ministers, Brian Faulkner and William Craig, were summoned to London by Harold Wilson. Wilson insisted on a package of reforms, which O'Neill announced at Stormont later in the month. Londonderry Corporation was to be replaced by an appointed development commission; sections of the Special Powers Act would be repealed; an ombudsman would be appointed to investigate citizens' grievances; and public housing would be allocated on a points system. However a key CRA demand – universal adult suffrage – would only be 'considered' for local government elections.

The momentum built up by the Civil Rights movement could not be stopped by O'Neill's announcement, significant though it was, and a march planned for November in Armagh was to go ahead. Ian Paisley organised a counter-rally and though police attempted to block him and his followers from the town, he avoided this by entering the town the night before in a convoy of cars. By midday, about 2000 loyalists had occupied the town centre and refused to leave. The Civil Rights marchers avoided confrontation but the police seized considerable quantities of weapons from loyalists who arrived the next day only to be stopped by the police roadblocks.

Also in November, Dublin intervened when the Taoiseach, Jack Lynch, announced that in a united Ireland, the government of the Republic would agree to separate parliaments in Belfast and Dublin.

In December, under pressure from within his own party, as well as from the street protests, Captain O'Neill decided to appeal directly to the Northern Ireland people. In his now famous 'Ulster at the crossroads' speech, he appealed to the civil rights leaders to take the heat out of the situation and give his government time to introduce reforms. After this speech, planned civil rights street protests were called off. However, William Craig furiously attacked O'Neill's speech and was immediately sacked.

At the end of the year O'Neill's position looked strong and a Sinn Féin spokesman in Dublin stated that the Civil Rights movement had achieved more in a few weeks ". . . than decades of IRA activities." However, this optimism would not last long.

# 1969 The Beginning of the 'Troubles'

On New Year's Day 1969, the People's Democracy began a march from Belfast to Derry. Much of its route was through Protestant areas and all along the route Protestant protestors made it clear that they regarded the march as a republican invasion of their territory. However, the march had not been banned, so the police were obliged to protect it. A major ambush was laid for the marchers at Burntollet Bridge, near Londonderry and crowds of men wielding various weapons attacked the marchers. Many were injured as the police provided little protection from the mob. Further trouble resulted in Derry itself and by the end of this period Northern Ireland was once more convulsed with violence.

At the end of April, following a number of loyalist bombings, which initially were blamed on the IRA, Captain O'Neill resigned. Many of his political supporters, believing that the civil rights campaign had turned into a republican terrorist one, had threatened to desert him. However, O'Neill was replaced by his cousin, Major James Chichester-Clarke who declared his intention of continuing with O'Neill's reform programme.

The summer marching season spawned more inter-community violence in Belfast, and elsewhere, reaching a peak in the 'Battle of the Bogside' in Derry after an Apprentice Boys' march on 12 August. A confrontation between local people and the Protestant marchers got out of control and developed into a full scale confrontation with the police, which lasted for two days. The first use of CS gas in Northern Ireland was by the RUC during this battle. However, the police were fought to a standstill by the rioters. The Irish government sent troops to Buncrana, a few miles over the border from Derry, and called for UN troops to be deployed in the Province. Hearing the news, many Catholics took to the streets in provincial towns to take the pressure off Derry by stretching thin police resources even thinner. There was serious trouble in Coalisland, Strabane, Dungannon, Dungiven, Armagh and Newry.

Stormont was forced to turn to London for help and on 14 August, the 'Battle of the Bogside' ended when the first British troops were deployed in Derry. Derry was now calm, but elsewhere the violence had flared, particularly in Belfast. The police were under siege in their Hastings Street station, situated at the bottom of Catholic Divis Street. That night, as the police, followed by Protestant mobs, moved in on the rioters in Divis Street, along the streets linking Divis Street with the Protestant Shankill Road, shots rang out. Within minutes a full-scale gun battle was raging, the police using heavy machine-guns mounted in Shorland armoured cars. Protestant mobs petrol-bombed houses in the streets connecting Divis Street and the Shankill Road. Fierce fighting also erupted in Ardoyne, a couple of miles away in the north of the city.

By the morning six people were dead or dying and over 100 houses and a dozen factories destroyed. Barricades constructed from telegraph poles, paving stones, hijacked buses and other vehicles were erected on the Falls Road. As a result, on 15 August, British troops were also deployed in Belfast. However, they were too thin on the ground to prevent further violence from erupting over the next two nights. Further properties were destroyed and another person killed.

The violence of July and August resulted in ten deaths; 154 people were treated for gunshot wounds and another 745 were injured. Sixteen factories and 170 homes were destroyed, 417 homes damaged and the cost of the damage was estimated at £8 million.

# 1969–71 Internment

Initially, in Catholic areas, British troops were welcomed as protectors against loyalist violence, and so were preferred to the RUC. However the GOC, Lieutenant General Sir Ian Freeland correctly predicted that this honeymoon would not last long – and it didn't. His soldiers were still acting in support of the Stormont government and not on behalf of the Westminster administration. The London government had committed the troops as a last resort and intended to pull them out again as soon as possible. Some parts of Northern Ireland were in virtual rebellion and there were 'no-go' areas where the security forces did not dare enter. Military commanders told the politicians that they could re-take these areas in three hours, but it if they did it would take three years to get out again.

Gradually the army convinced local activists to remove the barricades, which were replaced by white lines, which the security forces would not cross. The

*BCT Daimler CVG No 448 is used as a barricade on Divis Street. It survived but was destroyed at Turf Lodge on 24 January 1974.*

British Home Secretary, James Callaghan, visited the Province in a further attempt to calm the situation. He was well received in Catholic areas, while his statements

in support of the Union helped calm Protestant fears. However, at this point the Labour government planned no major political changes such as abolishing Stormont and returning Northern Ireland to direct rule from Westminster.

On 10 October 1969, it was announced, following the recommendations of the Hunt report, that the 'B' Specials were to be disbanded, the RUC disarmed and a new part-time force (the Ulster Defence Regiment) formed. The UDR would be under army and not police control. An Englishman, Arthur Young, replaced the head of the RUC, with the new title of Chief Constable.

These changes resulted in serious rioting on the Shankill Road in Belfast on Saturday 11 October. The first policeman to lose his life in the current 'Troubles', Constable Victor Arbuckle, was killed in those riots. The army was deployed in support of the police and eventually the rioting abated. Soon after, military police, accompanied by unarmed police, were able to enter the Catholic Lower Falls and the Bogside without opposition.

As 1969 ended, calm had once more descended and hopes for peace rose once again. However, on 29 December, it was reported that there had been a split in the IRA. A dissident group, dominated by northerners had set up what they termed the 'Provisional' wing of the movement. These activists disliked the Marxist path the IRA's Dublin-based leadership was following and were unhappy with the fact that the movement had virtually no weapons available when the violence had broken out in Derry and Belfast. In fact, when the Troubles had broken out in August, the IRA in Belfast was virtually extinct. Even the RUC Special Branch reported that the IRA had been caught unawares by the upsurge in violence and were "... largely unprepared in the military sense".

The Provisionals quickly established themselves in the new Catholic housing estates on the fringes of West Belfast, though for a period the Official IRA retained its hold on the Lower Falls and Markets areas. At first, the Provisionals were small in number and confined to Belfast. In the early months of 1970, they operated with caution since most Catholics still trusted the army. In fact, the army had more trouble with Protestant mobs still smarting from the reforms forced on Stormont by Westminster. However, the Provisionals capitalised on several instances where the army dealt insensitively with Catholic communities, and a steady stream of new recruits began to join their ranks.

However, one particular incident led to a major shift of Catholic feeling against the troops; the Falls curfew. A Conservative government, headed by Prime Minister Edward Heath, was returned to Westminster on 18 June and on 3 July, the army and police raided a house in the Lower Falls and uncovered a large cache of weapons. A massive protest developed and the military high command gave the order for a curfew in the area, which was to last for thirty-five hours. Once the curfew was in place, the army launched a house-to-house search. Both the Provisional and Official IRA opened fire on the army. The troops returned the fire and killed three people with a fourth being killed by an armoured car. This curfew is now regarded as a having been a major political blunder. Following it, hundreds of volunteers joined the Provisionals and the Catholic community's acceptance of the army was replaced with outright hostility.

The summer of 1970 saw a major bombing campaign by the Provisionals and by the end of the summer, there had been hundreds of explosions throughout Northern Ireland. 1970 also saw the beginning of the break-up of the Unionist Party. This was presaged in April by Ian Paisley's by-election victory in Captain Terence O'Neill's old seat. Four days later, the Alliance party was formed. The Social Democratic and Labour Party (SDLP) also came into existence in August of that year.

Looking at the bigger picture, it was clear that the new Heath government in London had no better idea than its predecessors of how to deal with the Northern Ireland problem, other than simply relying on the army to ensure that there was no more than "... an acceptable level of violence".

# 1971–72 The Fall of Stormont

1971 saw violence continuing to grow with serious rioting in January in Belfast, although the violence was not confined to the city. In March 1971 the Northern Ireland PM, James Chichester-Clarke resigned and was replaced by Brian Faulkner who for many years had had ambitions to be Prime Minister. The level of violence continued to escalate through April and May. During June and July, the army was faced with violence from both communities, there being considerable Protestant rioting as well as intercommunal violence during the months of July and August. The SDLP withdrew from government in July in protest at the refusal to hold an official inquiry into the shooting dead by the army of two men in Derry.

On 9 August, internment without trial of republican suspects, a policy Faulkner was very keen on, was imposed in nationalist areas right across Northern Ireland. This was followed by terrible violence. Many now believe that internment was a major blunder, not only because it was entirely directed against one community, but also because it failed to net the leading Provisionals. Many commentators maintain that the army had advised against it and it is now clear that the police intelligence, on which the arrests were based, was hopelessly out of date. Internment was a gamble taken by Brian Faulkner with the acquiescence of the British PM. The days which followed internment were the most violent since August 1969. During August, there were about 35 violent deaths and about 100 explosions. Thousands of Catholics fled over the border and several hundred Protestants moved to Liverpool for safety. Right across Northern Ireland mixed areas disappeared and were replaced by segregated ones.

In September 1969, Ian Paisley called for the creation of a 'third force' similar to the now disbanded 'B' Specials. At the end of the month, he launched his own political party, the Democratic Unionist Party (DUP), as an alternative to the Unionist Party. The Protestant paramilitary group, the Ulster Defence Association (UDA) was set up in the same month.

The Provisional IRA reacted against internment with great ruthlessness. During August, September and October, through the planting of hundreds of bombs, they made a concerted attempt to destroy Northern Ireland's economy. Between internment and the end of the year, 73 civilians, 30 soldiers and 11 policemen lost their lives due to violence.

1972 dawned without much hope of improvement. However, matters although bad, took a serious turn for the worse on Sunday 30 January when paratroopers shot 13 civil rights marchers in Derry. Reaction to what became known as 'Bloody Sunday' was violent and was not confined to Northern Ireland. The British embassy in

Dublin was burned down and the Official IRA bombed the headquarters of the Parachute Regiment in England.

The PM, Edward Heath, had let Faulkner's government take control of security policy in August 1971. Now Heath was convinced that Stormont was incapable of handling the situation. On 24 March 1972, Faulkner and his ministers were summoned to London where they were told by Heath that he intended to transfer control of security, including the RUC to London, end internment and appoint a Secretary of State for the Province. Faulkner and his government refused to accept this and resigned whereupon Heath prorogued the Stormont parliament, replacing it with direct rule from London. Little did he, or anyone else, think, that more than 20 years later, direct rule would still be in place.

In spite of the introduction of direct rule, the Provisional IRA announced its determination to continue its campaign. However, there was a short-lived ceasefire that lasted from 26 June until 9 July. Each side accused the other for its breakdown.

Attacks continued after direct rule was established, the worst by far of which was on 21 July 1972 when 22 bombs exploded in Belfast, including at Oxford Street, Great Victoria Street and Smithfield bus stations. Nine people were killed on a day that became known as 'Bloody Friday'. Three large bombs were set off in Derry and others elsewhere in the Province. A few days later, in an operation named *Motorman*, the army moved in in force to dismantle the no-go areas that had been set up in both republican and loyalist areas throughout Northern Ireland.

## The Power-sharing Assembly

Heath appointed William Whitelaw as the first Secretary of State for Northern Ireland and he set in train a complete overhaul of local government. The contentious area of housing, which had provided one of the initial sparks of the civil rights campaign, was removed from local government and placed under the control of the newly formed Housing Executive. In addition, local councillors would henceforth be elected under a system of proportional representation. Under the reorganisation of local government, Belfast Corporation was replaced by a new City Council with much more limited functions than its predecessor. In the world of public transport, Citybus Limited was created out of what had been the Belfast Corporation Transport Department and given to the management of Ulsterbus to run.

However, the major initiative of this period was the setting up of the Northern Ireland Assembly. This was established after a major conference held in Sunningdale, Berkshire, in December 1973. The British government intended to use this new assembly as a way devolving power once more to Northern Ireland, but under power sharing structures involving both Catholic and Protestant representatives. The other big change was that the new structures were agreed by not just by the Province's party leaders, but also by the British and Irish governments, the first time the Irish state had been formally involved in the political affairs of Northern Ireland. The Chief Executive of the Assembly was to be Brian Faulkner, leader of the Unionist Party and the Deputy Chief Executive, was to be Gerry Fitt, leader of the SDLP. In the middle of December, the IRA signalled its view of the Sunningdale Agreement by detonating six bombs in London.

The Assembly began work at the beginning of 1974. However, the governing body of the Unionist Party, the Ulster Unionist Council, rejected the Sunningdale Agreement. As a result, Brian Faulkner resigned as leader of the party, taking his pro-Agreement group of Assembly members with him. Unionist parties opposed to the Agreement formed a new grouping, the United Ulster Unionist Council (UUUC). In the Westminster general election held in February 1974, 11 of the 12 MPs returned for Northern Ireland constituencies came from the UUUC, the twelfth being Gerry Fitt of the SDLP. Faulkner's group failed to win a single seat.

In Westminster, the same election resulted in Heath's Conservative administration being replaced by a Labour government headed by Harold Wilson. Wilson backed the new assembly, but it was having little success in providing an effective administration for the Province because of a combination of Unionist opposition and IRA and loyalist violence. Matters came to a head in May 1974 when a grouping of Protestant workers, calling themselves the Ulster Workers' Council, organised a strike focused on the Province's heavy industries and power stations. It began on 14 May and, backed by the street muscle of the UDA, quickly spread across Northern Ireland. So many buses were seized in Belfast during this strike to make barricades, that the Citybus withdrew most of its services. To make matters worse the UVF exploded car bombs in Monaghan and Dublin, killing 37 people and injuring over 100 more, mainly in Dublin.

The military chiefs and their political masters in London were unwilling to commit the army to try and restore order on the streets or even to move into the power stations to restore a proper service. As a result, on 27 May Brian Faulkner resigned and the Assembly was finished. It was replaced again by direct rule from London, which would only be brought to an end by the implementation of structures set up under the Belfast (Good Friday) Agreement in 1998.

# The IRA Campaign

These constitutional experiments – the failed Assembly and its successor the Constitutional Convention, an attempt to find an agreed way forward – cut little ice with the IRA. It intensified its bombing campaign with the dual purpose of keeping up the pressure on the security forces and through the destruction and dislocation of commercial life, to persuade the British to withdraw from Northern Ireland. It also started to carry out operations in Britain with the bombing of a military coach on the M62 in February 1974, the Guildford bombing in October 1974 and the Woolwich and Birmingham pub bombings in November 1974. In addition, a vicious campaign was waged between the military and the IRA in nationalist-dominated rural areas, particularly south Armagh where by the end of 1975, 30 soldiers had been killed. This was in addition to a continuous series of tit-for-tat sectarian killings all over Northern Ireland.

Nevertheless, between 1976 and 1977, the security forces had some success in their campaigns both against the IRA and the loyalist paramilitaries. This was reflected in a fall in the number of Troubles-related deaths and bombing incidents. In April 1977, Ian Paisley attempted a re-run of the UWC strike action of 1974, but lack of public support and firm action by the security forces resulted in his 'Constitutional Stoppage' failing totally. Later the Chief Constable was able to declare that 1977 had been the least violent year since 1971.

However, the claim by the Secretary of State, Roy Mason, that the tide had turned against the IRA, proved to be premature. The Provisional IRA's Dublin-based leadership had been replaced by a new northern command that had reorganised the movement into very efficient companies and active service units. Along the border, the IRA also began to adopt the organisational structures and tactics of the SAS units now deployed against them.

In Dublin, the British ambassador was killed in 1976 when his car was blown up. In Northern Ireland, 12 people were killed in 1978 in the La Mon Hotel bombing. This bomb was one of a series of 20 devices that had been set off all over Northern Ireland, targeted at an already reeling tourist industry.

In 1979, there was a series of successful Republican operations against British targets. In March, the British ambassador to the Netherlands was shot dead in The Hague. A week later, Airey Neave, Margaret Thatcher's close advisor and Northern Ireland Secretary of State-apparent was blown up in his car as he drove out of the House of Commons car park. In August, 18 soldiers were killed in a bomb ambush at Warrenpoint and the same day the Queen's cousin, Earl Mountbatten and three others were killed in Co Sligo when Mountbatten's boat was blown up.

The Conservative Party, under Margaret Thatcher returned to power in May 1979. In spite of pressure from the army for a more 'robust' military response, Thatcher, through her Secretary of State, Humphrey Atkins, initially attempted to kick start a new political initiative. However, this got nowhere. To the fury of many loyalists, Thatcher then met with the Irish Taoiseach, Charles Haughey, in attempt to chart a joint strategy out of the political and security quagmire that was Northern Ireland. However the promising start made by this meeting, quickly ran aground on the reef of a new crisis: the hunger strike at the Maze prison.

# The Hunger Strikes

Following the phasing out of internment, the government expected Provisionals at the Maze prison to be held under the same conditions as 'normal' prisoners. The Provisionals refused to accept this and in 1976, in an attempt to be treated as political prisoners, began a 'blanket protest' where they refused to wear prison clothes, followed in 1978 by a 'dirty protest' where they smeared their cells with their own excrement. The IRA also launched a campaign against prison warders and by January 1980, 19 had been killed.

The government refused to meet the Provisionals' demands and in March 1981, the Provisional IRA's commanding officer at the Maze, Bobby Sands, began a hunger strike. During his hunger strike, he was elected MP for Fermanagh-South Tyrone. After 66 days without food, on 5 May, having resisted all pleas to give up the strike, he died. The hunger strike continued and between 12 May and 20 August, nine more hunger strikers died. Riots took place during Sands' hunger strike, erupting with even greater intensity after every death as the Provisionals stepped up their attacks on the security forces.

James Prior replaced Humphrey Atkins as Secretary of State in September. Through contacts in the Catholic Church, he hinted at concessions. On 3 October, the hunger strike was called off. Three days later, it was announced that prisoners could wear their own clothes, in addition to other concessions. During the 217 days of protest, 61 people had died, 30 of them members of the security forces.

Although Thatcher was praised by much of the British press for her 'magnificent obstinacy', the Foreign Office privately held that the whole episode had been a major diplomatic disaster for Britain in the Republic of Ireland and overseas. In addition, in Northern Ireland, the main result of the hunger strike was a spectacular increase in support from within the Catholic community for Sinn Féin, the political wing of the Provisionals. This marked the beginning of the shift of emphasis in the Provisionals' strategy from military to political activity.

# The Anglo-Irish Agreement

In November 1981, Provisional Sinn Féin adopted the approach of contesting elections, while at the same time supporting the IRA's campaign of violence, the 'Armalite and Ballot Box' strategy. The party began to win local government seats and in August 1981, in Fermanagh-South Tyrone, Bobby Sands' election agent, Owen Carron, took the Westminster seat.

In order to cultivate the Catholic vote, the Provisionals began to switch their emphasis away from commercial targets, which cost nationalist jobs, to security forces and political enemies. The Provisionals shot dead the Official Unionist MP for South Belfast, the Rev Robert Bradford, in his constituency office in November 1981. In December 1982 the Irish National Liberation Army, an even more extreme group than the Provisionals, blew up the Droppin' Well pub in Ballykelly, near Derry. This was a pub frequented by troops, and 12 soldiers and five civilians were killed and 66 others were injured.

In the Westminster general election held in June 1983, the President of Provisional Sinn Féin, Gerry Adams, defeated the veteran SDLP MP Gerry Fitt in West Belfast. This new strategy of the Provisionals alarmed the governments in both London and Dublin. It was soon being predicted that Sinn Féin could eventually replace the SDLP as the main nationalist party. As a result, the Taoiseach, Garrett FitzGerald tried to improve relationships with Britain after the disaster of the hunger strike and so encourage Northern Ireland nationalists opposed to violence.

To look for ways forward out of the conflict, FitzGerald set up the New Ireland Forum in May 1983. However, the following year, Margaret Thatcher summarily dismissed all the recommendations contained in the Forum's report, and to make things worse she did it very publicly on television. Unionists, who had refused to take part in the Forum, also rejected its recommendations. In spite of this setback, Thatcher maintained contacts with FitzGerald and the Anglo-Irish Intergovernmental Council, set up in 1981, continued to meet regularly.

In October 1984, the IRA bombed the hotel in Brighton in which Thatcher and most of the Tory top brass were staying during their annual conference. Five people were killed and many others seriously wounded; the Prime Minister was lucky to escape death. However, this incident increased her determination to effect change and in November 1985 the two premiers announced the Anglo-Irish Agreement.

# 1985–91 The search for a solution

The key innovation contained in the Anglo-Irish Agreement was an 'Intergovernmental Conference', headed by the Secretary of State. This would meet regularly to discuss cross-border co-operation and other matters. It would be serviced by a permanent secretariat of civil servants from both Britain and Ireland, which would be based at Maryfield, just outside Belfast. Once approved by the parliaments in London and Dublin, the Agreement would be registered with the United Nations as an international treaty.

The Agreement came as a shock to Unionists. They had not been involved in its construction and, in fact, were convinced that after Margaret Thatcher's 'Out! Out! Out!' outburst dismissing the conclusions of the New Ireland Forum, that a huge gap existed between London and Dublin. In particular, they were appalled that Dublin would now have a formal say in the affairs of Northern Ireland and saw this as a Trojan horse, which would result eventually in a united Ireland. They were also enraged by the fact that although they had not been consulted at any stage in the drawing up of the Agreement, it was clear that the SDLP, through the Dublin government, had had an input. However, the Republicans disliked the Agreement as well. They were only interested in a British withdrawal, not arrangements that facilitated the British remaining in Ireland.

The Unionists determined to oppose the Agreement with all the resources at their disposal. So was born the 'Ulster says No' campaign. However, having learned the lessons of the failure of the Assembly in 1974, the two governments designed this new Agreement to be impervious to Unionist protest. Although a rally in Belfast in November 1985 attracted 200,000 protestors, and in spite of the continuing Unionist protests over the next few years, the Agreement remained in place. A campaign of non-cooperation and civil disobedience by Unionists only led to sporadic episodes of violence and disorder.

By the next set of general elections in London and Dublin, the Agreement seemed to be accomplishing one of its key objectives. In the June 1987 Westminster election, Sinn Féin's vote fell and in the Republic's election held the same year, Sinn Féin failed to win a single seat.

The IRA continued and stepped up its campaign of violence, targeting not only members of the security forces, but civilian organisations having any dealings with them. By the early 1990s, a pattern had evolved of murders carried out by loyalist paramilitaries and the detonation of very large bombs by the IRA. Two in particular are of note, the bombing of the Remembrance Day wreath-laying in Enniskillen in November 1987

*Wright-bodied Mercedes minibus No 840, based at Londonderry, was wrecked in August 1992 when a controlled explosion was carried out on a suspect package left on board. No 840 was subsequently rebuilt to resemble a 1930s charabanc, complete with opening roof. It is anticipated that this vehicle will be operating on the Causeway coast in 2006.*

**Will Hughes**

where 11 people were killed and 63 injured, and a huge bomb planted in the City of London in April 1992. In this attack on London's financial heart, three people were killed, 75 injured and millions of pounds worth of damage caused in damage to property and buildings, several of which were virtually destroyed.

The Anglo-Irish Agreement improved links between Dublin and London and bomb attacks such as that at Enniskillen severely damaged the republican cause. However, it was not all plain sailing for the two governments. Although the Agreement remained intact and operative, relations between London and Dublin suffered a series of setbacks, the greatest of which resulted in March 1988 from the shooting of three unarmed IRA activists in Gibraltar. This was followed in Belfast by an attack on their funeral party in Milltown cemetery by a loyalist gunman, Michael Stone, in which three more people were killed and several injured. Three days later, during the funeral of an IRA volunteer killed by Stone, two soldiers in civilian clothing in a car strayed into an area where mourners were gathering.

When challenged by a steward, they panicked and one of them drew a gun. Assuming they were loyalist gunmen, the men were dragged from their car by the mob, stripped naked and shot dead, all in front of TV cameras, there to record the funeral.

On 23 August 1988, under the terms of the Anglo-Irish Agreement, the Gardai handed over an IRA suspect to the RUC, at the border. This was followed four days later by a second republican suspect. That night in a massive protest co-ordinated by the Provisionals, there was a huge spate of hijackings in West Belfast; Mackie's factory on the Springfield Road was attacked, as was New Barnsley army base. Large scale rioting also took place in Newry, Strabane and Derry.

The Gibraltar killings and the subsequent violence in Belfast, coupled with increasing worry in Dublin about the operation of British justice and security policies in Northern Ireland put a strain on relations between the two governments. However, in spite of all this, the Anglo-Irish Agreement remained intact.

Despite the improvements in London-Dublin relations and the achievements of the Anglo-Irish Agreement, the IRA was still a major force to be reckoned with. There was no sign of when or how Westminster could extricate itself from having direct responsibility for governing Northern Ireland and with the local economy slowly bleeding to death, the cost to the British taxpayer continued to escalate.

## 1992–98 The ceasefires

On 2 January 1992, Secretary of State Peter Brooke announced a new formula for political talks. Once again, an attempt was to be made with local politicians to find a set of constitutional arrangements that might end the violence. A few days later, on 4 January, the IRA responded by exploding an 800lb bomb in the centre of Belfast followed the next day by a 500lb bomb, also in Belfast. Over the next few months, large bombs would be detonated again in Belfast, Lurgan, Bangor and Coleraine. This bombing campaign would continue into 1993 and 1994 and include targets in Britain.

In the Westminster election held on 10 April 1992, as a result of tactical voting by Shankill Road unionist voters, the Sinn Féin leader, Gerry Adams, lost his seat to the SDLP's Dr Joe Hendron.

Brooke's talks eventually began on 29 April. The loyalists began a ceasefire at midnight on 30 April, but republicans failed to respond. When talks broke down in July, the loyalist ceasefire was ended.

During 1993, John Hume, leader of the SDLP, had a series of meetings with Gerry Adams, leader of Sinn Féin, looking for a way to end the conflict. At the same time, the British government was having secret contacts

*The burned-out shell of Citybus (Metro) Scania L94UB/Wrightbus Solar No 803 (UCZ 8803) lies at the side of the road in Cambrai Street, Belfast early on the morning of 14 September 2005. No 803 had been hijacked late on 12 September when running back to depot. At the time of writing it was the last Translink bus to have been burned.* **Paul Savage**

with Sinn Féin. On 15 December 1993, the two premiers, Britain's John Major and Ireland's Albert Reynolds, made a joint declaration inviting Sinn Féin to talks if the IRA ended its campaign. On 31 August 1994, the IRA announced "a complete cessation of military operations." This was followed on 13 October by a loyalist ceasefire.

In November 1995 the US President Bill Clinton, made a triumphal visit to Northern Ireland, but even while he was there, the IRA were moving a bomb to London, having decided to end its ceasefire. The IRA ceasefire ended on 9 February 1996 when the bomb was exploded at Canary Wharf in London.

Violence had returned, but amongst the politicians who continued to work for a solution was a newcomer, former US senator George Mitchell, appointed by Bill Clinton. Talks with all the major parties were set in motion. Initially Sinn Féin was excluded as the IRA's campaign of violence continued. However, it was admitted to the talks after the Provisionals declared a second 'complete cessation of military operations' on 20 July 1997.

# 1998–99 The Belfast (Good Friday) Agreement

In May 1997, a Labour government returned to power. Initiatives begun under the previous Conservative government continued into 1998 under the new Prime Minister, Tony Blair. Headed up by his Secretary of State, Dr Marjorie (Mo) Mowlam, talks continued between the representatives of all the parties. Of the main parties, only the DUP was not represented at the talks as it had withdrawn from them the day after the Provisionals had declared their ceasefire. George Mitchell chaired the talks, and the US President took a close and personal interest in their progress.

Both Tony Blair and his counterpart in the Irish Republic, Bertie Ahern involved themselves to a significant degree in the talks and finally on 10 April 1998, Good Friday, all the participating parties, announced an agreement. A power-sharing, devolved government would be formed and it would include representatives of parties representing paramilitary groups. Their involvement would be

dependant on the maintenance of their ceasefires and a 'decommissioning' of their weaponry. The UDA declared a ceasefire on 14 May followed by the Loyalist Volunteer Force the following day. The UVF had been on ceasefire since October 1994.

In May 1998, the Agreement was approved in a referendum held throughout Ireland, although the margin of approval by Unionist voters in the north was narrow. An Assembly was elected, and an Executive created.

# The Post-Belfast (Good Friday) Agreement period

Since the Belfast (or Good Friday) Agreement was signed, the patterns of direct terrorist attacks on public transport have largely ceased, but not completely. For example, a relatively-new Metro (Citybus) Volvo double-decker, fleet number 2927, was destroyed in the Woodvale area of North Belfast on 4 August 2005 during rioting associated with an internal loyalist feud that was going on at that time, while two buses were hijacked and destroyed, in North Queen Street, Belfast and Conlig, Co Down, over the weekend of 10/11 September 2005 during disturbances following the re-routing of an Orange Order parade in the northwest of the city. A relatively new Scania low-floor bus was also burned in Cambrai Street on 12 September 2005 during the same disturbances.

In addition, the low level violence associated with general hooliganism continues to be a problem; attacks by young thugs using stones, golf balls and catapults firing ball bearings are all too common. These attacks are not specific to public transport but represent a manifestation of the general decrease in law and order some, but not all of which can be laid at the door of more than three decades of the 'Troubles'.

Disagreements about paramilitary weapons decommissioning and policing policy still bedevil the smooth operation of the devolved institutions set up under the Good Friday Agreement. The IRA formally stood down its volunteers in August 2005 and although the loyalist paramilitaries have by and large reduced their military campaigns, violence has not yet been removed completely from the streets of Northern Ireland.

# OPERATING IN ADVERSITY

## Introduction

During the various episodes of political unrest which have afflicted Northern Ireland during its 85 year history, transport services had to be maintained as near normal as possible. In spite of all that was going on around them, bus company managers did their best to run their companies on a day-to-day basis, as well as plan for an uncertain future, while their staff and crews tried to maintain normal levels of service to the public.

In this section, key factors affecting the operation and development of the bus industry during the period covered by the book are identified. However, before dealing with the main phase of the current episode of civil unrest, we will look briefly at two earlier periods which gave Northern Ireland's transport bosses a foretaste of what was to come.

## Prelude: The IRA's 1950s campaign and the 1964 Divis Street riots

### The 1950s Campaign: November 1956 to February 1962

Given the vulnerability of the Ulster Transport Authority's bus fleet at the time, with many buses scattered all over the country in small depots or parked in open yards, and considering the damage that the Ulsterbus and Belfast Corporation Transport Department /Citybus fleets sustained in the campaign which began a decade or so later, the Province's bus services got off relatively lightly during the 1950s IRA campaign. All the attacks took place in rural areas and affected only UTA vehicles. No attacks occurred in Belfast so the vehicles and services of the BCT were unaffected.

The IRA did seriously target public transport, but tended to focus more on the railways, blowing up track, signal boxes and bridges and in one daring action in March 1958, they sent a runaway goods train crashing into the GNR's Foyle Road station in Derry.

In addition to those caused by IRA attacks, further problems for the UTA, Great Northern Railway and Londonderry and Lough Swilly Railway's bus services resulted from government action such as the imposition of local curfews and road spiking.

The first foretaste of trouble took place on Sunday 11 November 1956 when, for the first time in five years, buses travelling between Greencastle, on the northern shore of Carlingford Lough, and Kilkeel were searched by Customs officers. The number of incidents affecting the bus industry increased during 1957. The final attack on a UTA vehicle took place in March 1959 after which the campaign gradually petered out. Brief summaries of these incidents follow.

### 1957

| | |
|---|---|
| 23 January: | A bridge, between Maghera and Dungiven was damaged and closed for a week. For UTA bus services on the Derry–Maghera route, passengers left one bus, crossed the bridge on foot and joined another bus on the other side. |
| 17 February: | Buses were used when two bridges near Carrickmore, on the GNR railway line between Omagh and Pomeroy, were blown up. A shuttle bus service, between Omagh and Dungannon, was put in place. This was a foretaste of many similar incidents on the NIR network, mainly on the Belfast Dublin line, more than two decades later. |
| 29 March: | A fire gutted the UTA's freight and bus depot at Station Road, Dungiven. Five buses and a lorry were destroyed in a blaze that was started in the early hours. Replacement buses were sent from Belfast and Derry. |
| 27 April: | At 11.00pm, an attempt was made to hijack a bus as it made its way from The Battery to Cookstown, in Co Tyrone. Two men were standing at a bus stop and when the vehicle pulled up to let them board, one rushed to the cab and the other to the rear door. The driver was ordered out of the bus at gunpoint. However, he asked to be allowed to move the bus to the side of the road to allow a car to pass and the hijacker agreed. The driver then swung the bus across the road and blocked it, at which point the raiders panicked and fled. The bus continued on its way. |

5 July: An attempt was made to burn a UTA bus near Coagh, Co Tyrone. Several windows were broken and seats set on fire. The vehicle was damaged, but not destroyed. The bus was parked in a privately-owned yard. When the crew came for it before 8.00am, they found the seats smouldering.

13 August: The Newry curfew:

In August 1957 the government imposed an 11.00pm to 5.30am curfew on Newry. This was kept in place for four weeks. Late buses to Rostrevor, Bessbrook and Camlough were cancelled.

10 October: About 11.00pm an attempt was made to burn down Armagh bus depot. Night staff were held at gunpoint by four men while others poured oil over the vehicles and attempted to set them alight. When the raiders left, the staff phoned the fire brigade and then tackled the fire. They had it extinguished by the time the fire brigade arrived and damage was negligible.

*On 29 March 1957, a fire gutted the Ulster Transport Authority bus depot and freight yard at Dungiven, Co Londonderry. Five buses were destroyed; the remains of two can be seen here.*

*A GNR Gardner bus turns at the spikes on the Newry–Omeath road; these were erected in January 1958, by order of the Ministry of Home Affairs at Stormont. To avoid a long detour, the GNR ran its buses to the spikes and then passengers walked to a waiting bus on the other side of the obstruction. The spikes were eventually removed in June 1959.*

*Left:  Leyland PS1 single-decker No B8712 was badly damaged when a bomb was placed in its cab whilst parked at Rostrevor, Co Down, on 7 April 1958. It was repaired and returned to service.*

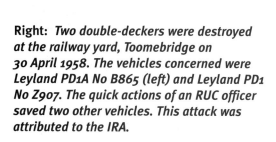

*Right:  Two double-deckers were destroyed at the railway yard, Toomebridge on 30 April 1958. The vehicles concerned were Leyland PD1A No B865 (left) and Leyland PD1 No Z907. The quick actions of an RUC officer saved two other vehicles. This attack was attributed to the IRA.*

This pattern of incidents of 1957 continued into **1958**.

28 January:     The Newry–Omeath–Carlingford road was closed and spiked at the border, by order of the Stormont Ministry of Home Affairs. This was the first closure of an 'approved' border crossing road. The GNR operated six buses each way Monday–Friday with additional services on Saturday. In order to avoid a 20-mile detour, the GNR ran its buses to the spikes and then passengers walked to a waiting bus on the other side of the obstruction. The GNR delivered a protest to the Northern Ireland government via the Dublin government. In September 1958, the company was awarded £475 (about £7000 at 2005 values) compensation against the Ministry of Home Affairs. The spikes were eventually removed from the Newry–Omeath road in June 1959.

4 February:     The Derry–Letterkenny via Killea approved crossing road was spiked by order of the Northern Ireland government. As a result, Lough Swilly buses had to make a four mile detour via Carrigans. The Swilly management stated that if the road remained spiked for any significant length of time, they would have to consider raising fares. In addition, the double-deckers used would have to be withdrawn because of the unsuitability of the diversion route. The company normally carried about ½ million passengers per year on this servce. The use of the Carrigans route would mean alterations in bus schedules and extra mileage.

23 March:       An explosion at Rasharkin in Co Antrim, late on Sunday night, extensively damaged two buses.

**Above:** *The remains of the Ulster Transport Authority Leyland Royal Tiger, No G8983, hijacked and burned at The Battery, near Coagh, Co Tyrone, on 10 May 1958, are seen here at Duncrue Street, Belfast awaiting disposal. One of the double-deckers burnt at Toomebridge can be glimpsed to the right of the picture.*

**Right:** *UTA Leyland PS1 single-decker No B8668 was destroyed in an arson attack at Feystown, near Glenarm, Co Antrim, on 8 November 1958. Locals claimed that this attack was carried out by a disaffected former Ulster Transport Authority employee.*

They had been parked for the night on a piece of waste ground on the Ballymoney Road. A bomb had been placed in the cab of each bus, but only one exploded. This wrecked the engine and damaged the bus generally and the second bus suffered blast damage.

7 April: At 10.50pm a bus parked on waste ground at Rostrevor was badly damaged by a bomb placed in its cab. The front of the bus was wrecked and all its windows blown out.

30 April: Two double-deckers were destroyed in the railway yard at Toomebridge, Co Antrim. Quick action by a policeman, who drove them away, saved another double-decker and a single-decker. The blaze, started amongst the four buses, was discovered shortly after midnight and took the fire brigade 1½ hours to bring under control.

10 May: A UTA Royal Tiger travelling from The Battery to Cookstown, in Co Tyrone, was stopped by a group of armed men near the village of Coagh. They ordered the crew and three passengers off the bus before setting it alight. After this attack, the third in the area, the UTA announced that it was considering suspending the service.

| 17 May: | Following police enquiries into the burning of the bus at Coagh, three men from Cookstown were taken to Belfast prison for detention under the Emergency Powers Act. Altogether, seven men from the Cookstown area were held in jail following intensive police enquiries. |
|---|---|
| 8 November: | A UTA single-decker bus was completely destroyed in the early hours of the morning at Feystown, near Glenarm, in Co. Antrim. The bus, on private hire, was parked outside a dance hall when a fire started. The driver of the bus was sitting in the back seat when he heard glass being broken in the cab. He moved forward to investigate, but as he did so the front of the bus burst into flames. The driver escaped unhurt but the bus was destroyed. (Although officially blamed on the IRA, local people claim that a disaffected ex-UTA employee, who had been seen earlier at the dance, destroyed this vehicle.) |
| 23 November: | The Gardai launched an inquiry into the firing of shots at a UTA bus parked in Clones. The bus had brought about 60 members of the Co Fermanagh Church Lads' Brigade to a service at Clones parish church. It was parked outside the church when seven bullets were fired into it, smashing windows and damaging the bodywork. |

By the end of 1958, the IRA's campaign had almost run out of steam so there was only one incident in 1959 which affected the UTA.

**1959**

| 14 March: | Three masked men set fire to a UTA bus in Crossmaglen, Co Armagh on the night of 13–14 March. Police said that three masked men ordered two passengers who were sitting in the bus to leave before pouring inflammable liquid inside and setting fire to it. The police extinguished the blaze. The outbreak was confined to the back seat and little damage was caused to the vehicle. |
|---|---|

# *The 1964 Divis Street riots*

A short foretaste of the type of mass street disturbances that was to become common a few years later was experienced in Belfast during the few days of the Divis Street riots of September/October 1964. Many of the ingredients that would later combine to cause the huge explosion of the 'Troubles' were present in those few days of civil unrest, which took place during a Westminster parliamentary election campaign.

Tuesday 29 September:

> After the Rev Ian Paisley threatened to lead a march of loyalists up Divis Street to remove an Irish tricolour from the Republican Party's election office, the government instructed the police to confiscate the flag under powers contained in the Flags and Emblems Act. When the police removed the flag, rioting crowds brought traffic virtually to a halt. Missiles were thrown at passing buses and other vehicles. During several hours of rioting, trolleys were pulled down from a passing trolleybus and crowds hammered the sides of buses caught up in the traffic jams. Bus crews took unofficial strike action and for a short period refused to go near Divis Street because their buses were being attacked.

Thursday 1 to Wednesday 7 October:

> The confiscated tricolour was replaced by a new one, and on the afternoon of 1 October, police moved in and removed this second flag, also by force. Renewed rioting, where the crowds kicked the sides of passing buses, followed this incident. Serious rioting took place on the night of 1/2 October. During these riots, trolleybus No 174 was hijacked and an attempt made to set it on fire.

> Despite loudspeaker pleas from the Republican Party calling for the rioters to disperse, the crowd remained. Each time they were asked to leave, they stepped up their attacks on buses, cars and the police. Trolley replacement poles were taken from trolleybuses and used as weapons. About 1.00am, a second attempt was made to set fire to No 174, but firemen extinguished the blaze. However the bus was so badly damaged, it never went back into service.

> The UTA re-routed its buses away from the Lower Falls on 2 October, but the Corporation issued a statement that they would try and maintain services. Further rioting took place on 3 October, with more attacks on passing buses. In one of these attacks, a rock was thrown at a bus, broke a window and injured a passenger. After windows had been broken on two buses, trolleybus services on the Falls Road were withdrawn.

> By 6 October, the riots had petered out and bus services were finally restored the following day.

*The remains of three buses – a BCT Daimler Fleetline, a BCT Daimler CVG6 and an Ulsterbus Leyland PD2 (right) – destroyed on the Falls Road. Research indicates that the date is March 1971 and the vehicles concerned are, left to right, BCT Nos 697 and 362 and Ulsterbus No 696.*

# The 'Troubles' 1968 to 1996

## Introduction: 1968–70

Saturday 5 October 1968:

> This date is considered by many as the start date of the recent Troubles. A civil rights march in Derry, organised by members of the Derry Housing Action Committee and supported by the Northern Ireland Civil Rights Association was stopped by the Royal Ulster Constabulary before it had properly begun. The RUC then broke up the march by baton-charging the crowd, injuring many people, including a number of MPs. This was all filmed and there was world-wide television coverage of the event.

> Following this incident there were two days of serious rioting in Derry between the Catholic residents of the city and the RUC. This unrest then spread to other nationalist areas in Northern Ireland. The genie was out of the bottle!

During this period, these were the type of incidents that increasingly were reported in the media:

**1969**

23 April:       Buses caught up in Falls Road rioting.

2 September:   Riots and barricades on Protestant Donegall Road.

27/28 September:

> Riots on the Shankill Road after the Hunt report on the future of the RUC. A bus was commandeered at Townsend Street.

*Buses were frequently hijacked and used as barricades. Belfast Corporation Harkness-bodied Guy Arab III No 286 was used to block Thompson Street, in the Short Strand area of the city. Fortunately, No 286 survived this incident and is now preserved. Although undated, this photograph must date from around 1969, as No 286 was withdrawn from service in 1970.*
**Jonathan Miller collection**

By 1970 the Troubles were really biting and their impact was being felt in two important ways. Firstly, with the lurid TV coverage of street rioting in Northern Ireland's towns and cities, tourism was beginning to suffer and tour operators were starting to cancel their operations in the Province. Secondly, on the operational side, falling passenger numbers were driving down revenue and forcing transport operators to increase fares to try and make ends meet. With the BCT's financial situation deteriorating, there were also the beginnings of speculation on a possible merger of Ulsterbus and the Transport Department.

Here, I want to give an overview of some of the matters that transport managers and workers had to deal with. I have divided these into 'Troubles-related' issues and 'Organisational' issues. Because of the sheer volume of material, I have only been able to illustrate each area with a few selected examples.

**Troubles-related issues:**

| | | |
|---|---|---|
| Killings and injuries on buses | Rioting and hijackings | Threats from paramilitaries |
| Some close shaves | Effects on tourism | Robberies |
| Depot bombings and bus burning | Bus stoning and vandalism | |

**Organisational issues:**

| | |
|---|---|
| Corporate reorganisations | Operational issues |
| Impact of government transport policies | Industrial disputes |

# Troubles-related issues:

## *Killings and injuries on buses*

Over the years of the Troubles, a number of people were killed or injured either on buses, transport property or while waiting at bus stops. On some occasions the killings were deliberate, targeting busmen or passengers for various reasons. On other occasions they were accidental. Injuries suffered by passengers and bus workers ranged from the very serious to minor.

Elsewhere in this book is a section devoted to the busmen who lost their lives, but here I have included what I hope is a representative sample, drawn from just between 1972 and 1977, of the dozens of incidents of death and injury which occurred during the Troubles. I have also included a few detailed examples of some of the more serious incidents which made the news.

### 1972

18 January: In East Belfast, armed men shot a BCT bus driver, Mr Sydney Agnew (40) dead in his home. The police said that he was not a member of the security forces and knew of no apparent motive for his killing. The dead man was to have appeared as a witness in a case involving the hijacking and burning of his bus, which was due for hearing later in the week. The deposition of the murdered man was used in court on 20 January when three men were imprisoned for the destruction of the bus. The killing of Mr Agnew was given as a reason for abolishing juries in Troubles-related trials and so influenced the decision to set up the no jury 'Diplock' courts.

11 February: A woman was injured by a bomb thrown from a car at the BCT canteen in May Street, Belfast.

16 February: In Derry, a 47-year-old Catholic bus driver, Thomas Callaghan from Limavady, a member of the UDR was shot dead. As he drove his bus through the Creggan estate in Derry, he was taken from his bus by a group of gunman. Three hours later his body was found hooded with his hands tied behind his back; he had been shot through the head.

29 March: A 35-year-old woman, Mrs Ruby Johnston, from near Newtownhamilton, who was severely burnt in a petrol bomb attack died from her injuries. Mrs Johnston died two months after the bus she was travelling in was attacked by a republican mob. A petrol bomb thrown into a bus had landed in her lap before exploding. The bus was en route from Armagh to Newtownhamilton when it was attacked in Lower Irish Street, Armagh. Two petrol bombs were thrown through the windows and Mrs Johnston was set alight when the front part of the bus, where she was seated, went up in flames. The driver carried her out and with the help of some young men put out the flames. Other passengers on the bus were able to escape through the bus's emergency door.

7 April: Peter Sime (22), a soldier in the Kings Own Scottish Borderers, and based in the joint army/police post in the Henry Taggart Memorial Hall in Ballymurphy was shot dead by an IRA sniper. A BCT bus was travelling up the Springfield Road when it was stoned and had a window broken. The driver stopped the bus outside the Henry Taggart Hall to allow his conductor to go in and report the incident. L/Cpl Sime came out of the base to talk to the conductor and while they were talking, L/Cpl Sime was shot.

21 May: On Sunday, a hijacked bus taken from the Carr's Glen terminus went out of control on the Ballysillan Road, slewed across the road and hit a pole which fell on 46-year-old Richard Oliver outside his home, killing him. The bus driver had been told he would be shot if he didn't hand over his bus.

26 June: During an armed robbery on the post office in Pettigo, the postmaster and a bus driver, who was mistaken for a policeman, were shot and wounded.

26 July: Two soldiers were shot and wounded as they went to investigate the hijacking of a Corporation bus in the New Lodge Road area of Belfast.

10 October: Sixty-seven-year-old Robert McKenna was killed when a bus driver lost control of his bus on the Glen Road in Belfast. The driver was knocked unconscious after being stoned by a crowd of about 20 teenagers. Mr McKenna was pinned under the bus which went out of control and veered off the road.

8 November: Joseph Kelly, a 47-year-old man from Turf Lodge was shot dead while coming home from work by

bus. Mr Kelly worked in the Hughes Tool factory on the Castlereagh Road. When the bus he was travelling on reached Castlereagh Street, it was flagged down by two men. One man ran upstairs while the other stood guard over the driver on the pavement. The man upstairs shot Mr Kelly at least six times with a pistol. There was only one other passenger on the bus at the time of the shooting. The driver then drove his bus to a nearby army post to raise the alarm.

31 December:   In Belfast, a bus was stopped on the Springfield Road by a man waving a flag. When it halted gunman fired about 18 shots into it wounding four people.

## 1973

1 February:   One man, Mr Patrick Heenan (50), was killed and nine others injured in a hand grenade attack on a workmen's bus in Cherryvalley, Belfast. The men, all Catholics, were working on the new St Patrick's school at Kingsway Gardens. According to the passengers, a limping youth walked across the road in front of the bus forcing it to slow down, a second man then threw a brick through a window of the bus while a third man threw a hand grenade through the broken window. The killing of Mr Heenan precipitated the first internments of loyalists.

2 March:   A BCT bus driver, Patrick Crossan (30), a Catholic, was shot dead at the wheel of his bus in the Woodvale Road area. All BCT transport was brought to a halt by the decision of bus crews to stay off work until after the driver's funeral. Ulsterbus services stopped running in the evening.

10 June:   A 50-year-old bus driver, Samuel Rush, a Protestant from Newtownards, was shot dead while driving his Ulsterbus on the Albertbridge Road in East Belfast. His bus was caught in gunfire from loyalist gunmen firing at troops. About a dozen passengers had a narrow escape because with the driver dead, the bus crashed into a Saracen armoured car at an army checkpoint. Bus services in the Ards Peninsula were affected on 13 June when bus crews held a 24 hour strike in order to attend Mr Rush's funeral.

9 July:   Dorothy Lynn (46), who had been badly burned when a bus was set on fire on the Cliftonville Road, died in hospital in Belfast. The attack had taken place on 4 July when seven buses, as well as several lorries, were hijacked and burnt in North and West Belfast. Gunmen boarded the bus on which Mrs Lynn was travelling (No 2863), took the driver's money, sprinkled inflammable liquid around the lower deck and then set the bus alight. Unable to get down the stairs for the smoke and flames, passengers on the top deck escaped by breaking a window. However, Mrs Lynn was unable to escape.

## 1975

20 January:   Twenty-one year old IRA volunteer Kevin Coen, a native of Sligo, was killed at Kinawley, Co Fermanagh in an attempted bus hijack at the border. He was one of a group of four men trying to hijack a CIÉ bus travelling between Dublin and Donegal. The bus was on the northern side of the border, on the road between Enniskillen and Swanlinbar, when the attempted hijacking took place.

*On 4 July 1973 Citybus Daimler Fleetline No 2863 was hijacked and set on fire on the Cliftonville Road, Belfast. Mrs Dorothy Lynn was badly burned and died several days later.*

Mr Coen was shot by a soldier travelling with a group of other soldiers in an unmarked civilian car. Passengers on the bus had to dive for cover, but there were no injuries.

2 May:  A Citybus inspector, Alexander Millar (54) was shot in Ardoyne bus depot. Two men entered the depot, confronted Mr Millar in an office and then shot him three times. He died later in hospital. Mr Millar was described as a 'captain' in the UDA in newspaper death notices.

July 12:  An Ulsterbus was stoned on the Ormeau Road and the driver's window was smashed. He lost control of the bus and a pedestrian was struck. When the driver went to his assistance, he was set upon by a crowd and beaten up and had to be taken to Dundonald Hospital for treatment.

The same day, a bus in East Bridge Street was also stoned by a mob and a passenger injured.

## 1976

21 January:  Gunmen ambushed a South Eastern Education and Library Board school bus in Co Tyrone which was being driven by an RUC reservist. A bullet grazed his arm, and two girl passengers escaped uninjured.

25 January:  David McDowell (26), an Ulsterbus driver, a Protestant and member of the UDR was shot dead at an army observation post at Middletown, near the Armagh–Monaghan border. Mr McDowell had stopped his bus at the army post and was talking to soldiers, when one of them accidentally discharged his gun, killing the busman.

17 June:  Two men, Brendan Meehan (48) and Gerard Stitt (21), were murdered by two gunmen on the upper deck of a bus travelling down the Crumlin Road. Both men were from Ligoniel and were travelling separately when they were shot. The bus was driven to the nearby Mater Hospital, but the men were dead on arrival.

13 September:  The driver of an Ulsterbus was burned about the face and hands when a gang set fire to his vehicle at Station Road, Greenisland. Police said at least one of the gang was armed.

## 1977

10 May:  A Protestant Citybus driver, Harry Bradshaw (46), was murdered by two gunmen on the Crumlin Road during the UUAC strike.

20 May:  School bus driver and RUC reservist, Robert North (52), was killed near Benburb in Co Tyrone. He was driving his bus at the time and was on his way to collect children. His bus was hit by 15 bullets.

2 June:  A Citybus driver was attacked with a knife by two passengers at the Cregagh terminus. They slashed the driver's arm and he had to be taken to hospital.

27 August:  A bus driver had to have nine stitches in his head after being forced to jump out the side window of his burning, hijacked bus. Two youths boarded the bus on the Crumlin Road and then set it on fire.

12 October:  A Western Education and Library Board school bus driver was shot dead in an ambush near Ballygawley

*13 May 1977 and bus crews are attending the funeral of Driver Harry Bradshaw who was shot three days earlier whilst driving his bus on the Crumlin Road during a loyalist strike.*

in Co Tyrone. The driver, Frank Canavan (47), a Catholic, was shot dead in mistake for a colleague, a member of the UDR, who should have been driving the bus but who was off ill that morning. A bullet grazed a schoolgirl passenger, the only other person on the bus at the time. The gunmen then hijacked a second school bus, which had arrived at the scene and drove off towards Carrickmore. They forced the bus driver to pull across the road in front of a car which they then hijacked and which was later found abandoned about six miles away.

## More detail on some of the incidents

### 25 January 1976: The death of driver David McDowell

In January 1976, a soldier at an army checkpoint accidentally shot Driver McDowell dead in his bus.

The Ulsterbus was halted at the Middletown border checkpoint when the shooting occurred. Three hours before the fatal shooting, the military post had come under attack from gunmen operating from across the border. A part-time member of the UDR, David McDowell had, on a previous occasion, survived an IRA ambush in which he was slightly injured. His empty bus, en route from Monaghan to Armagh, pulled in at the checkpoint and two soldiers got on board. He was shot as he sat behind the wheel talking to one of them. The soldier involved thought he had 'cleared' his weapon after the earlier battle.

### 17 June 1976: Murder on the Crumlin Road decker

In June 1976, one of the most cold-blooded murders of the Troubles was perpetrated on two Ardoyne men travelling on a bus down the Crumlin Road.

The two Roman Catholic men were Brendan Meehan and Gerard Stitt. They had boarded the city-bound bus near Ardoyne and had been sitting on the upper deck, on opposite sides of the vehicle. Two gunmen in the bus shot them in the head from behind. The driver heard the shots and thinking the bus had come under attack, accelerated his vehicle. The two killers came downstairs and ordered him at gunpoint to stop before jumping off. The driver drove his bus immediately to the Mater Hospital. However, both victims were found to be dead on arrival.

### 10 May 1977: The murder of driver Harry Bradshaw

One of the worst episodes associated with the Troubles was the murder of Citybus driver Harry Bradshaw at the wheel of his bus on the Crumlin Road during the 1977 UUAC strike. Harry, a married man with young children and a Protestant, had worked for Citybus for five-and-a-half years.

His murder was a blatant attempt to intimidate bus drivers into stopping work during the loyalist strike. Later his wife spoke about his death. Mrs Bradshaw said her husband had shown ". . . a quiet determination to go to work and get others to work" in the face of the Loyalist bullyboys.

Her husband had been threatened with kneecapping by republicans on one occasion when he worked on the Turf Lodge route. But on the Monday of the week he was shot, a woman passenger had hit him over the head with her umbrella when he drove a bus down the Shankill Road because he hadn't stayed off work and joined the loyalist strike.

Mrs Bradshaw said her husband was a true Ulster loyalist. He wouldn't stop working on the orders of the UUAC. Loyalty for Harry, she said, was doing a day's work and paying his taxes. He was loyal, she said, not only to the Queen and country but to his family as well. He had to work to support them.

"I can't blame Mr Paisley for what has happened, but I can't say he's free from blame either" she said.

### 5 September 1979: Attempted murder of Citybus passenger

On Monday 27 August 1979 the IRA struck twice. In one bomb attack they killed a large number of soldiers travelling in a convoy near Narrow Water Castle on Carlingford Lough. In a second bomb attack, on the other side of Ireland, they killed the Queen's cousin, Lord Mountbatten, and several of his party who were out sailing on his motor cruiser.

On 5 September, the day of Lord Moutbatten's funeral, an attempt was made to kill a young man as he travelled to work by bus. It is worth noting that this attack took place in an area where there had been a number of actual and attempted murders on buses, including that of Driver Harry Bradshaw.

The young man, John Smylie (21), was a married man from Ardoyne. He was shot three times in the face and back by a gunman who boarded the bus at the junction of the Oldpark Road and Manor Street.

Another passenger described what happened. The bus came to a halt and two men got on board. One of them remained at the cab but the second man, wearing an anorak and a balaclava helmet and who had a revolver made straight down the bus towards Mr Smylie who was about three seats from the rear. The driver shouted for everybody get down but the gunman took no notice. He opened fire on Mr Smylie from about three feet away. It was all over in a few seconds.

An acquaintance of the wounded man said that he boarded the bus opposite the Sacred Heart church and the gunman probably knew that anyone getting on there was likely to be a Catholic.

## *Some close shaves*

3 October 1972: A bus driver at the Braniel terminus found a fountain pen on his bus. The pen was booby-trapped and exploded when lifted. When it exploded, three-inch tacks were fired into the roof of the bus. Afterwards, police issued a warning against touching any suspicious objects found in public places.

30 May 1973: Passengers had a narrow escape on a bus hit by gunfire aimed at troops in East Belfast. Later a bullet was discovered lodged in the bus.

10 February 1978: Eight children and a bus driver had a lucky escape when a bomb attached to their bus fell off and detonated harmlessly between Ballymoney and Rashsharkin. The driver was a member of the UDR.

8 August 1980: During internment anniversary riots in Derry, an Ulsterbus operating on the Lone Moor Road was hijacked by four youths. Two of them drove the bus down Westland Street and jumped off the vehicle as it gathered speed. It crashed into a concrete pillar and an electricity distribution cabinet

*Daimler Fleetline double-deckers Nos 2804 and 2821, an unidentified Alexander-bodied single-deck Daimler Fleetline and ex-London Transport AEC Swift No 77 (ex-SMS 429) were destroyed along with 15 other vehicles in an attack at Citybus' Falls Park depot on 1 February 1980.*
**Belfast Telegraph**

*Twenty-six vehicles were destroyed in a firebomb attack on Armagh's Ulsterbus depot on 27 April 1982. Three of the five Leyland Leopards in this line-up can be identified. From left to right we can see Nos 514, 515, ?, 1545 and ?. The destruction of 26 vehicles in this attack was the biggest, single loss in the numerous attacks which were perpetrated on the depots of Ulsterbus and Citybus during the Troubles.* **Belfast Telegraph**

before coming to rest against the door of a house. None of the residents were injured, but an elderly woman was having breakfast, ". . . when the bus suddenly appeared in the front door." She had to be treated for shock.

The removal of the bus was delayed because of the danger from the damaged electricity cabinet, but when it was being towed away by an army unit who were assisting the Ulsterbus officials, youths stoned the bus and smashed its windows.

## Depot bombings and bus burnings

### Depot bombings

Ulsterbus and Citybus depots were a constant target for the terrorists during the period of the Troubles, and continue to be so to a lesser extent right down to the present time. Few depots escaped attack and most of the important ones were hit repeatedly over the years. Generally, attacks were designed to cause damage and destruction to property, but from time to time injuries or deaths resulted.

The attacks on Falls Park depot on 1 February 1980, when 19 buses were lost, on Ardoyne on 29 February 1980, where 21 buses were destroyed and Armagh on 27 April 1982, where 26 were destroyed, constituted the greatest vehicle losses suffered in single bombing incidents.

Opposite is a sample of incidents from two of the worst years of the Troubles, 1972 and 1973.

**1972**

2 January:       Kilrea bus depot was slightly damaged by fire in the early morning.

31 January:     Two single-deck buses and one double-decker were destroyed by fire at the Ulsterbus depot in Magherafelt following a heavy explosion.

27 February:   Four single-deck buses were set on fire in Dromara, Co Down. They were parked in an overnight parking area behind the local police station. Two buses were saved and two were destroyed.

4 March:        A bomb exploded at the Falls Park depot. It had been smuggled into the depot, which was also an army base, in a busman's ticket machine box.

22 March:       A car bomb exploded in the car park behind Great Victoria Street bus/rail station in Belfast. Eighteen people, mostly in the Europa hotel, were injured. Most of the glass panels in the station's roof were blown off and two trains and the bus departure area were wrecked. A second, smaller bomb went off about ten minutes later. This seems to have been designed to hit the security forces who had moved in to examine the area. However this bomb caused no injuries.

13 April:        A 50lb bomb wrecked a considerable part of Ulsterbus's Smithfield depot in Belfast. Five buses were destroyed and twenty damaged and buildings were wrecked, but there were no injuries. Two armed men, who told the employees that they had twenty minutes to get out, placed the bomb. Fifteen minutes later it exploded, wrecking the centre of the shed where the buses were parked.

*Great Victoria Street bus and rail station was itself bombed on 27 March 1972, a few days after the incident noted above. Northern Ireland Railways BUT railcar No 133, which had been new to the Great Northern Railway in August 1958, lies wrecked in the station.*

*Damage was also caused to the departure stands in the adjacent bus station, although services were operating as normal when this photograph was taken shortly after the attack. At stand 2, a Leyland Tiger Cub can be seen loading for a journey on service 26 to the Co Down village of Dromara.*

| 18 April: | Three small bombs were thrown into Short Strand depot from Anderson Street. Two buses were damaged. |
|---|---|
| 19 April: | For the second night in succession, two bombs were thrown into Short Strand depot. One bus was damaged in the attack. |
| 26 April: | The army defused two 40lb bombs at Smithfield bus station. They had been left as parcels on a lorry parked in West Street. The depot and the surrounding area were evacuated for most of the day while the bombs were made safe. |
| 28 April: | Six buses were destroyed in a fire that followed two explosions in Claudy. The buses had been parked in an open yard. |
| 1 May: | An attempt was made to smuggle a bomb into Falls Park depot, where troops were billeted, on board a bus. However, a sentry making a routine search found two suspicious packages under the back seat. He ordered the driver to take the bus out of the depot. A 10–30lb bomb later exploded. |
| 20 and 21 May: | Two buses were taken from Carrickfergus Ulsterbus depot. One was destroyed by fire on the Marshallstown Road but attempts to set fire to the other, at Greenisland, failed. |
| 28 May: | Eight people, six men and two women, were killed in an explosion in Anderson Street, beside Short Strand depot, when an IRA bomb exploded prematurely causing massive devastation. Four IRA members were killed in the blast. Debris and body parts were later found in the depot by staff on night duty. (An eye-witness account of this incident appears in the 'Personal Recollections' section.) |
| 26 June: | A bomb that had been planted by two armed men wrecked part of the Ulsterbus office at Edward Street, Newry. |

21 July: Bloody Friday:

| 2.10pm: | A car bomb explodes at Smithfield bus station. Many buses damaged but no injuries. |
|---|---|
| 2.23pm: | A suitcase bomb explodes at York Road railway station causing extensive damage but no injuries. |
| 2.48pm: | A car bomb explodes at Oxford Street bus station. Six people are killed and 40 injured. One Ulsterbus employee casualty was Tommy Killops, killed in the parcels office beside where the bomb went off. Depot Manager Jack Campbell, who was standing beside the car that contained the bomb when it went off, was stripped naked by the blast, blown on to the roof of the depot and was seriously injured; the soldier he had been talking to was blown to pieces. |
| | Those killed in the Oxford Street bomb were: |
| | Stephen Cooper (19), soldier; Philip Price (27), soldier; William Crothers (15), Ulsterbus employee; Robert Gibson, (45), Ulsterbus employee; William Irvine (18), Ulsterbus employee; Thomas Killops (39), Ulsterbus employee. |
| 2.48pm: | A bomb hidden in a van exploded in the upper yard at the Great Victoria Street bus/rail station. Four buses were wrecked and 44 damaged. |

**21 July 1972:    Blasts at Belfast's bus stations**

Blasts at Smithfield, Oxford Street and Great Victoria Street depots: One of the worst depot bombing incidents of the Troubles took place on 21 July, a day that has since become known as 'Bloody Friday', when the IRA launched a series of bomb attacks in Belfast's city centre. The security forces were overwhelmed and were unable to clear some of the sites, resulting in many civilian deaths.

All three of Belfast's Ulsterbus depots were bombed, with a considerable loss of life resulting from the Oxford Street bomb. No one was killed in the blast at Smithfield, but a soldier and a girl were injured by the Great Victoria Street bomb. However, the worst casualties occurred at Oxford Street depot where six people were killed and many more injured.

The Oxford Street bomb had been planted in a stolen Volkswagen estate car and it left seven people dead and dozens injured. Witnesses later described how badly mutilated bodies were flung yards away by the blast: how two soldiers were blown to pieces seconds after they had stepped from their armoured personnel carrier when the bomb exploded: and how frightened bystanders had no time to get clear before the blast.

Witnesses said the two soldiers who died had just got out of their vehicle when the bomb went off. The bus station was devastated. The bomb had been placed beside the depot manager's office. It destroyed the nearby cafeteria and glass and debris was scattered everywhere. Police and troops had to collect the mutilated bodies in plastic bags. Some body parts were flung up to 30 yards away by the blast. A fleet of ambulances took the injured to hospital and fire appliances were needed to fight the blaze which followed the blast.

There was extensive damage at Smithfield depot where 30 buses were badly damaged. As with the other bombs that day, the bombers gave little warning of their intentions. An inspector said that the first warning he got that there was a bomb was when a couple of young people shouted in to his office that they had been told to warn him that a bomb had been planted. The bomb was in a green BMC 1100 car. It went off about half an hour later, but everybody had been got clear. The force of the explosion tossed a large section of the corrugated iron roof into the street below. Heavy metal doors placed across the depot entrance after a previous bomb attack were lifted off their hinges and hurled into the street. The garage was left full of wrecked buses. Several nearby shops and homes also suffered blast damage.

At the Great Victoria Street station blast, a soldier and a girl were injured when a bomb went off in the Ulsterbus bus storage yard near the Boyne Bridge. Several buses in the yard were destroyed in a fire which followed the explosion. More than a hundred people who were standing at the bus terminal had lucky escapes as debris from damaged buses crashed down around them. The soldier was injured as he tried to move people off the Boyne Bridge to safety. Murray's tobacco factory beside the bus station also suffered blast damage. One bus driver arriving with a full bus saw what was happening, turned his vehicle and took his passengers to safety.

Another bomb blew a massive crater at Northern Ireland Railways' York Road station. A passenger saw a package being left by a youth and a girl. She warned a railway employee who raised the alarm. The station was only just cleared when the bomb went off. Fortunately, there were no injuries.

*Some of the destruction caused by the car bomb at Oxford Street bus station on 21 July 1972.*

*An interdenominational memorial service, arranged by Jim Kilfedder MP, was held at Oxford Street one week after what came to be known as 'Bloody Friday'.*

| | |
|---|---|
| 26 July: | Around midnight, a 15lb bomb destroyed three buses and damaged seven others at Ballynahinch depot. |
| 28 July: | A religious service was held in the ruins of Oxford Street bus station. About 300 people attended. Jim Kilfedder, a Unionist Westminster MP, arranged the service. It was timed to take place within minutes of the previous week's explosion. Catholic, Church of Ireland, Methodist and Presbyterian clergy officiated. |
| 18 October: | The Ulsterbus depot at John Street, Dungannon was bombed and set on fire. |
| 22 December: | A 50lb bomb left in a car in Duncrue Street exploded damaging Ulsterbus's head office. There were no casualties. |

**1973**

24 January:    A bomb at Hill Street in Belfast damaged the traffic offices of the BCT.

8 February:    During extensive Province-wide rioting following the UUUC strike, four buses were taken from Lisburn depot and one of them was set on fire.

26 February:   In Newry, the newly rebuilt Ulsterbus offices were damaged again by a bomb.

18 May:        Two explosions took place in Belfast, one at Great Victoria Street rail/bus station and the other at Queen's Quay railway station. Damage at Great Victoria Street station was considerable. The Great Victoria Street bomb was in a suitcase. Both bombs had been left in the stations' lavatories. A third bomb left in the lavatory of Lisburn railway station was defused, but a Belfast-bound train had to be evacuated.

22 May:        In Dublin, a bomb that had been set to explode at the Busaras (Dublin's central bus station) six months previously was found amongst unclaimed luggage. The timing device had been faulty.

21 June:       A 100lb car bomb left on the Boyne Bridge exploded shortly after the area had been evacuated. A telephone warning had been received, but the caller gave no time for the explosion. The bridge is alongside Great Victoria Street bus and rail stations so bus and rail services had to be suspended for a time. Debris was scattered for hundreds of yards and parts of the destroyed car landed on the railway lines. Buildings in the area, including the Europa hotel, were damaged in the blast. There were no injuries.

20 July:       Three people were injured and 20 buses damaged at Smithfield depot in Belfast by an explosion at the Bus Bar at the corner of Winetavern Street and Smithfield Square. Six of the damaged buses were write-offs.

2 August:      The army defused a bomb planted in the city's main bus depot in Derry.

12 October:    Bombs exploded at Great Victoria Street rail/bus and York Road railway stations. (A bomb also wrecked a train on the Bangor line, although the crew and passengers all escaped before the bomb went off.)

20 November:   Explosions damaged the Ulsterbus depot in Derry.

30 December:   Bombs damaged a school bus depot in Enniskillen.

## Bus burnings

During the early 1970s, the loss of buses due to rioting was extensive. In several cases, passengers lost their lives in these attacks. Below is a brief selection of incidents, all from 1972 and 1973 which give a feel for what was going on during this period.,

**1972**

31 January:    Buses were hijacked and burned in Andersonstown in Belfast. A bus en route from Dungannon to Omagh was stopped and burned by three masked gunmen at Carrickmore.

1 February:    Buses were hijacked in Belfast and BCT services were withdrawn on some routes. One bus was set on fire at the Glen Road terminus. Another two buses were hijacked and used to block the road. For the second night in succession, a bus was hijacked and burnt in Carrickmore. The same driver was involved as on the previous night. Later in the night, a Tyrone Education Committee bus, which had been parked at the Catholic school, was also set alight. Both buses were used as barricades to block the road. Ulsterbus withdrew services from the village.

2 February:    Two buses were burned in Ardoyne. Donegall Place in Belfast was sealed off while the army checked a bus for a bomb.

3 February:    In Belfast bus services to seven city areas were withdrawn and other services re-routed as rioters had damaged nine buses since Monday. Seven were damaged on Wednesday, including the two burned in Ardoyne.

5 February:    Armed men held up an Ulsterbus travelling from Enniskillen to Belturbet, near the border. The bus was set on fire.

*Two Daimler CVG6s have been hijacked on the Springfield Road in this 1972 incident. The one not on fire is believed to be either No 386 or No 430; it had been working on the cross-town route to Fortwilliam, on the Shore Road.*
**Courtesy Raymond Bell**

| | |
|---|---|
| 9 February: | During the Republican-instigated 'Disruption Day' some buses were burned in Newry. In the previous fortnight, 16 BCT buses had been hijacked on the Falls Road and six set on fire. |
| 4 March: | A school bus was hijacked and set on fire by four armed men in Newtownbutler. |
| 16 April: | Buses were hijacked and burned on the Springfield Road in West Belfast during heavy rioting in the city. All services were withdrawn in the area affected. |
| 12 May: | Six soldiers were shot on the Whiterock Road when investigating two hijacked buses which had been set on fire. Three buses were destroyed at Desmond's shirt factory at Swatragh. Masked and armed men used petrol to set the buses, which had arrived to bring workers home, on fire. |
| 20/21 May: | In Protestant East and West Belfast, BCT buses were hijacked and two burned during rioting. |
| 22 May: | BCT buses returned to most routes after two buses were destroyed and four others hijacked over the previous weekend. |

The IRA called a ceasefire which lasted from Monday 26 June to Monday 10 July

| | |
|---|---|
| 9 August: | The anniversary of internment: Two buses were hijacked and burned on the Falls Road during disturbances and all services to West Belfast were withdrawn. |
| 26 August: | A BCT double-decker bus was hijacked and burned at the junction of the Springfield and Whiterock Roads. |
| 6 September: | A Protestant crowd hijacked and burnt a bus on the Shankill Road and troops fired rubber bullets into the crowd. |
| 7 September: | A group of youths attempted to burn a bus in the Shankill area of Belfast. The youths were arrested. |
| 13 September: | Four masked men hijacked an Ulsterbus at Eglinton, near Derry. They ordered the driver to take the bus to a nearby quarry where the passengers were ordered off. The bus was set on fire and the driver assaulted. |
| 13 October: | A CIÉ bus was attacked with petrol bombs on the Killea Road, near Derry. |
| 10 November: | A single-deck Ulsterbus was burned at Lismacarrol between Derry and Dungiven. The bus went on fire shortly after the driver parked it outside his home. |

### 1973

| | |
|---|---|
| 5 January: | A double-deck bus was set on fire in Shipquay Street, Derry. The top deck was badly damaged. |
| 2 February: | Following the detention of a number of men relating to the hand grenade attack on the workers' bus in Cherryvalley, rioting broke out in East Belfast and two buses were burned. |
| 21 February: | A CIÉ express bus en route from Letterkenny to Dublin was stopped and set on fire by men in army uniform on the Aughnacloy–Ballygawley road. |
| 24 April: | A bus was hijacked and burnt on the Falls Road. |

| | |
|---|---|
| 4 July: | In Belfast, armed men hijacked seven buses and two lorries in Catholic areas and set them on fire. In one incident, when a bus was set on fire on the Cliftonville Road, the petrol ignited before the passengers had time to leave and five people were injured by burning, two of them seriously. In Derry, just before 9.00pm two buses were hijacked on Racecourse Road. One was set on fire and destroyed but residents saved the other bus and an off-duty bus driver drove it back to the depot. |
| 6 July: | A bus was hijacked and set on fire on the Glen Road, Belfast. |
| 9 July: | Seven BCT buses were destroyed in attacks by mobs during the evening. They were set on fire after the passengers and drivers had been forced to leave at gunpoint. |
| 14 August: | In Derry, buses were withdrawn from the Creggan area after two buses had been hijacked and set on fire. |
| 2 September: | Armed men at the Ulsterbus depot in Lurgan set four buses on fire. |
| 10 October: | In East Belfast an Ulsterbus was hijacked and burned by masked youths. Further attempts to hijack buses failed when passengers chased the youths away. |
| 28 November: | In Belfast, bus services to the Falls and Ardoyne were withdrawn after buses had been hijacked and set on fire. |
| 29 November: | In West Belfast three buses were hijacked and set on fire and the Falls, Springfield and Grosvenor Roads were blocked for a time. This action was part of a Province-wide action by the IRA to disrupt communications. |

### July 1973: Bus burnings and the black taxis

There was some suspicion that in certain parts of Belfast, buses were being destroyed as a way of boosting the custom of the self-styled 'peoples' taxis'. A flavour of this can be obtained from the following two sets of events.

During the night of 10 July, mobs burned buses in Belfast in what seems to have been a co-ordinated campaign. What made the burnings even more reprehensible was that they occurred shortly after a woman had died from injuries received in the previous week's arson attacks on Citybus vehicles by IRA gangs. Two firemen were injured fighting one of the blazes at Finaghy Road North.

Seven buses were set on fire in different parts of the city within minutes of each other. The attacks began with a bus hijacking at the Falls Road/Donegall Road junction at 6.15 pm. Three further buses were burned out on the Falls, and the gangs also attacked buses on the Glen Road, Shore Road and Antrim Road.

After these attacks, a story started to circulate that the Provisional IRA may have planned the attacks to force people to use the 'people's taxis' instead of the buses. The theory put forward by the security forces was based on their suspicions that the IRA had been putting pressure on some of the taxi-men for more protection money. So, this theory went, in order to increase the takings of the 'peoples' taxi service, the Provos decided to force public transport off the routes serviced by the taxis by burning a few buses.

If this theory was true, then the plan worked because buses were put off the Falls, Glen Road, Turf Lodge and diversions were introduced in other danger areas. A Citybus spokesman later said that he did not know when services would be returning to the affected routes, only that it would not be for a while.

### Mr Heubeck's bomb removal activities

One aspect of Werner Heubeck's work which always made the news was his willingness to remove suspect bombs from his buses. Contrary to popular, and some media opinion, he was extremely careful about how and when he did this, and only acted when he was absolutely sure that the 'bomb' in question was a hoax. He assessed each situation with great care before he made any move, usually quizzing, in great detail, the driver on whose bus the device had been left. On a number of occasions, having done this, he left the bomb to the security forces to deal with as he knew it was the real thing.

The reason Heubeck took these calculated risks was because the army's use of 'controlled explosions' to disable a bomb usually wrecked the bus as effectively as the bomb itself would have, even though the device left on the bus was often a hoax. His efforts in removing hoax bombs and driving buses to safety when real bombs had been planted in depots, undoubtedly saved Ulsterbus and Citybus a considerable amount of money. Not to be outdone, some of his senior managers also removed suspect devices from buses.

It is worth noting here, however, that for his work as Managing Director of Ulsterbus/Citybus Werner Heubeck was awarded an OBE and received it from the Queen at Hillsborough Castle on 11 August 1977.

Below, are a few examples of Mr Heubeck's bomb disposal activities.

7 August 1975: Mr Heubeck removed a suspect bomb from the rear of a bus in Donegall Place, near the centre of Belfast,. The bus was inside the city centre security cordon. The suspect device had been found on a seat inside the bus, around lunchtime.

The area was sealed off and evacuated while army personnel started to examine the parcel. However, Mr Heubeck boarded the vehicle and carried out the package which turned out to be an empty cardboard box.

When asked why he had taken such a risk, he dismissed the incident. He said that during his life he had done many things and this was just one of them.

6 January 1977: Werner Heubeck, once again took matters into his own hands by removing a suspect bomb from a hijacked bus in Co Fermanagh. He boarded the bus and carried out the suspect package. The bus had been hijacked by gunmen near Derrylin on the night of Thursday 6 January and had been placed across a road with its lights left on.

Mr Heubeck travelled from Belfast to where the bus had been abandoned. He arrived at the scene with the local depot manager, Mr George Breen, and area manager, Mr Bill Ferris. The army had not cleared the vehicle so before Mr Heubeck was allowed to board the bus he was required to sign a form declaring that he was prepared to take full responsibility for any risk to himself. The indemnity form stated that he was 'fully aware' of the risk he was taking

Once on board the bus, Mr Heubeck removed the package with the aid of a hook. The army later confirmed that the suspect device removed by Mr Heubeck was a hoax. Because the lights had been left on, the bus's battery was low and before the vehicle could be moved it had to be jump-started from a second bus brought up for that purpose.

16 August 1979: On this occasion, Mr Heubeck drove buses at risk away from danger after an incendiary attack on the company's Newcastle depot.

Incendiary bombs had been found by drivers coming on duty and army bomb experts had ascertained that, during the night, bombs had been placed on four of the 16 buses in parked in the depot.

When he was told of the problem, Mr Heubeck immediately drove down to Newcastle. When he arrived at the depot, he moved the buses parked beside the ones with incendiaries on board. Once this was done, the army bomb team went into action and defused the incendiaries planted on the four buses.

While the army were dealing with the bombs, Newcastle depot was operated from the street and a company spokesman said that all services ran normally.

Once he had moved the buses away from danger, Mr Heubeck left Newcastle and by lunchtime was back in his office in Belfast.

12 October 1980: In this incident, Mr Heubeck carried a bomb off a hijacked bus parked outside the McCrory Park army base on the Whiterock Road.

Two youths had hijacked the bus at the junction of the Glen Road and Shaw's Road shortly before 4.00pm. They ordered the driver to take the bus to the Monagh Community Centre where a milk churn was loaded on to the bus. The driver was then ordered to drive the bus to the army base. Once there, the driver raised the alarm.

The army bomb squad arrived but, before they could deal with the device, Mr Heubeck appeared on the scene, boarded the bus and carried the milk churn into the street.

When army experts later examined the churn they discovered it was filled with stones.

### Citybus boss Max has a crack

12 April 1979:   Max Hale, Citybus Operations Manager, got himself into the papers in April 1979 when, in the manner of his boss Werner Heubeck, he removed two suspect bombs from buses in Belfast. The Samaritans had received a call claiming that one of the buses, which had earlier left the Falls Road depot, had a bomb on board.

The suspect devices were discovered on buses on the Falls Road and Durham Street. Mr Hale asked for permission to deal with the devices, which was given by the security forces. He then boarded the two vehicles and dealt with the suspect bombs. First he dealt with the bus at Durham Street, where the parcel was sitting under the rear seat. He lifted the parcel and when the wrapping was removed he found that it was empty.

The device on the second bus also turned out to be a hoax.

### Ulsterbus boss Bill has a thrill

16 December 1980:

Bill Ferris, Western Area Manager for Ulsterbus, also decided to take a leaf out of Mr Heubeck's book when a suspect bomb was placed in one of his buses in Derry.

He removed a suspect bomb from a bus which had been hijacked at the Racecourse Road in Shantallow. A plastic dustbin had been loaded into the vehicle by two men and the driver told to park the bus on the Derry–Buncrana road. Traffic was held up for more than two hours and residents had to be evacuated from their homes.

The army were on the scene, and, with their permission, Mr Ferris went into the bus, tied a rope to the handle of the bin and started to drag it up the aisle. The bin got caught up on the seats and the lid fell off. When he examined the bin, Mr Ferris could only see ashes inside it. The 'bomb' which the hijackers had said would explode in thirty-five minutes, was just ashes.

## Rioting and hijackings

Amongst the most enduring images of the early years of the Troubles are the television and newspaper images of battles between rioting crowds and armed troops and police with one or more wrecked and possibly burning buses caught up in the middle of it all. These images had a negative impact on the bus industry right from the start, hitting passenger numbers, particularly in Belfast. They were also a major contributory reason for the poor financial performance and demise of Belfast Corporation's Transport Department in the early 1970s. Moreover, they had a significant negative impact on the tourist trade in the Province, and to a lesser extent in Ireland as a whole since many overseas tourists and tour operators made no distinction between the two parts of the island.

In subsequent years, incidents involving attacks on buses, depots and passengers became an almost everyday occurrence. Opposite are some examples selected from 1971:

*One of the MH Cars-bodied Daimler Fleetlines delivered to Belfast Corporation in 1962–4, No 680, burns fiercely at Clonard, on 3 February 1971.*

| | |
|---|---|
| 2 January: | Groups of Republicans boarded a number of buses in Turf Lodge on Saturday afternoon and ordered conductors not to collect any more fares because the buses had been 'liberated'. |
| 13 January: | In the culmination a night of incidents, BCT Daimler CVG6 No 382 was hijacked and was crashed into a row of houses. A fusillade of stones was thrown at an Ulsterbus in which five people were injured. Bus No 382 was later recovered. |
| 3 February: | During riots in the Clonard Street area of Belfast, following on army searches, a crane truck and a BCT Fleetline double-decker bus were hijacked, used as a barricade and then set on fire. |
| 4/5 February: | Riots in Clonard area: BCT Daimler CVG6s Nos 374, 427, and 428 were hijacked. After an emergency meeting, the BCT withdrew its bus services to the city's trouble spots until further notice. |
| 6/7 February: | BCT Daimler CVG6 No 354 and Fleetlines Nos 655 and 661 hijacked. |
| 9 February: | BCT Daimler CVG6 No 355 hijacked in Castle Street in the Belfast's city centre. |
| 5 to 8 March: | Rioting on Falls Road. Lesson Street barricaded with buses during a shoot-out between the Official and Provisional IRA. CVG6s Nos 355 and 362 burned on Friday and Fleetline No 697 on Saturday. |
| 11 April: | In Derry, 11 soldiers were injured in clashes with crowds after they had recovered a hijacked bus. |
| 16 June: | In Derry, bus services to Lone Moor Road were suspended following the hijacking and destruction of two buses. |
| 21 July: | Riots on Grosvenor Road, Belfast. Two buses were destroyed. |
| 26 July: | Buses burned in Belfast. |
| 6 August: | A machinegun attack was mounted on Springfield Road army post from a hijacked bus. |
| Monday 9 August: Internment: Major rioting follows all over Northern Ireland. | |
| 9 August: | An Ulsterbus was damaged in Irish Street, Dungannon. |
| 10 August: | An Ulsterbus was burned in Pomeroy, Co Tyrone. |
| 5 October: | Four buses were set on fire in Belfast |
| 7 October: | In Belfast various bus services were withdrawn for the third night in succession because of hijacking and violence. |
| 14 October: | Seven buses, all in service, were hijacked and burned in Belfast. Three were destroyed at Alliance Avenue in Ardoyne, Monagh Road in Turf Lodge and Short Strand. Two were set on fire at the Ormeau terminus and another at the Cregagh terminus. Armed men at Dawson Street, on the Antrim Road, hijacked a double-decker, opposite the entrance to Girdwood army barracks. All the attacks across the city occurred within minutes of each other. All services were withdrawn by 7.00pm on Thursday and Friday nights. |
| 16 October: | Four buses were set on fire in Belfast during the afternoon. Gunmen also set fire to a single-deck Ulsterbus near Coagh, Co Tyrone. |
| 23 October: | Soldiers escorting a damaged bus into Falls Park depot came under fire. Three soldiers were hit and were taken to hospital. Four buses were set on fire in Belfast. |
| 25 October: | A single-deck bus was destroyed near Kilkeel after three masked men set it on fire. |
| 16 November: | On the Whiterock Road in Belfast, a gunman ordered the driver and passengers off a bus and then set it on fire. |
| 1 December: | In his annual report, the BCT General Manager, Mr Robert Adams, said that nearly £1 million in revenue had been lost due to the civil disturbances. |
| 23 December: | Armed men hijacked a bus in Co Fermanagh, drove it across the border and set it on fire. |

Although not in 1971, I just had to include this next one!

17 January 1972: In Belfast, seven detainees being held on the prison ship HMS *Maidstone* escaped from the ship, swam ashore at 6.30am, hijacked a bus in the Harbour Estate, drove it to the Markets area and abandoned it there. The men were clad only in their underwear and were dripping wet when they hijacked the bus. They all escaped.

## Effects on tourism

**July 1969:**   **CIÉ and Wallace Arnold cancel their tours**

In 1969, following the riots in Derry and Belfast, CIÉ cancelled all its tours to Northern Ireland.

In July 1970, it repeated the action and the company announced that all its touring coaches had been diverted away from Northern Ireland and it was intended to maintain this situation until 19 July. The position would be kept under review and it was possible that the tours would be resumed.

There were no figures available for the number of visitors being diverted away from the North but it was confirmed that they were mainly tourists from Britain and the US. The reason given for the cancellations was that many foreign tourists considered Ireland, as a whole, a trouble spot

In the same month, Wallace Arnold followed suit. Wallace Arnold was a leading British holiday tours firm, based in Leeds. It decided to pull out of Northern Ireland for the 1970 season because of fears that that its customers might become involved in civil disturbances. The firm decided to cancel its Northern Ireland coach tours en bloc.

The firm, which during the season ran between two and five tours a week, had found that cancellations were making many tours unviable. They noted that many of their customers were very uneasy about coming to the Province. They stated that their tours in the Irish Republic were also suffering but they had, up to that point, not had to cancel them.

One of the main reasons that Wallace Arnold gave for pulling out of the Province was the hijacking of buses in Belfast to form barricades. The firm, which used Ulsterbus facilities, was afraid that its coaches could be hijacked too.

## Bus stoning and vandalism

## Bus stoning

In the 1950s and early 1960s, windows in bus shelters, telephone boxes, buses and trains were rarely vandalised. However, by the mid 1970s, as a result of the breakdown in social order resulting at least in part from the Troubles, this had all changed and public property was now fair game for teenage hoodlums.

The problem of the stoning of buses, generally unrelated to any particular street disturbances, built up gradually but reached a peak in the mid 1970s with multiple attacks occurring virtually every day, mostly in Belfast and usually in the same handful of areas, both nationalist and loyalist.

To illustrate this aspect of the Troubles, I have selected some the incidents which took place in just two months, September and October 1978, one of the worst years for this sort of activity. A large proportion of all the incidents recorded in that year involved stone throwing at buses. The results were broken windows and injured drivers and passengers.

7 September:   A number of youths stoned three Citybuses, two in the Oldpark area and a third at Ballymurphy. Nobody was hurt in the attacks.

16 September:   A window was broken in a Citybus by stone-throwers in the Ligoniel area.

30 September:   Windows were broken in a Citybus by stone-throwers in West Belfast. An Ulsterbus was hijacked and set on fire by four youths in the Twinbrook area. A stone-throwing crowd attacked firemen and police when they answered a call to put out the fire. The bus was destroyed.

3 October:   A Citybus was stoned on the Oldpark Road. A number of windows were broken, but there were no injuries.

4 October:   A number of Citybuses were stoned; one on the Antrim Road, one on the Ravenhill Road, and one at Springmartin terminus.

6 October:   In Belfast, schoolboy vandals wrecked a Citybus taking them home. As the bus was taking them down the Antrim Road, they tore out all the light fittings, upstairs and down and then tried to set fire to the bus. The bus was stopped at the junction of Clifton Street and North Queen Street where the fire was extinguished. The bus suffered smoke and scorch damage.

| 8 October: | Loyalists on the Craigavon Bridge in Derry stoned coaches carrying republican marchers back to Belfast from a civil rights anniversary march. |
|---|---|
| 10 October: | Two buses were stoned and had windows broken in the Oldpark area of Belfast. |
| 12 October: | Two buses were stoned, one on the Shankill Road and one at Monagh Road. |
| 13 October: | Two buses were stoned on the Oldpark Road. Windows were broken. |
| 14/15 October: | Several buses were stoned in various parts of Belfast over the weekend. |
| 18 October: | Buses were stoned at Cliftonville Circus, the Oldpark Road and Woodvale Roads in Belfast. |
| 19 October: | Four buses were damaged by stone-throwing mobs, two on the Crumlin Road, one on the Springfield Road and one on the Manse Road in Newtownabbey. No injuries were suffered in any of the attacks. |
| 24 October: | A bus was stoned at the junction of the Woodvale Road and Ardoyne. One man was injured. Two buses came under attack from stone-throwers on the Crumlin Road. |
| 26 October: | There were five stoning incidents in Belfast – at Carlisle Circus, Oxford Street, East Bridge Street, Shankill Road – and one in Lisburn. |
| 29 October: | A husband and wife and two girls were hurt in five separate attacks on buses in Belfast. These were at Glencairn terminus; Oldpark, Ligoniel and two took place on the Crumlin Road. |

In late October 1978, the problem of attacks on buses was publicly addressed by Mr Heubeck and the police. In 2006 we still await a solution to the problems they identified then.

**31 October 1978: Police and bus operators appeal to stone throwers to stop.**

Interviews were given to the local media by Mr Werner Heubeck, in his role as Citybus MD, and RUC Chief Superintendent, Seymour Dobson. They noted that vandals, who were usually teenagers, had carried out more than 260 attacks on buses in Belfast during 1978. The attacks were more numerous in the north and west of the city, although stoning incidents were recorded in all parts of Belfast.

The two men said that they believed that the situation was getting so bad that it was only a matter of time before someone was killed in one of the incidents. (In fact, on 10 October 1972, a 67-year-old man had been killed when a bus driver lost control of his bus on the Glen Road in Belfast, after he had been knocked unconscious by stones thrown by teenagers.)

To illustrate the severity of the problem, it was pointed out that the night previous to the publication of their appeal five people were injured in six separate attacks on buses in Belfast.

Attacks on the city's transport system had rocketed during 1978 with more than 200 stoning incidents recorded by police. Not all the attacks came from people throwing stones and incidents had included:

> Seats thrown out of the top deck of a moving bus
>
> A fire started on a top deck by children.
>
> A 15-year old girl in hospital with a fractured skull after a window was smashed.

Both men made a plea to the perpetrators to stop these activities before they killed someone.

Mr Heubeck was unable to give figures for the damage caused in the attacks but his main worry was that sooner or later someone would die on a bus either through fright or because an injured driver would lose control of the vehicle. Chief Superintendent Dobson, the head of the RUC's community relations section backed up Mr Heubeck's position stating that there was a clear risk that someone, eventually, would be seriously injured or lose their life in one of these incidents.

Citybus operations manager, Max Hale, also warned of the dangers to elderly passengers. He believed that sooner or later an elderly person would die through a heart attack because of a stoning attack.

Chief Superintendent Dobson admitted that police could do little to stop the attacks because when a patrol got to the scene of a stoning the perpetrators usually had vanished. He added that the solution had to be in talking to the children and their parents. He referred to his own visits to schools to talk to children about the dangers in attacking buses in this way.

Following up on the 1978 appeal noted above, in November 1979 the police announced some statistics quantifying the effect of stone-throwing on the provision of bus services in Belfast.

**21 November 1979: Some statistics on stoning attacks on buses.**

Chief Superintendent Dobson stated during a seminar that attacks on buses had almost tripled during 1979. He said that there had been 914 attacks on buses to date compared to 350 for the whole of 1978 and 286 in 1977. A survey carried out between July and November showed that the problem was worst in West Belfast, followed by the Shankill, North Queen Street, the New Lodge, the city centre and south of the Lagan. Most attacks occurred on Saturdays and the worst times were between 3.00 to 5.00 pm and 7.00 to 9.00 pm. Mr Dobson said the number of attacks during January and February was low but increased in the spring and then tailed off in the holiday months of June and July. September was the worst month for attacks.

In one evening, 56 bus windows were broken in the city. Most attacks were carried out by teenagers. The vandals were costing Citybus around £150,000–£200,000 per annum.

Mr Dobson suggested that drivers should get increased protection possibly through protective windscreens. These would lessen the danger of buses going out of control through the driver getting hit. Citybus did eventually institute a programme of fitting armoured windscreens to some of their fleet of Bristol RE single-deck buses.

# Vandalism

An unpleasant side effect of the civil unrest was the massive increase in vandalism and general thuggery in the community. This was manifested partly in a growing number of attacks on buses and their drivers.

Since the onset of the Troubles in Northern Ireland, vandalism had reached epidemic proportions and the bus companies had to spend large amounts of money every year to make good the resulting damage. It was in an attempt to reduce the costs of vandalism that cameras and the greatly disliked fibreglass seats were introduced into both companies' fleets. It was also part of the reason for phasing out double-deckers as passengers' activities on the upper deck could not be properly supervised by drivers.

**July 1976: Trying to beat vandalism**

In July 1976, Citybus and Ulsterbus announced that they were going to try and reduce the damage done by vandalism. They launched a poster campaign which had the aim of enlisting the help of the public in dealing with the vandals. An extensive publicity drive was mounted, with posters calling for public help being placed in every vehicle in the companies' fleets. The posters read:

"Vandalism increases your fare, reduces your comfort. Help us combat the wreckers by reporting offences to company officials or to school principals."

Mr Irvine Millar, Projects Manager of Ulsterbus, said that evidence showed that the vandals were almost exclusively teenagers, many of them school children. Mr Millar admitted that the problem of vandalism was difficult to overcome. He confirmed that the two companies estimated they spent around £75,000 each year repairing torn seats, broken windows and erasing graffiti. The companies had also begun to fit fibreglass seats to buses, particularly in the back of vehicles where the problem of vandalism was worst. Mr Millar admitted that these seats would mean a reduction in comfort for the ordinary decent passenger.

He also pointed out that the cost of dealing with vandalism had contributed to fares increases.

# *Threats from paramilitaries*

Attacks on buses has been a feature of the Troubles right from the outset, but sometimes these assaults were deliberately organised by paramilitaries to achieve certain ends. We have already come across the suspicion that some of the bus-burnings on the Falls Road were deliberately orchestrated to boost the earnings of the taxi drivers, and so their kickbacks to the IRA.

Opposite are some further examples of the kinds of threats bus operators faced from the activities of paramilitary organisations:

## May 1974: The first loyalist strike

The Ulster Workers' Council (UWC) strike took place between 15 and 28 May 1974. Except within nationalist areas, the strike brought Northern Ireland's economy to a standstill.

The strike was called by a coalition of loyalist politicians, trades unionists and paramilitaries in protest at the political and security situation in Northern Ireland. They were also very unhappy with the Sunningdale Agreement, which would have given the government of the Republic of Ireland a say in the running of the Province.

Many commentators believe that the strike was successful mainly because it drew on the sense of alienation that had grown in the Protestant community since 1969. However, an important factor in its success was the support given by key workers in the power generation, gas and petrol distribution industries. Other reasons can be found in the effectiveness of loyalist paramilitaries in blockading main routes thus preventing people from going about their normal business, and the inept security response of Harold Wilson's Labour government at Westminster.

All bus services, except those in nationalist areas, had to be withdrawn as buses were hijacked and many crews threatened.

The strike succeeded in bringing down Northern Ireland's new power-sharing Executive. The government of Northern Ireland then reverted to Westminster where it has remained, Good Friday Agreement notwithstanding, more or less ever since.

What follows are some of the key incidents affecting public transport which took place during the period of that strike:

| | |
|---|---|
| Tuesday 14 May: | The Ulster Workers' strike begins. |
| Wednesday 15 May: | There were several attempts to hijack buses in Protestant areas. |
| Thursday 16 May: | In Belfast, the entire Citybus fleet was withdrawn at 8.10am because of hijackings. Members of the UDA had taken many buses for roadblocks. The police later recovered nine buses intact. |
| Friday 17 May: | The buses ran normally. Ulsterbus crews were on strike. This ended and services were due to resume the following Monday. |
| Saturday 18 May: | Buses ran normally. |
| Sunday 19 May: | The UWC announced a complete shutdown of all industrial and commercial businesses, including public transport, though buses ran normally on Sunday. |
| Monday 20 May: | In Belfast, buses ran only on three routes through mainly republican areas – Falls Road, Glen Road and Whiterock Road. |
| Tuesday 21 May: | At around 7.45am many vehicles were hijacked. Two buses were used to block roads in Derry. Four Ulsterbuses were hijacked in east Antrim. Citybus in Belfast only operated on three routes in Catholic areas of the city. |
| Wednesday 22 to Tuesday 28 May: | |
| | Citybus in Belfast operated only on three routes in Catholic areas of the city |
| Saturday 25 May: | It was announced that normal Citybus services would be resumed on Monday. |
| Monday 27 May: | Long-distance CIÉ buses were still running to various points in the Province. However in spite of the announcement on Saturday, Citybus still only operated the three routes in Catholic areas of Belfast. All services were withdrawn in the evening. |
| Tuesday 28 May: | Brian Faulkner resigned as Chief Executive and the Assembly falls. |
| Wednesday 29 May: | Apart from Catholic areas, no buses ran in Belfast in the morning. The UWC announced that public transport could restart. At 1.00pm all bus crews were asked to report to their depots in the afternoon and a skeleton service was started in Belfast, except for areas in the east of the city. |
| Thursday 30 May: | Bus services were back to normal. |

## September 1976: Loyalist paramilitary hijackings

In September 1976, the UDA embarked on a hijacking spree in protest at alleged brutality by warders against their members at the Maze prison. This lasted for several days and quite a few buses were destroyed. During this episode, a UDA leader gave an interesting insight on why hijacked buses were often set on fire. His analysis is probably just as valid when applied to republican areas.

The UDA's protests started on 13 September and were centred mainly in Belfast and Newtownabbey. Buses were hijacked from about 7.00am to mid-morning in the Shankill, Rathcoole and Monkstown areas. At noon the police said seven buses had been hijacked and set on fire. In east Antrim, where the hijackings began, one bus was destroyed, and two others damaged. On the Shankill three buses were set ablaze, and on the Crumlin Road another was set on fire. A Citybus spokesman said the vehicles were write-offs. One Ulsterbus driver received burns to his face and hands when a gang set fire to his vehicle at Greenisland.

When asked about the damage caused during the spate of hijackings, Mr Tommy Lyttle, a UDA spokesman on the Shankill area responded, "Some of the lads got a bit over-enthusiastic. We don't want any damage to private property. We don't really want any burnings but we've really got very limited means of protest. Road blocking is probably the most effective protest. But if a bus is just put across the road it's not really news. If it's burnt, it is news."

### September 1976: IRA bomb Pennyburn depot

The Provisional IRA targeted not only members of the security forces, but those supplying them with goods and services. As a result, in 1976, Ulsterbus was threatened because from time to time it provided buses for the movement of troops.

To underscore its threat to those providing services to the security forces, the Provisional IRA bombed Pennyburn depot on 10 September, destroying four buses. In a statement following the bombing the IRA said that the depot was attacked because Ulsterbus vehicles transported soldiers to and from Belfast docks. They warned that if Ulsterbus continued to move troops it would remain a target.

A spokesman for Ulsterbus said that as a public service company it

*Acrid smoke billows from buses on fire after an IRA bomb attack on the Ulsterbus garage at Pennyburn, Londonderry, in September 1976. AEC Reliances, Bedford VAMs, Bristol REs and Leyland Leopards can all be seen.*
**Belfast Telegraph**

could have no other policy than carry anyone requiring transport. He added that this had been the company's policy since the start of the Troubles.

Ulsterbus crews in Derry staged a march protesting against the depot bombing and the IRA's hijacking of buses.

### May 1977: The second loyalist strike

In May 1977, an attempt was made to rerun the 1974 strike. The key political figures behind this venture were the Rev Ian Paisley and Mr Ernest Baird of the Democratic Unionist Party (DUP). As in 1974, they had the backing of the UDA, but on this occasion, not of the majority of the unionist community. When the strike was declared, UDA street muscle proved inadequate to bring the Northern Ireland economy to a halt. In addition, the security forces made a greater effort to keep the economy moving than they had done during the 1974 strike. In common with most other sectors of the economy, both management and workers of the Province's bus companies were determined to keep the wheels turning.

Below, again are some of the key events during that strike:

| | |
|---|---|
| Monday 2 May: | UUAC strike begins. |
| Tuesday 3 May: | A gang hijacked an Ulsterbus on the Albertbridge Road and its tyres were let down. |
| | In Omagh, most of the fleet was sabotaged during the night with sugar put in their |

| | |
|---|---|
| | diesel tanks. Thirty-eight buses were affected. Citybus services were suspended on the Crumlin Road, the greater Shankill area and the Braniel estate. Some other services turned short of their normal termini. There were also diversions on some Ulsterbus services. |
| Wednesday 4 May: | About eight hijacked buses, with their tyres deflated, were used to block roads in East Belfast. Buses that were hijacked were not damaged. Several buses were attacked by youths throwing missiles on the Newtownards Road in Belfast. At a mass meeting, Citybus crews in Belfast voted to keep working. Operations were similar to Tuesday's except that some late services were restored. |
| Thursday 5 May: | United Ulster Unionist Council (UUUC) coalition breaks up after disagreements over the backing of the UUAC strike |
| Friday 6 May: | Two buses were slightly damaged by fire, one at Balmoral and the other near Queen's University. The fires were put out by the fire brigade. Other services were as on previous days. |
| Saturday 7 May: | A bus was stoned in Bangor. The driver was treated for cuts. |
| Sunday 8 May: | A bus from Derry was stopped in Belfast's loyalist Sandy Row by six youths. The passengers were ordered off and an attempt was made to burn the bus. |
| Tuesday 10 May: | School bus services in parts of Fermanagh and Tyrone were hit when drivers refused to take out their vehicles because of intimidation by the Ulster Freedom Fighters. Twenty out of a fleet of 80 buses were affected. |
| | Citybus driver Harry Bradshaw murdered at the wheel of his bus. Mr Bradshaw was a Protestant and a driver with Citybus. He was shot by the UDA on the Crumlin Road when he had stopped for passengers. All bus services were stopped for three days after his killing. A colleague had been wounded by a gunman at the same stop the weekend before. |
| Wednesday 11 May: | A meeting of over 700 Belfast busmen held at TGWU headquarters Transport House voted to stay off work until after Harry Bradshaw's funeral on Friday. Mr Heubeck and union leaders also rejected an offer from the Secretary of State, Mr Mason, for armed guards to be placed on buses. Busmen felt that this would make them even more likely to be terrorist targets. |
| Thursday 12 May: | A bomb was planted near the Ulsterbus depot in Bangor. A bomb was also detonated on the Belfast to Bangor rail line. No buses ran in the greater Belfast area but Ulsterbus services were almost back to normal elsewhere in Northern Ireland. |
| Friday 13 May: | Harry Bradshaw's funeral was held in Glengormley. A fleet of fourteen buses brought busmen from all over Northern Ireland to the church. |
| Friday 13 May: | UUAC strike called off |

## Robberies

Bus drivers became soft targets for opportunistic thieves during the Troubles. However, it didn't become a major problem until the end of 1975. In the early years of the civil unrest, even when buses were hijacked, the crews were often allowed to recover their ticket machines and cash. But, as the years passed, the number of robberies on drivers increased. Many of these took place in Belfast, particular parts of the city being favourite haunts for the thieves. Robberies took place in both Loyalist and Republican areas, usually at termini located in or near certain housing estates. On numerous occasions the robbers were armed with guns, knives or other implements such as iron bars or hatchets.

Below are some examples from 1976 of the sorts of incidents which occurred, during certain years, on an almost daily basis.

| | |
|---|---|
| 12 January: | Millisle: A man and woman at Moss Road waved down a bus travelling from Newtownards. When it stopped, two armed men ordered the driver to hand over his takings before taking him out of the bus and hitting him over the head with a gun. |
| 22 March: | A bus driver was robbed at Ligoniel terminus. The gang who stole his takings later held up another driver in Short Strand. |
| 29 March: | Armed robberies were perpetrated on two Citybus drivers, one at Short Strand and the other at Springmartin terminus. |

| 2 April: | A Citybus driver was held up and robbed on the Springmartin Road. |
| 7 April: | Four masked and armed men robbed a bus driver in Park Avenue in Derry. Another driver was robbed in the Waterside area by a group of youths. |
| 19 April: | Three men robbed a bus driver at Donegall Road terminus. |
| 8 July: | A 17-year-old youth from the Glencairn area of Belfast and a 16-year-old juvenile appeared in court charged with robbing a Citybus driver with a hatchet. They were charged with the robbery of £30.87 from the bus and with using an offensive weapon. |
| 16 August: | In Newry, three masked men, one armed, robbed the Ulsterbus offices in Edward Street. |
| 4 October: | A bus driver was robbed by three youths at the Ballygomartin Road terminus. |
| 30 December: | A Citybus driver was robbed by two youths on the Whitewell Road. |

This pattern of robberies continued for the rest of the troubles and beyond, with an incident taking place, at the time of writing in July 2005, in which a NIR conductor on a Belfast to Bangor train was robbed of his takings at knifepoint.


# Organisational issues

In addition to the problems caused directly by the civil unrest, managements of the bus companies also had to contend with the normal problems associated with running their businesses. Below, I have sampled just a few of the issues and problems they had to deal with in the run up to and during the worst years of the Troubles.

## *Corporate Reorganisations*

### 1966: The end of the UTA

1966 was an important year in the transport history of Northern Ireland. The Ulster Transport Authority, set up in 1948 to provide an integrated road/rail transport system for the Province, had only one more year of existence left. The new boards and chief executives of Ulsterbus, Northern Ireland Railways and Northern Ireland Carriers had been appointed and these 'shadow' managements were beginning to take up the reins of control. The Coastal Bus Company, the first independent bus company since the formation of the state-owned Northern Ireland Road Transport Board eliminated all private bus operators in 1935, commenced trading on 26 April in the Portrush area, and the following day Sureline Ltd began operations in and around Craigavon.

However, not everyone involved with the public transport scene approved of these changes. In January, shortly before his death, George Howden, ex-chairman of the UTA and a man with an illustrious career behind him in both the Great Northern Railway and CIÉ, denounced the changes the government had put in train to dismantle the Province's public service ethos, integrated public transport system and replace it with competing companies operating on a purely commercial basis.

The UTA announced its plans to introduce one-man-operated buses and later in the year Belfast Corporation Transport Department's first o-m-o buses made their appearance on Belfast's streets. In a portend of things to come, Falls Park depot was severely damaged by fire. However, in this instance, it was just an accident. Four buses were destroyed, but 16 were driven to safety by staff.

The increasing dominance of the motorcar was signalled by the announcement of the Belfast Corporation-sponsored Travers Morgan and Partners consultants' survey into traffic in Belfast. This would recommend plans for a largely car-based transport strategy, including an elevated urban ring road, for the city.

### 1967–1968: Werner Heubeck arrives

Ulsterbus's new managing director, Mr Werner Heubeck, a German originally from Nuremburg, would figure largely in the story of how the Province's bus industry would cope with the Troubles. By the time he came to Northern Ireland, Mr Heubeck had become a naturalised Briton. Although a soldier in the Wermacht, he had spent most of the Second World War as a POW in the USA. He had come to England in 1948 and over the years had held an assortment of jobs, some of them at a junior level.

**Werner Heubeck**

A charismatic personality with strong views on how a business should be run, at Ulsterbus he headed up a management team which, against all expectations, turned the loss-making UTA bus operation into a profitable business. To top it all, this was achieved in the space of just one year without decimating services. A year into his tenure he was able to report that Ulsterbus, a publicly-owned company, was making money, instead of as in UTA days, losing it. In its first year under Heubeck's leadership, Ulsterbus made over £600,000 and this was achieved without reducing passenger numbers or raising fares.

One must be careful of applying national stereotypes, but many observers feel that Heubeck's business style owed a lot to his German background. However, it is clear that Heubeck himself was grateful to Britain for giving him his chance to show what he could do in the world of business. He is on record as saying that the kind of career he was able to follow in the UK would have been impossible in Germany for him, a boy who had finished school at 18.

Heubeck brought the skills of a professional manager to the problems of Northern Ireland's bus industry. Before he joined Ulsterbus, he had managed a paper mill in Scotland. His view was that Ulsterbus was simply a business and would respond to the same sensible management techniques as any other business. He observed when he joined the company that if he was not running Ulsterbus, he would be just as happy running a factory somewhere else in the UK.

When Heubeck took the on the job of Ulsterbus's MD, he admitted to knowing nothing about transport. Before he came to Northern Ireland to be interviewed for the job, a key part of his preparations was to spend the weekend before the interview, which was held on a Monday, travelling around Northern Ireland on buses observing how things were done. By the time he went into the interview he thought he could make the Northern Ireland's buses pay their way. To the surprise of some of the key players in the old UTA bus operations side, Heubeck was able to persuade the panel, and he got the top job.

One of the skills that Heubeck demonstrated over and over again to those who worked with him was that of knowing how to relate to ordinary workers. He mixed easily with the men and I recall seeing him one evening in the 'dundering-in' that passed for the men's rest room in Smithfield depot, wearing a cape and deerstalker and playing chess with a driver while a couple of other men looked on. Early on in his term as MD, he organised a coach trip for employees across Europe to Yugoslavia, which he went on himself. My father was on that trip and for years afterwards often recalled it with pleasure. As will be noted from interviews elsewhere in this book, trades union representatives recognised and respected him as a firm, but fair bargainer.

He saw a big part of the problem of UTA losses as being excessive overheads, so one of his first decisions was to cut these by £300,000. He also analysed the duties, which were the number of journeys a crew would do in a day's work, and concluded there was far too much slack in them. For the launch of Ulsterbus, he had the duties re-drawn much more tightly. As a result, he was able to reduce the number of duties required by 25%, without affecting the number of services operated.

I remember as a new conductor in Smithfield in 1967, just weeks after the start of Ulsterbus, comparing the new duties which we had to operate with the old UTA ones which were still up on the board. Even to my inexperienced eyes, the increase in the amount of work to be done on the Ulsterbus shifts compared to the UTA ones was startling.

Also, the conducting school that I had attended had been held in an office in the old Belfast Omnibus Company's depot in North Street, just across the street from Smithfield depot. It was the only office still being used in that building and I recall exploring the corridors and looking into lots of empty, recently vacated UTA offices, a testimony to Heubeck's overheads-slashing exercise. Years later, in 1973, as a junior manager in the company, I remember wandering about a similarly recently-deserted building in Utility Street which until the formation of Citybus had been the well-populated HQ of the Belfast Corporation Transport Department. It had received the same cost-cutting treatment.

In his first year as MD, and for a number of years thereafter, Heubeck focussed totally on his mandate from government to make the buses pay, and he did this to the exclusion of all else, refusing to spend money on what he regarded as 'extras' like the re-vamping of bus stations. He agreed that many of Ulsterbus's public facilities were of extremely poor quality, but he was adamant that money would be spent on improving them only when it could be afforded. In the event, Ulsterbus embarked on a programme of depot improvements in the early 1970s, although still mindful of the need to make economies, the new stations would be of spartan simplicity.

Once Heubeck's abilities became clear, it wasn't long before movers and shakers were talking about him taking over the operations of the Belfast Corporation's Transport Department as well, and merging it with Ulsterbus. However, it took the growing losses caused by the Troubles, plus a local government reorganisation in 1973, before a reluctant Heubeck got the chance to work his magic on Belfast's red buses, too.

## 1973: The formation of Citybus

After much speculation over the years, and a couple of false starts, between 1973 and 1975 the assets of the Belfast Corporation Transport Department were finally transferred to a new private limited company called Citybus. The new entity started operating in 1973, but the legal problems associated with the transfer were not all sorted out until 1975.

As an example of an earlier attempt to involve Mr Heubeck in the affairs of the red buses, a special meeting of Belfast City Council in July 1970 rejected tough takeover terms offered by the Ulsterbus boss, although it made it clear that it was still willing to talk to Ulsterbus on possible areas of co-operation to try and achieve economies. At the time the Transport Department was trying to stem losses of around £90,000 per month, a huge sum at the time for an operator the size of the BCT.

At that time Heubeck's terms for merger were:

> Ulsterbus would have total control;

> Any increases or changes in the fare structure would be a matter for Ulsterbus;

> There would have to be a satisfactory agreement immediately with trades unions on wages and wage demands covering the next two years;

> While Corporation members might be represented on the board of Ulsterbus, they would not be there as delegates from the Corporation.

Although a separate legal entity, Citybus, as it was eventually set up, shared a top management with Ulsterbus although at operational level they remained distinct entities. At the time this change took place, the BCT was still in serious financial difficulties, much of which could be laid at the door of the civil unrest. It was, however, a convenient time for central government to make the change since, following on the imposition of direct rule from London, local government in Northern Ireland was being reorganised with many of its powers being transferred to new centralised agencies. Since Belfast was the only local authority in Northern Ireland to have its own transport undertaking, it made sense to transfer it to the control of the successful Ulsterbus team.

Werner Heubeck had never been keen on the idea of taking over the loss-making Belfast Corporation Transport Department. But, as he makes clear elsewhere in this book, he didn't really have a choice, the operation being handed over to him by government in 1973 at the height of the Troubles. Although he instituted economies in the new company, it took some time before he could eliminate the losses.

## 1995: Translink

In 1995, as part of the new approach of government towards the provision of public transport in Northern Ireland, Ulsterbus, Citybus and Northern Ireland Railways were brought under a common board of management. A new brand name, 'Translink' was adopted for the integrated public transport service to be offered by the three companies.

This was a return to an operational structure not unlike that of the UTA. Although there was to be a single management team, the original corporate structure of three private limited companies under the Northern Ireland Transport Holding Company, a statutory corporation, was retained and, unlike the situation in the rest of the UK, public transport still remained ultimately under state control.

Key targets for the new organisation were set out in a booklet produced by Translink in 1997, *Moving Forward on Public Transport*. These tatrgets were to: develop a common brand identity for Northern Ireland's public transport industry, to strengthen road/rail co-ordination, and to develop an integrated fare system.

A common corporate identity was established by adopting a common corporate colour, green, a common livery for both the Ulsterbus and Citybus fleets and a single corporate logo to be used by all three companies on their vehicles and publications. The brand name 'Translink' was to be displayed prominently on all vehicles, documentation and publications.

In addition, Translink has been developing a number of integrated road/rail terminals. The first of these, the Europa Bus Centre/Great Victoria Street railway station in Belfast predated the establishment of Translink and was not originally planned as an integrated concept. The first planned integrated terminal to be completed was at Bangor. Coleraine has also been given the integrated treatment and Portadown is scheduled to receive an integrated terminal, this being earmarked for development as a key transport node with a road/rail interchange and a park-'n'-ride facility. Another road/rail park-'n-ride facility is planned for Templepatrick on the recently re-opened Bleach Green–Antrim stretch of the Belfast–Derry line.

New computerised fares issuing technology has been introduced in all three companies with the capability, it is claimed, to operate an integrated ticketing system between road and rail transport providers. Bus/train timetables, showing the road/rail connections, have also made a re-appearance after nearly thirty years and a programme of replacing the spartan early Ulsterbus bus stations with new modern facilities is well advanced.

# Impact of government transport policies

During the period of the Troubles, the bus companies, as state-owned entities, have had to deal with successive government ministers and their transport policies, or lack of same. In the 1960s, under the Stormont government, a major study had been carried out which recommended a roads-based policy for Northern Ireland. If it had been fully implemented, this would have resulted in a web of motorways radiating from Belfast and a major elevated ring road around the capital. Public transport took very much second place in these plans, with the bus industry only slightly ahead of the railways in the thinking of government ministers.

When the 'direct rule' ministers took over in 1973, thinking changed, partly because of the failures of car-centric policies elsewhere, but mainly because the British government was not prepared to spend the money necessary to complete these grandiose road schemes while also funding the vastly expensive security apparatus made necessary by the Troubles. Public transport therefore moved more to centre stage. However, years went by while various ministers, parachuted in from London, attempted to devise a policy that was reasonably acceptable to Northern Ireland political opinion and which London was prepared to fund.

The following extracts give a flavour of the arguments that went on over the years. In them, the process of arriving at the transportation structures now in place can be seen evolving.

### 1974: Review of the Transport Strategy for Belfast.

In spite of the continuing Troubles, some moves were initiated to improve the overall public transport situation with a review of the 1966 Travers Morgan transportation plan for Belfast. This very car-centred plan was shelved and the Secretary of State established a 'strategic review', giving public transport a much higher profile.

#### 7 November 1974: Ring road plan shelved

In November 1974, the government announced that plans for Belfast's urban motorway ring road were to be shelved and the city's transport problems to be examined afresh. They were to be the subject of a 'strategic review'. One proposal was to build a link road connecting the M1 and M2 and extend this link across the Lagan with a new bridge in the harbour area.

The decision was welcomed by most political groups. John Laird, Unionist Assemblyman for West Belfast, who had been pressing for such a review, welcomed the announcement and outlined part of his vision for the future:

> I hope the review will take in every form of transport for the greater Belfast area. I don't know what the complete solution is but I will be pressing for the consultants to consider pulling up the public transport service by the bootlaces and taking the emphasis off private transport. I can see the day when the motorist will be excluded entirely from the city centre and more and more people using public transport. Large car parks on the edge of the city should be considered.

#### 1977–78

In 1977 the discussion on the future shape of the Belfast area transport system continued. Pressure was being brought on government to reconsider their rejection of the idea of building a rail link between York Road station and Central station. A significant gap existed between the Transport Users' Committee, which favoured a public transport solution to Belfast's transport problems, and the Belfast Chamber of Commerce, which wanted a roads-based solution.

### April 1978: The Way Forward

After a long period of gestation, including a bad-tempered public consultation period, in 1978 the government finally announced the £100m transportation plan that would determine the shape of the transport system in and around Belfast for decades to come. It was announced by the Secretary of State Mr Roy Mason on 28 April at the City Hall and included:

- A dual carriageway link between the M1, M2 and the harbour.
- A six-lane cross Harbour Bridge linking the M2 to the Sydenham by-pass
- A rail link between York Rd station and Central Station following a cross-river route
- An increase in the bus fleet serving Belfast by about 50 buses.
- A central bus station to be built for Ulsterbus
- A central ring road 'box' to take the traffic round the immediate city centre area.
- The south side of the box to be linked with a new bridge over the Lagan near the Gasworks.
- Extensive pedestrianisation in the city centre.
- Donegall Place restricted to bus and service vehicle use only.
- Car parking policy to discourage all-day parker commuting to the city centre to be introduced.

The cross harbour rail link, originally omitted from all three alternative transport strategies put out to public consultation, because of public pressure had been included in the new plan.

With regard to the detailed plans for bus services in the Belfast area the government accepted that buses would provide the bulk of public transport in the city and would be an important part of future transport arrangements for Belfast. The review committee had recommended an increase in the Citybus and Ulsterbus fleets in the city by about 50, increased bus mileages operated and substantial additional manpower, and the government had accepted these recommendations.

It was also announced that a proposal by the review committee that a new central station should be provided for Ulsterbus at Great Victoria Street would be considered by the government. The committee also proposed building a road link from the Boyne Bridge to the M1 motorway but recognised that this could create problems for the bus operators.

The government also accepted that the cost of concessionary fares on trains and buses should not be borne by the transport budget.

A government spokesman acknowledged that the bus companies had had to cope with the difficult security situation, terrorist attacks on buses, bus drivers and bus depots. They also had to face competition from black taxis and the demand for evening services to the city centre had declined dramatically.

### The saga of Belfast's central bus station.

The 1978 plan outlined above, mentioned the plan for a new central bus station to be built at Great Victoria Street.

As far back as 1969, the Belfast Transportation Plan had recommended a single bus station for Belfast. This would have been built on a site taking in both the existing Smithfield depot and Smithfield market and would have incorporated a high-rise office development.

It was later decided that the Smithfield site was too small and in 1976 attention turned to expanding the Great Victoria Street depot once the railway had moved out on the opening of their new Central Station. However, this scheme was snookered by plans put forward by the DoE to remove the Boyne Bridge, thus threatening to split the Great Victoria Street site by a busy road.

In 1978, the Oxford Street depot, right beside the new Central railway station, became a candidate, provided it could be expanded into the adjacent, but derelict May's Markets area. However, Belfast City Council had ambitions to build a concert hall on this site, and this eventually knocked the Oxford Street idea on the head.

Smithfield depot was destroyed by the IRA in 1978 and was not rebuilt, services being moved to a congested Oxford Street depot and although there was much discussion in the press, the plans for a new central bus station stagnated.

Eventually, it was decided that the main Ulsterbus depot would be located at Great Victoria Street and the Europa Bus Centre was opened in the late 1980s. This was supplemented later by a new, smaller depot at Donegall Quay, close to the site of the Oxford Street depot when the latter was demolished to make way for the City Council's Waterfront Hall. Ulsterbus were happy with the idea of operating from two depots as they had learned the importance of having a fall-back position if one depot was destroyed in a terrorist attack, as had happened with Smithfield.

## Operational issues

Some of the operational issues affecting the BCT/Citybus and Ulsterbus during the height of the civil unrest included the introduction of one-man buses, the token system, and standee buses; the phasing out double-deckers; eventually replacing the token system with multi-journey tickets; introducing express buses into Belfast; coping with the necessity, and the public relations problems of having to impose high fare rises; and finding vehicles for special one-off events such as the Pope's visit, and Peace People rallies.

Management also had to field criticism from local politicians over various issues, including standards of passenger facilities at depots and lack of concessionary fares for pensioners. In addition, in the early 1970s, Ulsterbus introduced female conductors and several years later female drivers, with far from universal approval from their male employees.

Furthermore, scores of second-hand buses had to be sourced from Great Britain to make up the losses suffered as the result of the civil unrest. As this subject will be covered elsewhere in the book, I will not refer further to it here.

### 1969–70: One-man-buses and tokens

During 1969 and 1970 the Belfast Corporation Transport Department introduced one-man-operated buses and the associated token system, as the following facts demonstrate:

Between 19 May and 30 November 1969 one-man-operation was introduced on the Glengormley, Dundonald, Braniel, Ormeau, Castlereagh, Stormont, Broomhill/Carr's Glen, Donegall/Ligoneil and Silverstream/ Ligoneil routes.

Double-deck o-m-o was introduced on the Bloomfield, Carr's Glen, Ormeau, Mount Merrion, Malone, Ballygomartin, Glencairn, Springmartin, and Downview services.

On 18 February 1970 the token system was introduced. All other Citybus routes were converted to o-m-o by the mid 1970s. Ulsterbus also converted to o-m-o by the mid-1970s though without getting involved with such complications as the token system.

## Fares increases

The Troubles hit passenger numbers severely on both Ulsterbus and the BCT. Evening services were particularly badly affected. Ultimately, this would play a major part in the demise of the BCT and the formation of Citybus.

As well as the financial disruption caused by the civil unrest, Northern Ireland's bus companies, in common with all other business in the UK, would have to cope with increasing levels of inflation. This would become a major problem from about 1973 until the early 1980s and during this decade the real value of money would be slashed dramatically. This problem would not ease until the late 1980s.

### July 1970: An Ulsterbus fares increase

In July 1970 Ulsterbus tried to compensate for inflation and falling revenues by increasing its fares. Mr Heubeck estimated that Ulsterbus losses the previous year, as a result of the Troubles, were around £100,000. Private Hire work had also been hit badly by the civil unrest. People were not travelling on the ordinary afternoon tours because they did not know if they could get home again in the evening. As usual, Mr Heubeck was forthright in his explanation for the need for the fares rise. He said in a statement announcing the intention to raise fares:

Fares have to go up by a substantial amount. The troubles in Northern Ireland have got to be paid for by the people of Northern Ireland. We had hoped that this would not be necessary, but we have suffered last year and now have got to keep going.

At the same time the Belfast Corporation Transport Committee announced that they were seeking Government financial assistance to help keep the fares down in Belfast. The Committee decided at a special meeting to seek a meeting with Brian Faulkner who at that time was the Minister of Development in the Stormont government.

### August 1975: A Citybus fares increase

Fares rises were always unpopular and usually generated headlines in the local press. Early in the life of Citybus, Heubeck decided that there was a need to raise fares. This was to try and reduce losses, to recover revenue lost as the result of the Troubles-related fall in passenger numbers, and to offset the effects of the rampant inflation with which the British economy was plagued.

However, in 1973–74 Citybus was still £500,000 in the red and it was expected that the 1974–75 figures would be even worse in spite of the economies Citybus management had put in place. The previous increase in fares had been in March 1975, but in order to keep the company's finances in line with inflation, it was calculated that another increase would be needed before the end of the year. So in August 1975 it was announced that fares would probably have to go up before the end of the year

The year's accounts for the whole NITHC group indicated that the overall loss for the group would be in excess of £700,000. However, the biggest part of that loss was expected to come from Citybus.

Two other recurring themes emerged during the end of year financial review for the group; one concerning the losses Citybus was suffering because of operation of the black taxis and the other was the losses resulting from fare dodging, made easier because of the weaknesses in the token system introduced by the BCT.

The 'people's taxis' in Belfast were costing the company about £1million a year in lost fares. Mr Heubeck was constantly frustrated by the reluctance of the authorities to do anything about this as he regarded these taxi operations as, at best, just within the borders of legality. The company was also losing a lot of money through people failing to pay the correct fares and it was estimated that more than four million journeys were being made each year by fare dodgers.

### 1971: Decimalisation

D-Day in both the UK and Ireland was 15 February 1971. On that day the United Kingdom changed from using 12 pence to the shilling and 20 shillings to the pound to 100 new pence to the pound. Bus crews had to be familiar not just with the new UK coinage, but also that of the Republic Ireland. Both currencies circulated freely in the two parts of the country until the Republic of Ireland entered the European Monetary System in 1979 at which time the values of the two currencies diverged.

It is worth listing some of the other problems that the bus companies were having to deal during that February as well as coping with decimalisation:

3 February:     During riots in the Clonard Street area of Belfast, following on from army searches, a crane truck and a BCT Fleetline double-decker bus were hijacked, used as a barricade and then set on fire.

4/5 February:   Riots in Clonard area: BCT Daimler CVG6s Nos 374, 427 and 428 hijacked. After an emergency meeting, the BCT withdrew bus services to the city's trouble spots until further notice.

6/ 7 February:  BCT Daimler CVG6 Ns 354 and Daimler Fleetlines Nos 655 and 661 hijacked.

7 February:     Riots all over the Province; bus services disrupted.

8 February:     Ardoyne depot bombed. Riots Antrim/New Lodge road. BCT No.565 hijacked.

9 February:     BCT Daimler CVG6 No 355 hijacked in Castle Street.

15 February:    Changeover to decimal coinage day.

26/27 February:

                Rioting in Markets area. Buses burned in Cromac Square.

## March 1971: the Troubles, express buses and traffic congestion

A meeting of the Belfast Corporation's Transport Committee held in March 1971 illustrated a number of operational issues of interest during the 1970s:

The BCT's General Manager, Mr Robert Adams, reported that bus receipts had dropped by one-third during the outbreak of rioting in February when services were stopped altogether in riot areas. The chairman of the committee, Councillor W Spence, referring to the attempted hijack of buses the day previous to the meeting, said that if, ". . . these people do not behave themselves these buses will be taken away altogether."

In spite of the growing impact of the Troubles, Ulsterbus and the BCT were still looking for ways to improve services. This March meeting saw the beginnings of what would eventually become the highly successful Citybus 'City Express' service. The Transport Committee agreed to try out an express bus on the Dundonald and Carnmoney routes, in addition to the normal services. Coming into town in the morning, the Dundonald 'express' would not pick up passengers after Knock, and Knock Road would be the first stop on the way out in the evening rush. On the Carnmoney route the first stop would be Glengormley.

However, the Transport Committee refused to approve a proposal that the Castlereagh buses should turn at the Albert Clock, or that the Oldpark service should turn at Upper Queen Street to avoid the city centre traffic congestion. Councillor Alfie Ferguson, deputy chairman of the Committee, opposed stopping the Castlereagh service at Albert Clock because he claimed that the 10,000 people using these services were paying two tokens to get into town so were entitled not to be put off four or five stops early. In addition he noted that many people from the north, west and south of the city had to make a cross-town trip to get to work at various Castlereagh factories and so an Albert Clock turnabout would mean a long walk for these workers from the city centre.

However, radically, for the time, he suggested it would be better to take the cars out of the centre of the city than the buses.

## February 1975: Women drivers

At the start of 1975 there was a flurry of media interest in Ulsterbus's announcement that they intended to introduce women drivers. Although female conductors, or 'clippies,' (the term 'clippie' never caught on in Northern Ireland), had been a common feature in Great Britain for years, Ulsterbus had only introduced women conductors in 1970. The BCT never did, even during the two World Wars.

However, some of the men in Smithfield depot did not approve of the idea of women behind the wheel. On Saturday 15 February 1975 Ulsterbus made an announcement that it was to take on women as drivers. There was an immediate protest from Transport and General Workers Union busmen in Smithfield depot who claimed that this would undermine wages, and they threatened a stoppage. Although the other main union, the Municipal and General Workers Union, refused to back this stance, the Smithfield men received support from Eugene O'Callaghan of the TGWU who claimed that though, in principle, he had no objection to women drivers, the Ulsterbus announcement was in contravention of an existing agreement with the union.

However, at the end of the month, after a new pay agreement was reached with the Ulsterbus management, the TGWU dropped its opposition. In May, Betty Scott of Smithfield qualified as Ulsterbus's first woman driver. Betty had been one the first group of women conductors that the company had taken on five years earlier.

However, it was not until 20 September 1978 that Citybus's first woman driver, Kathleen McMahon, started work.

## April 1975: End of conductors and double-deckers

In April 1975 it was announced that the face of public transport in Belfast would change dramatically as both double-decker buses and conductors were gradually be withdrawn. The announcement of the intention to stop using double-deckers was made on the introduction of the first of a batch of 170 new vehicles, which, perhaps surprisingly, included 40 Leyland Atlanteans, the last new double-deckers Belfast would see for nearly a quarter of a century.

## September 1975: Standee buses

Another innovation which caught the media's attention was the proposal to introduce high-capacity standee single-decker buses as a cost-cutting exercise. Trials of a couple of these buses had been carried out in Belfast over the previous year and in September 1975 Citybus decided to give them a semi-official launch.

Eventually, these unpopular 'cattle trucks' became the standard type of single-decker bus to be used in Belfast. They had almost the same nominal passenger capacity as the double-deckers being withdrawn, though much cheaper to build, maintain and operate.

### 1975: Concessionary Fares for pensioners

During the 1970s, the management of Ulsterbus and Citybus came under continuous pressure to grant concessionary fares to pensioners. Mr Heubeck refused to do this on the grounds that elsewhere in the UK the government made up losses to bus companies due to the granting of concessionary fares. In Northern Ireland, the direct-rule ministers refused to contemplate this for Ulsterbus or Citybus.

However, by 1975 a scheme was in place whereby over-70s were able to travel on Citybus between 10am and 12.30pm and 2.30pm and 4.30pm for 4p. There were no reduced fares on Ulsterbus. Eventually, once government had agreed to underwrite the scheme, concessionary fares were introduced on both Ulsterbus and Citybus.

### November 1976: Republican Clubs and public transport

The Republican Clubs/The Workers Party, which had evolved out of the Official IRA, took a keen interest in the development of public transport and this is illustrated by the proposals they made to the Transport Review for Belfast. Some of the ideas contained they put forward have since come to pass, but others are still matters for discussion and debate.

In a statement released to the press on 6 November 1976, Republican Clubs/TWP proposed free car parks and free express buses and bus and cycle lanes for Belfast

A novel aspect of their submission was the proposal to establish three traffic 'collars' around Belfast. The outer collar, two miles from the city centre would be a ring of major public car parks. These would be free with free express buses leaving every five minutes during rush hours for the city centre. Only buses, service vehicles and short-stay cars and vans would be allowed through. The second collar would be half a mile from the city centre and would contain free car parks linked to the city centre by buses. The only other traffic allowed would be buses, essential service vehicles, and cars owned by local residents. The third collar would be an inner-city collar ½ mile from the city centre. Most cars would be banned within this zone. Only buses and essential services vehicles would be allowed through.

Other proposals included:

- Pedestrianisation of most streets around the City Hall.
- Linking the Belfast–Larne rail line to the Bangor line by a new bridge across the Lagan to run alongside a road bridge linking the M2 to the Sydenham by-pass.
- Scrapping all bus fares, as well as the token system because it penalised workers in far-flung housing estates.
- The construction of cycle lanes and new multi-storey car parks.

### December 1976: Tickets not tokens

Werner Heubeck made it clear at every opportunity how much he disliked the token system he had inherited from the Belfast Corporation Transport Department and which had been introduced in February 1970. However, he had to obtain permission from government before he could remove it. In December 1976, the system that would eventually replace the tokens, the multi-journey ticket, was trailed in the media by Citybus. At this stage, however, what was being outlined was not quite the system that was finally adopted, the multi-journey card system introduced in April 1978.

On 15 December 1976, Citybus released a statement announcing that it was considering a long-term plan to phase out tokens. The company had calculated that fare-dodgers on Belfast buses had cost it at least £½ million during 1976. They pointed the finger firmly at those passengers who didn't use the correct number of tokens to pay for their journeys. It was suggested that a decision on replacement of the token system could be taken in about six months once agreement with the Government had been achieved.

Citybus management had become dissatisfied with the token system, the principal reason being that many commuters making a 'two token' bus trip only put one token into the ticket machine and only a blitz on buses by inspectors could successfully cut down on this type of fare evasion. There was also the problem of 'token hoarding' each time a fresh rise in bus fares was rumoured, leading to shortages of tokens and loss of revenue for the company.

It was made clear that Citybus management were already looking at alternative methods for paying fares and had studied systems being used in other major European cities. These included a method where passengers would buy books of tickets at retail outlets in the same way as Belfast commuters purchased bags of tokens. The tickets would be automatically cancelled in a machine by the passenger on entering the bus. The driver need not be involved at all in the process. Compliance would be enforced by inspectors with powers to levy substantial on-the-spot fines.

Another factor putting Citybus off the whole concept of the token system was the sheer physical problem associated with the handling of bus tokens. Each week Citybus had to process and recycle several tons of them. And finally, there was the fact that tokens were, in themselves, items of value and so were the target of thieves.

So, what Citybus wanted was to find an alternative, fraud-proof way of issuing tickets where the driver would not have to handle an excessive amount of cash while at the same time retaining the use of one-man buses.

In December 1976, Citybus was finally able to announce that talks had started between the government and Mr Heubeck, over future plans for the bus services. As well as confirming that Citybus were considering phasing out tokens in favour of a flat-rate fare, it was announced that tougher penalties for bus and rail fare-dodgers were also on the agenda.

## 1977: Citylink service looking shaky

In 1977, a year into the provision of the Citybus 'Citylink' bus service linking the new Central station to Belfast city centre, it was looking as if the service might have to be scrapped because of low levels of patronage.

However, in fact, it was retained, having been eventually taken over from Citybus by Northern Ireland Railways and survived in one form or another until the 2005 'Metro' re-branding of Belfast city services. It was then replaced by a provision allowing train passengers to travel free into and out of Belfast city centre using ordinary stage-carriage services.

## 11 June 1977: Award for Citybus driver

A month after the murder by loyalists of Harry Bradshaw at the wheel of his bus, another Citybus driver, Hugh McClune received an unexpected award for his services to transport, the British Empire Medal. He received the award in the Jubilee Birthday Honours list. Hugh had thirty years service when he received the award, the last fourteen of which had been based in Falls Park depot.

In an interview after the award had been announced he said, referring to the problems of working through the Troubles:

> We could have had an award for the whole staff for this is a team award. If everyone had not pulled their weight there would have been no award. Everyone from inspector to the mechanics has worked hard particularly through the troubles. But I can't understand why they have picked me. I'm just an ordinary driver. If the road was there I took my bus along it. I know Belfast busmen have had a hard job keeping the vehicles on the road during the Troubles. I have had buses burned and windows smashed like everyone else.

## May 1978: Pat-on-the-back time

Since the start of the Troubles, both Ulsterbus and BCT/Citybus had taken a hammering from terrorist action, both directly through death and injuries to staff, and loss of vehicles and facilities, as well as indirectly through loss of business due to potential passengers staying at home. However, in spite of this, the companies were in a sound financial position, something very rare at that time amongst bus companies elsewhere in Britain and further afield.

Statistics released by the two companies in May 1978, gives a useful rain check on the scale of vehicle losses suffered up to that point, as well as the excellent financial results being achieved under Mr Heubeck's leadership. The key numbers were:

- A fleet size of 800 Ulsterbuses and 300 Citybuses
- To date, Citybus and Ulsterbus had each lost more than 300 buses, worth £15 million in total
- In 1977 Ulsterbus made more than £2 million and Citybus £500,000

The successful financial performance announced was all the more creditable when it is remembered that the weekend previous to the figures being released there had been yet another attack on the Ulsterbus depot in Dungannon. Derry, another regular target had also suffered a recent attack.

The spokesman complained that although the two companies did get government subsidies, these were much less than what was being received by comparable companies in Great Britain. This was in spite of the fact that they were the only UK bus companies making money.

Between August 1969, when the Troubles had really started, and May 1978 nearly all 25 main Ulsterbus depots had been hit. This was in addition to the daily attacks on and burning of buses, mainly those of the Citybus fleet. A spokesman noted that in the rural areas losses were nearly always of vehicle parked in depots whereas in Belfast buses were mostly lost when running in service.

In its statement, Milewater Road announced that increasing numbers of single deck buses to replace those destroyed were being bought second-hand, primarily from London Transport and operators in the north-east of England. The first of the London buses had arrived in 1977 and about 50 were already in service. As well as the second-hand buses, about 100 new buses were being bought every year.

### May 1979: Depot facilities criticised

Councillor Will Glendinning of the Alliance party, who was a regular critic of the lack of passenger facilities at depots, surfaced again in May 1979 with another attack on Ulsterbus for the poor conditions at Great Victoria Street station. He said the conditions at the station were a disgrace and he encouraged the public to make their complaints known.

Mr Heubeck countered by saying that since the station was likely to be replaced within two or three years by a new station at Maysfield, he could not justify expenditure on facilities which would only be used for a short time. In a letter to the Ulster Tourist Development Association, Mr Heubeck accepted that facilities at the depot were unsatisfactory but pointed out that there had never been a waiting room at the Great Victoria Street terminus.

The UTDA had expressed concern because the depot was the arrival point for the airport bus and they were concerned that the depot would give visitors a poor first impression of Belfast.

Mr Heubeck's statement on there never having been passenger facilities at GVS was not strictly true, because before the railway station closed and the bulk of the passenger facilities there demolished to make way for the building of the Europa hotel, bus passengers had been able to use the railway waiting, buffet and toilet facilities.

# Some Special Events

### 1976: The 'Peace People'

The 'Peace People' movement was started by two West Belfast women, Mairead Corrigan and Betty Williams. Mairead Corrigan was an aunt of three children killed when a car driven by an IRA team went out of control after the driver was shot dead by an army patrol in West Belfast. The women began to hold a series of 'Peace Rallies' in an attempt to mobilise ordinary people on both sides of the sectarian divide against the violence occurring all over Northern Ireland. The two women would be awarded the 1976 Nobel Peace Prize for their efforts. Their 'Peace Rallies' provided good business for Ulsterbus and Citybus, providing transport for both supporters and opponents of the Peace People.

### 1979: The Pope's visit to Ireland

At the start of August 1979, an announcement was made that, in September, Pope John Paul II would pay a first ever papal visit to Ireland. This would place significant strains on the Province's public transport undertakings, given the larger number of people who would want to attend the open-air masses he would be celebrating in various parts of the country.

The Pope was to arrive in Ireland for a three-day visit starting on 29 September and two key events during his visit would be open-air masses in Dublin and at the Knock shrine. In order to ease some of the transport problems the Diocesan committee set up to deal with the visit, had a sub-committee solely to co-ordinate transport arrangements. Ulsterbus and Lough Swilly were each invited to have a representative on this sub-committee.

By August, an Ulsterbus spokesman was able to confirm that to date they had bookings for 60 coaches for the

Saturday and Sunday of the visit but that the situation was still fluid. He confirmed that the company did expect to receive more bookings when the full programme was announced and that they expected to reach saturation point and start turning people away.

It was hoped that special trains from Derry to Dublin would be able to take some of the pressure off the buses but once again, the number of trains it would be possible to run would depend on the amount of rolling stock available.

An Ulsterbus spokesman ruled out speculation that additional buses could be brought from Great Britain to help out. This would not be viable because it would be too expensive to ship them over to Northern Ireland and the charge would have to be passed on the customer. In addition, all buses would have to undergo a Northern Ireland PSV test before they could go into service here.

There had been speculation that the Pope might also visit Northern Ireland, but in the event this did not happen. However, the Pope did celebrate a mass just south of Dundalk and this resulted in a massive operation by Ulsterbus and Citybus to get the crowds from north of the border there and back safely while still maintaining normal services at home.

### 1991: The Tall Ships Race

In July 1991, the International Tall Ships Race visited Belfast. It was arranged that the ships would anchor in Pollock Dock, close to York Road railway station, and that as many visitors as possible would be encouraged to travel to the venue by public transport. By his own admission, Frank Clegg, an operations executive with Citybus, says that the company completely underestimated the numbers of people who wanted to visit the spectacle. In the event, it is estimated that over a quarter of a million people poured into the docklands area to see the 80-plus vessels, which included the 400 foot Russian sail training ship *Sedov*.

The small fleet of buses originally allocated to the shuttle service, had to be quickly strengthened for the four days of the event. The visit culminated in a huge carnival in which about 2000 members of the ships' crews took part and which included a magnificent fireworks display.

When the ships left, sailing in convoy down Belfast Lough, additional public transport facilities, both road and rail, had to be put on to transport large numbers of people to various points along both shores of Belfast Lough to allow them to view the ships' departure.

# Industrial disputes

### 1976–79: Strikes and threats of strikes

In spite of the Troubles, normal industrial relations problems continued. Below three accounts from between 1976 and 1979 illustrate the sort of on-going problems that management and union leaders had to deal with. Two of the stories illustrate that factors related to the 'Troubles' were involved.

#### September 1976:

A group of about 60 drivers in Craigavon went on strike over various issues, including having to operate o-m-o double-deckers and drive second-hand buses brought in from England to replace buses lost to terrorism. This led to a standoff between the striking drivers and Werner Heubeck. School services were particularly badly hit.

The strike began at Lurgan depot when 30 drivers walked out. It then spread to Portadown where a further 30 men walked out. It was not possible to operate bus services out of the two depots although services continued to operate into Craigavon from other depots.

The strikers were protesting against having to drive o-m-o double-deckers at the same rate of pay as single-decker buses. There were also some demands for the re-introduction of conductors. It was also stated by the drivers' spokesman that the men objected to having to drive old buses which had been brought into service because of the destruction of vehicles by terrorists.

The strikers were not supported by their unions. Both the Transport and General and the Municipal Workers' Unions advised the men to return to work. The unions regarded the strike as being unofficial and they refused to make it official. Mr Heubeck made it clear that he was prepared to discuss the men's grievances, but only after they returned to work.

In the first week of October, Ulsterbus management issued an ultimatum that drivers on unofficial strike should return or face dismissal. This did the trick and the next day the company was able to announce that services in the Craigavon area were running again after the drivers called off their strike

A union official announced that talks would take place with management on the drivers' grievances. However, Mr Heubeck made it clear to the press that he also wanted to discuss with union leaders the reasons behind the excessive number of unofficial stoppages in Lurgan depot.

### July 1978:

This dispute followed on from the destruction of Smithfield depot and the move of its services to Oxford Street.

Ulsterbus services to Newtownabbey and Carrickfergus were hit by a 24-hour strike, ostensibly over a meal allowance. About 60 buses were off the road as a result. Again the stoppage was unofficial and it involved drivers who were based at Smithfield depot but who were operating from Oxford Street because their home depot had been destroyed in a bomb attack.

They claimed they were entitled to a daily £1.00 meal allowance because they were working away from their home depot. Werner Heubeck, in an uncompromising statement, made it clear that he had told the Smithfield drivers that they did not qualify for the allowance. "Smithfield depot is closed," he said. "The drivers are now based at Oxford Street."

*Former London Transport AEC Merlins in service with Ulsterbus at Lurgan. No 2506, formerly LT MB 312, on the left retains its London red livery while No 2517, ex-LT MB 364, has acquired a coat of Ulsterbus blue and ivory. Both vehicles had been delivered to LT in 1968 and had come to Northern Ireland in 1977. No 2517 moved to Citybus in March 1980 (see Citybus, Belfast's buses 1973–1988, page 93) and was later renumbered 674; it was maliciously destroyed in 1982.*

The strike was not a great success. An inspector at the Oxford Street depot said that there had been few enquiries from the public about the missing buses and he suspected that black taxis operating between Belfast and Rathcoole and Monkstown were carrying many of the passengers. People would also have switched to the trains from places like Whitehead, Carrickfergus and Greenisland.

### May 1979:

In early May 1979, Ulsterbus found itself in court defending itself against a claim that the company was not paying the correct level of wages to its workers

The unions took Ulsterbus to the Industrial Court asking it to adjudicate on a claim that the bus company was in breach of a section of the 1967 Northern Ireland Transport Act. If successful, this claim would have given the company's' drivers pay increases of more than £15 per week, backdated to January 1971.

A month later the courts ruled in favour of the unions' position, except that the pay claim was backdated only to January 1979. There then followed a squabble between the company and the unions over the precise meaning of the ruling and therefore the amount to be paid out. The unions called for an overtime ban to force the company to fall into line with their wishes. The ban was called off a few days later after the Court had clarified the position. Their clarification was in line with the unions' interpretation of the award conditions.

*Two unidentified Leyland PD3 double-deckers flank Albion Aberdonian No 62 amidst the tangled mess of what was Smithfield depot, on 21 July 1972. Ex-Edinburgh Corporation Tiger Cub No 1036 is on the left of the picture; the mangled double-decker on the right is a Leyland PD2.* **Belfast Telegraph**

*The remains of Citybus Eastern Coachworks-bodied Bristol REs No 715 (left) and No 781 block Springhill Avenue, West Belfast, on 11 March 1988. No 715 had come to Northern Ireland in April 1986 from the Eastern National Omnibus Company, Chelmsford, where it had been new in 1972, while No 781, also new in 1972, arrived in Belfast in December 1984 from United Automobile Services of Darlington.* **Mark O'Neill**

***Citybus Bristol RE No 2401 was hijacked and burned on the Shankill Road on 3 March 1987. Its remains were recovered and taken to Ardoyne depot, where it was caught by the photographer, for component recovery. The choice of advert applied to the rear of the vehicle was, perhaps, somewhat unfortunate!***
**Will Hughes collection**

# MANAGEMENT'S PROBLEMS

In this chapter, the main problems faced by the senior management teams of Ulsterbus and Citybus resulting from the Troubles are encapsulated in this fascinating interview given by Werner Heubeck in January 2002 to Ruth Graham as part of the *Routes* project.

Another senior manager with Ulsterbus, Irvine Millar, who was involved in the operational side of running the company, gives a valuable insight into the view of things from the company's Milewater Road headquarters during the difficult years.

In his interview, Frank Clegg who joined the Belfast Corporation Transport Department fresh from school as a junior manager describes vividly how the Troubles impacted on the BCT between 1968 and 1973 when it became Citybus Limited. Frank stayed with the 'red buses' after Citybus was formed and is a senior manager with Translink at the time of writing.

Finally, there is a brief summary of the report prepared to identify the financial loses being suffered because of black taxi competition on some important bus routes.

## *Werner Heubeck, Managing Director*

## Introduction

Like almost everyone else in Northern Ireland, the Troubles caught the managements of Ulsterbus and the Belfast Corporation Transport Department by surprise. Werner Heubeck said that when he took over the job of Managing Director of Ulsterbus, he had intended to stay only long enough to get the company on its feet before moving on to pastures new. However, once the Troubles took hold, he decided he could not leave and stayed to steer the company, and later Citybus, through the worst years of the civil unrest.

WH    The start of Ulsterbus was quite dramatic and to the best of my knowledge nothing like that has ever been done either before or since. We finished under the Ulster Transport Authority on a Sunday night and to operate all the services we needed 1600 duties. Now a duty is a piece of work for which you need a driver. Monday morning, we started the same services and the public didn't know there was a change – the buses looked the same – they didn't realise there was a change – with 1200 duties. Now you imagine a 25% reduction – and because we formed the company in April at a time when the cash flow from fares and everything was in excess of outgoings – we started building up immediately a positive cash balance. Now before we did that, I said to my chairman, "Look we better go to the bank and get an overdraft". Now at that time (don't forget this was over thirty years ago) half a million pounds was an awful lot of money. So we got an unsecured overdraft – we had no security – I'm sure they spoke to the Government and the Government must have approved but as far as we were concerned this was an unsecured overdraft and the way the timing fell there was more money coming in than going out. So of course we built up a positive balance and after a few weeks I went to the bank and said, "Thanks very much but we don't need to make use of your overdraft." Now the effect on the business community must have been sensational because nobody believed this could be done. But it was and, of course, it enabled us to gain their confidence. You see people were beginning to trust me whereas before I was an unknown entity who could talk but that was all. So it created the foundation, which enabled us to deal with the Troubles, when they finally came, in an important way, which I will explain in a minute.

So within two years I was really thinking of leaving again because I only went over there to sort out public transport and it was done. But then, the Troubles started and I couldn't leave and I will try and explain that also.

The beginning was quite harmless. It was civil rights marching and such but there was an incident at a place called Burntollet Bridge which is just this side of Londonderry from Belfast where the civil rights marchers marched from Belfast to Londonderry and a lot of Protestants stood. The bridge goes over . . . there's a sort of embankment and the Protestants gathered there and stoned them. I knew there would be trouble and I went up because we had buses on hire to bring them back. I called up and the road was littered with stones. Now this looked terrible but the number of injuries was not all that great because from a distance you can dodge a stone. But it was, in those days, a shattering event. The first person I met was our inspector in the car, so I flagged him down and I asked him what had happened and he said, "Listen boss. It was rough," because nobody had ever really faced a stoning crowd from two sides. I realised then that this was going to take on a much more serious edge and that it would not be over quickly. Then of course the shooting started and the riots in Belfast. The Troubles had really started in earnest.

Now, as far as I'm concerned, public transport-wise, the most important lesson occurred in an incident on the Glen Road. This was before I became responsible for the red buses. In those days, the City Fathers still ran the red buses and the only reason they got dumped on me was that they were beginning to start needing money. So they went to the Government and said, "Look will you bail us out?" And the Government said "Not at all!" and took the buses off them and gave them to me and said, "Run them. And sort them out on the same basis as the blue." This happened to coincide. Now the last thing I wanted was the red buses because the Troubles were already beginning to cause serious problems. But the willing horse does it. Now you know where the Glen Road is? Above Falls depot there. An Ulsterbus was lying on its side on a piece of grass but it was not damaged so I got told and said, "Alright we will go up to retrieve it." But this was in the early days so I went to Andersonstown police station and we organised it and the army was already in Northern Ireland and the inspector said, "Listen, you will have to go up with an army escort." Well I couldn't argue. So I remember saying to the driver of the recovery truck "I'm going up with you in my own car but if anything goes wrong, we've got over 1000 buses but only one recovery truck, so if I give you the signal just unshackle and get out." So I went up with a police inspector and we stood there and the army was there and our men were there too and they had to right the bus first and they to pull it off the grass and there was a fire hydrant in the way which was a bit of a nuisance. The police sergeant and I were watching it and he said, "Listen, we haven't got much time." The dustbin lids were being rattled which was a signal for everybody to get inside. So I said, "I know. But if I shout on our fellows to hurry up then everything will go wrong." Within a very short time the shooting started and the first thing that happened was the lieutenant in charge of the detail came down – he had been shot through the jaw. Now it looked horrible but I am sure it was only a wound, which was sorted out later. So I realised that the army would have to retreat because they had nobody in charge. So I shouted to our people, "Unhook and get out!" And they did. And I waited until they had cleared off and I remember that I walked up the Glen Road for a few yards and a couple had strayed into this – totally uninvolved so I shoved them into an armoured vehicle and said, "Don't get out until they tell you to." and I was that mad that I refused to go in the armoured vehicle. I just turned my back and walked all the way down to the Falls depot.

And there was an aftermath. When I got to the Falls depot, there was the driver of our recovery truck and he had been shot through the arm. It wasn't serious, right, but he had a lump as big as that with the blood pouring out. Anyway, by that time I already knew enough about who to speak to etc, etc. And I said, "What's the big idea of shooting at us!" "Oh well you came with the army." So I said, "Listen, I was there" – and this went in a very roundabout way – I never met anyone who really needed to get the message. Anyway, I said, "I was there" and they all knew I was there "and the shot was not fired from a distance. There was not a soldier within range near the recovery truck driver." And I said, "Whoever fired that shot aimed deliberately at a working man trying to earn his living." This was in . . . it must have been 1971. There was any number of occasions when people were lying in a hedgerow with guns watching us recovering vehicles. We were never fired on again. Now the first lesson that I want to impress on you is this. When you are dealing with these situations where the rule book has gone out of the window and you have to find your own solutions – if you make one mistake or if you put yourself at somebody else's mercy and become beholden to somebody – you are sunk. And the one leads to another and you can't do your job.

I decided at that incident. I said, "The army and the police are to be kept away from the buses completely."

Now this was not immediately achieved but I established relations with the police – I had to because I had to know what was going on etc, etc. And my standing then was such that I was being trusted because when you go out and don't sit in your office and face the reality on the street, you don't have to reassure people, they make up their own mind. So I tackled the police and the army. I went to Lisburn headquarters and said, "Listen, you've got to understand one thing. This is not going to be over in a short time." They were setting up a thing called the Ulster Defence Regiment, which were part-time soldiers, and of course they were mostly Protestants. I said, "Understand one thing – driving a bus and playing soldiers don't mix." Now I couldn't stop them and three of the employees who were murdered were murdered not because they were workers on the buses but because they were part-time soldiers.

Now I wasn't popular saying that but I decided that no one – not the government, not the unions, nobody – was going to run the buses, except me. Now this was put to test time and time again. The most famous one was when quite a long time later the IRA attacked public transport – not only public transport, but we got the brunt of it – two successive Fridays. These things always happened on a Friday because then the weekend was there and they could watch television etc, etc, and on the second occasion, drivers were being attacked. Also, unfortunately, a woman was burned to death because it was a hot afternoon and the idiots used petrol instead of diesel to set the bus on fire and it flashed and caused a fireball and the woman was burned to death. The man who did it also got burned but he managed to jump off. So that was it – I said, "Stop the buses." I will come back to this in a short while.

I knew, whenever there was serious trouble in Belfast, the next day Londonderry would follow suit so next day I was on my way to Londonderry. When I got there, there was a phone message saying that I had to go to a meeting at Stormont. I had stopped the buses on the Falls Road, so I turned my driver out of his seat because I had to break the speed limit and I did that rather than asking him. Anyway I drove to Stormont and we made it. We had to go to a meeting, a big meeting about the Troubles, and the colonel who was representing the army took me aside and said, "My general thinks that you should restore the services." So I said, "Thanks very much for tipping me off." And in we went. Eventually his turn came and he had to say his piece because he had been instructed so I said – there were police, civil servants and the army – "Look, let's be clear, let the general run the army but I run the buses." I kept the buses off the Falls Road for five weeks because – I said, "Attacks on drivers are something I show no mercy for!" Do you know, they didn't even argue with me. I got no pressure to put them back. Eventually we restored it but it was me who decided when and I didn't listen to anybody.

So I will come back to this later on because this was a very important attitude on my part, which governed why we succeeded in coping and keeping going and, above all, why we never really had any serious trouble about attacks on staff. Losses of buses I accepted because whenever there is civil disturbance the first thing they do is turn over the trams and buses and set them on fire so I was gearing up myself for a long haul. Mind you, I didn't think it would last eighteen years.

Now at that time Citybus was dumped on me as well. I didn't want them because they had a different union agreement – their attitude to work, the way they worked, the way the duties were organised were all completely different to Ulsterbus – so all I did was, I left Citybus completely on its own with it's own Chief Engineer; they had their loyalties, you see, and if you merged they would get interfered with. I put one man in charge and he was the former Corporation operating manager and he ran them along with the blue buses in the Belfast depots.

By that time we were ready to face the Troubles. And the first thing now I want to explain is attitude because the key to understanding these issues had a lot to do with my own attitude which was, "I run the buses and no one else." Now let me deal with these things one at a time. I told the government I would maintain the services unless we lost more than 100 buses a year. And I kept that promise. Mind you, sometimes it was touch and go. There were three years running when we lost 115 but we managed. I've already mentioned that we told the army that the Ulster Defence Regiment and driving buses don't mix and I could not stop them joining but the army had to accept the consequences. I heard of incidents – the details don't matter – where some drivers had to carry their guns on duty. I mean concealed guns. Now the biggest thing I did when I became responsible for the red buses – the army was in occupation of all the three Citybus depots, that's Short Strand, Ardoyne and Falls depot – I went round and I was horrified. They were all next to republican areas and I said, "Sooner or later some idiot is going to plant a bomb and cause awful problems." So I went to army headquarters and said, "Listen, I want all of you out!" Now at first they didn't believe me, but when they realised I meant it, within twelve hours they had disappeared. Now that was important because I had already decided that the army and the police would have no role in protecting buses – you can't protect buses – so I said "Don't even try. You have to rely on something quite different," and of course secretly the army and police were glad that they didn't have to worry about the buses. "No matter, Heubeck will deal with it!" And what's more our own employees also preferred that because whenever a soldier went into a depot – we were completely penetrated by the UDA or the IRA paramilitaries – they knew what was going on and it was always a cause of friction. So my attitude of getting the army away from buses meant that I completely succeeded in preventing public transport (bus-wise) from becoming a political football. We were there for one purpose and one purpose only – get the kids to school and home again, get the workers to work and nothing else would be allowed to matter. This also helped me with the politicians because I knew we would have to face tough situations.

The worst one potentially was when a bus driver was shot in Londonderry; some Protestant bus drivers used this as an excuse to prevent them to drive on their duty. I allowed it for a while and then I said this has got to stop. There was a small core of about four or five drivers who refused to carry out their duty – now potentially that was dynamite – so I went round and said some words in the right places and said, "These drivers are going to be sacked by me and don't you go near this problem." So the unions knew and some of the local politicians were also told and those five drivers were sacked. Now that was a very important lesson because it drove home the point – I decide what happens – and if you use a sound argument for the wrong reason, you are going to suffer the consequence, and the unions didn't argue.

So you see what I'm driving at. I wasn't defenceless, I don't mean in a personal sense, I mean in the discharging of my duties and above all to ensure that drivers were as secure in what they were doing as I could possibly make it. I had a far bigger protection than guns or security forces; it was something that I will try and explain to you now. It's a concept called moral superiority. That means that when you face a contested situation – and it doesn't matter whether it's the government and me; whether it's the union, Mr O'Callaghan and me; whether it's the Ulster Defence Association or the IRA against me – I always made sure I had more moral plus on my side of the argument. Once I had that, I prevailed. Now this is something unfortunately that nobody ever appreciated. Of course, it takes courage but I knew I had the courage necessary not to start running out of steam halfway through a tight situation, and it worked time and time again.

There was one episode, and again this is one where I want you to be discrete in what you do with it, when the Hunger Strikers died. The first one went and nobody knew what was happening; it was really very tense. I didn't even go near the army or the police to ask for information. I said to the man in charge of Belfast – we knew Belfast was going to be the key because Bobby Sands was a Belfast man – so I said, "Right Max, we'll do a tour at 5 o'clock tomorrow morning, through Belfast and we'll decide then." So we did. He took one part of Belfast and I took the other, including Cromac Street and we met in his office down at the old Oxford Street depot, which is long gone now. I said, "I can see no reason why we can't roll the buses." He said, "I agree." So we phoned the police and said, "The buses are going to go out." And do you know, nothing happened.

And the point I am trying to make to you is, because I was there, I wasn't like an army major who was there for three months and disappeared, I was there every day. We developed a feeling for the situation which meant that we could trust our judgement, well we had to. We didn't take it lightly because we were conscious that bus drivers had to be sent in and the only allowance we made was, especially on Ulsterbus drivers coming in from the country, if there were serious riots in Belfast they were nervous and we made sure that they would not be punished for not being as brave as the boss was. But that was all. After a day they realised that they'd been a bit foolish.

You see, you would watch a street corner and you could tell from a distance if you were heading for trouble. So there was an expertise. These situations are really quite predictable, foreseeable, provided you are not in a state of panic – you've got to keep a cool head. I learned that very early on – before the shooting and the civil disturbances. The police in those days were called county inspectors and I realised that the county inspector knew what the crowd was going to do before the crowd had made up its own mind. Now this was crystal clear – all you had to do in those days was to mentally pace out or mentally measure the distance that somebody could throw a half brick and you stepped another ten paces back and you were alright – you could stand there calmly and watch what was going on. Provided you were willing to accept the responsibility, you could minimise the risks and as you gained experience you could judge the situation.

I remember once, there was one of those lunchtime riots outside the Royal (Victoria Hospital) on the Falls Road. So I left my car in the Northern Ireland Carriers yard which is right next to the Great Victoria Street bus station, where the freight depot is.

I walked up and yes, the place was black with people, there were double-decker buses . . . but what was significant was that the drivers stood not far away from the buses with their boxes where they had their money and their ticket rolls. They were responsible for them, so they always took them with them. I could see that they were only just waiting till it blew over then they would carry on. So I walked back and that's precisely what happened – so you can see that this is not as hair-raising as it is on television. Because when you are familiar with a situation you can judge exactly to what street corner you can go to or not.

So I really didn't have any trouble at all with the politicians. People like Paisley and Hume – I made it clear, *I* run the buses. If people have a complaint – people would write letters to their MPs with this complaint or the next – I said, "Tell them to get in touch with me. I will not let them down". Once they realised that they didn't have to worry about complaints from the buses it created goodwill and, of course, people accepted that not only I, but also the employees, were doing their best under very difficult circumstances and so they made allowances. They made allowances and, what's more, we acquired a standing. There was a time in Londonderry when the mothers said, "It's safe to let the children out! The buses are back!" This was perfectly true but events finally took over. Once the shooting started, it changed things. Now on the other hand we had to understand that we would also be affected. We couldn't expect to sail blithely through. I've already mentioned to you that I accepted that buses would be lost and I simply made arrangements accordingly to enable us to carry on. I also had to deal with a situation where drivers, going into estates after a riot, well, you didn't know what you would find. Well we did not oblige them to do that. What usually happened was that I, or the manager for Belfast, would take the first bus in, the driver would sit in the back and would see whether it was safe to resume. So again, the drivers were not being sent blindly into situations.

Now there were other things that were necessary. There were demonstrations and counter demonstrations and at one time one lot of private hire buses carried the demonstrators, the other lot carried the counter-demonstrators and third the police – to keep the two apart. You see? So we had to deal with these things as well. Some of the biggest demonstrations, especially over the Anglo-Irish Agreement, you were dealing with 80,000 people in the centre of Belfast. Well, they had to come in on the buses, nobody was going to take their cars. We very quickly learned how to organise these things. It didn't take any more than about three-quarters of an hour. We knew how many buses we would have and we knew how to route them. But people were coming and they would say, "We want to cross." and "We want to go the proper road." I would say to them, "You either go our way or you don't get taken, full stop." And they didn't argue.

Now the biggest problem we had was the effect on our financial position because people didn't go out at night, especially in Belfast; nobody went out at night for quite a few years. And, of course' the buses had to pay their way so I said "Look we've got to take essential workers to work, and we've got to get them home." I said, "Right, we'll take the workers home at six o'clock and after that we have a departure on the hour every hour." They all left from the City Hall and the inspector stood there and blew the whistle. The buses would come in a few minutes earlier to allow people to change and for an awful long time we had to survive like that. The loss, financially, was enormous but there was nothing you could do.

The government didn't help either by allowing the black taxis to mushroom the way they did. One can be very critical of the government but my main criticism was not that the black taxis took the hold the way that they did but because the effect was that every taxi fare had to be paid twice. We didn't get the money which we needed, right! The Inland Revenue lost out because many of those taxi fares were not declared as income so altogether it was a thoroughly unsatisfactory situation. Now given the situation that prevailed then, what really annoyed me was that the government didn't even try to cope with it. They made no attempt. They just allowed things to slide. The taxis took their passengers but they didn't take their kids to school.

There was poor St Louise's on the Falls Road, right. Sister Genevieve was one of the best people I have ever met. Everybody was terrified of her and she made demands on everybody. The governors of her school were terrified of her. When our managers couldn't cope with her any more, I was sent to talk to her. I only went to see her two or three times and I made it clear to her. I said, "I will do what I can for you but you are not entitled to tread on my territory to a degree that I can't cope with." You see, if you gave her a little finger she would take your hand! That was her nature, but once she accepted then that was it. You see, she respected that I was having problems too.

The taxis had a field day because they could come right into the city centre, make a short turn – there was a security gate – and we had to make big detours. So the time came when we had to go back on a normal route out of the city centre. I didn't know about it and the manager made the mistake of allowing the first bus to have passengers on. Well, as soon as they arrived at the security gates, the black taxis just blocked the road and started shouting abuse. So I was called and I arrived and there was the bus sitting and the first thing I did was I said, "Look," – we had two London taxis which were manned by inspectors to shuttle around on company business – "get one of those taxis and we'll put the passengers in." I said to one of the black taxi drivers, "Tell your committee chairman that we are coming back on Tuesday to go through." This was a Friday morning. So, on Tuesday we appeared on an empty bus. I said, "I want a driver who is not likely to lose his head," – not that we expected fisticuffs, that's not it – so I thought to myself that I better have a reporter present as well so I got hold of somebody from the *Belfast Telegraph*. He sat on the bus. We came to the same gate and, of course, the taxis blocked again. And the abuse! You see they saw their livelihood being threatened and so I could understand their point of view but I had a job to do and I was going to do it. I said, – there were only four people on the bus, myself, the manager, the driver and the reporter – "Sit completely still and don't move a muscle. Don't even look at anybody." And we did. One or two of them started thumping the side of the bus, which makes an awful noise but was harmless. And eventually the committee arrived – two or three of them – and so I asked the driver to open the door and he opened the door and I said to the committee chairman, "Look, we are going to resume the services," and I pointed to the driver and said, "That driver has as much right to earn his living as your drivers do to earn theirs. Tell them to open the road and let us through." He turned round and unblocked the road and we resumed the services. No soldiers needed, no nothing. Now that's what I call moral superiority. It takes courage. The reporter was terrified but he needed to be there just in case things went wrong. So you can see that when this effect has to cover a long period it is like a fungus that grows. It spreads in all directions and you may not see the effect, but it's there, and you can rely on it.

But we did have to make 350 jobs disappear in Ulsterbus because the demand fell away because of the increase in cars. But, by that time, when you do your job properly – I could see this coming and I said to the unions and I think O'Callaghan will confirm this – I said, "Look, we are going to have to cut down because the money isn't coming in." Then I said, "We can afford to take our time" and out of all the jobs that had to disappear I think only 15 were redundancies. Again, if you do your job properly you can afford to take the time but you've got to be on top of things not just struggling to keep your nose above the water.

I was far more effective against paramilitaries than I ever dared dream. There was, for example, an incident where, on the corner of the Newtownards Road, in the evening buses got stoned. It was young kids flexing their muscles. In that area it was Protestant muscle and not Catholic muscle, and, of course, there was a risk, especially at night when the driver couldn't see the stone coming, that there could have been an accident. And the media drew attention to this so the first thing I did was I went to speak to the press and the television and I said, "Look, don't publicise this. This is young children and the more publicity it gets, the more they will do it." And to give them their due, they did play ball. The stone throwing calmed down a bit. Now, it started again later but this time we got the feeling that it was an older age group. So I went to see somebody in the UDA. We knew how to get in touch if we had to. So I went and saw someone and explained that I expected them to stop the stoning. They came up with the usual feeble protests. I said, "Look I wasn't born yesterday!" And I have a classic phrase which always works, "Just do your best!" So they tried to get one on me and they said, "Here, you can do us a favour." I said, "What is it?" He said, "We have relatives going to Long Kesh. Will you give us a bus for nothing?" I said, "Nothing doing. Carry on stoning." And walked out. This really can be quite an important point because one day there was Protestant rioting in Belfast, on the Newtownards Road, and I had to stop the services. I was at a meeting in Portadown with the management and we got a message from the radio room of the red buses saying, "We are getting phone calls saying that if the buses don't go back they will burn all the bus depots." So I carried on with the meeting because they couldn't just burn all the bus depots and I completely ignored them. But it came on again, you see they persisted, "When are you going to put the buses back?" And of course the inspectors stalled them by saying they only did as they were told. So I said, "OK. The meeting is finished." We were going to have some lunch and the manager and I went to deal with it. So I told him to lay on a meeting, not on the Newtownards Road in East Belfast, but in West Belfast because I knew enough about the rivalries between East and West Belfast. The meeting was laid on and I made it perfectly clear. I said, "We'll decide. If the buses can operate they will operate but if they are stopped, no threats will make me change my mind." And I used that also in republican areas in the country if they attacked buses. I went to meetings where you didn't ask who was at the back of the hall and I made it clear, I said, "The buses are there to take passengers to where they want to go and home again. If they are left alone they will operate and if they are not, they won't." The unspoken understanding was that they might burn the odd bus and nothing would be said.

So the message I must make clear, too, is that although the bus drivers might have felt very vulnerable at times, they weren't without protection. There was a guardian angel watching over them and the casualties – well, we had about 13 people killed – Mr Hesketh made a calculation and the only thing he forgot was the first bus driver who was shot at home because he was a witness to something. That was on the red buses when I wasn't responsible.

Now I mentioned to you that the army and police were happy to leave us alone and by and large they did. If something happened I made certain enquiries with the police but I never dealt with the army because the army for much of the Troubles was useless. Their thinking was different and they were as much alien to us as they were hated on the Falls Road. But we also got plagued with suspect devices. Now that was not on the cards when I took my decision that the army and police were not to be involved. I had to face up to what to do about it and I decided that it was working so well that we had to let it continue and I made it clear that we did not want the army or the bomb disposal people unless we really needed them. Now, it didn't always work because sometimes a bomb disposal man got there first, in which case we let them get on with it. But there were several reasons and I'll deal with the depots first because, don't forget, it wasn't just bus drivers I had to deal with there were also fitters, etc.

It didn't suit our book at all to have army personnel in bus depots. First of all, if we called them about a suspect device we would have to abide by their way of doing it. The bomb disposal man has very strict instructions about what he can and can't do because, if he blows himself up, the government has to pay a pension to the widow, so he was not a free agent the way it would appear and that would take time and there was nothing we could do. We had to wash buses, fuel buses and get them ready so it didn't suit our book at all and also soldiers were like a red rag to a bull for some of our employees. So, we didn't want them. I gave instructions that I was to be informed first and then I would decide whether I was to inform the army and by and large it worked and the army quietly accepted this. Nothing was ever written down about this. It came into being and because it worked. It suited everybody and it was allowed to continue.

I can recall at least two attacks. We had 67 buses squashed together in the Ardoyne depot because it was an old tram depot and I remember one Sunday morning when the IRA put eight bombs into the depot. I was in there because I was working every weekend in the joiner's workshop. The inspectors on duty had the sense to wait until the IRA had cleared off before they called me. They knew I was there but they also knew I had a gun and that I wouldn't have hesitated to use it. So they called me and I said, "Right when was it?" A good 15 minutes had elapsed so I said, "That's dicey." These things have timers and if you are there within the first five minutes then you are usually OK to take a risk but once ten minutes had past then it became a problem. So I said I would get my gear. I kept ropes and hooks and things in the boot but as I was walking back the first bomb went off. So I said, "How many were there?" There were four fellows, which meant eight bombs – two each. So I waited – now they didn't all go off together – they were dotted all over the place. So after about the fourth bomb I said, "Listen we are getting out now." We knew exactly how fires developed. We also knew that diesel tanks don't rupture; they are like a flamethrower and the fire hoses out through the nozzle where you put the fuel in. So we had enough expertise to know that, but the gate at the top was locked from the inside (due to vandalism) and we had no means of getting over it. So I had to run through the whole of the yard to open the gate and then we drove out the buses. Instead of losing 67 buses we lost seven.

The rule was very simple, if somebody stepped on a bus – Protestant and Catholic employees – they all took their turn and if somebody saw a bus with a bomb on they simply shouted to the others, "Don't go near this one." They create a fireball. If you're inside the bus, you're dead. But if you are outside the force is not enough to blow the windows out and cause a lot of damage, so it was quite all right to drive the next bus away. You see, I knew that – experience tells you – but when it was over, one of the yardmen said, "Boss, I've never seen you run as fast as you did." Because the place was on fire, any moment another one could go off but you see that's simply called 'going beyond the call of duty'. Nobody could have touched you or accused you if you hadn't done it but by doing it you put yourself into a very strong position when you have to make somebody come down in size and that is really my contribution to the employee's safety. There were quite a few people who said I would not live to see retirement because of what I was doing. In other words, somebody would set me up. I always knew that this was not likely to happen. My reasoning, which of course was instinct, was that I never rubbed the nose of the IRA or the UDA in it when they did something involving buses. I judged and acted when it was all right to act and they had achieved their objective of causing a delay of a few hours or whatever they were trying to do and that really worked. It was pure psychology and I understood this. I never called terrorists by bad names because they simply saw things in a way that you can't judge by ordinary standards. And somehow or another that enabled us to survive eighteen years of the Troubles.

## *Irvine Millar*      *Projects Manager (Ulsterbus), later Inspector General*

# Introduction

Irvine Millar joined the newly formed Ulsterbus in 1967 from London Transport, where he had trained as a manager. He started in Ulsterbus as a Personal Assistant to Werner Heubeck, the company's new Managing Director and went on to occupy senior management positions in Ulsterbus/Citybus right through the period of the Troubles. In this interview, he gives an illuminating insight to the problems facing the companies from the perspective of a member of the senior management team.

**MC**   *When did you join Ulsterbus and in what capacity?*

**IM**   I joined as PA to the MD and started at the beginning of 1967. 1 January had been one of the dates for commencement of Ulsterbus but didn't happen and when I started the date had been moved provisionally from February to the beginning of April. It was then moved again to 17 April which became the final date. So I did have technically three months of employment with the UTA which now and again I claim credit for; but I really came to join the new company.

**MC**   *What attracted you to Ulsterbus?*

**IM**   Firstly, I am married to a girl from Donegal, so I was familiar with Ulster. Also I'm from Edinburgh. When I worked in London, I rarely saw my parents. We were in the position where we had to devote much of our holidays to alternately visiting Scotland and Donegal. So it seemed like a good idea to get closer to both Edinburgh and Donegal and that was one aspect of it. Also my colleague from London Transport, David McCracken, had moved across about three years earlier as Road Passenger Manager designate for the UTA but he never got beyond the 'designate' because they froze all appointments and promotions when they decided to disband the UTA and break it up into units. Now, he was fairly happy because he had made a reasonably good impression with the new MD when he was appointed. Werner was appointed about 18 months before the start date and David was working closely with him. We kept in touch and he had come to our wedding in Donegal. He put me wise as to the appointments that were going to be made. Area Manager jobs were advertised so I applied but they felt that I wasn't quite ready for Area Manager but Werner wanted me and offered me PA. When I came over, David was able to show me around the depots and help me get my bearings.

**MC**   *What sort of work did you do as PA?*

**IM**   It was all sorts of technical and advisory things. I got the Fleet Control department which at that time consisted of two people. In terms of executive responsibility, that was it. But the job was more ideas, a think tank sort of thing; bringing ideas in from elsewhere. David was also in this PA capacity at that time, and between us we did the fleet allocation for the new company, planning where all the vehicles should be allocated, trying to achieve some policy objectives in terms of standardisation within depots and things like that. There was a lot of work went into that initial allocation. A lot of vehicles were moved around the country and in terms of service development, what sort of services we should be going for and how we should be improving those services and improving the profitability and productivity of resources. Werner wasn't a transport man, so he wanted that sort of expertise to be personally available to him separately from the Area Managers themselves because I suppose he wanted some means of sounding their ideas out on others.

**MC**    *Were you in charge of the schedules?*

**IM**    No. Schedules had been a centralised function under the UTA, but once the initial schedules were done for the new company, they were decentralised down to the Area Managers. The concept was that Area Managers should run their own areas, as profit centres. The depots were also individual profit centres and were to be autonomous units within their areas. I had more involvement a couple of years later after I became Projects Manager and became part of the senior management structure. Then I was responsible for things which crossed area boundaries; if there was a need to look at something or intervene at the 'big picture' level. So I took on, at that stage, things like fares and fares policy, publicity, timetable production, those things that were done centrally for the whole company. Also anything which went outside the Province, eg, cross-border services, tours, etc. I also took on the commercial side. We also developed later into Scottish services as part of the commercial side.

**MC**    *What were the couple of years before the 'Troubles' started like?*

**IM**    When we started, we were all geared up to the whole idea of running purely a bus company and doing it successfully. We started off at Easter, in April, and we made a really big effort to make an impact on Easter tours and things like that. There were a lot of new buses out, the Bedford VAMs. There had been a lot of change, but I didn't detect much negative feeling from the staff. One-man-operation (o-m-o) was a big thing. There were still crews on double-deckers, but everyone understood, and accepted, that this was only until such times as there were buses available which would allow those duties also to be converted to o-m-o.

One of my first big jobs, which overlapped with the beginning of the Troubles, involved me spending several months in Derry. At the start of 1968 we had been told by Derry City Council to leave the Strand Road bus station site. This followed on from one of the first decisions that Werner took. To explain; my very first brief when I arrived in Northern Ireland had been to study the Derry city services and recommend what we should do with them. There had been a debate within the company as to whether they were profitable or not. As the result of my study, Werner took the decision to unilaterally cancel an old agreement which had been entered into in the 1920s by HMS Catherwood and Londonderry Corporation when that company took over the Corporation's city bus services. Under this agreement, Catherwood paid a proportion of the city service's profits to the Corporation. This amount was calculated by setting the revenue per mile on the city service, against the cost per mile of Catherwood's whole operation. In time of course, this became the NIRTB's whole operation and then the UTA's whole operation and so into Ulsterbus. This calculation was still showing a profit for Derry city services which was then being split with the city council. My calculations showed that this was a very inaccurate figure because the average cost of operating the city services was much higher than the Ulsterbus average, which was based on country operations. In fact, I showed that the Derry city services were barely breaking even, though I also recommended that they were worth holding on to. But based on my work, the decision was taken to cancel the agreement. There was little that Derry City Council could do about this, as the agreement was fifty years old and long out of date. They weren't in a position by then re-negotiate it either. However, in a fit of pique they told us to get our bus station out of their premises, the old Strand Road market. So we were put out of there, though they were pretty grotty premises. As a result, I set up what I sometimes called the 'string of pearls'. We managed to persuade the council to allow us to share their car park at Foyle Road. Here we located the bus station; we had a pay-in office across the road in the back of a chemist's shop; we took over office accommodation in an old, closed, mill building, which became the area office. Then there was a vacant site further down

Foyle Road where we placed the bus wash and refuelling point. We also had the garage down at the old GNR station and finally we used part of the GNR trackbed on the other side of Craigavon Bridge where the railway museum is now, as a parking area. We had everything strung out down that line. I did look at other sites. Pennyburn, where we are now, was one I looked at, but they were going to need far too much work and expense which at that time we could not afford. What I came up with was done on a shoestring and was only to last for about five years. But as these things do, it lasted for about 20 years. The Pennyburn depot was built later and that replaced all the stuff at the bottom end, but the present Foyle Road passenger terminal was only rebuilt as late as about 1990.

**MC** *So, the company was up and running and over the first couple of years, 1967 and 1968, it was just getting on its feet when things in Northern Ireland start to unravel politically. Can you remember the first incidents where you realised that things were starting to go wrong?*

**IM** Very much so. At the start of 1968, our Area Manager in Derry, James Heuston, was involved in a car accident and was going to be off for several months. As I mentioned earlier, something needed to be done about the fact that we had been told to leave our Strand Road depot by Derry Council, so I was sent up as Acting Area Manager. James Heuston came back in the autumn more or less on a full-time basis, but though my work was scaling down, I was asked to continue coming up to Derry a day or two per week because I had set in motion a number of property developments and relocations following from our need to get out of Strand Road. As a result I was in Derry during the summer of 1968. My wife and I had rented a house on Chapel Road, which overlooks Craigavon Bridge. Come the protests, the rioting, Burntollet and so on, there we were looking down on the Craigavon Bridge with a grandstand view of the water cannons and all of that. So I was there when the trouble started in Derry. The people who say that the trouble started in Belfast are wrong. It started in Derry and then spread to Belfast. It was 1969 before things got bad in Belfast – Ardoyne and the Lower Falls.

As well as that, the fact that I had the fleet responsibility meant that I had to deal with any fleet losses. Our policy was, keep the services going, so I had to be ready to replace any losses. As long as we had new vehicles coming in, one or two a week, that was enough to plug the gaps. The buses that were due to be replaced would perhaps be kept in service, maybe reallocated, instead of being withdrawn. We didn't tend to throw a new vehicle into a gap caused by malicious destruction. We had a planned allocation of new vehicles worked out beforehand to try and spread them fairly across the company. If there were losses, we might take half life vehicles out of an area to ensure that replacements for riot losses were of a reasonable quality. This was some sort of compensation for a depot that might have just lost a nearly new vehicle. Of course after a while the losses increased to the point where we could not cope with them just with new vehicles coming in. We then had to buy second-hand vehicles as well. I had a hand in this, in allocating them and pressurising the engineering department to get them on the road when they arrived in Northern Ireland. We also developed the technique of having a reserve of vehicles which were still in running order, perhaps not fully PSV'd, but still in reasonable running order, and keeping them that way for a few months as back ups until we were able to dispose of them.

**MC** *Was there a point where senior management realised that the civil unrest was not going to be a short term problem, but that it was going to last?*

**IM** I can't actually remember that as a point in time but we did recognise from the start that this was a pretty fundamental political problem and wasn't just going to go away. I remember talking to colleagues on the commercial side, especially after two or three years of unrest, of how great it would be when peace breaks out. Well it didn't, at least not then anyway. It was pretty bad at that time and we just hoped that it wouldn't get any worse.

In the early days, it wasn't nearly so destructive. They would hijack vehicles to block roads, but they didn't burn them. We would get the buses back. For example, at the end of 1968 or beginning of 1969 there was the incident concerning the first Bristol RE taken in Derry. Now at that time the REs were brand new. It was taken and used as a barricade. James Heuston, the Area Manager, went and negotiated that if he brought them an old bus, could he have his new bus back? At that time in Derry, we used a Land Rover as a towing vehicle. The Land Rover towed an old PS1 to this site. They took the Bristol out, put the PS1 in its place but then discovered that it was several feet shorter than the Bristol so didn't fill the gap. So they took the Land Rover as well to fill the space!

*Ulsterbus No 2490, the former London Transport 'Red Arrow' AEC Merlin MBA 460, is seen amidst the remains of buses destroyed in Londonderry. This 1969-built vehicle had come to Citybus in November 1977 but wasn't operated. It was transferred to Ulsterbus in 1978 but returned to Citybus in 1980 and was destroyed in an attack on Ardoyne depot on 16 December that year.*

There were other cases on the Falls Road where buses were taken and eventually recovered several days later. Then there was the mysterious case where a Tiger Cub was taken but our local people couldn't find it in the barricades. There was, however, a report of it having been seen down the Newcastle/Kilkeel direction, although we couldn't confirm that. Eventually, we did get it back, but where it had been in the meantime, we're not quite sure. We don't know for certain if it was used to transport people or other things around. It was just one of a number of mysteries that occurred during that period.

Then things started to get worse. Whatever they took, they burned. We found that we did not get vehicles back unless we got them very quickly. You will remember the incident in Kilkeel where we lost, I think, eight vehicles? That was one of the first instances of vehicle damage, especially on that scale. Immediately, I went and looked at the second-hand market. I remember going to Northern General and finding four AEC Reliances there and another four Reliances in Manchester, in the hands of a dealer. I brought back the details and we discussed it at senior management level but concluded that we didn't need them. We decided that the devils we knew in our own fleet were preferable to those we didn't know and we wouldn't take somebody else's cast-offs. Now they probably would have been okay. The main problem was that they weren't identical either mechanically or from the point of view of bodywork. We were very keen on promoting standardisation and I couldn't find a batch comprising a single model. That decision not to buy second-hand was okay at that time. We must have had some new vehicles coming in so it was just a matter of holding on to our own cast-offs a bit longer. That was more acceptable to both our engineering and operating staff because we were used to the vehicles and we knew their eccentricities and so on.

But there soon came a time when I had to point out that our old vehicles were getting older. Here we were with a fairly aged fleet that had had almost no new vehicles for three years before Ulsterbus started and we wanted to maintain our replacement programme which was geared to replacing vehicles after 14 to 16 years. We didn't want to be extending the life of the vehicles on beyond what we could cope with because if we did, we would run into problems. We had had a few instances which indicated that there were vehicles which were not capable of having their lives extended, except at exorbitant cost. Some of the older vehicles' wooden-framed bodies were rotting and it was beyond economic viability to start overhauling them to keep them on the road. It would tie up resources which were needed to carry out the repairs to put 'quick jobs' back in traffic. Eventually, especially as the number of casualties mounted, and where the losses were exceeding the number of vehicles we were planning to withdraw and so eating into our total fleet size, we recognised that we were left with no option but to go looking for second-hand vehicles. We made a number of purchases – 10, 15, 20 at a time – and then Mr Heubeck had the idea of going to London. London Transport, a huge operator, was bound to have a lot of vehicles of the same standard and specification. So that's where the Merlins came in, followed by the Swifts, which were an even bigger disaster!

In fact, the Merlins were quite a reasonable vehicle. But they were designed for urban use and so weren't really suited to our type of operations. The Swift was a much less reliable vehicle. We found that perhaps one in ten of the Merlins would fail to reach Stranraer. With the Swifts it was two or three in ten that failed to reach Stranraer or Heysham, or arrived under tow to be ferried across. That wasn't a good sign. So really the service we got wasn't great. Some of the Merlins gave good service, but the Swifts had a very poor record.

It was then that I pointed out to Tom Campbell, the Citybus Chief Engineer, that the National Bus Company were withdrawing Bristol RELLs. By that time, after 1975, we were well standardised on the Bristol RELL as the Citybus vehicle. Tom liked them; they had Gardner engines, which as an ex-Corporation man he liked, so he jumped at the idea and from then on we got a steady stream of second-hand Bristols. He negotiated with the various National Bus subsidiaries and if one couldn't supply us, they passed us on to another who could. In fact, National Bus around that time consolidated their disposal of serviceable vehicles through a subsidiary company based in Lincoln and whatever vehicles were fit for future use went to this centre, were checked over and sold on. So we got quite a few out of that operation, as did the Swilly.

**MC** *You weren't attracted by second-hand Leyland Nationals?*

**IM** No. We had taken a policy decision not to buy Nationals. In fact we only ever owned one and we had no interest in buying them second-hand. The Bristols suited our needs far, far better. We also got some batches of Leopards and various other types for Ulsterbus operations over the years.

**MC** *Who paid for all of this? These buses didn't come for free.*

**IM** It was all initially paid for out of Ulsterbus's own funds. We did get compensation, under a government scheme, to which it was committed by legislation. The theory is that government is responsible for maintaining law and order and therefore has to compensate for loss of property, if they fail to maintain law and order. So if the loss was proved to be due to a malicious act, and the legislation was fairly clear on this, there had to be proof of, I think it was three or more individuals, and some other details which I can't recall, but if that was proved, then the Chief Constable would write a certificate. Once we got the Chief Constable's certificate we would then get compensation for the market value of the vehicle. Now initially the market value was based on the age of the vehicle and to break even we had to try and buy a replacement of a similar age. We had a table drawn up showing the different types of vehicles and their ages so if we lost one we could read off that the agreed figure would be such and such.

A number of things happened to dislodge that system. Our accounting department made a mistake. To explain. We got, from 1974 onwards I think, a grant of 50% on new vehicles. That was a national scheme although we didn't get it as early as operators across the water. However, that depended first on us buying the vehicles so if we didn't buy the vehicles first, we didn't get any grant. So for our normal intake of new vehicles, we got this grant. It was extended in Northern Ireland for longer than in GB because of the trouble we were having in maintaining our fleet. So you could say there was an element of compensation in that. But, under the regulations across the water, the fact that payment for the bus had been grant-aided had an expiry time period attached, five or ten years, I can't quite recall. Also, the bus had to be of stage carriage operation standard. So, because of this rule, in GB there were luxury coaches coming out with stage carriage doors fitted. That and a few other things meant that they met the regulations, so they got the grant. They also had to be used for 50% of their mileage on stage carriage, so the coach operators would use them on coach work in the summer and then on their bus work in the winter to balance the mileage. But, and this is important, after the requisite number of years had expired, the grant-aided status of the vehicle lapsed and the operators could use them as they liked. So, they could use them purely as coaches and did not have to balance the mileage.

However, those rules didn't apply in Northern Ireland. There was no expiry date, so if the vehicle lasted twenty years, the government still considered that it was 50% grant-aided, and therefore its value, according to the government, was only half of its actual market value. As a result of this system, if the vehicle had been grant-aided initially then its compensation value was cut by 50%. I considered that policy to be fundamentally unsound because, in fact, there were two separated objectives involved here. The grant aid scheme was to assist companies to modernise their fleets, to encourage one-man-operation and that sort of thing, while the compensation scheme was to do with the breakdown of law and order and having to replace equipment that shouldn't have been destroyed in the first place. If we lost a grant-aided vehicle, we still had to go out and buy a replacement and if the vehicle destroyed was, say, five years old and worth £5000, we would have to spend £5000 to replace it, but would only be compensated to the tune of £2500. That was unsound, but unfortunately, our accountants gave way and we had to adopt that system. Also, there should have been a cut-off point, similar to GB, after which the grant wouldn't have been taken into account when calculating the compensation.

MC  *So Ulsterbus ended up having to pay part of the replacement cost for destroyed buses out of its own pocket?*

IM  Yes. But because they were second-hand vehicles they were low cost compared to having to pay for new ones. It didn't really affect our investment in new vehicles. It was for the same reason that we started the programme to re-body buses.

MC  *I was just going to ask you how that scheme fitted into the overall picture.*

IM  Yes. The work needed to recondition chassis was greater on some vehicles than on others but we did get quite a number done. But there were a number of other vehicles in the pipeline that were never completed. One of the problems was that this work was spread around the depots and they would work on reconditioning chassis when they had time. But when a vehicle came in needing a spare part,

*Leopard No 1591 (SOI 3591) is one of the rebuilt vehicles referred to above. It was constructed from the chassis of No 1347 (AOI 1347) and is now preserved by the Irish Transport Trust. It is seen here at Llanfairpwllgwyngyllgogerychwyrndrobwll-llantysiliogogogoch, Anglesey, when returning from the 2006 Llandudno Transport Festival.* **Paul Savage**

the fitters might take it off the chassis and so, gradually, they were cannibalised to keep other buses running. This meant it was always an uphill struggle to get the reconditioning work completed. You found yourself ordering up parts which you had already ordered up for that chassis previously. So, some of them were never finished.

But we were refused grant on those vehicles, even on half of the price of the new body which would be fitted for us by Alexanders. The new body was half the price of the vehicle, but we got no grant aid for it because, under the regulations, the finished article wasn't classed as a new vehicle. Consequently, re-bodying an old chassis cost us as much as a new vehicle and getting the grant on it. For that reason there was no real advantage to us in pushing this programme. Had there been a proportionate saving to us, as against the cost of a new vehicle, we'd have continued the scheme. But the government's rigidity in applying the regulations killed off that programme.

**MC**  *How do you think the Troubles affected the way the company evolved? For example, did the Troubles hold back privatisation?*

**IM**  They probably did. But I wasn't much involved in that aspect of things. That was more the MD's territory. There was a stage where we were close to being privatised but we managed to stave it off and I'm sure that the Troubles were a factor in this. Perhaps it was to the advantage of the organisation that we didn't

*Leopard No 1337 (4037 WZ), which had been purchased by the Irish Transport Trust for preservation, became a victim of the Troubles when it was destroyed in an arson attack at Antrim depot on 14 October 1990. This incident also saw the destruction of Ulsterbus Leyland Tiger No 1159, Leyland Leopard coach No 1998 and Bristol RE No 2597. No 1591 (SOI 3591) (see previous page) later became an appropriate replacement.*  **Jonathan Miller collection**

*The remains of Citybus Bristol RE No 2261, also a vehicle which had been rebuilt and rebodied, are recovered following its hijacking and destruction at Spamount Street/North Queen Street on 17 February 1992. Bristol REs Nos 2488 and 2566 were also hijacked and destroyed in the same area on this day.* **Mark O'Neill**

go down that line. It was recognised that we had developed an expertise in maintaining services through the difficulties applying in Northern Ireland and it was also recognised that potential buyers would undervalue the company because of the Troubles. So, in that sense the Troubles were an advantage in that helped delay the spectre of privatisation.

From the passenger service point of view, certainly some of our objectives in terms of developing the business and making services more attractive were put on hold, indeed evening services almost disappeared. Late evenings were slimmed down and down almost to nothing on some routes. No-one wanted to come into Belfast in the evening. There was very little entertainment activity. Some of the Falls Road services were handed over to the Corporation because they were no longer attractive to operate. The Corporation could not avoid the difficulties. They had to run their services on the same roads anyway, so all that happened was that their buses would run out a bit beyond their original termini to our old termini. So, the Glen Road, Shaw's Road and Ladybrook services went over to the Corporation. It had always been Heubeck's intention to develop the express services across the Province because he saw them as the way forward. But this development proceeded slowly and some of our experiments weren't very successful and didn't catch on. By the time the Goldline network was launched by Ted Hesketh around 1990, things were much better politically.

At that time we had the first ceasefire which then broke down and then we had the second ceasefire. People said that we lost business because of the breakdown in the ceasefire, and we probably did. But I did some extensive probing into the figures and it actually proved that the damage to our passenger numbers started with the ceasefire, ironically, not its breakdown.

**MC**   *That's odd.*

**IM**   Yes, that was everybody's reaction. I explained the numbers at various meetings including ones with government, but I don't think anyone really believed me. But looking at the figures, the downturn in passenger numbers quite definitely started when the ceasefire came in. It wasn't really visible in a major way until we'd got a full year's figures to allow comparisons to be made. I thought that the phenomenon wasn't unreasonable because here we had people using the buses often because they didn't want to risk using their own cars to go into a town where they worked or shopped, in case they would get caught up in something and lose their car or have it damaged. They would take the bus instead; they were with other people, and by and large the bus, particularly in country areas would get in and out unscathed. But when the ceasefire came along, it gave people more confidence in using their own transport. If you think about it that way, you can see that that might well explain, at least in part, the fall in numbers. Then there were the people who didn't use cars; the end of the ceasefire knocked their confidence so they travelled less so this was another step down in the numbers travelling.

**MC**   *You would have thought that it would have gone the other way with the ceasefires boosting numbers.*

**IM**   Yes, that's true. Now going back to the early years, our passenger numbers fell but because we were obliged to watch the situation closely and respond quickly, we were still able to maintain a reasonable profit margin in Ulsterbus. When we took on Citybus in 1973, it was already running at a big loss but we gradually whittled that down until they were breaking even. The Corporation always complained about something they called the Aberdeen clause. It was something to do with support from the rates.

**MC**   *Yes, I think it was to do with the fact that the rates could be supported from profits made by the Transport Department, but the Transport Department could not be supported from the rates.*

**IM**   Yes, public transport couldn't be supported from the rates. But why Aberdeen came into it, I don't know. This was one of the reasons why they were in a bad way when we took them over. In the reorganisation of local government the government didn't want local authorities to have transport powers. Belfast was the only one that was using them. Derry had powers but had long since handed them over, initially to Catherwood as I said earlier. They were the only two authorities which had transport operating powers and the government wanted to kill this off. So it made sense, given the financial trouble that the BCT was in, to hand it over to the experienced bus operator, Ulsterbus, merge the two and run it under the wing of the Holding Company.

**MC**   *The two companies weren't really merged, except at the top, until recently, were they?*

**IM**   They were up to a point. A civil servant can, at the stroke of a pen, transfer an undertaking from one statutory body to another. So they transferred the Transport Department from the Belfast Corporation to the Northern Ireland Transport Holding Company. At that point it was called Citybus Services. It wasn't a limited company and it was a couple of years before it was made a limited company. But in terms of the actual integration, yes, virtually at a stroke, all Head Office activities were merged. Some people came over from the BCT to Milewater Road, and all the Head Office departments took on the management of the equivalent Citybus functions. Max Hale, as Operating Manager and Tom Campbell as Chief Engineer, were the senior BCT people who came over. The people above them, including the BCT General Manager, Robert Adams, left. So, Citybus was in effect an operating department, equivalent to an Ulsterbus area, headed up by Max Hale. Within a few years there was further merger by adding the Belfast Ulsterbus depots to it. So at that level, there was substantial integration. Below that we didn't integrate because the decision had been taken to keep Citybus as a separate limited company with a separate staffing. The two staffing agreements, the one covering Ulsterbus operating staff and the one covering Citybus people, were different. But gradually, over the years we were able to merge some aspects of the staffing agreements. Of course, the unions always wanted whichever was the better of the two agreements to apply to both companies. That was a constant battle.

We also achieved quite a lot in terms of fleet standardisation. There was very little difference in the specs between Ulsterbus Bristol RELLs and Citybus's. Those vehicles could be switched, and were switched from company to company with little or no problem. Some staff moved about from one company to another on promotion or transfer and that wasn't a big issue. Here and there the unions still had demarcation issues between the two lots of staff, but after several years we were eventually able to draw on Citybus drivers for the tour pool.

There wasn't the need to push integration any further and with all the other problems we were having to deal with, the Troubles deflected our attention from completing the merger. We didn't push it along as forcibly as we might otherwise have done. I don't think any great harm came of it, though we were criticised for not having done it.

MC    *In some of the newspaper reports of the mid 1970s merger always seems to be on the horizon, but never actually happens.*

IM    It's still not a merger. Metro is just a trading name, a brand image. Citybus is still there. They have rationalised some of the operating boundaries between the two companies but I don't think that was necessarily an advantageous thing to do. I was one of the ones who held out against that sort of thing because Ulsterbus is far more efficient than Citybus. It is a much lower cost operation and to extend Citybus boundaries at the expense of Ulsterbus means that you are getting no additional revenue. In fact, depending on the level of the fares you might be getting less revenue, for a higher operating cost. However, they've done it now with Metro and we'll see what comes out of it. They are talking about the extra passengers being carried by Metro, but have these increases been offset against the loss of passengers suffered by Ulsterbus? What is the overall picture across the two companies? I'm not sure if the sums have been done. If the sums are done, they might have a trumpet to blow and, if so, I would be happy but reading between the lines I have a feeling that they want to keep quiet about that.

MC    *Another thing that comes through, and I remember it myself because I was involved in it for a short period, was the whole question of the black taxis and Heubeck's hatred of them. Have you any views on that whole business?*

IM    What happened there was that when they were hijacking buses and burning them, we had to withdraw services. We kept going as long as we could but for the safety of passengers and staff we had to withdraw services from time to time. It was more because we were concerned with staff safety than concern for the vehicles. Then, of course, the local activists made a big issue about it. You know how good their PR can be in areas like West Belfast. They made a big thing of it and they put on their own operation. They bought second-hand taxis and flooded the road with them. Once they had done this, they wanted to keep them going.

Politics being what they are, the Protestants had to set up the same thing on their road to keep level with the nationalists on the Falls. Then we found that a fair number of passengers on the Falls road, on principle, supported the black taxis because they represented their political objectives and they were the sort of people who were reluctant to support the 'establishment' bus service. There was very little we could do about that. So we had to respond with reduced frequencies and reduced services. We delayed it for a period, but eventually we had to trim services back. The irony of it was that the taxis couldn't cope in the peak. We were still getting the peak load, but were suffering in the off-peak. That made it more difficult for us to achieve savings because the buses still had to be there to cover the peak periods, but we weren't getting the off-peak revenue to help pay for those vehicles. But that is a common public transport issue everywhere, the best way to balance peak and off-peak work.

MC    *Didn't Heubeck want the government to back him on the taxis issue?*

IM    Yes, but as was said at Gerry Fitt's funeral recently, the government at the time was spineless. The taxis weren't legal, but the government wasn't prepared to take them on. One of the ironies of the situation was that initially the black taxis operated without tax, insurance or anything else. But, if you remember at the time of one of the Middle East conflicts, there was a threat of fuel rationing. The government was planning to issue fuel vouchers but to get these you would have had to produce a valid tax disc and so on. So, all of a sudden the taxis sprouted tax discs. Then there was an issue about insurance. At one point, I heard that the government had managed to nobble one of the major insurance companies not to cover the taxis. But that didn't last long.

MC    *Yes, however, somebody in West Belfast organised a way around that problem, a self insurance setup I think, which got them off the hook.*

IM    Well, you see, we were self-insured. We inherited that from Citybus. Ulsterbus moved on to the same system. So it was almost impossible for the government not to allow another organisation to be self-insured.

But we did what we could. We did manage to prevent black taxis from spreading to some other routes.

They tried to set up an operation in East Belfast, on the Newtownards Road. But they made some tactical mistakes. I think the people of Dundonald and Ballybeen were realistic enough to see that they might lose their bus services. Also, the taxis were only going to go as far as the lower Newtownards Road but not across the bridge into the city. That, of course, cut a significant proportion of their potential. That scheme only lasted a week or two.

Citybus did use taxis as patrol vehicles with the idea that they would be less visible, but we lost one or two of them. We suspected that this happened because some of the black taxi people needed spare parts! Then there were times when we thought we were gaining passengers on the Falls Road and we would have one or two hijacking incidents and our numbers would fall back again. We suspected that these hijackings were triggered by the taxis seeing a loss in revenue and they had methods of dealing with this problem not available to us!

The taxis were a by-product of the whole political situation. There was also the fact that they were a very good revenue source for paramilitaries, a good cash flow. They also provided employment for ex-prisoners.

**MC** *Another thing that comes up over the years, and I'm not sure if the Troubles had any impact on it or not, was the whole question of whether or not to provide a central bus station in Belfast. Can you shed any light on that?*

**IM** I remember a councillor, a Unionist from Annadale or somewhere like that, and he used to say the most terrible things in the City Hall about the bus stations. But the City Council weren't keen on having a central bus terminus and they wanted to shunt us elsewhere. The planning service diligently hunted for alternative sites. For a start, three Ulsterbus stations was not the most efficient setup, but was just a historical thing, like having three main line railway stations in Belfast at one time. We looked at putting all services into one depot, but we couldn't get a big enough site. Then, after Smithfield was hit, we cottoned on to the fact that if we moved into one station, the bombers could put us out of action. When we had three bus stations, we could manage comfortably if we were reduced to two, as was shown after the destruction of Smithfield. That was just within Ulsterbus. If you added Citybus, a central location for Citybus and Ulsterbus would be very difficult to achieve

Heubeck basically didn't believe in bus stations. On the continent they generally didn't have much in the way of bus stations. Buses left from an open square with negligible facilities for staff and passengers. He took pleasure in showing us that in various places. That partly explains why in country areas, though we did improve the depots, the standard in the early days were very basic, minimum cost buildings. Ted Hesketh brought a different view to developing premises. The first was Dungannon. Although it was opened when Heubeck was still in charge, Ted was allowed to run that project and once he took over, we saw the building of places like Omagh, Enniskillen and so on. Architect designed, distinctive; they stood out above and beyond the functional minimum. So during the Heubeck period any idea for building a central bus station in Belfast tended to be given short shrift.

During the redevelopment of Smithfield there was some consideration given to making Smithfield a central bus station but that was to replace the three Ulsterbus

*Twenty-one vehicles, including these unidentified Leyland Leopards, were destroyed at Belfast's Smithfield depot on 12 June 1978.*

depots, it wasn't to include Citybus and, as I have said, we didn't pursue it once we realised how vulnerable it would leave us.

Then the idea of a central location for Citybus began to be promoted. One of the sites we were asked to look at, and this was relatively recently, after Heubeck had gone, was off Queen Street, that whole block where the police station used to be. We got as far as working out a design to see how many bus routes we could get in using a design where passenger and staff facilities were placed above the departure stands. I think from the point of view of accessibility to vehicles, it wouldn't have got too far for it was always going to be a problem to get passengers to approach on an upper level and then go down stairs to an island departure area. Nevertheless, we tried to see what we could get into that very limited site.

But I remember making an argument at one of the meetings when public representatives and various other were present, by asking, "Do you really feel that the centre of your city should be tucked up a back street, in Queen Street?" And they all looked at me. And I said, "Look, go back in history. In the 1920s and 1930s, where was the centre of Belfast?" "Oh," they replied, "The centre of Belfast was Castle Junction." And I said, "Why was it at Castle Junction?" No answer. So I answered my own question, "It was the tram terminus. It's where all the trams turned. That was the centre of the city!" In other words, where public transport is, is perceived to be the centre of the city and over the years the centre has moved along to Donegall Square and that area now, around the City Hall, is the city centre. But it is the presence of public transport which makes it the city centre. If you take public transport away from there, you are in danger of creating a new city centre somewhere else. That was an argument which impressed a number of people, though not all of them. There were a few more meetings after that but gradually the Queen Street proposal was dropped and we are still in Donegall Square.

There was also a proposal then to take the buses out of Royal Avenue. We made a strong case against it and managed to convince the traders who were all for the pedestrian scheme. We carried out some market research which showed the percentage of their customers who used public transport to get into the city so the traders realised that if public transport was pushed away round the back of the city centre, they could lose a large number of those people. We pushed for the solution that Royal Avenue should be a bus and pedestrian zone like is found in many continental cities. That didn't actually happen, though what we have isn't far off it.

**MC**    *Are there any particular incidents to do with the Troubles you can recall which have stuck in your memory?*

**IM**    Oh, yes. This first story didn't involve one of our vehicles, but a CIÉ one, an M-class Leopard. It was on the Newry–Dundalk service was hijacked at the border and a bomb placed inside. The British army came along and looked at it, and walked around it, and hummed and hawed and then said, "No, we can't deal with that. The bomb is in the Republic of Ireland." So the Irish army came along, looked at it and said, "We can't deal with that, because the entrance to the bus, to gain access to the bomb is in Northern Ireland." That vehicle ended up being totally destroyed, I think by someone setting off the bomb with a bullet. It was tipped over the hedge and the chassis could be seen lying there for several years afterwards.

When the security checks were on in the city centre there were quite a few cases of items of lost property being found on buses and causing incidents. Sometimes these were innocent enough, but some were probably intended as hoaxes. Then someone from the company had to go and lift the item off the vehicle. Often Werner (Heubeck) was called to the incident, though Max Hale also dealt with some of them. The army would deal with it if it was definitely a device, but often it was far quicker to get someone from the company to move it if it was 99% certain that it was lost property. The army's 'controlled explosion' would turn a bus inside out (see photo on page 13). Sometimes the bus was repairable, but not always.

This next story gives you some idea of the care Werner took when he decided to lift a suspect bomb of a vehicle. He didn't lift bombs rashly. One of the newspapers described him erroneously as a munitions officer in the Wermacht. He wasn't, but that kept on coming up because it was in their files. He hadn't been in the army long enough to develop that kind of expertise. At least that's what he told me. But he had enough savvy and he would always talk to the people involved. If a driver had been hijacked he would talk to the driver and find out how the bomb had been put in and whatever else he knew about it. He would talk to any other witnesses available. Then there were various things known about bombs at that time, for example, they were usually assembled with things like timers out of street lamps. Well, there was this case in Derrylin and Werner heard about it and decided to go look. When he got there he talked to the driver, the local police and so on. He then came to the conclusion that the Provos had closed the road for a reason. They needed the road closed maybe to allow them to shift stuff or something like that. It was clear that if they didn't get the bus rescued, the headlights had been left on, the battery was going to be flat and they wouldn't be able to start the engine. So Werner decided that it would be safe to have a go. Enough time had elapsed, he judged, several hours, so he would go and check it out. He opened the cardboard box which had wires sticking out of it and found it contained a pile of bricks!

He was his own man and hadn't much time for those in authority if they were being obstructive. On one occasion, a small bomb had exploded outside the Unionist Party's HQ in Glengall Street. There was also a suspect bomb in the salt box at the corner of Glengall Street and the Boyne Bridge. As a result, the security forces closed Glengall Street and so Great Victoria Street depot. Passengers were milling around outside the Europa Hotel, unable to get to their buses. Werner showed up but he and his staff were prevented from getting into the depot by police and army. So, he organised a group of drivers to go up the side past Murray's tobacco factory, and over the back wall into the depot. He then formed up a convoy of buses up in the bus park which he led out of the depot, along Glengall Street and into Great Victoria Street to provide services for the passengers. The police were jumping up and down with rage as this fleet of buses ploughed through their forensic gathering outside the Unionist HQ. That was Heubeck, and he got away with it!

I remember another incident involving Werner at the Madrid Street triangle in East Belfast. This triangle was effectively a traffic island, rimmed with big concrete flower pots. A bus had been hijacked at the side of the island, and Heubeck brought the bomb out through the emergency door and left it on the traffic island as far as possible from the surrounding buildings. He then got the bus away. Next thing he was called up on the radio. "Mr Heubeck, the army want you back at Madrid Street." "But I have cleared that bomb and got the bus back in the depot!" he said. "Yes," replied Citybus control, "But the army still want you back." He went back and the army said, "Look, we can't get our robot in between these concrete flower pots to deal with that bomb. So since you put it there, you get it out!" So they made him go in and move it out to where they could get at it!

There was also the story of Werner arriving in Larne after the security checks had started. This was told to me by the Sealink manager. Werner had built a beautiful big oak dining table for his wife who was living in Edinburgh for security reasons. During the Troubles he was considered to be 'at risk' as one of the establishment elite and had a weapon for personal protection. However, at this time he was well into his woodworking phase. He had some final finishing with French Polishing to do. When he pulled into the security check in his car, the security man rushed off to his boss and said, "There's a man just going through there and he's got a big Jag but in the back he's got a box with wires coming out of it and a strong smell of solvents or something. I'm not very happy with it." At that point Werner came out of the toilet and walked across the terminal building. "That's him there!" exclaimed the excited security man. Our Sealink colleague, said to his man, "Relax. You're all right, that's the Managing Director of Ulsterbus!"

**MC**   *How did you find working with Werner Heubeck?*

**IM**   He was certainly a change from what I had been used to before. David McCracken had been working with him for a year or more before I arrived and he put me wise to some of his characteristics. He was inclined to reject ideas very quickly but he would often think about them afterwards and on a number of occasions the idea would resurface a few months later. That would have annoyed some people, but I didn't mind. I was happy that the idea had been adopted. Sometimes if he rejected one of my ideas at a meeting, I would go to his office later and speak to him. I would suggest that maybe he had been a bit too quick to dismiss the idea and would ask him to listen again. Sometimes he would but on other occasions he would say, "It's your department. It's on your head. Go on, do it." There were things that I know he wasn't very interested in and wasn't very supportive of, but he let me do them. That was one of the great things about him. He did let us get on and use our initiative and do things in spite of this initial impression that he was overbearing.

Another thing about him was that he had a terrific depth of human understanding, but it was kept under wraps. It wasn't something that he let generally be known. There were some people with problems that he took a special interest in. Even after he retired he still had this sort of involvement in the communities where he lived. But he didn't make a big thing about it and didn't want it to be widely known.

He didn't intend originally to stay in Northern Ireland. I remember during my first few days when he was taking me round, we were driving along Royal Avenue and he said to me, "I may be only here for a year or two. I regard myself as a professional manager and I can turn my hand to managing any business." But, public transport grew on him. The challenge grew on him, particularly the challenge of the Troubles. Dealing with the Troubles was something he revelled in and I can't think of anyone else that I know who would have made as good a leader. He was a tremendous leader and he held the support of the company and his employees because of his ability to lead through the most difficult situations. I can think of lots of other senior managers who would lead from afar but Werner wouldn't make somebody else do something that he wasn't prepared to do himself. And people responded to that. Max Hale was a bit like that too, but I feel he was following Werner's example. He wasn't having Heubeck coming in and lifting his bombs!

# Frank Clegg, Operations Manager (Citybus)

## Introduction

During the worst years of the Troubles, the managements of Ulsterbus, Belfast Corporation Transport Department and later Citybus had to juggle with buses, duties, timetables and routes to keep services operating. Interviews with staff, set out elsewhere in this book, illustrate what this meant in practice. In addition, during certain periods of the Troubles, buses were destroyed at a phenomenal rate. There was no way that these losses could be replaced through normal purchasing from vehicle manufacturers. As a result, management scoured the UK for suitable second-hand vehicles that could be quickly pressed into service to fill the gaps being inflicted by the almost daily malicious destruction of vehicles.

Over the years, buses from London Transport and many other mainland companies were put into traffic in Northern Ireland. For those readers interested in the detail of the vehicles obtained from these sources, more information can be found in the companion volume to this book, *Citybus: Belfast's buses 1973–1988* by Will Hughes (Colourpoint 2005).

In the following interview, Frank Clegg, an operations manager first with the Belfast Corporation Transport Department and later Citybus, describes how Belfast Corporation's transport department coped with the shock of the onset of the Troubles. He then goes on to describe in detail how services were kept going during the years which followed when buses were being destroyed in large numbers.

He tells of how every six to eight weeks he would lead a team of drivers to London to collect a batch of second-hand buses to replace those destroyed in rioting and depot bombings. Often the number of buses destroyed during the weekend's rioting would exceed the number he had brought back.

In one incident, which is redolent of the account of how at the battle of Stalingrad, new Soviet tanks would drive straight off the factory production line and into battle, Frank describes how one ex-London bus was driven off the boat, quickly refuelled at Short Strand depot and went straight into service on the streets of Belfast.

Often these buses entered service in their original owner's colours, time having permitted only a change of destination screens and the application to the vehicles of 'Citybus' or 'Ulsterbus' stickers. If they survived mechanical failures or the depredations of the rioters long enough, they would eventually be repainted in Ulsterbus or Citybus colours.

Not all the buses so acquired would go into service. Because of the difficulties in obtaining spares, some vehicles were bought purely as a source of spare parts to keep other vehicles running.

FC As a teenager I was particularly interested, not so much in the vehicles, as in the whole area of route planning and timetabling. I used to take the old Corporation transport timetables and devise new services, timetables, and so on. I would then send them in to the Transport Department, to Robert Adams, the General Manager, no less – the sort of thing you would do at that age.

 I left school after my 'O' levels and had to go out to work. I applied for a job with the Belfast Corporation and at the interview decided to stick my neck out and ask for a placement with the Transport Department. I got started in the Transport Department and was happy that I had got a reasonable position.

What happened then was that my new colleagues had made some enquiries about me and on the second day after starting in the Traffic general office in Utility Street, a big tall chap called Ernie Shimmon, from the schedules office, comes walking in and called out, "Where's this fellow Clegg who thinks he knows about timetables!" The schedules office was just across the corridor from the general office. Of course, as a young lad, I didn't know what to do. Those schedules guys were the cream of the department. "Right", he said to me, "In there!" Pointing to his office. My boss, a soft, quiet sort of man protested, "Hey, my staff . . .", but to no avail. I went into the big office and there were about four in there working. What they used to do was that when they came to the school holidays or any other major change in schedules, they would literally cut the old schedules up and stick the pieces they needed to keep on larger sheets of paper.

**MC**   *Real cut and paste?*

**FC**   Exactly, real cut and paste. Of course, Ernie's sitting there. "I'll show you how timetabling's done," he says, "I'm doing the July duties." And he's sitting there cutting and what have you, and I'm looking over his shoulder. And he says, "What are looking at that for?" And I says, "I'm just looking at what you are doing." "Away and get yourself a brush and shovel and brush up!", came the reply. As he was cutting, all the unneeded bits of paper were going here, there and everywhere, so my initiation to timetabling was to brush up all the bits of paper left lying around the office!

The first major project I got involved in was the withdrawal of the trolleybuses, which were withdrawn in May 1968. This was, of course, peacetime. My first real job was to have some involvement in this and I was able to show that I did have some inkling of what I was doing. My job was in the creation of the new omnibus duties to take over from the trolleybus duties out of the Haymarket depot. We brought Daimler CWA and CVG rear platform buses back on to the roads to allow the trolleys to be withdrawn. The new Daimler Roadliners and AEC Swifts, which were to become the first 'one-man'ers, were in storage.

I always remember that at the peak periods the trolleybuses were carrying full loads. It was the last time, I regret to have to say it, it was the one and only time in my career when we took the period between 8.00am and 9.00am, counted the number of seats available on the trolleybuses on the Glen, Falls and Whiterock Roads, and the same thing at 3.00pm and 5.00pm. Then using 54 and 56-seater buses we worked out how many vehicles we needed to replace the equivalent number of seats provided by 68-seater trolleybuses. That was the last time I remember getting to that fine level of detail. You would have been in the same situation with Ulsterbus on routes like Rathcoole.

**MC**   *Yes, that's right.*

**FC**   Those were the last of the days, before the Troubles, where you had to virtually replace seat for seat, remembering that different vehicles had different seating capacities. Never have we got down to that level of detail again, which is an unfortunate commentary on the volume of traffic being carried by public transport since.

The next big thing was the introduction of the 'one-man'ers, the first route being to Stormont on 24 March 1969 and then on 19 May, the Antrim Road group of services. Unfortunately that was the last pre-Troubles group of services that I had to deal with and from then on the Troubles took over.

The Troubles started around July–August. They came, we know now not out of the blue, but they did come as a shock. The memories of that time were basically that we had to evacuate down to the Naval Air Yard at Sydenham. We were lucky that by that stage the trolleybuses had gone. The Naval Air Yard was the only place of its size which was secure and perceived to be in a safe area that could be acquired quickly and all depots were evacuated down there.

We were operating on emergency schedules, which were produced overnight and I remember doing the timetables along with my colleagues in the BCT's HQ on the Donegall Road. In those days, with the photocopiers of time, you had to mix the chemicals and they were very messy. I wore my old Sullivan Upper school jumpers when working the spirit duplicators because you got covered in the blue ink they used. Awful, awful things. And writing by hand on the carbon paper they used. We had neither enough paper nor chemicals to deal with the situation, so armed with these core timetables and special work cards, I remember walking down the middle of the Donegall Road to the City Hall. Things were so bad that the middle of the road was the safest place to walk because of the bonfires and stuff scattered around the place. We went down to the City Hall and we went searching for photocopiers. There was no one else in work from any other Corporation department. But we were the Transport Department and part of the Corporation, so we got permission to go into the City Hall. I think we managed to demolish and break every photocopier in succession trying to get the stuff we needed copied.

At that time, 90% of our operations were crew-based, so we were dealing with both drivers and conductors. What we did was produce basic timetables, say, based around a one hour running time. We photocopied these standard ten-minute timetables, then wrote in the destinations on to the standard templates and then we cut them up ready for distribution to the crews. It was as crude as that, not terribly sophisticated. What we had to deal with was where we could

*Buses heading off from the Sydenham By-pass to take up service in July 1970. On arrival at the Bridge End flyover, drivers and conductors would be allocated work, the shifts which could then be operated being dependent on the number of men who had managed to get to work.*

safely operate. So a certain route might be operating only to a certain point, for example. In some areas there was total disruption. On the Falls Road, for example, we were off for days on end. On certain roads we were diverted or operating only partial routes. Ardoyne, for example, was difficult. But we were trying to piece together services as best we could.

From a staffing point of view it was difficult. We were operating from the Naval Air Yard and our people were coming from the Falls, Ardoyne and what have you. Transport was not like it is today with most people having their own cars, so we had to get them there. We had difficulty in getting them there on time and certainly at the start of the day. We then had to match up a driver and a conductor. We separated the air base up into sections, one being Falls, one Short Strand and so on; we tried to operate these areas as if they were depots. We tried to set up what were in effect mini-depots. Staff operated out of a bus converted into an office. We were taking pay-ins in the bus office and so on.

Now, I'm not certain whether this happened the first time we were in the Naval Air Yard, though I think it was the first time, we thought we could see if we could get exclusive use of a lane on the Sydenham by-pass. We were given the flyover near Short Strand, the road had a slightly different configuration to what it has now, and we positioned ourselves there and allocated the work, pairing up drivers and conductors. We were standing in the middle of the by-pass allocating work. We would reach a point where we had exhausted our initial crews and were trying to put extras on, for example at the peak hours. I'm not suggesting that we were producing full timetables, but bear in mind we didn't know how many buses we were going to get or how many staff would turn up or when they would turn up. So we had to match up staff and I would find myself standing in the middle of the by-pass writing out extras, eg journey to Oldpark, 8.15; journey to Ardoyne 8.35, etc. Then a bus would come up and I would give this rota to the crew. In the afternoon you had to repeat the same operation, but at least then you could do this in the city centre and use your inspectors.

MC    *So men reported for work at the Air Yard, collected their bus then drove up to the flyover and you allocated them their work?*

*Three burning Belfast Corporation Transport Daimler CVG6s are used as a very effective roadblock on the Falls Road in October 1971.*

FC    No, not quite. Some of the staff were allocated their duties at the Air Yard. Where you had specific work to allocate, this was done in the Air Yard. But it was the spread drivers that you were using to fill in the gaps that you allocated work from the flyover. You would then tell them that after doing that piece of work, they were to report in to the city centre where you could then use them to cover other bits of work, eg meal breaks etc.

MC    *So you were flying by the seat of your pants with those people?*

FC    Yes

MC    *How long did that last before you could get back into the depots again?*

FC    In 1969, It lasted for the guts of two weeks.

MC    *What sort of vehicle losses did you suffer at that time?*

FC    The bulk of the losses were the rear entrance vehicles, the CVGs and what have you. You are talking a fair number of buses, many used as barricades. However, bear in mind also that in the Corporation we were moving to one-man-operated (o-m-o) buses at that time. So we were fortunate in that that conversion was taking place at the same time as the Troubles were happening. This meant that the losses were of basically the rear entrance vehicles, buses that we would have been withdrawing in any case.

However, the new Roadliners were on the road from 24 March 1969 and the Swifts from 19 May. Now wait a minute. In fact we must have been out of the depots for longer than two weeks because I remember that on 1 September, Dundonald was going on as the first of the double-deck Fleetline 'one-man'ers and when they went on we were still out of the depots. So the first conversion to the double-deck one-man buses was done operating out of the Naval Air Yard. So we must have had to stay in the Air Yard into the second week of September or thereabouts. It was difficult to handle the conversion because we were out of the depots. We were trying to train men to become one-man-operators and we were trying to get them on to new duties we also were trying to get off the emergency schedules, even though we were operating out of a different place. We had negotiated a deal with the unions on additional running time and I remember that at the start that extra amount wasn't too bad but as the years went on the unions got wiser as to how to get more generous extra time for inconvenience, etc, and it became more expensive for us from that point of view.

So basically we went from serious Troubles in 1969 to a bit more on and off during 1970 and early 1971. Then in 1971 the problems became bigger and more difficult after internment. Now that was bad! It was then we were off certain roads for in excess of a week over the internment period whereas it was days, two or three days being more the norm in earlier years. As I remember it, we had to cope with more body destruction to vehicles in 1971, whereas in 1969 there was more burning of vehicles. But we lost more vehicles in 1971 than in 1969 and there were a lot more roads affected. It was a lot harder to deviate and operate round the trouble spots than it had been before.

The new Fleetlines were coming in in 1971. But we got to the situation where things were extremely difficult because of the scale of the losses we were suffering. Even the losses of rear entrance vehicles was hitting hard because they had been taking the brunt of the attacks over previous years. Two areas where we suffered extreme difficulty were the loss of window glass and the loss of screw-in light bulbs. Generally speaking we had to shuffle window glass between vehicles and it got so bad that we were generally down to two windows on each side of the vehicle with glass in them. I think it was two downstairs and three upstairs.. You weren't supposed to go below that. You were never supposed to go under four light bulbs, especially upstairs in the vehicle, because of the safety issue. Now what happened was that the conductors would build up their own wee supply. So the bus would go out in the morning with a full supply of them, but then the first conductor didn't want to be caught out so he would take a few out. So that's when we got into all sorts of bother with those issues. However, the buses were still PSV'd with window glass missing.

**MC**   *Just with hardboard or something in their place?*

**FC**   Generally speaking, it was hardboard or whatever they could come up with. Because we couldn't get the glass. There would have been instances where the upper deck would have been closed off at night for safety reasons because there were no lights in it. At night, when you had fewer passengers and there were only a few bulbs left in the bus, it would be better to switch those you had to the lower deck for safety reasons. The bulbs were a special order and we simply couldn't get them, so our stores ran out.

**MC**   *I suppose most new buses were fitted with strip lights and that explained the difficulty of getting the bulbs?*

**FC**   Yes. The other problem was that as the kids got to know about this, they started pinching them and throwing them out of windows and so on. So that became a problem, too, in 1971 and 1972 and that's when it really started biting

**MC**   *How did it start to affect passenger numbers and revenues? Were you involved in that side of things?*

**FC**   Oh we had a tremendous drop in revenue and passenger numbers. It did hurt us badly. 1969 was difficult but 1971 and internment, basically broke us. Bear in mind that we had routes like the 77 Gasworks–Waterworks route, which was completely severed but had been a profitable, if not the most profitable, omnibus route we had. Now not as profitable as Falls trolleybuses, but it was not possible to be as profitable as Falls trolleybuses. And by 1972 the 77 route had degenerated into only five journeys in the morning peak and five in the afternoon. Outside that it was carrying nothing because it was crossing the sectarian divide. Anyone having to travel went into town and out again rather than risking the cross-town route. As well as that we had curtailment of evening services; people weren't travelling in the evening, so there was a progressive cutting back of evening services. By 1970 the black taxis had started on the Falls and slightly later the Shankill and Shore Roads. The Falls service frequency had degenerated too.

So we had bus losses and staff losses to deal with. Staff were leaving because they didn't want to deal with the new environment they were experiencing. It wasn't called trauma in those days, but if you had been hijacked and forced off your bus, it had an effect. So now there was difficulty in getting the work covered, set alongside the constant reduction in service levels. There was also the ongoing conversion to one-man-operation, which was reducing the number of staff that we required. With regard to the latter, it is fair to say that in a certain way, the effect of the Troubles was to ease the problem of shedding staff required by the conversion to o-m-o.

**MC**   *I suppose your staff costs were falling because of o-m-o at the same time as your revenue was dropping because of the civil unrest?*

**FC**   Yes, but not enough to keep us afloat. You see even the benefits of the cuts in staff costs couldn't keep pace with the fall in revenue.

It was after internment I presume the Transport Committee of the Corporation started to talk to Werner. The Corporation had decided to divest itself of the Transport Department.

**MC**    *Yes, and local government reorganisation was coming up as well.*

**FC**    Yes, that was coming up, too and there was no stomach for keeping on what was becoming a very difficult department to maintain. It was always having problems, even though most were not of its own making. So basically 1971's problems continued through 1972. Then came March 1973 and the takeover by Ulsterbus. We tried to operate during the UWC strike in 1974. We operated from the city centre, just working out timetables standing on the street.

At the takeover by Ulsterbus, what could be done was very limited because of the engineering workload and the staff required. We were still maintaining vehicles that should have been taken off the road. The final conversion to one-man-operation was in March 1975, but we still had to retain about six of the Daimler CVGs, which operated mainly on the Downview service. It was supposed to be one-man-operated, but we simply didn't have the vehicles. So we also retained conductors. We had redeployed some conductors because we had new routes, like Four Winds, coming on stream. There was a bit of an exchange of routes with Ulsterbus around 1971–1972. BCT took Four Winds, Glen Road, gave away Tullycarnet, took Shaws Road, took Ladybrook.

**MC**    *Erinvale?*

**FC**    I think so, but I'd need to firm up on that. When we took on a new route, someone used to be sent up on the first morning to make sure that everything was running properly. I was the junior member of operations staff, so I didn't get Four Winds, etc, but was sent up to the Shaw's Road/Glen Road turning circle. I must admit I was more than a little apprehensive. When I got there I stood out like a sore thumb as a non-local, so to speak. So, I'm standing there taking bus numbers, and the black taxis were also operating to the turning circle. Things were pretty crude in those days, not like now, and there was this boyo up there at the turning circle, too. At first, in my naivety, I took it that he was providing some kind of operating, timetabling support for the taxis. But he was doing no such thing. He was collecting dues or suchlike from the taximen. He sees me and he says, "Hey, what are you doing?" And I says, "I'm up with the buses." "I'm with the taxis," he replied. I remember him coming up to me at the end and says, "You wouldn't give me a wee lift down?" So there he was, after collecting the dues, none of the taximen would give him a lift down in their cabs! I had to get him on the bus and say to the conductor when I showed my pass, "He's with me!" Innocent times in a way.

The other problem cropped up when we took over the like of Four Winds. You see, at a terminus the o-m-o Corporation men wouldn't reverse their buses. They had to have a turning circle. It was written into their agreement. So because there were no turning circles at these places, we had to deploy conductors up at these turning points. What with tea breaks and travelling time up and travelling time down, when I think of the actual amount of work we got out of these conductors, turning the odd bus every twenty minutes or so! Crazy, you know. But it was a way of re-deploying conductors, of course, and avoiding redundancies.

On the takeover by Ulsterbus, initially very little change was made. A '2' was added to the front of the fleet number, the legal name on the side was changed, and for a while the Corporation crest was retained. I understand that circumstances were difficult but I have always felt that a great mistake was made by not stamping some sort of mark on the company at that time to mark the change to Citybus.

**MC**    *Yes. I remember when I was in Milewater Road seeing a logo designed for Citybus but it was never used.*

**FC**    There was no sense of change amongst the operating staff, unlike what happened when Ulsterbus was set up. Really, there was no change until recently when Metro was set up. Even the agreement the men were working under was the old National Working Agreement with all its inefficiencies, that has long disappeared in GB; a relic from BCT times.

It was very crude in the early days with regard to the payment of wages. I remember the late Frank McGrogan going around the depots, lifting the takings, bringing them to Head Office, bagging them up and using them to pay the staff. You were getting paid, but not necessarily in notes. You see, at the break-up of the BCT, the clerical staff all left. Unless you were an eejit like me, and interested in buses, you got a transfer out of the Transport Department. There was a period of about nine months when everybody knew what was happening and scrambled to get out, so there were few clerical staff left at the end.

**MC**  *Yes, I remember that few clerical staff came over to us from the BCT.*

**FC**  It's also why we had so many inspectors. Inspectors were doing clerical work. During Ted Hesketh's era I was always getting hammered, "Why have we so many inspectors?" The chief clerk in a depot, for example, was graded as an inspector. The reason for that was that at the changeover there was nobody else to do the work, so by default the inspectors took it on. Now once that happens, it is very difficult to reverse the process.

**MC**  *So basically, at the changeover, your entire backup from the City Hall vanished?*

**FC**  It vanished.

**MC**  *And there was nothing to take its place for a while?*

**FC**  Well, the theory was that Ulsterbus would, within its resources, provide this backup. So any function that could be amalgamated was. But everything was very tight.

**MC**  *It was. For example, I recall two payrolls being run with the same staff on the same computer that we had previously used to run one.*

**FC**  Yes, we tried to run all the processes and fire-fought at the same time.

So, the pace of changeover to one-manning accelerated because Heubeck wanted to cut costs. As a result, between 1973 and 1975 we completed the process of changeover. Conversion had only started in 1969 and we did the difficult cross-town routes first. The simple end to end ones came later. One of things I didn't like about this accelerated process was the waste that became built into the system. In the early days, we were able to keep running times tight. But as we accelerated the changeover process, in order to get agreement on it, we were giving more time away. The men's representatives were making claims that they couldn't do the runs in the times we wanted. A load of nonsense, mostly. Part of the problem was that we had such complex routes, for example around Glengormley.

This extension of running times led on to another problem; a shortage of buses to implement this rapid acceleration in o-m-o. The rear-entrance fleet was collapsing around us. Those inherited by Citybus had been battered and bashed over the years and were in a pretty bad state. That's when we took in the 1300-series Leopards from Ulsterbus. You remember them, with the yellow stickers? They were the first buses to actually carry the 'Citybus' name. All that happened to those buses was that they got the stickers and token machines. We also got the ex-Edinburgh Tiger Cubs. We used those on the Stormont service. We put them on poorly patronised routes, but with the Stormont run we hit the morning civil servant rush. But the Edinburghs couldn't climb the hills with all the civil servants on board. So they had to get off and walk behind the bus while it went up the hill!

**MC**  *Yes, I remember those buses well. I recall operating to Four Winds and experiencing them crawling up the hill to the estate in first gear, at about 5mph. They were awful.*

**FC**  We were back in the Naval Air Yard a couple more times, but in time part of it became Belfast Harbour Airport and the available space became less and less. Then we started to use McNeill's yard, down Duncrue Street here. We tended not to be out of all depots when we used McNeill's yard, just Falls and Short Strand, and Ardoyne on occasions. Then in the 1979–80 period, during the time when depots were being bombed and we were losing a lot of vehicles we hit the buffers and we entered into . . .

**MC**  *The glorious phase of London Transport buses?*

**FC**  Exactly, the glorious phase of London Transport buses. Well, don't ever believe that London Transport had any sympathy with the poor buggers who were getting their buses burnt in Northern Ireland. London Transport simply saw it as an opportunity to offload . . .

**MC**  *. . . a number of excellent quality vehicles?*

**FC**  . . . those bloody Merlins that had given them nothing but bother. Now, they played a clever move in that with the first ones, they gave us the opportunity to send our engineers over and select the 20 vehicles, the fully seated group that went into Short Strand, as I remember. I now believe that they did some work to those vehicles. We definitely got sucked in with that first group of vehicles. There is no doubt about that. After that there was no selection. The vehicles were taken 'as seen'.

From then on it was a different story, as I know to my cost. Every third or fourth Friday I would take a group of volunteer drivers, people who were generally off the weekend, and for them it was an attractive jaunt across. They saw it as a jolly for which they were being paid. This view would last until the Sunday when they finally realised what they had let themselves in for.

We went over on the London express coach – no expense spared – the bit from Stranraer being generally operated by Western SMT. We were all right if we got on the regular working, but if they knew we were a group of drivers we could end up travelling from Stranraer to London on a service bus! We would sleep on this thing which might have been used on its previous duty to work schools or something like that. We would arrive the next day in London and the drivers could then have their day on the town; all these Paddies over in London with all its attractions. I remember to my cost.

We had an engineer and a group of drivers to get the buses home. We would set out with the buses from one of the London depots. However, we always got a smile from the London boys. I remember that; we always got a wave and a smile from the men in wherever we were collecting the buses, whether it be in one of the London depots, like Southend or from London Country depots. You remember, the buses came from various arts and parts. One of the worst was the second group, the ones with the big turnstiles in them.

**MC** *I remember those; 6d in the turnstile.*

**FC** Yes, the second group. That was in the middle of winter. I remember us at Tebay Services – I knew every motorway service area – Tebay Services with the snow thick on the ground and the poor engineer underneath those buses trying to nurse them on up the road. We tried to aim to make Carlisle on the first night. We had collected the buses on the Sunday and we were booked into one of the hotels in Carlisle Ulsterbus used on the tours. That was supposed to be a highlight of the trip and was to encourage men to volunteer. I was able to hold out the prospect of a slap-up meal and luxury accommodation – God help them. Little did they know of how unlikely it was they would get this slap-up meal. Generally they would be eating sandwiches at two or three in the morning and out again at 6.00am for Stranraer.

One of the pitfalls I had to cope with was what the men would get up to on their Saturday in London. I remember once visiting one of those strip joints. I had to play along, keep some sort of control, or risk losing them altogether. We got a taxi and he drove round in circles half a dozen times with these Paddies in the back and then came to this place where he knocked the door. He got his tenner for bringing us to it and in we went. You had to get signed in because technically it was a club.

One of the boys with us was a shop steward. It was always better to have a shop steward, for obvious reasons, particularly for the return trip on the Sunday because some of the men would have, reasonably enough, thrown up the head given what they had to cope with.

Anyway, this shop steward, Joe-Boy, was a hard man and we were fortunate that we had him with us. We went down into the club. They came round with the drinks; well, there were no prices with the drinks so you can guess where this story is going. It comes to the end of the night and the bill was presented for about £360.

**MC** *My God! £360 at 1970s prices?*

**FC** Yes, about £10 or something like that for a beer, you see. There was no way we could pay that kind of bill. The only thing that I had was my fuel money for the next day and if I'd used that it would have been the sack for me. We were in trouble. So Joe-Boy, said, "Do you know where we are from?" playing the Northern Ireland card. As he threatened, and faced down the heavies at the door, the rest of us scarpered. Well, I got out through a wee window in the toilet but I don't know to this day how everybody else got out, other than to say they did and we lived to collect the buses the next morning!

At least that occasion was worth acknowledging. It was better than some other occasions where we went to places where we paid £4.00 to watch a ten-minute film of some dame taking her pants off. After that all it was good for was having a good sleep. I remember those times where you paid £4.00 to have a good sleep! It was a crazy situation.

Then there were the evenings when our men would provide the entertainment in some working men's club. We were generally able to get in to one of these clubs. They were the best of whole lot. What would happen as the night went on, the floor would be opened up for entertainment. Our boys were great at filling the holes in the entertainment and generally it ended up where the rest of the night was free. They were getting free drink because they were providing the entertainment. I didn't drink, so it didn't matter to me, apart from worrying that with all the free drink would they be able to get up the next morning to bring the buses back to Northern Ireland.

It was crazy; I remember us leaving Carlisle and doing the journey to Stranraer feeding the fuel into the engine because the fuel line was blocked. The engineer had lifted the trap over the engine at the back and had rigged up a big plastic container to provide a direct feed into the engine. I had to sit holding this thing. Every so often he would go over a bump and this thing would get dislodged. Also, because of the hard water in the London area, other problems would develop in the engines because parts of the water cooling system would be furred up with scale.

Another problem was, most of the buses were fitted with 45 gallon tanks. Now, the price differential for fuel between the motorway services areas and ordinary service stations in those days was high, much higher than today, so we were generally careful about where we re-fuelled. On one occasion we got a group of Merlins. Some were London Country but they were fitted with 40-gallon tanks. But, of course, nobody had told us that. Another problem was that we were a driver short on that trip. Now, I had no PSV, and had never driven a bus. But, either we brought one bus less back, or I drove the bus!

**MC**   *And just hoped you weren't pulled in?*

**FC**   I was. It was on the motorway. We came to a section of road works. Of course I'm trying to stay between the white lines but we came to these narrow coned lanes at the road works and I'm not used to the width of the vehicle so I demolished a line of cones. So I got pulled in. Yer man says, "What are you up to?" So I told him we were bringing these buses back to Northern Ireland to replace so many buses burnt since we left, you know, played the sympathy card. And he let me off. I was lucky; he didn't ask any more questions. He says, "You need to be a lot more careful! I hope you boys don't drive like this at home." Anyway we got to Carlisle eventually.

On the same trip, the next morning and I'm driving. By then, we were on the A75, you know that road, if you break down you block everything. The next thing I come across a bus stopped. I pulls in and goes over. "It looks as if she's out of fuel," says the driver. "Not at all," I said, "It couldn't be." I had the receipts for the fuel, you know, the usual routine. You had to bring back receipts so that what you spent could be accounted for to the last penny! So then the engineer in the van behind pulls up and has a look. "I think she's out of fuel," he says. So I said, "How could that happen?" He went off in the van with the container to get more fuel. I drove on and round the corner was another bus sitting stopped. By the time I got to the third one, the police appeared. They pulled in and were absolutely flaming. "Who's in charge of these buses?" I replied, "I am, constable, is there some trouble?" "There's eight of your buses scattered all over this A75!", came the reply. Of course they all had 40-gallon tanks and had all run out of fuel. So we had to get fuel for them all and top them up. Now I don't know if you've ever looked for a petrol station on that road. There aren't too many.

The other problem was getting them over on the boat. That was the only area where I got any dispensation from those accountants upstairs, because eventually I was able to convince them that in order to get the buses across, I couldn't get receipts for the additional amount it took to actually get them on the boat. You see, because we didn't know when we would arrive, we couldn't book in advance. I had always had to put that payment down to 'miscellaneous expenses'. It didn't matter whether you went Cairnryan or Stranraer, you always got a big smile because they knew they had you.

Never, in all the trips I made, 16 or 17 of them, do I remember getting the full complement over. If I got 60–70% of them over, I was doing well. Once I had to go back down to London because on that weekend, we had lost more buses at home than we were bringing over. But we did eventually cotton on to the various moves being pulled by London Transport.

At the time we were bringing in the Merlins, we were operating the Citylink service on behalf of NIR. It started off, as you remember, with ex-BCT Swifts, but then we put on the Bristols. But as far as we were concerned, the Bristols were a waste of a good bus on this service. They were taken off, and the service went down hill because it ended up with all the scrap of the day. The morning I drove the bus in from England at the end of the trip I was talking about a moment ago, and I was never gladder to see Short Strand depot, as soon as we arrived one of the batch was refuelled; a set of Citylink stickers was slapped on, not straight, not over the previous owner's name, London Country, just slapped on the front and the sides and she was put straight out on to the Citylink service. By the way, it wasn't the bus I drove in, because it had – ahem – a few scrapes on it. The reason we were able to put the bus straight out like that was because on the Citylink service they didn't need ticket machines.

Some of those LT buses operated with Piccadilly Circus and suchlike showing on the destination blinds because the men thought this was great and you couldn't get them to change it.

However, after we had exhausted the Merlins, we went for the Swifts. Oh, God, the Swifts!

**MC**     *You went from bad to worse?*

**FC**     Bad to worse it was! But once LT saw we had an interest in the Swifts they came thick and fast and we able to build up a bank of them. For example, we were able to put them into service when Smithfield was destroyed. There were spare Swifts that were transferred over the night that Smithfield was bombed. That's how we got Smithfield's services moving again, with Citybus Swifts along with a load of scrap from other depots.

But the London Transport era was awful and was I glad when we started to bring in Bristols.

**MC**     *From the north of England?*

*Former London Country Bus Services, Reigate, AEC Merlin MBS 292 became Citybus No 651 in 1980. This was one of the vehicles to which Frank Clegg refers above; it came straight off the boat and into service! It is seen here outside the now-closed York Road railway station, operating a journey on the Citylink service.*                                                **Will Hughes**

**FC**    Yes. They were good buses. That was a good time.

Not knowing the number of vehicles you had for your services, and having to adjust, especially peak hour services, to take account of that, was extremely difficult. Once we got over the Naval Air Yard period, we tried to operate out of May Street. Our offices were at 43 May Street had and had been inherited from the BCT; They very cramped. We had used it in BCT days when we had had to get out of Utility Street because that area had become a hot spot.

(MC    *At this point Frank starts to talk about Werner Heubeck*)

*Three former London Transport AEC Swifts – SMS 688, SMS 722 and SMD 64 – are seen undergoing preparation at Falls Park depot in 1979. They became Citybus Nos 45, 57 and 71 respectively. Note the tram lines still in situ, even though Falls Road trams had been withdrawn in 1938.*

The reason that Heubeck got doing his own thing, apart from the influence of his particular personality, was because the powers-that-be wanted public transport in Belfast to operate.

**MC**    *As a political gesture?*

**FC**    Yes. In other words, if public transport in Belfast wasn't operating, then things were seen to be very bad. Therefore, the deal always appeared to me to be, "You keep the buses running and you'll be left alone." It was at this time that we had the episodes of lifting devices off buses. It filtered down the line, from Heubeck and Max Hale, the Chief Traffic Officer, on down. I lifted a device off one bus, but I knew it was safe before I did so. Heubeck was a very shrewd man, very careful. It was a myth that he would have walked in, thrown caution to winds and lifted a device off a bus. Never in my experience did he do that. He always had done his research. He always had the driver at hand and had questioned him as to who had put the device on, where it had been put on, what did they say, where were you told to take it to, what was it like, etc. I never knew of him to lift off a device where he had not talked to the driver first. He only took his decision after weighing up all the facts. What he did have, of course, which made him unique, was that he had been given the authority to do it. And that was because of, in my opinion, this pact or whatever you wanted to call it.

**MC**    *Gentlemen's agreement?*

**FC**    Yes, which give him the authority to do it as part of this non-interference deal on the operations side.

**MC**    *Yes. Reading what Heubeck himself says, it seemed to boil down to "You let me be and I'll run the buses. I'll do it my way and I don't want any interference from government"*

**FC**    Getting back to the operational difficulties, we always had a tricky situation when we had been off roads as to when we would go back on them again. That was difficult for two reasons. First off, I must put on record my admiration for our drivers and in earlier days our conductors. Whatever run-ins I had with them over schedules or whatever, the one sure thing was they did keep the buses running. A certain amount of what they did was out of respect for Werner Heubeck and to a lesser degree Max Hale, who was originally Chief Traffic Officer and later Area Manager. The problem was, if you had been off a road for a while, you were probably operating out of a different location and operating different routes. You were probably having an easier time than you would be having on your normal duty. Therefore when it came time to go back on a road you would not have been jumping up and down with enthusiasm.

The tradition was that a route was 'opened up' by a shop steward and you generally used them to drive the bus. Now here I must say that, normally, religious persuasion never entered into the picture. That is one thing that we here in the bus industry are very proud of, that religion was never a factor. Drivers went everywhere. However, to pick up on the point I was making, the other practice when opening up a route was that we always used a shop steward of the other persuasion to that of the area the route was operating through.

**MC**    *I didn't know that. That's very interesting. A clever bit of psychology there.*

**FC**    There were wee things like that done, that when you look back on them now were done for good reasons and in their own way achieved results. Another thing was that we did not publicly advertise that the route was back in operation. We always tried to give it a bedding-in period. Then we made the announcement.

In earlier years, when I was involved in producing the schedules, I worked most of my time in the office; at that time I couldn't drive. However, I later learned to drive and would go out in the black taxis that Citybus used for mobile patrols. By the way, the choice of black taxis was tactical, to blend in, so to speak, into the landscape. However, in the end we had to put the yellow 'Citybus' stickers on to them. That was because the taximen weren't happy. At that time we had new black taxis and their taxis were quite rough. Anyway, I used to drive these things at night with inspectors, keeping an eye out for trouble developing. We couldn't get people to drive them sometimes, so I would go out with an inspector when a route was coming back on. We were operating in front of the buses, scouting out the territory, so to speak. I knew how to get offside quickly if needed.

**MC**    *Those black hacks had a great turning circle*

**FC**    Yes, and how to drive up a footpath and so on. They were good days. I know it's awful to say that, because they were difficult days, but you know what I mean.

In recent years, we have had to deal with missile throwing, and a lot of it targeted at drivers. It's bad enough. But I wonder how some of our present drivers would have coped if they had been operating during the real bad times. However, during the real bad times the drivers were not the targets. I could count on the fingers of one hand, the number of times drivers lost their money. They were generally given time to take their money. They were usually directed to a phone or told where a public phone was, because it was the vehicle that was wanted. At times you could even sometimes exchange the vehicle. You had the contacts to know that they wanted the bus as a barricade.

**MC**    *Yes, I remember that that happened in Derry, where they took a good one out and put a scrapper in its place.*

**FC**    Well, it happened in Belfast as well. As I was saying, the driver was normally protected. We'd have got a phone call to say that the driver was on his way in but the bus had gone up in smoke. The safety of the driver was important. Significant efforts were made to search for the drivers. During those days of the hijackings and burnings, with the exceptions of individual instances, like what happened to Harry Bradshaw, generally speaking the injuries to staff were not severe.

**MC**    *Yes, in the cases of Harry Bradshaw and Sydney Agnew, it was the driver who was deliberately targeted, not the bus.*

**FC**    Yes. When a colleague was killed, it was difficult because we wanted to maintain a service to the public but equally we wanted to show respect to the deceased. Sometimes what happened was driven by emotions and it may not have been done the way we wanted, but we had to bite our lip to a degree and take it on the chin. What I mean of course was the disruption. And then we had to try and get things back on course again as soon as possible. It was a combination of weighing up what was reasonable to do, what was right to do and the service to the public.

We also went through a difficult period with the police, some of whom wanted buses off because it made life easier for them. If there were difficulties in an area and we wanted to maintain services into that area, sometimes that didn't concur with the police's view of the situation. In other words, the bus then became a nuisance because either they were going to have to rescue it or it was going to result in a lot more form-filling if damage was done to the vehicle. So we had some difficulties there.

In the early years of the Troubles we were hit because the army were in all the depots. Between 1969 and 1971 the nationalist community accepted the army. That all changed in 1971 and we were affected because we were associated in some degree with the army. That was always in the background. Of course, the bus was an easily manoeuvrable barricade associated with authority.

**MC**    *Heubeck put pressure on the army to get out of the depots when he took over.*

**FC**    Yes he did, because he recognised the association and the difficulties their presence was creating for staff. The other thing from a staffing point of view was the depot code. You know how each bus had a depot code? Well that became a problem in Belfast. They had to be removed. With us, buses from a depot could be operating anywhere in the city. The driver on a bus at any particular time could be from any depot. The only time you knew that the driver on a bus is from the depot shown by the bus's depot code was first thing in the morning and last thing at night, because once it came to driver's meal break, he would hand over the bus to a driver from any depot. However, the thugs knew that the bus had to brought in or home by a driver from that depot so they were identifying at night the religious persuasion of drivers, particularly Falls drivers from the 'F' code on the buses. That's why the codes came off.

Then we had the era, during the 1980s, where the taximen were being targeted for assassination because of their religious persuasion. Up until then, there had been virtual freedom for our drivers to move about between depots. But this tended to result, in the case of Falls in particular, in drivers of one persuasion dominating. I remember at one time there was only one Protestant driver in Falls. So although we took the codes off buses, the hoods still knew that buses from particular depots operated certain late night services. Therefore we took action to move drivers around and mix them more from a religious point of view and if a new driver came into the company, a person who had no access to the driver's personal details allocated them at random to a depot. These were issues that weren't there at the start of the Troubles but which developed as things moved on from the 1970s right up to the late 1980s.

Then we moved from the hijackings into the depot attacks and we were losing a group of vehicles and that's when things became extremely difficult. That's when we got in the old Ulsterbus Bedford VAM/Duples and we had to look for a driver who could handle them. They did very little work. The other ones we got were the semi-automatic PD3s. They were sent to the Falls. That was the time when we were grabbing anything. For example, with the PD3s, here were a few vehicles which could be operated by our men because they had the same gear shift as the Fleetlines. There were even times when particular vehicles were allocated to particular drivers.

Another big change during the 70s, related to school buses. When I came in to this job, the number of school buses was few, about 20–25, if there were even that many. Belfast Royal Academy and the Model, for example, had their own buses. Suddenly, with the Troubles, we had this problem. Children couldn't cross interfaces and so on and we ended up with these long, winding school routes. We went from simple services and simple routes to a period when the numbers of commuters were in decline. The number of peak hour services was going down. At the same time there was an increase in demand for school buses. So, in the afternoon at 3.30 you had this increase in school work. In effect, we went from being an organisation where the afternoon peak was the workers coming home to one where we were turning out buses to bring the school children home. By the 1980s we found that we had no work for those buses to do after the schools were dealt with. The shipyard was virtually gone and other places like that were gone or in decline, places which had in the past supplied passengers for the afternoon peak but we were still faced with an ever increasing demand for school buses.

The increase in demand for school transport was jacked up because of what happened in Ardoyne with the Everton, Somerdale, St Gabriel's schools sectarian problem. At the time the government stepped in to deal with the resulting problem of soldiers being attacked at the Ardoyne/Crumlin Road junction. That was the first time that the government had stepped in to deal with a schools problem, and the way the government dealt with it was to bus the kids. Everton were bussed at 3.10, Somerdale at 3.30 and St Gabriel's at 3.50. This was all started with best of intentions but it required the use of 12 to 14 buses. Then everyone else got to hear of it and pressure built for similar services elsewhere. The Antrim Road schools wanted it and others wanted it. Then we had complaints from some schools, why should our school day finish at 3.50 when the school down the road finished at 3.10?

At the start the Community Relations Council paid for the extra buses but then it ended up being shunted from pillar to post as to who paid for them. Nobody had a budget for them. Then you had the problem of Our Lady of Mercy School. I always felt sorry for them that they were not treated justly. They always had to have school buses because of where they were located, but because of that their kids had to pay; they never got the free bus transport that these other schools nearby were getting and I never could understand that. The whole North Belfast area was a real problem in this regard. We ended up with a situation where the school bus was always the answer.

*Ulsterbus Leyland Leopard/Marshall No 1192 was a second-hand purchase in March 1979 to help cope with the toll of destruction. It had been new to Southdown Motor Services, Brighton, in 1967 and is seen here at Ballycastle, parked beside the long-closed narrow gauge railway station. Most of the former Southdown vehicles were pressed into service in National Bus Company green, with Ulsterbus fleet names applied.*

| | |
|---|---|
| **MC** | *To whatever problem there was?* |
| **FC** | Yes, you reduced the police presence and reduced the army presence by the provision of school buses. I remember us being summoned up to meetings where the great and good were present all around the table. We always knew where it was going to end, with the provision of more school buses. We are still suffering from the results of this policy, because we can't get rid of them. |
| **MC** | *It must be a massive drain on the company's resources* |
| **FC** | Yes, and it has never been recognised. It's a hobbyhorse of mine, the fact that the real costs of providing those buses has never been recognised nor has the impact on normal services. We came to the point where we couldn't always meet the needs for normal services. We had to lift buses out of normal services to use on schools work. |

Since the introduction of Metro recently, that has stopped. We don't lift buses out now. In the old timetable we did lift buses out and put them on to a schools run, but even though Metro went on line in February 2005, we're still fighting with some schools that want their dedicated school bus back. With Metro, we put on a normal service that still carries the children.

The other significant thing that came out of the Troubles was the fleet changes that followed on from the behavioural changes of passengers on the top decks of double-deckers. This is tied in with the Heubeck fibreglass seat era. The issue was that sustaining one-man double-deck operations became difficult because of the vandalism and other bad behaviour upstairs. As a result, we converted to a single-deck fleet in Citybus. This lasted until improvements in video technology, and some general improvements in behaviour in recent times, allowed us to reintroduce double-deckers.

**MC**   *How has that worked out?*

**FC**   Oh, very good. One of the positive factors seems to be related to the length of the vehicle. The old 11 or 12 metre vehicle was too long for city operations. The new ones are just over ten metres and they suffer very little damage to bodywork. Also there is very little damage now being done upstairs so the costs of operating the new 'deckers are very encouraging.

**MC**   *You mentioned earlier the issue of compensation. When vehicles were damaged or destroyed, particularly new vehicles, how was compensation claimed?*

**FC**   It was based on age of the vehicle and its life expectancy. There was a formula for calculating the claim and (the late) Frank McGrogan used to administer it. However, over the years, the compensation system got tighter and tighter. They wouldn't pay the first £100, and then the first £250 of a claim and then they started to manipulate the statistics to knock out some of the claims, and so on.

There was also the issue of compensation for injuries to drivers. We have an Assault Pay agreement. Of course, we have normal sick pay, but it was never an exceedingly generous scheme. There were always penalties associated with the sick pay scheme. But Assault Pay was entirely different. Under this scheme the rule was that if you were assaulted, you should not be penalised through a loss of any earnings that you could have accrued. The calculation of Assault Pay was partly based on the overtime that a driver had done over the previous thirteen weeks. However, once on Assault Pay, we had the devil's own job to get them back off it again, as you can probably appreciate.

Of all the controversial issues we had to deal with over the whole of the Troubles, the Assault Pay scheme was the most difficult. We had to make sure that what the driver claimed had happened had actually happened. That was important, because the difference between sick pay and Assault Pay was fairly substantial. We had to have some system for getting them back off it. That involved sending them to the company doctor. There was also a psychologist involved. It was a difficult balancing act.

When an assault took place, the police were notified. What usually happened was that a driver would ring in, or if he could, bring his bus into the city centre. If he needed to be taken to hospital that would be done. Radio Control would notify the local police station. At some point the driver would have to pay a visit to the police station to give a statement. The driver would then come in, the next day or when he was fit, fill in a form and be interviewed about the details of what happened. A manager would then have to sign to authorise the assault pay.

**MC**   *How long did Assault Pay last?*

**FC**   At the start it wasn't time limited. But later it was limited to ten weeks. Then there was a cap put on it. In a few cases, I must admit, I would have had a doubt about whether a genuine assault had happened, especially if the pattern of previous overtime working supported this suspicion. You see, there were drivers who went through their career with us and were never assaulted. They worked the same cycle of duties as men who were being assaulted four, five, six times. What I'm getting at is you were getting the same names coming up over and over again. However, it is a very hard thing to prove.

**MC**   *Was this a purely company provision?*

**FC**   Yes, it was in an agreement with the unions.

**MC**   *How did you reduce or get rid of it?*

**FC**   Oh, during wage negotiations, we whittled away at it. We didn't increase it or it didn't get a cost of living increase, that type of thing.

Fortunately now assaults are not as common, but it was a very difficult problem during the post-first ceasefire period. The time we really started to experience problems from assaults, was after the first ceasefire and it got even more difficult after the second ceasefire. If you think about it, the young people who had been brought up during the Troubles and who may have had some affiliation to paramilitary organisations, couldn't do what they had been previously used to doing or being instructed to do. So what's the next best thing?

**MC**   *Go and beat up a bus driver?*

**FC**    Throw something at him, or rob him. So we got the targeting of drivers with missiles; we got the robberies that we never had had before; we got the specific targeting where it was not only the vehicle they were after, but the driver too. That became more and more difficult with the increase in assaults. Drivers then began to genuinely develop stress and trauma and we had to get more professional medical people involved.

I remember the times when I would have to interview drivers and try to encourage them back, of talking through things with them, and me with no professional qualifications whatever to do it. In the early days, I'd maybe arrange for a man to have a day or half day in the driving school and then encourage them to go back to work, and it generally worked. But later it all became more and more difficult and you found yourself counselling in the true sense. I wasn't qualified for it and people would say, and were entitled to say, "What are you doing?" They would say, "You're not out there; You don't know what it's like." Which was fair comment. The other point was that when I was out knocking about in the late 1970s, the drivers knew me. I was seen as being involved, you know, driving into trouble spots ahead of the buses and so on. When I went to Short Strand in 1985, I don't think anyone ever said to me, "You don't know what it's about. You don't know what you're talking about."

Knowledge of your people and being seen out and about was very important. Heubeck placed great importance on that, on mingling and always being out and about. And there was many a bus that he drove, as you know. We were unique in that respect. In GB, there were the National Bus Company subsidiaries and the big municipals and in none of them were the management known for mixing with the men, whereas we had the opposite philosophy and I always believe that that was a great advantage.

*The mangled remains of Citybus Bristol RE No 2223 lie at the rear of Falls Park depot awaiting a one-way trip to the scrapman's yard. Any useful bits will be salvaged before disposal. No 2223 had been destroyed at Wellington Place, in Belfast City Centre, on 7 July 1990, by a firebomb left on board.*                                                          **Mark O'Neill**

Then, by the 1990s, in my view things started to go the wrong way and we began to get swamped with paperwork. One of the things about computerisation is the amount of paper it generates.

What you've got to remember, too, is the change in expectations that occurred between the Heubeck and Ted eras (Ted Hesketh, Werner Heubeck's successor as MD). Heubeck was a man for his time. The one description of him that was so, so true, is that. He was a man who was out there, mixing with the men. But don't ask him to sit at his desk writing long reports; don't ask him to sit explaining things to government ministers; don't expect him to explain what he was doing to ministers or have to ask for anything. But by the Ted era, all that had all changed. I was brought down here as Ted's PA because he recognised that he was weak on the operational side, which, of course, is where my experience lies. People didn't understand that things had changed by the time Ted took over, and that Ted's management style would never be the same as Heubeck's.

MC    *Yes, I can understand that. People had moved away from just hoping that the buses could be kept running in any shape or form, to looking for a quality service.*

FC    Yes. That's why the seating was improved again. Seats went back into the standee buses; video cameras were installed; new vehicles were fully seated; bus shelters were erected. Also there was more and more legislation to deal with, generating more paperwork and systems were not as relaxed as they had been when Heubeck was in charge, when he could operate with minimum paperwork.

Another of the things that I haven't mentioned which were associated with the Troubles, was the Peace People and their rallies. There was a period when they were holding these regularly. They were great times because city-based vehicles, these vehicles that had never been out of Belfast, were now going around the country, doing that work. Then there was the Pope's visit and the huge number of buses needed to deal with that. They were good times with people co-operating and mucking in. The London trips, the Peace People, the Pope's visit; they all lifted drivers who had been driving in difficult situations in Belfast. It let them do something different and that was a morale boost. Then in Ted's time came other events, like the visit of the Tall Ships.

On my gravestone will be an epitaph, something that was recorded at a Citybus works council. The Tall Ships were coming but at this meeting we were arguing about some service changes and overtime levels. There was a discussion about where we would get the drivers to do the specials associated with the Tall Ships and I said, "These Tall Ships. What are you talking about? We'll have two buses and a third as a standby." And that's minuted! (*Author's note: Citybus could barely cope with the huge numbers of people wanting to see the Tall Ships. It turned out to be one of the biggest public events Belfast has ever seen.*)

Then we had the balloon carnivals as morale boosters. Although we were moving into this post-Troubles area, the problem was that our drivers and the emergency services were still getting hit. Bus drivers felt that while everyone else was getting the benefit of this post-Troubles improvement, they weren't getting the full benefit because of the expenditure of excess energies by some young people in attacking buses.

MC    *To conclude, what are your strongest memories of this period?*

FC    What I remember most, especially during the 1969 to 1971 period was horrendous hours; the late nights and working all night on occasions. The Ulster Workers Council Strike was a particularly dreadful time. At that time I lived on the Belmont Road. We were operating out of May Street in the city centre. To get into work, I used to leave the house at about 4.30–4.45am and make my way across to the Sydenham by-pass. I was then able to get into town by walking down the by-pass because the army had kept it open. If I had tried to walk down the main road, I would have been stopped by paramilitaries at the barricades and questioned. Once I got over the railway bridge at Sydenham railway station, I knew I was all right. Then I was coming back home at ten at night, walking up the Sydenham by-pass.

MC    *I was working here in Milewater Road during that strike, and I remember having to get in to work. I lived in Andersonstown, so it was easy enough for me to get into the city centre, but then I had to get out here. But I recall Brian Gordon, the Company Secretary, sitting out there in the lobby, personally checking everybody in. He was checking, at every level, who was coming into work and who wasn't. And to give everybody their due, we had virtually a full complement in here during that strike.*

FC    It was the same with the drivers. Where other industries fudged it, there was no fudging with us. Being in public transport, you can't fudge it.

# 'People's taxi' competition

## Introduction

By 1973, Ulsterbus and, even more importantly, Citybus were losing a lot of money because of the operation of so-called 'people's taxis' in Belfast. These had originated in nationalist West Belfast at the start of the Troubles during periods when the normal bus services had been withdrawn by the Corporation due to civil unrest. They were so successful that the operation was quickly copied on the loyalist Shankill and Shore Roads. On both sides of the sectarian divide they were believed to be under paramilitary control, or at least subject to their influence.

Werner Heubeck wanted the authorities to clamp down on these activities and to help him make a case for this, he decided to try and quantify the amount of traffic being lost by his companies to the taxis. In order to gather the necessary data he set up three teams to carry out a survey of taxi traffic for a week. After threats made on the first day of the survey by paramilitaries, the investigation was continued under cover.

In order to try and estimate the numbers of cabs operating, the registration of each black taxi was recorded as it passed the observers; also noted was its direction of travel, the approximate number of passengers and the time. For purposes of comparison, the same details were noted for buses that passed.

Enough data was gathered to make a reasonable approximation of the losses in both traffic and revenue that the company was suffering and this information was used by Mr Heubeck in his fruitless attempts over the years to have the authorities close down or curtail these taxi operations.

What follows is a summary of the internal report published in August 1974 based on the data gathered in the survey. The statistics contained in this document were what Mr Heubeck used to demonstrate the losses Citybus was experiencing as the result of the illegal black taxi operations.

The appendices to the report are not included.

## Taxi Competition

Taxi competition against Citybus services occurs on these routes:

|  | Estimated no. of taxis* |
| --- | --- |
| Falls Road | 240 |
| Shankill Road | 140 |
| Shore Road | 40 |
|  | 420 |

(* It has proved difficult to estimate this exactly, as the majority carry English registrations with a large variety of suffix and prefix letters which are not easy to record in a census.)

Operation appears to be organised by some outside body (the Provisional IRA and the UDA) and there is a degree of positive support for the taximen. Equally there is a block of passengers who will only use Citybus. Opinions vary, but the general impression is that positive choice represents 20% at each end of the spectrum, leaving 60% who will take the first available transport.

Normal fares are comparable with Citybus token fares, ie, 10p, or 5p on short journeys. Children 5p for any length of journey. Old Age Pensioners pay full fare on the Falls Road, but reductions appear to be available on the Shankill. The fare advantage is that passengers travel paying cash at the token fare, not at the higher cash fare for Citybus. This is particularly important on the Falls Road.

The approximate percentage of total traffic carried by the taxis on each route is:

| | Mon–Fri | Sat | Sun |
|---|---|---|---|
| | % | % | % |
| Falls Road | 66 | 70 | no census |
| Shankill Road | 43 | 52 | 52 |
| Shore Road | 21 | 33 | 31 |

This suggests that:

The lower weekend frequencies provided by Citybus, together with the lack of a pronounced peak, make it a more practicable proposition to get a good day's work out of a taxi on Saturday or Sunday;

That drivers normally engaged on other work are available to drive a regular man's taxi;

The taxis do particularly well in off-peak periods again when frequencies are reduced;

The taxis are at full stretch during the peaks when Citybus occupancy improved sharply;

On the figures obtained we would be unable to cope with the peak traffic on the Shankill if the taxis were not operating.

The estimated loss of revenue is:

| | Falls Rd | Shankill Rd | Shore Rd | Total |
|---|---|---|---|---|
| No. of Mon–Fri passengers | 10,000 | 6,500 | 1,850 | |
| x5 | 50.000 | 37,500 | 9,250 | |
| Saturday | 9,000 | 8,500 | 3,000 | |
| Sunday | 3,000 | 1,800 | 700 | |
| Total per week | 62,000 | 47,800 | 12,950 | |
| At 10p per passenger | £6200 | | | |
| Add Whiterock Road | £1500 | | | |
| Total per week | £7700 | £4780 | £1295 | £13,775 |

This gives a figure of approximately £700,000 per annum.

# THE TRADES UNION PERSPECTIVE

## Introduction

There are two interviews in this chapter, with Eugene O'Callaghan and Liam Hughes. Eugene and Liam gave these interviews to Ruth Grahm as part of the *Routes* project.

Before taking up the position of full-time trades union officer, Eugene O'Callaghan had been a bus driver. In his role as a senior trades union representative for the Transport and General Workers Union, he had many dealings with Werner Heubeck and it is clear that both men often worked closely together to deal with the impact of the Troubles on the bus industry.

At the time of his interview, Liam Hughes had worked in the bus industry for thirty-five years and lives in Dungannon. He started off as a conductor with the UTA then he went on become a bus driver in 1968. He also spent some time as a bus-driving instructor and was Controller of the Cookstown Ulsterbus depot. His post at Cookstown was the first post of Controller to be set up. He was also a shop steward for twenty-five years and a senior shop steward for much of that time.

*(Author's note: In his interview, Liam Hughes covered all aspects of being a busman. I have used only the parts of the interview relating to the impact of the Troubles on his job.)*

## Eugene O'Callaghan, TGWU Senior Officer

EO'C   The trains have had problems but they are minor and insignificant in comparison to what the bus drivers went through. Now I was a bus worker for the best part of 40 years both as a driver, as Chairman of the Bus Council, Chairman of the Branch, Regional Committee Representative and as full-time trade union official.

Werner Heubeck made a very significant contribution and if it wasn't for some of the decisions we both had to take during the time, some of which weren't very popular, possibly we would have had no bus industry. He did make a very, very significant contribution. In those days, times were tough and people were really frightened to go back onto the streets so we had to take decisions because if we didn't the whole thing would have collapsed and the thing would have increased in intensity and made room for others from paramilitary organisations to take up the places we would vacate with our bus services. There were a lot of other things to be taken into consideration – children who had to get to school and old people having to get in and out of their homes, all of these things – and we did suffer very, very significant losses. For instance we had 11 people who were murdered, killed and we had an excess of 1400 buses which were totally destroyed. We had thousands and thousands of windows smashed and we had a considerable number of buses which were partially destroyed and on some occasions they could lose as many as 20 buses in one night. For instance when Smithfield bus station was bombed and burned out – we took an awful hit – I think we lost 20 buses that night. Oh, Dungannon, Falls, Ardoyne, various depots which were on the frontline interfaces had very serious losses but we were able to man and put a fleet out the next morning.

That was something that Werner made a significant contribution to. We were able to purchase maybe a hundred, I don't have the exact figures, of old buses that had been made redundant on the mainland and there was an agreement with the union and Werner and we got bus drivers over and they drove them down to the boats, put them on the boats, parked them down at the airport and we cannibalised them in such a way as that, for instance, if we lost 20 buses in a night, we had 20 more buses ready to roll in the morning, so we were never without a service.

Now as I said earlier on, there was a very large number who received very, very serious injuries and were hospitalised; one man got as much as 90% burns when petrol bombs were thrown into the cab of the bus. They were very, very seriously hurt. We had those who suffered significantly from stress and various other health factors and were permanently damaged and we don't know because we have never had proper statistics of the number of wives and mothers who suffered because it's very traumatic to be sitting at home at night knowing that your husband's out on the road, knowing that he's on that bus on his own and you listen to the radio and you hear, or you see on television, that there is severe and serious rioting in that particular area and your husband is on it. You don't know what condition he is coming home in. You don't really know or can put a finger on the number of wives, mothers and so forth who suffered.

I was one of the ones who was in the awful position that whilst it was the aim of paramilitaries to put transport off the road I was the main front line man myself, with Werner Heubeck, in keeping buses on the road and for that reason we could become prime targets. But you just put it down as part of the job.

For instance, I think it was Dillon you called him, who was injured at Carlisle Circus when they threw the petrol bomb in. Mr Heubeck sent him on a holiday to Canada, him and his wife you know and paid for it and there were other matters like that, which he doesn't want to mention.

Heubeck showed a great degree of courage. People would say that was because he was an explosives expert in the Rommel corps before he was taken prisoner in the desert. I don't know about that, I don't know whether it's true or not but I know he did go on the buses and he did carry off bombs and you could rest assured that anybody who was injured or if anything happened to them he visited their homes and, without saying too much, he was generous.

Now, I was there on Bloody Friday when the car bomb went off in Oxford Street bus station. Now we had five members killed in that explosion – Billy Irvine, a fellow called Carruthers, Tommy Killops, Jackie Gibson . . . That was – oh – we swept the body parts up with a shovel and put them in bags. Tommy Killops, God rest him, Tommy's kneecap was found up around the flour mills; there used to be a flour mill there at the time. I arranged all the funerals. I arranged for immediate financial aid for the wives to make sure they didn't go short, and the Union, immediately, without any qualification or red tape, we were able to donate £1000 to each home immediately and we provided free legal aid and free legal representation and we received, in all cases, quite significant compensation. It's a remarkable feature of the Troubles that the then depot manager was a man called Jack Campbell. Jack was standing beside the bomb when it went off and he wasn't killed but he was badly injured, and again, you may find this funny, but Jack insisted that I was the man who would represent him and get him legal aid and all the rest. There was that kind of camaraderie between the various people. So I did Jack's case and we got him compensation and all the rest.

Harry Bradshaw, now let's see, the loyalists twice had strikes. The first one – we held out for a while then towards the end of the day the company decided that it was too dangerous and that we would have to come off the road. The second one was called by Paisley and his cronies. I think that was in 1977 and we intended to maintain the service and that was it. And we had a fellow called Harry Bradshaw who was shot dead and Jim Rutherford who was also shot but he didn't die; he survived. Harry Bradshaw – I arranged for the funeral and all that as well. I opened, at that time, a fund for them too – an old half-barrel tub, we would call it here, through the depot – donations from people – you know? We made a considerable amount of money which we were able to donate to the families. And in agreement with the Union, buses were off the road for two days and Werner Heubeck agreed there would be no loss of pay. After the funeral, Harry Bradshaw was buried in Carnmoney and I'd arranged a meeting for that afternoon with the intention of getting the buses back on the road the next morning, and the worst was this feeling that it would be rough and there was no way we would get them out on the road again. I arranged the meeting upstairs, in this building here [Transport House] and about 1500 of them were thronged into the hall, but, yeah, at the meeting, I convinced them that we were not going to be put off the road – we had made too much of a sacrifice to let it happen – convinced them! And we were back out on the road again. That was the straw that broke the camel's back, the loyalist strike finished!

**RG**    *It finished right after that?*

**EO'C**    Yeah, we were back, and you know, you're sitting at home and you're wondering whether to go work or not and you look out and see a red bus trundling past the door. You would say to yourself, "Well it mustn't be too bad, there's the red buses, I'll head out." And they did. OK, I came under sustained pressure at the time, which I'm sure Heubeck did and there were all sorts of threats but we broke it! We kept them out and you couldn't pay enough of a tribute to the guys who were there at that particular time, to the men who were there because, let's be honest about it, fellows are there doing their job and they get to have a low morale and that, but I really feel a bit aggrieved that they were going to take the credit for the people who were really there and really went through it all. You know there's a plaque in Oxford Street bus station for those who died and there used to be a saying, "They buried the dead and bandaged the wounded, then went back to work," and that's basically it.

Well this was it and I must say that I had great shop stewards at that time, all of whom were courageous – and who I would have differences of opinion with at meetings, arguing that this should be done and that should be done but the one thing that they were never lacking in was courage.

If we go back to the decision taken that all drivers drove all routes, no matter if he was a Catholic or a Protestant, then there was a safety idea behind it all as well. The bus drivers couldn't be targeted so easily because the paramilitaries couldn't be sure if it was a Catholic or a Protestant that was driving up the Crumlin Road or on the Falls Road. It was a significant achievement to keep the buses on the road at that time.

**EO'C**   There was a fellow called Billy Irvine and Billy was in the UDA. [Note: Billy Irvine was killed in the Oxford Street bomb on Bloody Friday] Billy was buried from Brown's Funeral Parlour on the Newtownards Road and the story was that the UDA would provide the 'Guard of Honour'. We said, "No. The busmen will provide the 'Guard of Honour' and if the busmen don't provide it, there will be no 'Guard of Honour'; the busmen won't be there." So the message got through and the busmen did it and the UDA didn't. Despite the fact that Billy was a member of the UDA and so forth, what people did outside their job was their own business, so long as you didn't bring it into the job and that was basically all that we were concerned with.

**RG**   *Yes, you would hire out buses to the GAA Clubs, the Orange Order and anyone . . .*

**EO'C**   We provided buses for everybody. Whilst we came under attack from both sides (buses were the first on the front line to be attacked), we provided buses for the Orangemen on the Twelfth of July, Black Saturday and other demonstrations and we also provided the buses for the republican movement for the burying of the Hunger Strikers, for their anniversaries at Bodenstown – for all of those things. We served the public without fear or favour of where they came from. One thing that we did insist on, and we made very clear, was that you would use the driver that we sent you and not who you might want. Do you know what I mean? In other words, if it happened to be a Catholic driver's turn to run the Orange Lodge that day, well, too bad, it was his turn. Neither would we tolerate you interfering in any shape or form or being abusive in any way to that driver, otherwise you wouldn't get the buses the next day. In that way we maintained the thing properly.

During the period of the Troubles, too, there was an effort made at one time by the Northern Ireland Office, and I think they had a degree of support, it was after Heubeck left, to privatise the buses and they attempted to do this through the back door by setting up the Mergers and Monopolies Commission to look into the question of how it could be done and what could be done and to, in other words, provide justification for that course of action. I led the delegation against it to London at the time and we presented the case to the committee which was set up to get it and we advanced a number of arguments. But I think that one of our best arguments was the question that whilst we remained a public undertaking it would be more difficult for any paramilitary organisation to put us off the road. And that private companies were only interested in profits and would be more open to intimidation. It was easier to go to a private man's house and intimidate him and to seek protection money and all the other things, which you couldn't have done with us. If they were put off the road for a while, well they just wouldn't go back to it. They wouldn't be able to sustain the losses. We also pointed out that if there was privatisation, obviously the paramilitaries would then move in, because at that time the black taxis were becoming more frequent, more numerous. The end result would be that different organisations would obviously acquire a big percentage of the work in their own areas, which they found to be lucrative. That in turn would fund the paramilitary undertakings. It would be a means of laundering money and it would be to the detriment of the youngsters who went to school because in travelling to school they had to cross all areas of the town whereas the black taxis, because they were run by paramilitaries, stayed in their own areas.

**RG**   *It must have been hard even keeping the buses going for the schools.*

**EO'C**   It was. It was very, very tough and we had a policy, too. There were times we had a few wildcat strikes, for instance if a driver got badly beaten up or something like that then emotion took over and there might be an immediate stoppage. Now one of the things that I insisted on, which was fully supported by the committee, was if we brought the youngsters to school in the morning, come hell or high water we would pick them up again in the afternoon. We wouldn't leave them stranded. When you equate that to what's happening today with some of the schools, particularly up at Ardoyne and so forth, it just makes you think.

**RG**   *Was there much difference then in the school runs? Nowadays I know some of the drivers have problems with bad behaviour.*

**EO'C**   Oh, we did have problems and I remember a particular run, Dundonald it was, we were having considerable difficulties and drivers were getting abused. I gave instructions and went to the school and said that we would withdraw the buses till they behaved themselves. We were then told that the UDA would put people on the bus and make sure that they were under control. We said no, under no circumstances. If anybody was on the buses it would be the schoolteachers and that would be it. So after a while of having to walk, various approaches were made and schoolteachers did find the boys who were creating the disturbances, and they were in a minority. They were left to walk or get to school whatever way they wanted. And that was the way we did it. You have to deal with circumstances like that and while the management wouldn't publicly agree with you, they were maybe, privately, behind you and would say, "Well what do you expect?"

As I said earlier on about the attempt at privatisation, I thought that we should have a back up system in case things went against us. Now I was sure they wouldn't because as I was coming out of the meeting I bumped into the chairman of the panel who said to me, and I was a lot younger at the time because he said, "Son, I don't know who briefed you but you pressed all the right buttons today. I don't think you have anything to worry about" and he just kept onwalking.

**RG**   *A lot of the bus drivers, I've heard, have had real back problems.*

**EO'C**   The back problems are bad but I felt that the damage that was done to people's lungs and their innards was very serious and when you added that to the stress . . . don't forget that a bus driver who left the depot in the morning to go up the road, and it's the first run at four o'clock in the morning and there's maybe been rioting the night before and he had with him his ticket register, his cash dispenser and his machine, it's just the bus and himself, nobody else. Whereas with the army or the police, when they went up, they had an armoured car and rifles and all the protection and these fellows set off with nothing, and that took tremendous courage. *You* try to imagine, setting off the day after one of your colleagues had been attacked and robbed and the bus was damaged or maybe they even tried to murder him and that was happening all round.

**RG**   *What happened to the conductors after the one-man buses were introduced?*

**EO'C**   They got their redundancy money and so forth. Some of them didn't want it but some of them went for it. Tommy Killops, Lord rest him, poor Tommy, he went to the training school and Tommy would say, "I'm never going to get this." I said, "It's alright Tommy, you've plenty of time," and he made it. He turned out to be a good wee driver.

**RG**   *Was he a conductor originally then?*

**EO'C**   He was a conductor. Then, in the final analysis, it got a wee bit much for him so we got him in, in charge of the parcel office; we did the best we could for all of them.

# Extracts from an interview with Liam Hughes, Shop Steward

## Introduction

Liam talked about the situation in Dungannon during the Troubles. He pointed out that in Dungannon there were more buses destroyed than in the other Ulsterbus depots (apart from Belfast and Derry). Seventeen buses were lost one night. Two bus staff were also shot dead; they were James Gibson (driver) and Stanley Arthur (cleaner). The first bus to be destroyed during the Troubles was a bus to Dungannon.

He also talked about the transition from the old buses with conductors, to the one-man-operated buses and the feelings of isolation that accompanied this change. He also talked about the fact that buses were a soft target for all and sundry. He recalls being hijacked by a young boy on a bus heading for Dungannon; the boy was so nervous that he could, quite easily, have let off a shot by accident. These were the kind of things drivers had to deal with in those days. He remembered going to Belfast one morning and finding a driver literally in tears. He was waiting on a bus to take him back to the depot after being hijacked for the sixth time that morning. Each time he had gone up the road he had been held up at gunpoint and a black taxi took him back down the road and every time he was sent back to do the run again. Losing a bus for the sixth time was the final straw.

He noted that the camaraderie of the job was the main balance to the stress although nowadays the tight time schedules have an effect on that.

LH    I have seven brothers and five of them have been shop stewards and I have a sister as well and she has been involved as well through the different jobs she did. My father was also a shop steward – he worked in the railways – and I have a cousin who was also a shop steward. Because of this, I was interested in the unions and I was interested in learning more. My confidence was brought on by being in the union, by being supported by the union and educated by the union, so I have a lot to be grateful for, very much so.

But I have to say, that the main man that would have been behind that would have been Eugene (O'Callaghan). Eugene was very conscious of educating his people; Eugene doesn't suffer fools easily, as I am sure you will have gathered. OK he couldn't decide who was elected in the depot but his influence spread out and, he had a team that supported him, and he supported them, so therefore it was a very good team; it was a very strong team. They had the confidence to make decisions, even if they were hard ones. He was instrumental in the position that busmen are in today in Northern Ireland – conditions-wise and employment-wise, very, very much so.

RG    *Things like pensions?*

LH    Yes, he fought for that and got it introduced and the men now have a very good pension – local government superannuation; there's not a better one you can get. All that sort of thing. As I said, I didn't always agree with him, but I respected him very much and he was a good officer and a good friend and he had the interests of his people at heart. And whether you liked him or not, if you were being honest and objective, you had to say that. He brought all of his men well up the grade and at all times he was very supportive of his people and, you know, if people had problems even outside the workplace, he would have organised help and welfare. He introduced a branch fund where everyone paid so much a week – you know, so that if people were having hard times they would have been looked after.

A true socialist, as I would put it – he definitely was that – sometimes he was abrupt with people – he didn't suffer fools easily – he didn't like people coming along with frivolous arguments – stupid things that were wasting time as he saw them – things that shouldn't get to that level – you did get your knuckles rapped if you came along with something that you should have dealt with yourself – because you really shouldn't have been there with an issue unless you had taken it through the process and couldn't get an answer at that level or whatever the case may have been. So you didn't come and get him to do your job for you. As long as you did your job you had his support, though, and he'd have left no stone unturned to deal with a situation such as that.

**RG** *He seemed to have a good healthy relationship with Heubeck as well.*

**LH** Well, Heubeck was the sort of man we all admired and the reason we admired Heubeck was when he gave you a yes, it was yes, when he said no, it was no, so that he would have said to you, "Well, you can take it to your union or whatever but that is my decision." Also on numerous occasions maybe a manager had agreed to something that he (Heubeck) wouldn't have agreed to, well, he would have brought that to Heubeck and he would have said, "I don't think you should have agreed to it but, if you did, I will honour it but it will not happen again." And that was Heubeck so therefore you had to admire a man like that. A lot of people have said that management since, well a different style, of course, but, you know they would say, "Oh no, that's not what we meant" but with Heubeck, before you left the room or before you left the meeting, you understood exactly what Heubeck was saying. It wasn't a matter of coming back and him saying, "Oh no, that's not what I meant", you were clear and that is why most people, although they didn't always agree with him, still admired him. That to me was very important, very, very important.

**RG** *Two pretty unique individuals there at that time.*

**LH** Oh yes, exactly, you couldn't have put it any more clearly – this only happens very rarely – that was exactly what you had. Heubeck again had the same sort of nature; he didn't suffer fools lightly either. He came from a regimental background – he was German – and he comes from that idea we have of Germans anyway, that they are a very regimental people and the way they do things very exactly. I had many a discussion and argument with him, being a senior shop steward, but I still got on well with him. I remember one day driving a bus out of Belfast and he got on the bus and – Heubeck would have done this regularly – "I will take her up the road for you," and he let me sit back and he drove the bus up the road.

**RG** *He enjoyed a wee drive now and again then.*

**LH** That was it, and as a matter of fact I have one of his famous hats that he wore. He gave me one, I still have it and it's the one he wore right through the Troubles, the one he wore every day. But that's what people admired about Heubeck, he was what he said he was and you have to admire that, though not necessarily like it. Personally, I did like him and I also respected him. But that doesn't say you had to agree with him all the time. He was very approachable, believe it or not. Heubeck would have walked into the depots and would have gone over and spoken to the drivers; he would come over to you, "Aah, Mr Hughes, what are you doing in this depot?" and all that type of thing. That's the reason he should be admired.

So as I say that's my experience of buses. I started in 1966, when I was eighteen, from a conductor to a bus driver to a driving instructor and I've ended up in Cookstown here as a Controller.

**RG** *Being a driving instructor must have been pretty interesting. Did you have to train any of the old conductors when the one-man buses came on?*

**LH** No I wasn't involved in that, that happened before I came on. It was an interesting job, I enjoyed it actually. I think the only part I didn't like was, I live in Dungannon, and it meant you were commuting every morning into Belfast and you were sitting in the traffic jams. Now I'm only ten minutes from work. But as a job, I enjoyed it and I would teach people to drive their motorcars in my spare time, as well. Sometimes I wonder if I should have stayed at it; it was a lot easier than what I'm doing now but this has its days, too.

Then there were the times when we'd have been taking the buses to the different demonstrations, you know, a nationalist or republican demonstration and the ones from the other side would have been watching for the bus coming. I remember a stone being thrown and I saw it coming and I was able to avoid it but the boy behind me, the stone came right through his windscreen and just missed the side of his face and embedded itself in the panel behind him. Now it was embedded: we couldn't pull it out; it had to be cut out. If that had hit him, oh he'd have been stone dead. The consequences of that action would have been horrendous. If you were driving one side, the other side, if they recognised that – and there might even have been individuals on the bus who were publicising who they were with flags or whatever – then obviously the buses would be attacked coming through certain areas.

You had to avoid certain areas but you always had the one d**khead, to put it bluntly, who would throw something out of the bus. That was the sort of thing drivers were having to put up with; it was one side today and the other side tomorrow. You know, somebody gets on a bus and it's, "Where are you going to?", not "Are you a Protestant?, Are you a Catholic?, Are you a Hindu?" You'd be going out one day taking Orangemen to a demonstration and the next day you'd be taking republicans to another demonstration; you were serving both sides of the community. You were going into all areas of the community because that was your job. Obviously if things got really bad in a particular area they would take the bus off but you just couldn't decide, "Oh I'm a Catholic, I'm not driving them Protestants" or "I'm a Protestant, I'm not driving them Catholics." If it was your duty you did it. OK, if it was overtime or something it might have been different.

I have had the experience where I have been known to the other side and you do get verbal abuse – you always get one or two like that. I have driven the other side manys the time and they've been more than nice to me but there's always the odd time when it happens. I have been called an Orange, black bastard in a Catholic area – you maybe did something to offend them, drove past the stop or something – and that's the laugh of it, because I am a Catholic. And vice versa, it has happened to me as a Catholic and it's happened to Protestants too – "Ya Fenian bastard ye." You hear these stories, you know the anecdotes – a comedy script writer just couldn't write them – and especially in Northern Ireland nothing is unbelievable you know. Things would have happened in reality and you can sit back and laugh at them now. OK, they were serious at the time but they were still incredible.

I have a nickname – I was always known in Dungannon as 'The Captain'. Where that came from is another wee anecdote for you. Heubeck came around all the depots when he took over and he was meeting all the people and we had a meeting one night and different questions arose. It was questions like, "If a situation arose on a bus, what do you do and who's responsible and all this . . . ". I had occasion anyway, as I was a shop steward, I put my hand up and Heubeck said, "Ah, Mr Hughes, I was wondering when you were going to ask a question." Because we had many a battle, I forget my exact question but anyway his response was, "Mr Hughes, you are like a captain on a ship. Once the bus goes out of the depot, you are the man who is responsible for that bus. You are in total control. You make the decisions."

Now the decision may have been a good one or a bad one but you were responsible and, ever since that day, I was nicknamed 'The Captain'. Yes that was Heubeck, "You are a captain." That's basically what the driver is though, when you think about it. As soon as he takes the bus out of the depot he is responsible for you and everybody who is on it, to take you from A to B as comfortably and safely as possible and if anything happens, he has to answer for it. It's a very responsible job which is done down. We do it down ourselves. We make little of the job. On the other hand, when you're sitting back home and your wife, daughter, husband or boyfriend gets on a bus, you like to think that they are going to get off again safely. If you get on a train or a plane, there is a responsibility and it's the same with the bus driver.

*The remains of a Bristol RE, thought to be No 2032, have been pushed to the side of the road in Shantallow, a Derry housing estate. No 2032 was hijacked and burned on 9 May 1987.* **Will Hughes**

# PERSONAL RECOLLECTIONS

In this section it is intended to give a flavour of what it was like to be working on the buses during this period. For every incident recounted below, there are many others that do not appear in this account. However, the reader should get a good idea of the dangers facing bus workers at this time as well as the ingenuity, dedication and bravery exhibited by many of them as they kept the services running as best they could. It is worth remembering, however, that these are personal reminisences and the events described are how the interviewees remember them many years on. They are not necessarily an accurate history of what happened.

Some of the pieces have been extracted from interviews collected as part of the *Routes* project. This project, sponsored by the Transport and General Workers' Union, was set up to record the history and experiences of the men and women employed in Northern Ireland's bus industry since 1970.

## *Author's experiences as a student conductor and (later) Ulsterbus junior manager*

One of my first memories of the impact of the Troubles was during the Falls curfew in July 1970. At that time, the army used liberal quantities of CS gas during the riots associated with the curfew. I was based in Smithfield depot, which was close to the Lower Falls. During one of the periods of rioting, the wind was blowing in our direction and both passengers and busmen were left coughing and weeping from the effects of gas being blown into the depot from the riot zone.

One of the problems that conductors had to deal with in Ulsterbus days, was that the pay-in office closed about 5.00pm and on a late shift, you were expected to take your takings home for safekeeping. On a busy shift this could amount of over £100, much of it in small (pre-decimal coinage) change. One night during the Troubles, around midnight, I was walking home up Shaw's Road, pockets bulging with cash, having got as far as Casement Park on the last red bus. Everything around me was pitch black, all the lights having been shot out by either the army or the Provos. It was as quiet as the grave. Suddenly, all hell broke loose; flashes and bangs and shouting everywhere. I had managed to stray into the middle of an ambush on a military patrol. I found myself in a shallow ditch by the side of the road with no idea of how I had got there. Clanking like a tank with all this cash in my pockets, I crawled along the ditch back down the road to comparative safety. With the weight of metal in my pockets, I couldn't have run even if I had tried! Once clear of the shoot-out, I made my way home by a longer, but safer route. After that, I left my night's takings in my box in the depot to take its chances there!

In 1970, after the Falls curfew when the Troubles started to get really bad on the Lower Falls Road, quite a few buses were hijacked and used to barricade the entrances to the narrow streets of terraced houses, which made up most of the area at that time. This was in an attempt to keep out the army and police. I remember seeing Fleetlines parked across some of the streets. They were jammed so tightly between the opposite walls; it looked as if they had been lowered into place by a crane! The only way you could get into the street was through the emergency door of the bus at one end and then out the passenger door at the other, opposite end! It took a lot of skill to get buses parked so tightly and I suspect people well used to driving them put them there.

*A fireman damps down the remains of a Belfast Corporation Daimler Fleetline double-decker.*

107

The other thing I remember was that the seat cushions from the buses fitted the windows of the houses quite snugly and provided excellent protection against missiles.

One afternoon, in the summer of 1972, I was in Great Victoria Street depot waiting for a bus home, when a coach drove into the yard with one half of its windscreen and several side windows smashed. When the bus stopped, I could see that it was fully laden. Several of the passengers were injured, and others were nearly hysterical. It also became clear that some of the injured passengers were Americans. This was the airport bus, and on its way down from Aldergrove airport, the vehicle had been attacked and an attempt made to hijack it. The driver, with great courage had kept going, but the mob had stoned the bus as it made its escape, and many of the passengers were injured. I have often wondered what sort of a report those visitors gave of Northern Ireland when they got home.

In the early hours of Monday 9 August 1972 the army and police moved into nationalist areas, in force, to round up and intern suspected IRA activists. In spite of the mayhem in the area we lived in (Andersonstown), my family managed to sleep through the whole thing! My father and I were both on a spreadover shift that week and the first we knew there was anything wrong was when we went out to get the early 105 bus into work. The bus wasn't at the Glen Road terminus, where we had expected to see it, but pulled across the top of Shaw's Road as a barricade. As well as that, in spite of the early hour, there were crowds of people roaming around. We were astonished. We then met a neighbour, another busman, who told us what had happened, so we decided to walk to Finaghy to catch the train into town. When we approached the hijacked bus, some men standing near it, when they saw us both in Ulsterbus uniforms, quickly let down the bus's tyres, thinking we might try and drive it away! Later that morning when I was conducting a workers' bus from Monkstown Estate to the Standard Telephone factory, all one could see were huge plumes of smoke rising over Belfast, one of the biggest being that

*Leyland PD2 No 612 and Leyland PD3 No 875, both with bodies built by the Ulster Transport Authority, await their next turns of duty at Smithfield depot. No 612 was withdrawn in 1970, following accident damage and No 875 was maliciously destroyed in the Greenisland area on 21 May 1972.*
**Photobus**

from Short Strand depot. I remember the passengers on the upper deck, mostly women, who had good view over the city, staring in silence and total disbelief at the sight.

I was conductor on a bus returning to Smithfield depot one evening (Wednesday 4 October 1972). It was well into a late shift and there were few passengers on the bus and even fewer people on the street. Because of the civil unrest, Belfast's streets were deserted after about 7.00pm. We were sitting at the traffic lights at the Art College, inward bound. There was no other traffic in the vicinity, other than a car parked up Donegall Street opposite the offices of the *Irish News*. Suddenly the parked car exploded. There was a flash, followed a split second later by a huge boom. When the shock wave hit, the bus rolled from side to side on its springs and the whole fabric of the vehicle seemed to ripple as if the bus was made of rubber. Our bus was a PD3, and at the time of the explosion I was, in time-honoured fashion, leaning over the bulkhead chatting to the driver. As the bus rolled and shook with the force of the blast, I remember clearly that the bottoms of my trouser legs flapped from side to side as if caught in a strong gust of wind. Fortunately, neither the bus nor its occupants suffered any harm and we were able to make our way back to Smithfield and several cups of very strong tea. However, Donegall Street was wrecked.

One night, after finishing a late shift, a group of Smithfield men, myself amongst them, caught the accommodation bus home. The company laid on this bus to get men home who had finished work after the last service buses had left. This was in the years when busmen owning cars was still fairly uncommon. Each Belfast depot took it in turn, week about, to provide the accommodation bus, which toured the three Belfast depots about midnight to collect the men and then leave them home. To be fair to everybody, a different route was taken each night so that the same men weren't always the last to get home.

That particular week it was the turn of Smithfield depot and the Smithfield night shunter, a dour character, was driving the accommodation bus. He selected a brand new Leopard for the run and before he left Smithfield, he turned on every light that the bus had, inside and out. This was odd, as generally the accommodation bus ran with all the interior lights out, so that potential passengers didn't try and wave it down. He headed up the Shankill Road to leave off the first men at Glencairn. I was next, on the Glen Road, so he headed across the West Circular Road and into Ballymurphy.

If I was worried about this, and I was, my Protestant colleagues were *very* worried. At that time, Ballymurphy and Turf Lodge were real republican hotspots and the army had built a huge fort dominating the area. In addition, every streetlight had been smashed so the place was deserted and in pitch darkness. Seemingly completely unconcerned, our shunter roared the Leopard flat out and lit up like the Queen Mary, right through the middle of this area. Most of the busmen were lying on the floor in terror; believe me, one was actually calling for his mother!

Sure enough, the four headlights and twin fog lights of the bus illuminated a military foot patrol. As they dived for cover, they opened up on the bus with rubber bullets. From the relative safety of the floor, all I could hear over the roar of the engine was the thud of the rubber bullets against the sides of the bus and our driver swearing fluently at the soldiers as he ploughed on regardless. We were lucky the bullets were only rubber ones! Thankfully, we got clear without any injury or serious damage to the bus. However, it seems when he got back to the depot, the shunter phoned the military base in Ballymurphy and lodged an official complaint! I doubt if much action was taken on it.

One evening I was on a late shift. About 9.30pm we were operating into the loyalist Monkstown Estate when our bus, a Leyland PD3, broke down just at the entrance to the estate. A local man was kind enough to let me use his phone to ring the depot to send out a breakdown truck, though I had some fun trying to get across to the inspector on duty who I was without saying my name in full. I reckoned that the name Michael Collins might not have gone down too well in Monkstown, even in those pre-Liam Neeson days!

Anyhow, safely back in the bus my driver and I settled down to wait for the breakdown crew. After a few minutes a police car pulled up beside us. The police came over to the bus and enquired if we were ok. Satisfied, they then drove off. Another ten minutes passed and an army jeep pulled in and repeated the process. They had gone about a quarter of an hour when an ice-cream van stopped beside us. Two men got out and approached the bus. They also enquired as to whether we were all right and went on their way when we assured them we were. They were the local UDA patrol! I was glad to see that breakdown truck arrive!

One 12 July, I was a conductor on a PD3 leaving Smithfield bound for Rathcoole with a rowdy but cheerful load of people who were heading home after watching the big Orange parade in Belfast. It was a hot day and the driver had left the sliding entrance door open to try and encourage a cool breeze through the bus. When we got to the junction of Winetavern Street and North Street, where we normally would have turned right down on to York Street, the police directed us to turn left, up towards Peter's Hill. When we got to Unity Flats, expecting to be able turn right along Upper Library Street, the police were there too and directed us to turn left along Millfield towards Divis Street and the Falls. We had no intention of going near Divis Street with that particular load and we planned simply to turn left again at West Street, go back into the depot and wait until the police had got their act together. However, as we turned into Millfield, panic suddenly spread throughout the bus and people started jumping off even though we were still moving. I was on the platform and was nearly carried off the bus in the mad rush by the upstairs passengers to get clear. It seems that someone had said that the bus was going up the Falls Road and the loyalist crowd were having none of that!

In the late summer of 1973, I had been away in England for a couple of months. I flew home early September on a flight that got into Belfast late in the evening. It was a horrible, wet night and when I boarded the airport bus at Aldergrove, there was only one other passenger on board. The bus was an AEC Reliance with semi-luxury body and so was fitted with high-backed coach seats. As we made our way towards the city, I was puzzled by the fact that the driver did not switch on the interior lights in spite of the fact that it was quite dark outside. In those days, the airport bus made its way into Belfast via Dundrod, the Horseshoe Bend and then down the Crumlin Road into the city. To my consternation, when we reached the top of the Crumlin Road, I could see that all the streets were barricaded and guarded by masked men armed with pickaxe handles and similar weapons. They all stood staring at the bus as it raced by, but made no move to interfere with it. Puzzled, if thankful at this inaction, I leaned over and looked down the aisle and through the windscreen. It was then I saw that we had an escort in front, a Land Rover with armed soldiers pointing their weapons at these vigilantes. A quick glance through the back window showed another Land Rover taking up the rear. In effect, the airport bus had been provided with an armed military escort!

By 1973, Ulsterbus and Citybus were losing a lot of money because of the operation of so-called 'people's' taxis in Belfast. These had originated on the Falls Road during periods when the normal bus services had been withdrawn by the Corporation due to civil unrest. They were later established on the loyalist Shankill and Shore Roads. On both sides of the sectarian divide they were believed to be under paramilitary control, or at least subject to their influence.

Werner Heubeck wanted the authorities to stop their activities and to help him make a case for this, he decided to try and quantify the amount of traffic being lost by his companies to the taxis. In order to gather the necessary data, he set up three survey teams, one located at Peter's Hill at the bottom of the Shankill Road, one in Falls depot at the junction of the Falls and Glen Roads and one at York Road railway station on the Shore Road. These were to carry out a survey of taxi traffic for a week.

As the most junior manager in the company (I started in this role in October 1972), I was allocated to the first shift at Peter's Hill, along with a senior Citybus inspector. We sat in the inspector's Morris Marina and noted the details on specially produced data sheets. In order to try and estimate the numbers of taxis operating, we recorded the registration number of each black taxi as it passed; we also noted its direction of travel, the approximate number of passengers and the time. For purposes of comparison, we also noted the same details for any of our buses that passed.

About 11.00am I went for coffee but when I returned about 20 minutes later, the inspector and his car had vanished. I headed back to Head Office and was told that shortly after I had left, the inspector had been approached by a number of men and told that if he didn't clear off, he would be shot. Interestingly, the same threat was made at about the same time to the men at the other two survey points.

However, Mr Heubeck was not to be thwarted and we resorted to subterfuge to collect the necessary information. For the rest of the week I travelled up and down the Falls Road as a front seat passenger in a company car or masqueraded as a driving instructor on a driving school bus, collecting the information as we travelled. The other teams did likewise.

When we later came to analyse the information, one piece of data caused some raised eyebrows. A

*A group of UDA men, armed with pickaxe handles, stand guard as Belfast Corporation Potter-bodied AEC Swift No 765 is used to block Agnes Street at its junction with the Shankill Road in 1971 or 1972. The bus survived this incident to pass into the Citybus fleet in April 1973. It was subsequently destroyed, on 19 September 1977.*

particular taxi was recorded as operating both on the loyalist Shankill and Shore Roads as well as the nationalist Falls. Some joker observed that it was probably being operated by the Four Square taxi company This was a reference to the Four Square laundry, a covert military operation that had recently been rumbled by the Provisionals.

Anyway, we gathered enough information to make a reasonable approximation of the losses in traffic and revenue we were suffering and this was later used by Mr Heubeck in his, as it turned out, fruitless attempts to have the authorities close down these illegal taxi operations.

During the Ulster Workers' Council strike of 1974, although buses were operating only in nationalist areas, most Head Office staff still made it into work. Some experienced extreme difficulty in getting to Milewater Road and I remember one man, the company cashier I think, having his car, which he had parked outside the offices, stolen.

However, I well recollect the reaction in Milewater Road on 28 May when it was announced that the power-sharing assembly had fallen under the pressures of the strike. There was much jubilation and celebration at this news on the lower decks, but great gloom amongst the ranks of top management. I recall one senior manager, who was neither a Catholic nor a nationalist, saying that in his opinion, the loyalist leaders had made a terrible blunder in bringing down the Assembly and that any future arrangement, whenever it was established, would be even less to their advantage than the Assembly had been. He was to be proved completely right.

*Daimler CVG6 No 2366 and Fleetline No 2823 at Glen Road terminus. No 2823 was destroyed but the author managed to save (older) No 2366. The only comment made at HQ was that it was a pity that he hadn't saved the newer Fleetline!*

One afternoon in August 1974 I was sitting at home, when my young brother came rushing in to tell me that there was a bus on fire at the nearby Glen Road turning circle. I grabbed my Kodak Instamatic and headed up to take some photos. When I got there, I saw two buses. One, Fleetline No 2823, was blazing from stem to stern. However, the other, a CVG6, No 2366, although damaged, with almost every window smashed, was otherwise intact. However, it looked as if she wouldn't last too long. No 2823 was parked up tight against her back and the flames were licking through the broken back window and up the staircase of the CVG. In addition, she had been doused with diesel. An army patrol was on the scene, but the soldiers couldn't move her. A couple had climbed into the cab to try, but the pre-select layout, with the gear selector under the steering wheel, had them foxed.

At the time, I was a junior manager with Ulsterbus, and had completed my training in the company's driving school and I knew how to drive a CVG. As a local, I also knew that this was not an 'authorised' IRA hijacking, but the work of hooligans. Therefore it would be safe for me to move the bus. I called the officer over, showed him my Ulsterbus pass and told him if he could make sure the bus was safe, I could move her. His soldiers quickly checked the bus; I climbed up into the cab and started her up. I had to knock out what was left of the windscreen with my camera so that I could see where I was going. With the army jeep right behind, I then drove the bus back to Falls depot and a rapturous welcome from the staff there.

On the way down the Glen Road to the depot, I saw a man standing at a bus stop carrying a car wheel. His car was parked on the other side of the road, up on a jack. He waved me down and I stopped. He jumped on the back platform and to this day I can see his face reflected in the driver's passenger mirror, as he stood holding his wheel, astonished, on the smouldering platform of the bus. At the depot, he jumped off, waved his thanks, and headed off towards the garage across the road to get his tyre sorted out. He is probably still dining out on that story!

A few weeks later, I had the pleasure of seeing No 2366 back in service, with a nice new back end fitted. As regards reaction at HQ in Milewater Road, the only comment that was made was that it was a pity that I hadn't managed to save the Fleetline!

## Jim Collins, retired Ulsterbus inspector (and author's father!)

I very nearly didn't last long after the Troubles began. In those days, I didn't own a car and usually, after a late shift, I would catch the last red (Corporation) bus as far as Casement Park terminus and walk the last mile or so to my home at the top of Shaw's Road. I would still be wearing my uniform, including my inspector's cap. One night, after the serious fighting had begun in Andersonstown, I was walking home when I heard footsteps coming up on me very quickly from behind. I turned to see who it was and saw two young men very close. At that moment one of them said, "Christ, it's only a bloody bus inspector!" And they sheered away. I'm sure they thought I was a policeman and were going to shoot me. It was a very close shave. After that, when I came off duty, I left my cap hanging in the inspectors' office!

One of the first casualties of the Troubles was the Alverno Hotel at the top of the Whiterock Road. Early in the morning following the torching of the Alverno, an Ulsterbus was heading down the Falls Road into town. As it was passing the bottom of the Whiterock, the crew saw a dishevelled, but otherwise well-dressed man with a suitcase, clearly in some distress, frantically waving them down. Although not supposed to pick up passengers inside the city boundary, they realised that something was wrong and let the man on. It turned out he was English and very, very angry. He said, "Wait until I get home and get my hands on that bloody travel agent. I said that I wanted to go to somewhere in Ireland for a few days peace and quiet and the idiot booked me into the Alverno Hotel!"

I was standing talking to a woman on the platform of Smithfield depot, when somewhere away in the city centre there was a huge explosion. Seconds later, the woman gave a cry and fell over. A piece of metal, as it turned out later, from the car bomb which had just exploded about a quarter of a mile away, had sailed over the roof tops and hit her in the ankle, breaking it. A few minutes later, after we had the woman made comfortable in the office until the ambulance came, I recovered the chunk of metal. It was a piece of the car's engine block and was still hot to the touch.

*(Sometimes hijacked buses were not destroyed but pressed into other uses. To get the gist of this story you need to know that in Ulsterbus there was a custom whereby drivers in buses passing each other raised their right arms in salute. This fraternal tradition, which wasn't a feature with Corporation or Citybus crews, went back to the UTA and NIRTB and, probably beyond, to coaching days.)*

We had been notified that a PD3 had been hijacked out in Rathcoole, (a huge, predominantly loyalist housing estate on the northern outskirts of Belfast.) The crew were ok and had returned safely to the depot and the police had been notified. A couple of hours later, another crew reported that the hijacked bus had passed them out the road near Carrickfergus. It was loaded with masked and uniformed UDA men, and was being driven by one such. However, as the bus drove past, the masked driver, in his paramilitary uniform, raised his arm in the busman's salute!

One evening, one of our double-deckers pulled up outside the depot. I noticed, with surprise, that it had a standing load downstairs, but the upper deck was completely empty. As soon as the bus came to a halt, the passengers and crew baled out as fast as they could. The driver ran over to the office, extremely agitated, to tell me that the bus had a bomb on board, upstairs!

*(To get the picture of what happened in this incident you have to know that Falls depot's entrance is right at a V-shaped junction where the Falls and Glen Roads meet. There is a small roundabout at this point and to get into the depot you have to drive around this roundabout, across the entrance to the Glen Road and through the depot gates. There was a security check at the gate and any vehicle entering the depot had to stop, effectively blocking the exit from the Glen Road. The depot was in a republican area where the army was not welcome.)*

In the early years of the Troubles, and the army were using the Corporation bus depots as billets and one of these was the Falls depot. One of our drivers was a hotheaded young fellow from Andersonstown, and a bit of a boy-racer with his bus. One evening he was driving his PD2 double-decker down the Glen Road and was, as usual, flying, when two military jeeps pulled across the road in front of him and stopped at the security check at the depot gates. They stopped, but he didn't – said later he couldn't. He hit one of the jeeps full tilt with his bus and knocked it, and its occupants, halfway down the Falls Road. There must have been injuries in that jeep. Anyway, next morning a squad of soldiers came to the depot looking for him. I am sure they believed he had rammed the jeep deliberately and were planning to give him a hiding. However, he hadn't turned into work. I heard later that right after the incident, he packed his bags, headed over the border and never came back.

One afternoon just as a bus was leaving the depot, the army arrived to warn of a car bomb planted in the street outside. Instead of just driving on clear, the driver stopped his bus, jumped out and ran away, leaving his conductor and passengers to do the same. As a result, when the car bomb later exploded, the abandoned bus was also wrecked. The driver was forever after known by the nickname 'Motor Mouse'!

While I was working in my office in Smithfield, a relatively new driver, a quiet, big, country fellow, walked into the office. Before I had a chance to ask him what he wanted, he said, "Jim, that's it. I'm away. It was nice to know you, but those b*****ds won't make an eejit of me." He walked out of the office and I never saw him again. A couple of minutes later his conductor struggled in, lugging his box, to tell me that his bus was abandoned, full of passengers, at a military road block a few hundred yards from the depot, up on Carrick Hill. It seems that when the soldiers set up their roadblock, they did it in such a way as to require vehicles passing through it to take a tight U-shaped path. When the bus arrived, the driver told the soldiers that there wasn't enough room to get the bus through. The soldiers wouldn't move their jeeps and the driver couldn't move his bus. A shouting match developed, at the end of which the driver got out of his cab, told the soldiers to move the f***ing bus themselves, stormed off and left them all to it.

Early on in the Troubles, when hijacking wasn't yet common, a Smithfield conductor, who was also a famous character in the depot, had had his bus hijacked two days in a row. On the third morning, he was coming into work on a Great Victoria Street bus when it too was hijacked. As he walked down the Falls Road with the crew of the hijacked bus, he mentioned his own recent experiences. The Great Victoria Street driver stopped, looked at him and said, "So you're that bloody Smithfield Jonah? We've heard about you. If I'd known who you were you wouldn't have got on my bus!"

Early one morning another Smithfield inspector took a phone call from this same conductor who lived in Andersonstown. "I can't get into work, Jim. There's a full scale gun battle going on up here and I'm on the floor of the phone box making this call!" "Catch yerself on, Robbie," replied the inspector. "What do you take me for? Get into your work!" "Honestly Jim, listen," replied the conductor. At that he opened the phone box door and held the handset outside. Right enough the inspector could here the rattle of gunfire in close proximity to the phone box.

A Smithfield crew in a PD3 was stopped by a crowd of UDA men who informed them that they were going to hijack the bus. The boot was full of parcels and the conductor had started out in the firm as a parcels boy. As cool as you like he informed the UDA 'warriors' that there was no way they were taking his bus until he had got all the parcels off it. And they didn't!

A conductor walked into the inspectors' office in Smithfield carrying a small box which he had found left on his bus. He thought it was lost property. When I went to examine it, I saw it was a bomb. We got the area cleared, but the bomb went off and wrecked the office.

# Frank McHenry, BCT/Citybus engineer, Short Strand depot

**MC**  *When did you start working for the Corporation?*

**FMcH**  I started in 1948 in Falls depot and transferred to the night shift in Ardoyne around 1950–51. At first it was only holiday relief, from June through to September. Gradually, as men retired, I went permanent on the night shift. I started in Ardoyne for two years and then after a retirement I moved to Short Strand. At that time, Ardoyne looked after Ardoyne's and Falls buses but Short Strand looked after the Haymarket trolleybuses and Mountpottinger as well. Gradually staff were reduced to two on the night shift. Eventually the other fellow left and I was left as the only engineer on nights along with a spark and a body-builder. The work involved ferrying buses between depots and testing them in the middle of the night.

**MC**  *What was it like working in the engineering side of the buses during the Troubles?*

**FMcH**  The army were in the Short Strand and took over part of the shed and built these huts, one at the back of the shed and one inside the shed, for soldiers to sleep in and they were on guard at the gate. The officers took over the upstairs in the ticket office and that was their HQ. The soldiers were in the huts they built, one inside the shed and one out the back, and then they built a third. That got on our nerves. The guys who were building these huts were getting danger money and we were working amongst them all the time and we weren't getting any danger money.

I was in charge the night the bomb went off in Anderson Street. I was sitting in the front office in Short Strand, at a desk. The office was glass fronted. Next thing I knew I was lying in the corner, with glass all around me. It was terrible; Anderson Street was next to the depot. There was a house and they were carrying a bomb out of it – three men and a girl – and the bomb went off. The sights I saw that night – this is gruesome – a head and shoulders blown right across the shed had hit a parked bus and slid down. Bits of bodies everywhere and a lot of buses were wrecked, the glass blown out of them. The army and police were there lifting bits of bodies, it was terrible. My wife had gone to Ballycastle for the weekend and on the Sunday morning the priest said a prayer for the people killed at the Short Strand.

She panicked and ran out of the church and down the main street and some man stopped her. He knocked up a chemist and got her a phone. I was home in bed when she rang.

The IRA used to attack the depot every so often and we couldn't get near it. We had to bring the buses down the Sydenham by-pass, to where the airport is now and you had to do your work by the light of a torch. One time the IRA attacked and the foreman, Archie Hayes, and me had to get down into the maintenance pit to make out the slate [list of buses available for service] because the bullets were whizzing about the shed.

Another time, one of the elite army units, the Coldstream Guards, I think, were in the Strand. They were all big, tall men, over six feet, but were the dirtiest soldiers you ever seen in your life. I said to one of them, "I thought the Guards were, you know . . ." He said, "Aye, that's all right when we're not on active duty. If we were back in barracks everything would be spit and polish." But they were running about in denims, army fatigues and their rifles were lying everywhere. I was actually fixing rifles for them. A fellow would come to me saying that his rifle was sticking and I would get it in the vice and try and free it up to him. The IRA attacked the place one night when the Guards were there. They were running out and one guy went running out with a sten gun and he ran through the wee gate. Whatever way he tripped, the gun went off and went off all over the place. When they came in after being out all night, about four or five in the morning, they came staggering back in again. I heard one of them saying to the other, "Did you fire any shots?" "Fire any shots?" replied the other guy; "I haven't fired this gun since I came here; if I had tried to fire this gun it would have exploded in my hand!" This is the Guards!

Another incident – they had built this big hut at the back of the shed and there was an upstairs and a downstairs in it. The upstairs was bunks and downstairs was a kind recreation area for the soldiers, table tennis and all that. What they used to do was bring in a projector for showing films; they used to show some of the best films. This projector came on wheels; it was a big thing and was sitting on the floor after the film was over. They had left it outside and this was about 6.30 in the morning. I was finished my work and was working at my car and this thing was sitting just in front of my car and this jeep came flying in. These four soldiers gets out and lifted this thing into the jeep and away they went. I didn't think anything of that. I went into that work that night and the RUC Special Branch and all were there and I said, "What's the matter, what's going on?" "Do you know anything about a projector, a film projector?" "Aye, it was sitting there this morning." "Well it's been stolen." "Well, if it's been stolen," I said, "It was the army that stole it." "What do you mean, it was the army?" "It was the soldiers who came in and put it in their jeep and drove away with it." They were questioning all the cleaners and what-like, more or less accusing us. They'd have needed a trailer to take it away! Do you know where they found it? In the UDA's headquarters about a month later. They sold it to the UDA. It was desperate.

MC          *Just like Sergeant Bilko!*

FMcH     Aye. They used to get all these great films; they got all the latest films, if you had time to watch them. A couple of our cleaners used to skive off and slip into the hut and watch the films, maybe for an hour and a half or two hours, so you had to watch them and go around the buses and make sure they had cleaned them right. It was a rotten oul' job though. You got people who had been sick in the buses and it had to be cleaned up.

The petrol the army used was all in two-gallon tins and one part of the yard was chained off and all these two-gallon tins of petrol were sitting there. The soldiers used to come in, "Want to buy some petrol?" I wouldn't put that stuff in my car! Little did they know that everyone in the place was knocking it off. If you went down into the pits, there were empty cans in there. But it was oul' two-stroke stuff and if you put it in your car, it pinked like hell.

MC          *Yea, you could smell it off their jeeps; there was a funny smell off it.*

FMcH     I got a couple of tins of it and I thought about it and I went to confession and said to the priest about it – stealing it. "What would you call that?" he said, "Sabotage?"

There were some good laughs, though it could be rough enough at times. There were some queer episodes with the soldiers themselves. One fellow, one of the shunters, lived away down the Shore Road and this soldier came into us in the office about half six on a Sunday morning and he said, "How would I get to Larne? I'm supposed to be on leave this weekend and I want to get to the boat at Larne and get across to England." This big shunter said, "I'll run you to Larne to get the boat." He knocked off about 7 o'clock. So he took yer man away. Next thing, there was a hue and cry. Yer man had gone AWOL and the shunter had helped him get away, to clear off to England!

They had a cook in the place. They had a kitchen set up and you could have got what you wanted off this cook. There were some of our cleaners who never took a dinner at home, but would get their food from the cook.

They had a wee Pakistani and he opened a shop in the ticket office, supposed to be for the soldiers, and he had drink there. They were only allowed two cans of beer a night, the soldiers, and they would come to you to get them a few more cans of beer and give you the money. You would go and get them more cans of beer and they would be half drunk every night. One driver used to cycle home at night. He used to live down somewhere before you come to Bangor. He got half tore buying these cans of beer and one night he got on his bike and drove it into the pits! Then the Pakistani got in a slot machine and they brought one into Ardoyne too. Two soldiers robbed the one in Ardoyne and they tried to blame it on the cleaners, but they found out that it was these two soldiers had broken into it and stole all the money out of it.

MC   *Did you ever have to go out when buses were hijacked?*

FMcH   Oh yes! I had to go out. I might have been sitting at home on a Saturday night, maybe about half eight, watching TV and the phone would ring, "Frank, there's a hijacked bus in such and such a place. See what you can do." So I'd get into the car and drive away to wherever it was and nine times out of ten they'd have stopped the bus but hadn't really done any damage to it and I was able to get it away from them. But sometimes they would have set it on fire and there was nothing I could do about it. But what I had to do, a whole lot of times, when they set it on fire and the oul' tyres had burnt, you had to get the wheels off and put new wheels on to get the chassis away. The nuts, with the heat, had more or less welded themselves on, so I had to chisel them off. I've seen me sitting down there at Beechmount at about 7.30 in the morning and I'm chiselling away, cutting these nuts off to get the wheels off. Finally, you get them off and get the new wheels on and get the oul' thing towed away. If they had set it on fire, it would only be scrap then. The gypsies used to take them when they were scrap, when they were burnt. They would come and take them away.

MC   *Did you ever have any trouble with the IRA threatening you?*

FMcH   Funny enough, I never did.

A few episodes when things happened. Some nights, I would drive into the Short Strand and the army would stop me, "Oh, you can't go down there, they are attacking the depot." And I would say, "I'm working in the depot." "Well you are not working there tonight!" And I had to turn and go back, then go up to Falls depot and ring through to say where I was. Then about 4 or 5 in the morning, when everything was all clear, I could drive back down again.

MC   *Where you there the night of internment?*

FMcH   Yes, I was there the nights of all them things. The only one I missed was the night the crowd from Short Strand attacked the depot. I suppose the IRA were leading them, but I was away on holidays in Tramore. Archie Hayes was the foreman and, funny enough, two days later he came down to Tramore on his holidays and he told me all about it, about them coming in and they were going to set fire to the place. You see, the fuel tanks in the Short Strand, you drive in the gates and there was something like 10,000 gallons of diesel oil in big tanks suspended up high. The buses drove in and were fuelled there and they were going to set those buses on fire that were underneath these tanks. They came into the office and were going to shoot all round them. They wouldn't let the fire brigade up into the Short Strand. They did set a couple of buses on fire.

MC   *I remember us coming into town the morning of internment and seeing the black smoke coming up from over Short Strand direction and wondering what was happening.*

FMcH   That was maybe the morning that they all attacked the depot and were going to set the buses on fire under the fuel tanks. Somebody told them that there was 10,000 gallons of fuel there and if you set that on fire, the whole of Short Strand will go up. But they did burn a few of the buses.

116

**MC**     *That would make a fair pall of smoke when they went up.*

**FMcH**   Every week the IRA would have a go at the depot because the army were in it and there were more bullet holes in that shed. You could see daylight shining through the holes in the side and in the roof. And even the army themselves; I remember one night – they went out in squads and would walk around the streets – there was maybe six of them and a corporal. When they came in at the gate they had to check all their guns and the bullets, but this particular night it was lashing rain and instead of checking them at the gate, they ran into the shed and whatever way this fellow emptied his rifle, it went off. Luckily it was pointing up and it went up through the roof. And if you heard the language that that corporal used at that fellow. I said to him afterwards, "If anybody had talked to me like that, I'd have shot him dead with that bloody gun. I wouldn't have let anyone talk to me like he talked to you." "Ah, this is the army, you have to take it," he said.

I used to tell them tales. There was a Scotch regiment in, the Black Watch. Every night, two soldiers used to parade around the depot, around among the buses, two wee Scotch men, and I said, "Are you going around the yard tonight?" "Aye, we are." "Wait till I tell you something," says I " See when you get to the back of that shed, and you are walking along and you find somebody walking alongside you, don't worry about it, he won't do you any harm." "What, are you talking about?" they said. I said, "Well you see this depot wasn't always a bus depot, and at the back there used to be a felt works," and I said, "They used to have a big guillotine for cutting the felt sheets." "One time one of the workers fell in and the thing cut his head off and he haunts the back of the yard. But he is only looking for company; he'll not say anything to you. He just walks along with you." "Well I'm bloody sure I'm not going around the yard!" one exclaimed, and they wouldn't!

One of the soldiers got shot going around the yard, and by one of his own men. One had a radio on his back and the other had the rifle. We used to leave a space between the buses so that you could drive a bus right round the shed. They were supposed to walk up this space, but these two, one night, instead of doing that, walked between the buses, you understand, three lines of buses parked there and they were walking in where the buses were instead of the open space. The guard at the gate, he can see up the yard which is all lit up, and the guy with the radio on his back with the aerial sticking up, he comes out from between the buses and this thing was sticking out. You would have thought it was somebody with a rifle, and he shot him, the sentry shot him! Only wounded him though.

**MC**     *Did you ever see Mr Heubeck?*

**FMcH**   Yes, he was always out and about. One night this bus came in and yer man says, "There's a bomb in this bus," and he said that there was a guy got off the bus and said there was bomb in it. He had driven in and was sitting at the pumps. "There is supposed to be a bomb in this bus," the driver said, so there's panic stations. They rang up for Heubeck. I said to yer man, "Drive it up there to a bit of wide open space, get out and leave it there." The army was there and wouldn't let any of us do any work, keeping us away from that bus. And then Heubeck came on the scene and he had on his jump suit. What he used to do every morning was drive his car a certain distance out into the country and jog for a while and then go back to the office. Heubeck wanted us to move the buses and the army wouldn't let us near them. Heubeck and the army had a bit of a row about it. The army said, "You're not moving any buses. We'll settle it." Eventually the army brought in a robot and they shot at the bus. It was a false alarm, but they made a big hole in the side of the bus. Heubeck was raging. "We could have had that bus away." He wanted us to get in and shunt the buses round the yard and the officer said, "No way, you aren't doing anything like that. Just stay where you are." Heubeck was a brave man. He actually carried a bomb out of a bus in the town, but he only made brief appearances at Short Strand and never interfered much. He tried to organise a holiday for the busmen to go to Germany and climb the mountains. I don't know whether he got anybody to go or not.

**MC**     *Did they ever actually bomb the depot itself?*

**FMcH**   They never bombed it; that was the only occasion, when the driver came in with the bus and it was a false alarm. But the IRA did attack the depot.

**MC**     *But that was mostly to get at the army?*

**FMcH**   Yes, It was the army they were shooting at. The army guys had night sights on their rifles, but they

never did any damage with them. A soldier said to me, "I don't know why the IRA are shooting at us. We're just numbers. It means nothing if they shoot me. They just put another soldier in my place. I'm only a number. It's the head men they want to shoot, at the officers, the generals. Shooting us isn't getting them anywhere."

They used to fight amongst themselves, too. It was terrible, the battles they had amongst themselves. One time – Richardson's was next to the Strand – it was lying empty and the army moved into it – and one night – the fuel pumps were near to Richardson's – I was over at the pumps and they had some guy, they must have picked him up somewhere, and they must have formed a double line and were making the poor guy run up between them and walloping him with truncheons. You could hear them f'ing and blinding and shouting at the guy, "Run, you so-and-so," and so on. I don't know who he was or whether he was one of their own or whether they had caught somebody.

Another night – there was gang over that end of town called the Tartan gang – and when the army came to the Short Strand at first, they used to let some of them out at night to go to the dances. It was a Protestant area so they would be safe enough, but a couple of the soldiers were beat up by this Tartan gang. A crowd of soldiers went out the next night to this place and emptied it; they got the Tartan gang. We heard them saying what they were going to do to them.

The army had a great racket running in Falls depot. See any cars that were stolen that were found by the police – they didn't burn them like they do now – they used to bring them into Falls depot and the army used to strip them and sell the parts to anybody who needed parts for their cars. It was a great racket. In every depot they had rackets running. After all, when you think about it, most of these guys were guys who had been on the dole in England and had joined the army. They were up to all the dodges. Anything they could sell, they would have sold it to you. They nearly would have sold you their guns if they could have got away with it. But they had to account for every bullet they had. Now, that soldier I told you about, when that gun went off, the corporal was saying, "You'll have to pay for that round!" They had to pay for any rounds that weren't authorised to use and they were checked every night when they came in to make sure that they had the same number of rounds as they went out with.

It was a hard life, too. When they came here first it was a pity of them, before ever they came into the depots. I was going to work and those soldiers were lying in sleeping bags on the footpath along the

Short Strand. That was the only place they had to sleep. Then somebody had the bright idea of moving them into the depots but it meant that every night they kept the gates closed. They had to open the gates to let you in. They searched your car and every night it was the same thing. They searched you coming in and sometimes they searched you going out in the morning. And my name being McHenry – I had a big box of tools in the boot with my name on it – they used to say, "What sort of name is that? Machinery?" "Not Machinery, McHenry," I'd say. Then they got to know you and it happened a couple of times to me – driving down the main street in Bangor – there was an army patrol. "Oh, Mr McHenry. Ok, go on ahead!" and everybody looking at me!

One morning after the buses went out, this pistol was found lying on the ground. It must have been under a bus. It was one of those guns for firing signal rockets, and you should have seen the army! They cleared the whole yard and put sand bags all round it; a wee gun lying there. And then they blew it up. It must have been thrown over the wall from Anderson Street and was lying underneath the bus and was only seen after the buses went out.

| MC | *Why did they leave the depots?* |

| FMcH | They left when they built the various big forts around Belfast – Silver City and the like. They were in the depots because they had no other place for them. They had a hard enough life, them soldiers. |

# Brian McCrory, Citybus inspector

| MC | *Brian, you joined the Belfast Corporation shortly before the lid blew off on things?* |

| BMcC | Yes, I joined in July 1969. I started as a driver. Most others were conductors who had converted over, but I came straight in as a driver. |

| MC | *How do you remember the Troubles starting?* |

| BMcC | At the time I had a conductor called Paddy Fennell, who later became an inspector, same as myself. I was out on the tear the night before. I got to bed about 2.00am and had to be up again for work at 5.00am. Anyway, I got to the depot and the only thing I had to do was to check that my bus had a full radiator. If you had a half-decent conductor, which of course I had, he would check it for you. The bus was already filled up so all I had to do was climb up into the cab, start it up and off we went. |

| MC | *What depot was this?* |

| BMcC | Falls. Of course, I didn't go into the office so I didn't see the notice up on the wall telling us that the buses were not to go any further than the Springfield Road. My conductor didn't see it either, which was surprising. So, to get into the town, we were supposed to go via the Grosvenor Road. Neither of us saw this notice; at that time in the morning it was none too bright, and of course, after the night before, neither was I!

When we passed over the Grosvenor Road junction, we started bouncing all over the road, over the paving stones that were lying all over the middle of the road, over railings that had been pulled off Dunville Park, and various other things like that; around cars that were still smouldering and so on. Of course, I'm looking at all this and Paddy comes up to the window behind me and shouts, "What the f***'s going on?" and I shouted back, "Paddy, you're as wise as I am! I haven't a clue!"

When we got to Castle Junction, I hadn't the heart to tell anyone that we had just come down the Falls. It was only then that we learned that we shouldn't have gone near the place at all! However, we made it in one piece and it was only then that we learned what had happened the night before; that the lid had come off in Bombay Street and various other places, and because of my inebriated condition I had heard nothing about it until the next day! |

| MC | *So that was the morning after the Bombay Street riots?* |

| BMcC | Yes. |

| | |
|---|---|
| MC | *I remember being in Divis Street that morning, too, and the complete mess it was in. I had just finished the first part of a spreadover shift and heard that there had been trouble the night before. I had made my way up Divis Street to see if my grandmother was okay. She lived near the Royal Hospital. I remember this guy stopping me and warning me to be careful because there were snipers about. There was this shopkeeper diverting traffic around the rubble of what had been his shop but was now spread half way across the road just opposite St Comgall's school. I wondered why there were no police there to direct the traffic!* |
| BMcC | Yes, part of St Comgall's wall and railings were pulled down too, as far as I can remember. So I took a bus down the road that morning. I hadn't a clue there was a thing wrong until we were in the middle of it. |
| MC | *So, that was the start of it?* |
| BMcC | Yes, that was the start of it as far as we were concerned, and all it did was get steadily worse from then onwards, on a daily and nightly basis. It was about three more weeks before we lost a bus. |
| MC | *So, the worst period would have been the early 1970s?* |
| BMcC | From the early to mid 1970s, you wouldn't have had a clue from one day to the next what was gong to happen. I went out one day to do a run up the Shankill and at first it was just a normal journey, a No 63 up to Glencairn. When I got to Glencairn all I could hear was the banging and booming all around. I could see clouds of smoke away in the distance, but I had no idea what was going on. When I was coming back down the road again, people weren't aware that there had been bombs going off, including one at Oxford Street. |
| MC | *So you were up the Shankill and you could still hear the bombs going off?* |
| BMcC | Oh yes. From the top of Glencairn I could hear them going off. You were high up there, you see, and you could hear them quite clearly and see the plumes of smoke going up. But it wasn't until I had got down into the town again that I realised some of the places that had been hit, including Oxford Street.

That day, I think I was the first to invent the two-way traffic flow past the Ritz. I couldn't get the bus around the City Hall because nothing was moving. The only way I could get from the Shankill was across Millfield, through King Street and up past the Ritz the wrong way against the traffic flow, and to a stop outside Cormac Hamill's hotel. At that point, a bomb went off at Great Victoria Street and the bus station, though I wasn't aware of where it was, even though I was sitting beside it with the Fleetline bus getting banged off the blinking telegraph poles. I was caught in the reverberation from the Great Victoria Street blast. I wasn't beside the bomb, but it knocked the bus around.

I had to turn the bus at Balmoral, though I should have gone on as far as Sicily Park. People, scared out of their wits, just hopped on the bus and took it wherever it was going to. All people wanted was to get on any bus; they didn't care where it was going, as long as it was going out of town. |
| MC | *Were you ever hijacked?* |
| BMcC | No, I managed to avoid that. The only incident that came close was one night in Turf Lodge about 1973. The whole place was covered in snow. I was a one-manner on a Fleetline. A youth got on the bus and indicated that he had a gun in his pocket and said that he wanted the bus. I said, "You can have the f***ing bus, if I can stop it!" I was actually sliding down the road with the tyre rubbing against the kerb to slow me down because I daren't put the brakes on! The passengers backed me up on that particular occasion and told the wee bastard to get off the bus, to f*** off and leave me alone; that all I was trying to do was get them home. |
| MC | *Were you ever physically assaulted?* |
| BMcC | No. I was robbed a few times at gunpoint, but never physically abused in any way. I was robbed on about six occasions while I was a one-manner. I never offered any resistance, because I never knew whether it was a real gun or not. |
| MC | *When you would go back to the depot and report that you had been robbed, how did the company deal with it?* |
| BMcC | They just tallied up what I was supposed to have and gave me whatever was necessary to get my cash flow going again and get me back on the road since I wasn't physically injured in any way. They were very pragmatic about it. The buses had to be kept running. As long as I wasn't physically injured, they didn't worry too much about it. |

120

However, some men weren't as lucky as I was. Some were shot dead. Harry Bradshaw was one, Paddy Crossan and Alec Millar – he was an ex-'B' Special and I think that had a lot to do with him being shot – Syd Agnew . . .

**MC**     *He was shot in his house.*

**BMcC**     I didn't know that.

**MC**     *As an inspector, what other things did you have to deal with?*

**BMcC**     Much of it was just trying to keep things moving as best we could. We tried to patrol the more difficult areas to try and make sure that we could get the buses through and get them back again. Sometimes you could get them into a part of the town, and then you couldn't get them back out again. It might not have been anything concerning the bus itself, but possibly someone hijacking a lorry further down the road and setting it on fire, or something of that nature preventing the driver getting his bus back again. In those days there was no radio communication with the buses so once a bus was out, the driver was on his own.

On one occasion I handed a Molotov cocktail to Ted Hesketh, completely unaware of what it was or who he was. The bomb was rolling all over the floor of the bus with flames and sparks shooting from it. It would have put you in mind of the old penny banger you used to get at Hallowe'en.

The bus had been hijacked and I was sent out to recover it. When we got it back to the depot, Mr Hesketh was there but I didn't know who he was or what his rank was in the company. At this stage, I was a bit pissed off having to go out a get buses that had been hijacked and bring them back to the depot.

**MC**     *Why did you have to do that?*

**BMcC**     We were driving the Corporation's inspectors' old black taxis, do you remember them?

**MC**     *Yes.*

**BMcC**     Well, Willie Graham and myself were given the job of going out in these taxis and getting buses back that had been hijacked or set on fire. God bless the fire service, they always seemed to be there. When a bus went up, they put the flames out and then we had a go to try and recover it. One of us took the bus while the other drove the taxi. We had to struggle the bus back to the depot.

On the occasion with Mr Hesketh, I got out of the seat in the bus with my backside nearly burnt off from the heat of the metal frame of the driver's seat, which was still quite hot. I bent down to pick this thing off the floor and hadn't a clue what it was, and I handed it to him and said, "This is more in your line of business than mine." I thought he was a well-dressed copper! I handed it to him; he stood and looked at it for a second, then dropped it and ran off the bus!

**MC**     *And you managed to keep your job?*

**BMcC**     Yes, I didn't tell him who I was!

**MC**     *Were drivers issued with any particular instructions in what to do in the event of a hijacking?*

**BMcC**     I don't think there were any official instructions issued by the company, but any driver I dealt with took the view that his first priority was to look after his own safety. We can always get another bus but we can't get another you. Let them take it. Just walk away from it.

**MC**     *Were many of the men robbed during hijackings?*

**BMcC**     On most occasions they were. They were told to get out of the bus and leave whatever money was in their tray and box. They would just get out and leave it all there. Sometimes they would have most of their money in their pockets and were able to get it away. Sometimes the money that was left went up in smoke along with the bus.

**MC**     *Did anyone, to your knowledge, ever approach the paramilitaries to try and get them to stop the hijackings on the grounds that they were only disrupting their own communities?*

**BMcC**     I don't know. I remember during BCT days, Max Hale who was Chief Traffic Officer took the buses off the Falls for three weeks. I imagine at that time somebody in the company would have had to speak to someone in the paramilitaries to get some kind of guarantees before the buses were put back on again, at least for a couple of hours in the morning and couple in the evenings, without interference, and then do what you like in between times.

**MC**     *Were there any suspicions that buses were being destroyed deliberately to allow the taxis a free hand?*

**BMcC**   I was never aware of that being the case, and no one ever said anything to me along those lines. I think that when the buses were taken off the road because of the violence, the taxi men simply saw it as an opportunity to make a few quid. As far as I could make out, it wasn't a deliberate policy of the people backing the taxis, but just the taxi men taking advantage of the situation on the ground.

**MC**     *When Citybus was set up, did you notice any change in management's attitude towards putting buses into dangerous areas?*

**BMcC**   Well, Mr Heubeck seemed to take the view that it was no good having buses sitting in depots doing nothing. It was better to get them out on the road earning money, whereas a few short years earlier, Max Hale was prepared to pull off the Falls for three weeks. He was more worried about losing buses than losing money.

**MC**     *Were any of the depots you worked in ever hit?*

**BMcC**   No. I was in all the depots at one time or another, but not while I was there. Falls used to come under sniper fire, shooting at the army.

**MC**     *How did you get on with the soldiers based in the depot?*

**BMcC**   I don't know. I was drinking too much of their beer! Do you think I was going to worry about soldiers when I was getting drink at half price? It must have cost McAnerney's a fortune!

**MC**     *Funny, Frank McHenry said something similar!*

**BMcC**   Yes, he was a fair, sound judge there! The army had cut-price beer and it didn't matter what time you came into the depot at night, the bar was always open. You didn't have to worry whether McAnerneys' was open or not because there was a bar in the depot!

Any snipers shooting from the cemetery or the Falls Park would have been trying to hit the soldiers on the periphery of the depot, rather than anyone in the middle of the depot. They wouldn't have been able to see us in the middle of the depot. "Well, we'll just have another beer and go home when the shooting stops!" Stop you laughing; that's what it used to be like on occasions!

**MC**     *Did the Troubles ever put you off the job?*

**BMcC**   No, strangely. The only test I ever passed was my driving test. When it came to the academics, I didn't have an awful lot going for me. But the one thing I enjoyed doing, was driving. It never entered my head at any time to pack in the job.

**MC**     *But you had a trade; you were a spark. You never thought of going back to that?*

**BMcC**   No, I did not. I was actually asked on one occasion by the director of the company I had worked for originally. But my answer was, "I don't care if the Belfast Corporation loses a million pounds a week, I've still got a job. You can't give me any guarantees that I would still have a job this time next year."

## Raymond Bell, Ulsterbus driver, Great Victoria Street depot

I started to work for Ulsterbus in 1973. I spent the first six months in Head Office, in the wages office waiting for an engineering job to come up. The wages office was not really my thing, but I did enjoy my time as a fitter. I was involved in small unit work, overhauling and repairing mechanical fixtures and fittings on buses and over the years I worked out of the company's main engineering complex in Duncrue Street as well as Smithfield, Great Victoria Street and Bangor depots.

I left the fitting side of things in 1981, not because I didn't like it, but because I felt it was time for a change. The engineering boys tried hard to hang on to me but my mind was made up. I fancied going to the driving, although initially I thought it would be lorries and so on as I had paid to put myself through the HGV test. However, I found it hard to get a job in this area so I applied to drive buses, got accepted and I've been there ever since.

I've seen a lot of people come and go over the years and although staff turnover is still high, it's not as bad as it used to be. It's the sort of job you have to be cut out for, though it's not bad if you have an interest in buses, like I have. You can make life hard for yourself, if you are silly. But for me it's like working in an office except that the scenery outside the windows keeps changing! If you are easygoing, it is a good job because, basically, you are your own boss.

Before I went to the driving, I had had experience of recovering hijacked buses as part of the engineering team. On one occasion, we went out to Twinbrook to recover a bus. The driver's nickname was Two-Stroke because he had a very bad stutter. He lived in Twinbrook himself and had stayed with his bus. A gang of young fellows had tried to hijack it but had been chased by a crowd of women. But Two-Stroke couldn't get her started again, so had sent for us to come out and rescue him. However, the incredible thing was, as he was telling us all this, and he was really wound up about it, he told it all without a single stutter! Under stress he stopped stuttering. We towed the bus to safety and then started her and Two-Stroke drove her back to the depot.

The day that Lord Mountbatten was blown up and the troops killed in the ambush at Narrow Water Castle, near Warrenpoint, I was detailed to take a CIÉ bus back down to Dundalk and bring back an Ulsterbus. When I got to the border at Killeen it was closed with a bomb scare or something so I decided to try the Omeath road instead. I hadn't been on that road for years and wasn't sure of my way to Dundalk by that route. Anyway, as I was heading towards the border a crowd of soldiers waved me down and wanted to know where I was going. In blissful ignorance of what was going on, I was sitting there in my blue overalls with no ID, in a CIÉ bus, just across Carlingford Lough from Narrow Water Castle. I explained I was taking the bus to Dundalk and then asked them if they knew the way. There I was, close to the border, in a CIÉ bus, asking British troops if they knew the way to Dundalk! I eventually explained the situation and they let me go, warning me to watch my step as the Provos were on the loose. I eventually got to Dundalk and drove home the same route with the Ulsterbus without a hitch. It was only when I got home that evening that I heard about Mountbatten and what had happened at Narrow Water.

During one of the loyalist strikes, they took a number of buses from Great Victoria Street depot, where I was based at the time. They used these to barricade Shaftesbury Square, Sandy Row and such places. Eventually we got word that we could take the buses back and we went with the police to recover them. However, before we could remove the buses, a UDA 'officer' insisted we sign a release form for each of them to confirm that they had suffered no damage! We wouldn't sign – we said we didn't have the authority. Eventually the Area Engineer turned up; he had the authority, so he signed! But the UDA rank and file had used one bus as a canteen. The UDA 'officer' made them sweep it out. "You didn't get it like that!" he said. There wasn't a mark on it or any of the others that were recovered.

The bomb which caused so much damage at Oxford Street depot on Bloody Friday destroyed two buses and there were quite a few others damaged with broken windows and the like. They were shunted over to Great Victoria Street with orders to get them sorted as fast as possible so that they could be back in service the next day. While we were working, Mr Heubeck arrived to see how we were getting on. He had a good look round and then he left, but shortly afterwards he re-appeared with two big plastic bags filled with fish suppers for all the men working late.

The first time I ran into trouble as a driver, it was an assault. I was doing the 18.00 to Poleglass. Two men with drink on them got on at the Royal Victoria Hospital. They walked by me without paying. I was faced with a choice. I could ask them for the money, ignore them or get the police. But I was one man against two so I decided to ignore them. They got off at Glengoland. As they were doing so, one of them caught my eye and asked me who I was looking at. I tried to just pass it off but he threw a punch that caught me on the side of the head. I hit my head off the driver's window and bruised my nose. I still have the mark. However, there is often a funny side to these things. A woman passenger, seeing me getting hit, jumped up and shouted after the thugs, "It's not his fault that the fares have gone up!" She thought that's why they had hit me!

The next occasion I was sort-of party to didn't affect me directly. I was doing the 17.30 to Lisburn and Alex Frazer, who is now an inspector, was in front of me with the 17.30 to Twinbrook. I stayed behind him because he was taking the short journey passengers and I was taking those going further out to Lisburn. He pulled up at Sinclair's Post Office in Andersonstown and I pulled in behind him. However, he sat there for ages and I could see people standing on the platform. Eventually I got fed up waiting, so I drove off round him and away on to Lisburn. Later I asked him what had been keeping him at Sinclair's and he told me that he was being robbed! Two guys, one with a sawn-off shotgun had got on and pointed the gun at his head. He asked the gunman to point it at the ceiling and take whatever they wanted. This was all at about ten to six in the evening! I had been sitting waiting behind him for about ten minutes and hadn't realised what was going on.

Over the years I lost three buses in hijackings. The first was Leopard No 1507. It was the day of the first marathon to be held in Belfast, on May Day. After the race was over, I was on my way to Twinbrook and got as far as the corner at the Giant's Foot on the Falls Road when I saw a Citybus Bristol pulled across the road. I told the passengers I was turning the bus and tried to do so. However, some of them wanted off and some dithered as to whether they wanted off or not and in the delay the hijackers saw me and whole crowd of them ran down and boarded the bus. The Citybus Bristol was now on fire, but the mob had run out of stuff to set my bus on fire. They told me to park my bus as close as possible to the burning one so that it would also catch fire. The crowd started to break the windows as I was manoeuvring the bus into position. I got off the bus and started to walk back to the depot, but when I gone a few yards I remembered that in my confusion, I had left everything in the bus; my coat, cash dispenser, ticket machine, everything. I ran back and got my coat and cash dispenser, but as I was moving away from the bus again a young fellow tried to take the dispenser. However, an older man stopped him and clipped him around the head saying, "Leave the driver alone, we only want the bus." That was the usual way when you were hijacked; they told you take your stuff and your money. I walked down to the Donegall Road terminus at the old Celtic Park and a Citybus was sitting there, the driver blissfully unaware of what was going on. When I told him, he high-tailed it back into town and dropped me off at the Europa. You could see the smoke from the burning bus from the depot. I wasn't injured, but I was shaken. All the buses were pulled off the Falls and I went to the canteen for a cup of tea. A little while later, inspector Brendan Deeds came into the canteen and asked if I was okay to drive. I said yes, thinking he wanted me to take over somebody else's duty, but no, he asked me if I could go up the Falls again and collect my bus! It hadn't caught fire and the police and fire brigade had rescued it. When they had arrived, the mob had taken themselves off. A Citybus taxi brought me up to it and I drove it back to the depot. It was all scorched up one side and all the windows were smashed. However, when I got it back to the depot, I removed my ticket machine and paid in! The bus was repaired and was soon back in service.

I lost my second one another night, when I was driving Bristol No 2274 on the 22.30 to Twinbrook. I had just reached the entrance to Twinbrook. There was no street lighting and it was very dark. I could just see what seemed to be the silhouette of a car. Then, in the pitch black I made out what were lots of people running towards me. Next thing the windscreen and side windows came in. Passengers were yelling and getting down on the floor. The bus was full of women coming back from bingo. With the passengers on the floor the mob must have though that the bus was empty because they threw a petrol bomb at the door. Luckily it bounced off back on to the road. I was told to put the bus across the road. I did so, got out and started to walk back towards Belfast. However, before I had got very far a fellow, one of the mob, called me back. A car drove up, a taxi. The man ordered the taxi-driver to drive me back to the depot. When we got there I asked what I was to pay. The answer was, "Nothing. I was told to take you here!" The taxi had, in a way, also been hijacked. But at least his car survived; my bus was burnt out.

The third bus I had hijacked was Tiger No 482, just fresh from an overhaul in Duncrue Street. I was coming back from Lisburn, out via the main road but back via the Falls. On the Stewartstown Road I saw a young fellow, about ten-years-old, at a bus stop. I stopped, but as I did so the wee fellow ran away. Four masked men with baseball bats, jumped out of hiding and on to the bus. I was told to put it across the road and then take my stuff and go. As I was walking away, they came running after me. They had changed their minds as to where they wanted the bus and had tried to drive it away. However, they had stalled it and couldn't get it going again. I went back and started it up for them. As they drove it away, they were smashing the windows. A local couple took me in and gave me tea. I was able to phone Citybus control and they sent out a Citybus taxi for me. The bus was a write-off.

Another day, I was coming down the Falls in Bristol No 2242. Just past the bottom the Whiterock, at almost the same place as the first place I was hijacked, I saw a Citybus Bristol pulled across the road, hijacked. I immediately swung my bus to the right and headed down the Donegall Road. But when I got to the junction with the M1, I saw the military had the big yellow security gates closed across the road. At that time, the old Celtic Park had been demolished and the area had been cleared to allow the building of what is now the Park Centre. The building site was surrounded by light wire fencing. I drove my bus straight through it, across the building site and that way got around the security gates. When I got back to the depot I was shaken, but the bus was fine.

My next bit of trouble was one evening when I was doing the 22.30 from Derriaghy to Belfast via the Falls. At that time all Ulsterbus services were diverted down the Grosvenor Road, so avoiding the Lower Falls. When I turned down the Grosvenor, there was trouble going on somewhere close by. A crowd ran out of some side streets and started throwing corrugated iron partitions, which they had taken from a nearby house-building site, at the bus. One of these sheets somehow caught in my front bumper and jammed itself, upright, between the bumper and the front of the bus blocking my windscreen. I had to drive back to the depot leaning over to see around this thing!

I had a very lucky escape on another occasion. I was trying to get back to the depot but the town was coming down with bomb scares and the police had diverted me round into Queen Street, you know, behind the Spires building. I was at the front of a line of traffic waiting to turn right into Howard Street when a bomb went off in a building in Brunswick Street, just opposite. The first I knew was when both windscreens came in around me. Glass was blown half way up the bus. I was covered in glass, much of it as a fine dust, but I didn't suffer a single cut.

Another day I was doing the 17.10 Derriaghy and was the 'sweeper' bus for the road. At Broadway a man got on. "Take me to the top of the Whiterock," he said. "You're on the wrong bus," I said. "You need to get a Citybus". However, he started to argue and then said he was hijacking the bus. At this point a man who had been sitting behind, reading his paper got up, walked up to yer man and hit him a smack in the head knocking him clean off the bus! "I'm working all day and a drunken eejit like that wants you to take him up the Whiterock? No way!" he said as he sat down again.

One night, it was actually Hallowe'en night, I was driving past Greenways heading for Twinbrook. All of a sudden a tremendous bang went off behind us and it actually lifted the rear of the bus. It sounded like somebody slamming a door right beside your ear. There was a stunned silence form the passengers. It turned out to have been a nail bomb thrown at two army Land Rovers travelling behind the bus. It blew a hole the size of a briefcase in the road. The bus was undamaged but I can tell you we got offside in a hurry!

One day I was on the early Newry. This was during the period of hunger strikes. When you got to Newry you had to do a run to Bessbrook before doing the return to Belfast. Off I went and at Derrybeg Estate I found myself in the middle of burnt out cars and lorries with broken stones and paving setts everywhere. Anyway, I zigzagged through, got to Bessbrook and made my way back without any trouble. When I got back an inspector came running over and said, "Just to tell you, don't go up near Derrybeg. There's been trouble up there." "Too late," I replied. "I've been up and back." The inspector couldn't believe it. They hadn't had a bus up there in two days and had lost two buses already. I put it down to the fact that I went up early in the morning, before the hooligans were out of bed!

The IRA left a bomb in Glengall Street one time, beside the Opera House. I was in the canteen and we were told to get out and back up the yard as far as the garage. When the bomb went off it felt like we had been lifted up and then set down again. Dust and debris came down on us like a mist. When we got back to the canteen, the door, which had been shut, had been blown open so hard that the handle was embedded so deeply in the wall that the door was jammed open. The engine of the van in which the bomb had been left was found in the yard where the buses were parked, sitting between two buses.

A driver called Victor Baldwin was hijacked at the top of the New Lodge Road. He got off the bus but stood and watched as two young fellows sprinkled petrol over the interior of his bus, starting at the front. When they got to the back of the bus, they found they had no matches. One of them then opened one of the sliding windows and asked Victor if he had a light! He didn't oblige them, and he wondered how these two geniuses expected to get off the bus once they had set it on fire.

One of the drivers I worked with was an argumentative little terrier of a man. A loyalist crowd who intended to hijack his bus stopped him. He started giving them gyp because he said he couldn't get home. They told him to take himself off but he kept on at them, yapping and shouting. Eventually, to get rid of him, they gave him his bus back and told him to clear off! He was lucky they didn't give him a hiding.

During the Drumcree confrontations, it was sometimes bedlam, other times they didn't bother us. On one occasion I was driving a bus to Lisburn, but was told in the depot not to go into the Old Warren Estate. At Hilden I spotted two UDA types in full uniform sitting on a settee by the side of the road. One of them flagged the bus down and said, "Don't you be taking your bus up to any of those estates. You'll get it taken off you." He then went back to his settee.

One of the men in Great Victoria Street had a bad limp, so was nicknamed 'Skippy.' He lived up in Ballybeen Estate. A driver taking a bus up towards Ballybeen was waved down by a group of masked and hooded UDA men. One of them warned the driver not to go in a particular direction. "Thanks, Skippy," answered the driver. "How did you know it was me?" asked the crestfallen UDA man, completely unaware that his limp had given him away!

In my experience, most hijackings took place in the context of wider political disorder or as part of football hooliganism. The exception was the May Day hijacking I told you about. Hooligans who had taken too much drink while watching the marathon carried out that one. As I see it, the buses were a symbol of authority, in a way, and destroying one was a way of retaliating against police or army authority. Setting it on fire makes good news, if a poor barricade.

Today a new type of low-level violence, stone throwing and so on, is now routine, even in well-to-do areas. I have a scar on my head that I got from a metal bolt fired at me from a catapult in broad daylight, at four in the afternoon. When it happened, I saw something out of the side of my eye coming towards the bus. I thought it was a wee bird or something like that. It broke the windscreen and hit me. I didn't feel it, but it stunned me and I lost control of the bus, which ran up a grassy bank and was stopped by hitting up against a small tree. I was lucky. The bolt skinned my head and opened quite a deep wound but it caused no serious damage. But, given where it hit me, an inch and a half down and I had lost an eye. This is a example of the thuggery drivers have to put up with today. This happened, not at the height of the Troubles, but in 2002.

*An Ulsterbus Derry City Services AEC Reliance burns fiercely at Rossville Flats during a Derry riot, July 1971. The bodywork on the Reliances used on the Derry city routes differed from those used elsewhere in having the emergency exit located in the rear, as opposed to midway along the offside. They also had a rear route number/letter box and were bus, rather than coach, seated.*

One of my mates wasn't so lucky. In Twinbrook he was hit with a ball bearing, again fired from a catapult. It knocked him out cold and the bus ended up on a grass verge. He was dumped on the ground and joyriders took his bus. The driver never fully recovered and he had to leave the job.

Another driver had his jaw broken in three places by a man because he wouldn't let him off at a road junction. He never came back to the job either.

## Derry and Strabane men

*(Author's note: The accounts in this section were supplied to me during a meeting at Foyle Road depot in Derry by Fred Buick (ex Area Manager), Michael Murray (ex-inspector/driver), George Gallagher (shop steward/driver), John Christie (ex-Strabane inspector), John Doherty (ex-cashier, Pennyburn depot), Eddie Doherty (ex-shop steward/Driver), and Tony McDaid (District Manager/ex-inspector.)*

## *Fred Buick*

At the start, hijacked buses were often recovered. It wasn't until the army started to go in to rescue them, that buses were destroyed. Then they began to be hijacked in order to lure the army into ambushes. There are about 1026 hijackings in my records, but the bulk of these vehicles were recovered. Very often, the men would go out and rescue the vehicles even though they often came under attack with stones and bottles. Operating staff would help inspectors and managers plan services by giving information on what was likely to be happening in the areas where they lived. It was a bit of a cat and mouse game, cutting services, diverting or turning buses short in order to try to avoid loses. At one time hijackings occurred at rate of 2–3 per day.

**An AEC Reliance is caught in the middle of a riot at Rossville Flats, Derry.**

The first Derry bus to be hijacked was No 76, an Albion Aberdonian, in 1968, but the real problems started in 1970. The first 'good' bus to be hijacked was a new Bristol RE. James Heuston the Area Manager didn't want to lose a new bus so he negotiated with the hijackers and offered an old PS2 in its place. They agreed and the old bus was driven up and crates of petrol bombs offloaded from the Bristol on to the PS2. However, the press had got wind of what was going to happen and the swap was recorded by a group of photographers and made the papers.

A bus was hijacked and a bomb put on board. Werner Heubeck, who was in Derry at the time, borrowed a driver's Vauxhall car, drove to where the bus was lying and attempted to remove the bomb using a fishing rod.

One night Pennyburn depot was attacked, a number of bombs were planted and several buses destroyed. The following morning when staff regained access to the yard, they found a Bristol RELL burnt to the floor, but her engine still running!

*Lough Swilly Plaxton-bodied Bristol LHL coach No 117 (7001 UI) burning in 1976. Generally, the Lough Swilly men weren't bothered by rioting mobs, although one man, Roy McMonagle, was hijacked in Co Donegal, had a bomb placed on his bus and was ordered to drive into Derry; he never worked again.*

*Leyland PD3 No 904 on Derry City Services route to Creggan, the only double-decker operated city service.*

Generally, the Lough Swilly men weren't much bothered. For the most part they were coming in from the Buncrana side of the city, and the nationalist crowds left them alone. However, one Lough Swilly man, Roy McMonagle, had a bomb placed on his bus on the Republic side of the border and was ordered to drive it into Derry. He never worked again he was so shaken by the experience.

Usually, when buses were hijacked, money wasn't taken from the drivers. They were usually told to get their gear and their cash and get off the bus.

A Catholic driver, John McGinley, was taken from his bus at Altnagelvin at gunpoint by a loyalist gang. Although threatening to kill him, they later let him go out in the country and he had to walk back to Derry covered in mud. I had actually gone to tell his wife what had happened when a phone call came in from a farmhouse, which the driver had managed to reach. He thought he was going to be shot because one of his kidnappers asked how many children he had. When he replied that he had six, the kidnapper said that he wouldn't have seven!

# Michael Murray

*(Prior to the incident recorded above, a driver, Thomas Callaghan, a Catholic who was in the Ulster Defence Regiment, had been taken from his bus in the Creggan and shot dead.)*

I had advised Tom a few days earlier both to leave the UDR and let it be known that he had done so, or else not drive buses in nationalist estates, as the fact that he was in the UDR was common knowledge amongst busmen. He didn't seem to be aware of the danger he was in as all he said in reply to my advice was, "You've only once to die." When I told him to, "Catch himself on," all he would promise to do was, "Think about it." Two days later, he was dead.

I was given an old 'schools' Bedford [a UTA-bodied Bedford SB5] and told to take it up to the Creggan and not bring it back. It was hoped it would be hijacked. However, the hijackers ignored the Bedford, which made it back to the depot, and hijacked a good double-decker that was following the Bedford around the estate.

Two buses had been hijacked in the Creggan. One was on fire, but the second was okay. I took a chance and made a dash for the second bus. Under a hail of stones and bottles, I drove it away. Later in the day, the bus I was driving was blocked by a van and a group of men surrounded my bus and threatened me for having rescued the other bus earlier. I protested that I was simply trying to maintain a service to the ordinary people of the area. I was warned off not to do it again. I was very frightened by that experience.

When going out to try to recover a hijacked bus, if it was isolated and no-one near, then there was a real chance it had a bomb on board. If it had been left near homes or kids playing around, it was probably safe. On one occasion, I recovered a bus where all its tyres were flat. I drove it back to the depot on four flat tyres.

Another occasion I was on the Dublin–Derry express. Not far from Derry, I was stopped by a mob that wanted to hijack the bus. It was a freezing night, and there were women and small children aboard. I reasoned with the leaders of the mob to let the bus through, which they did. However further down the road the army stopped me. They were suspicious as mine was the only vehicle to have come down the road for several hours and they wanted to know how I had managed it!

A CIÉ driver arrived in Derry on an assist bus and was curious to see the Bogside, so I brought him along. When we arrived, all was quiet but soon after a sudden commotion erupted. Before I could stop him, the CIÉ man ran like a hare back to the depot, all his worst fears seemingly realised!

Two drivers, Danny Collins and Joe Crane, on different occasions, were stopped and had bombs placed under their seats. Danny Collins was ordered to drive to the Guildhall. He never drove again after that incident. In another incident, a driver had his bus petrol bombed and the mob wouldn't let him out of it at first. I had a tear gas grenade land under my seat. It was one of the worst experiences of my life because I thought I was going to choke to death. I was told later that the way to deal with tear gas was to breath through a hanky soaked in vinegar.

## Fred Buick and George Gallagher

Buses used to be hijacked and driven up tight against Rossville Street flats. The idea was to draw in the army and police who would then be bombarded from the upper floors. An ex-Edinburgh Tiger Cub was hijacked and pushed up against the flats. So we decided to try to rescue it. The police wouldn't go near it. However, they did lend us steel helmets. We got into the bus and started to move it at which point part of a gas cooker crashed through the skylight narrowly missing Fred. As the bus was driven away petrol bombs were thrown. One petrol bomb in a milk bottle ended up inside the bus. As the bus made its way down Abercorn Road, Fred kicked the petrol bomb out the door where it crashed on to the footpath, near an old lady, and burst into flames. She lifted her skirts and rushed off in a panic. Fred said she was running so fast she nearly overtook the bus!

## John Christie

Very often in order to avoid rioting or risk of hijacking, buses would have to take a ten mile detour to make what should have been a one mile journey.

There were problems with out-centres such as Claudy, Dungannon, Limavady, and Dungiven. Buses were often set on fire. Usually one in the centre of a line was set ablaze thus damaging the buses on either side of it. When this happened, local staff often did their best to repair vehicles and get services back to normal. Drivers who often were also farmers with some mechanical knowledge, would work on the buses to repair them rather than waiting for engineering crews to come out from Derry. They did their best to maintain services, partly because they were afraid that all the buses would be pulled into Derry meaning a lot of extra travelling for them.

Because of losses and damage due to hijackings, there was such a shortage of buses. On one occasion, in order to get kids home from school, a bus with broken windows was partly roped off inside and the kids sat in the seats away from the broken windows.

On one wet night, a bus had been hijacked and set on fire near the graveyard in Strabane. A driver and I went out to try to recover it. We arrived in the middle of a gun battle between the army and the IRA. Bullets were bouncing off the wall beside which we were sheltering. Although badly damaged, the bus's engine was still running but the tyres on one side had been burst. When things had quietened down, we drove the bus away, the driver sitting in the still smoking frame of the bus.

*In September 1976, Derry bus drivers' staged a march to protest at the IRA's bombing of Pennyburn depot and the hijacking of buses.*

Strabane Square, which was the departure point for buses, was bombed. A bomb was left in a bag amongst a collection of kids' schoolbags, which they tended to dump on the footpath while waiting for their bus. I was chivvying the kids to remove their bags as they were causing an obstruction. However, as I was about to lift this one, a local alcoholic stopped me from touching it. He knew from the smell what it was and this led to the alarm being raised. The bag I was about to lift later blew up. I was a very shaken man for a few days after that incident.

*Strabane depot after a bomb attack in November 1971. Two Leyland Leopards – Nos 1419 and 1441 – and Bedford VAM/Duple No 1222 (left) were destroyed. The Leopards received new Alexander bodies in early 1973; the other VAM in this picture was repaired.*

*Ulsterbus Bristol RE No 2206 was destroyed at Pennyburn, Londonderry in February 1978, when almost new.*

## Eddie Doherty

When the army first arrived, they hadn't much idea of what to do, so if there was any sort of incident, they simply sealed everything off to prevent movement. However, on one such occasion, I found myself and my bus being surrounded by barbed wire by overzealous soldiers.

When a no-go area, the Creggan sometimes went for weeks without a bus being lost. However, after 'Operation Motorman', hijackings started again but to indicate that things were back to normal on the law and order front, political pressure used to come from above for the company to put buses back into the estate, even though the men knew that there was a high chance of them being hijacked.

On many occasions, duties just went by the board. Inspectors allocated runs to shift passengers as best they could. The men did respond well. This was probably due to the slow build-up of the Troubles. Men just got stuck in and sorted out the problems as best they could as they came along. Drivers helped fix buses, would drive buses without windows or even windscreens if there was no alternative. Sometimes men would be hijacked twice in one day. Nevertheless, they generally came back to their work the next day.

## John Doherty (describing the planting of a bomb in Pennyburn depot.)

I saw the bomber coming in carrying a bag but thought he was a BT engineer, who was expected. When I noticed the man running away I became suspicious. I found the bomb in a bag with a clock ticking on top (a Westclox, which someone noticed was running five minutes slow!) The smell of marzipan was the giveaway that it was a bomb. I had to pass the bomb to raise the alarm with other staff. One

*The remains of two ex-London Transport AEC Merlins – Ulsterbus Nos 2514 (LT MB 354) and 2510 (LT MB 658) – await removal from Armagh to the scrapyard in the late spring of 1978. Both vehicles had been destroyed in an attack on Dungannon depot on 7 May.*
**Will Hughes**

*In 1968, Ulsterbus put 20 Leyland-engined Bristol REs, with Falkirk-built Alexander bodies, into service at Londonderry. The disturbances which affected the city from 1969 took a heavy toll on this batch with just one, No 1058, not being maliciously destroyed; it is now preserved and undergoing a major restoration. These two Bristol REs, Nos 1064 and 1061, were lost, along with 17 other vehicles, in the attack at Pennyburn depot on 19 February 1978.*

*The smoking remains of Omagh-based Leyland Tiger No 427 of Ulsterbus lie at Sixmilecross in July 1996.*

**Mark McAleer**

133

female clerk panicked and wouldn't pass it. A double-decker was reversed up to a window of her office and she climbed into the bus through the upper rear emergency window. When the bomb went off, it wrecked the building and money was scattered across the yard. Staff ended up picking up notes and coins from all over the place. Because it had been raining, many of the notes stuck to the ground. There was a security man, but he didn't raise the alarm. Once he realised a bomb had been planted, he went and had a drink and came back later when it was all over.

Another time, a bomb was placed in the office just as all the takings had been bagged ready for removal to the bank. When the bomb went off, the building collapsed and burnt out. The following day the local kids then scavenged for the cash and were seen washing the dirt and ash off the coins to see what they had found.

Once, the bombers arrived disguised as painters. Their bomb was concealed in a paint tin. Staff became suspicious when they saw the men running down the fire escape shortly after they had arrived. The bomb went off and wrecked the building.

On one occasion, there was a panic when a parcel being sent by bus was heard to be ticking. However, it turned out to be a clock being sent for use in timing greyhound racing!

## Dessie Dixon, Ulsterbus driver, Ballymena depot

**News report: Monday 29 February 1988:**

*Ulsterbus hijacked on Antrim Road by a group of armed men. The bus was destroyed by fire.*

Below is a detailed account of this incident. It is worth remembering that all those other incidents had the same impact on the people caught up in them as this one had on Dessie Dixon and his passengers.

DD     I started with Ulsterbus in May 1983 as a driver in Ballymena depot. However, the incident in which I was involved took place on 29 February 1988. It was around the time that the IRA people were shot in Gibraltar. At that time in Ballymena depot we did the 120 service, this bus leaving Ballymena at 8.15 at night and travelling to Belfast. The service time on that route was 1 hour 22 minutes so you were arriving into Belfast at about 9.37pm. We were due out again at 9.40pm so we were just straight in and straight out again.

That night will always stand out in mind for a lot of reasons because it was my wife's birthday and our wedding anniversary. It was a Monday night so we had planned to wait to the weekend to go out to celebrate.

We went down the Antrim Road and you always knew going down the Antrim Road at that time of night that it was either very, very quiet or there was a fair few about. That night it was very quiet. There had been disturbances the weekend before, but I was told, "Go down in and see what everything's like and take it from there."

I went down in, but although it was very quiet the place was in darkness around the top of the New Lodge Road. The lights were all out, but we got down okay into Oxford Street. We were coming out again at 9.40.

At that time the radio taxis were floating about.

MC     *The Citybus ones?*

DD     Yes, and if they had come across any disturbance they would have been on the phone to Oxford Street to warn us. If that happened we would have been put out the Shore Road and up the Limestone or Fortwilliam. However, everything was quiet. I was coming back out with about 15 passengers on the bus and as we came around Carlisle Circus, everything was in darkness. Coming on up the road, because everything was in darkness, I was motoring along briskly when next thing I saw a big round pipe or something being rolled at me. It turned out later to be a big round industrial rubbish bin of about 7–8 feet diameter, on its side. It was near that nightclub, the Gregory I think it was called near, the top of the New Lodge Road. I saw that this pipe thing was going to hit me and in that situation you automatically slow down.

134

Then this guy whom I hadn't seen, jumped out from behind the bin. He had a balaclava on and a gun pointed at me. He was right at the front of the bus. I had 15 passengers on board and in that situation you don't take any chances, you don't be a hero. Then these other guys appeared from the other side of the road and approached us. Then I heard glass breaking down the bus where they were firing stones at the bus. When I opened the door these two guys with scarves around their faces came on and said, "We're taking your bus, mister." I said, "Ok, but let the people get out first before you take the bus." But the other guys were still firing things at the bus and the passengers were trying to shield themselves because the windows were being smashed in around them. I shouted, "Look, someone's going to get seriously hurt here." Then I heard someone shouting, "Stop the throwing!" The stone throwing stopped and they let the passengers get out of the bus.

Now I had my dispenser sitting and it was quite full because I had been working through the day. So I said to myself, "If this guy's looking money, he'll ask me for it." And I flicked off the dispenser as I was getting off. I wanted to get the ticket machine off too, but he wouldn't let me, shouting, "C'mon, c'mon, out, out!" So I flicked off the dispenser and I went out past him and he never asked for the dispenser, money or anything so they were not interested in the money.

We all got off the bus and I said to the passengers, "Come on and we'll all walk up here." We walked on up, and as we walked I turned to look back. When I looked back, I saw the guys get into the bus with jars, obviously petrol, and the bus was lit. The bus was a Tiger, fleet number 1062. We had got two buses, Nos 1060 and 1062 and at that time they were the two of the better buses in Ballymena depot. Within a short space of time the fire brigade appeared. They seemed to there within a couple of minutes. At that stage although the bus had been lit at the back, she was still probably salvageable and could have been got out. But as the fire brigade came down in, they were stoned and the front windscreen of the fire engine was put in. So they had to get offside.

I walked on up the road and I was looking around. The passengers were in a state of disbelief and there was this one wee girl in particular that we had to comfort because she was in a bad way. She was in tears. Then I happened to notice the lights on in the manse behind a Presbyterian Church, which was in operation at that time. So I told all the passengers to come up with me, I went up to the door of the manse and I knocked the door. It was the Rev Patton Taylor who was the minister. I haven't seen him since that day. I told him what had happened and I asked if the passengers could come in and get their heads sort of settled down, get calmed down. He said, "No problem. Come in." And he made everybody tea and helped calm the passengers down.

Within a short space of time, somebody must have seen where we had gone for the guys floating around in the radio taxis appeared. They radioed through what had happened. We sat there for about fifteen minutes just getting our heads together.

I was fine and okay. But just at that split second when that guy appeared around the side of the bin, or what I thought at the time was a pipe, a lot of things flashed through my head. You think are you going to see your wife and children again. You just don't know what's going to happen. Thankfully I am fairly easygoing and can take things in my stride and that night I handled the situation as best I could. I don't think I could have done anything more.

We were in the manse and then the police appeared. They said that they couldn't get the bus out, that she had been burnt. They said that they had to get us back to Ballymena. Now this one wee girl found it hard to understand why something like this could happen to her. I was trying to talk to her and tell her that the main thing was that everyone was okay. There was nobody hurt, that thankfully someone had been looking down on us so that nobody had been hurt. We tried to talk to her like that. Now she was from Ballymoney. Her father drove from Ballymoney to that church to pick her up because she wouldn't leave the manse. He must have known Belfast so he came and collected her. So she didn't go on the bus again.

After a while they said they would bring a bus out of Great Victoria Street and there was a driver, Eddie McGreevy, who came with a bus. He said he was taking us to Ballymena. We got everyone on the bus except the wee girl and someone who offered to stay with her until her father came to pick her up. The police also said that they would stay. Eddie got us in the bus and as we went up the Antrim Road, Eddie asked me how I was. I replied that I felt okay. I asked him how he was going to get back from Ballymena and he said that he would get a taxi back.

As we came up to the lights at Glengormley I said, "When you get through these lights, Eddie, pull over." He pulled over at the stop and I said, "Look, I'll take her on to Ballymena for I feel all right." He asked me if I was sure and I said, "Look, I'll take her on the Ballymena for I don't want to be keeping you out of your bed till all hours of the night." I was okay, and I wanted to get back behind the wheel. So Eddie left the bus and I brought it on to Ballymena.

By the time I arrived, word had got through and the depot manager, Tony Wylie, and the inspector, Sammy Reid, were there. I was a bit more emotional when I saw them. They wanted to know if I was okay. I said I was a bit shaken up, but otherwise okay. Sammy told me that he had rung my wife and told her that I was okay and that I would be home as soon as possible. I came home and my mother and father were there too waiting for me. I was emotional when I got home. It was probably when I got to bed that I fully realised what could happened.

I went into my work the next day and Sammy asked me how I felt about going back on the same run that night. I replied that I was a bit apprehensive about it. He asked me if I wanted the road inspector, John McCormick, to go with me for the rest of the week. I made the decision myself to go back. Some of the boys were saying to me to take a couple of weeks off and to take a bit of time to recover. I didn't know at the time whether or not there were any special payments if you had been hijacked. But my way of looking at it was I was okay and I wanted to get back up the road again. I knew if I didn't, it would get harder to go back. So I went back up the rest of that week and John went with me for a bit of moral support.

For the next two nights we were diverted down the Limestone Road because the trouble that had started that Monday night lasted for a night or two. We only went back down the bottom bit of the Antrim Road on the Thursday and Friday night.

The next evening, the Tuesday, North Queen Street police asked me to come and give a statement. So the early part of my shift was covered to let me go up and make the statement. Making the statement annoyed me a bit because the CID officer was asking things like, "Do you think this was a real gun?" I said that in a situation like that, you don't really care; you assume it's the real thing. He wanted to know if I had recognised any of them. Well, they had masks or scarves up so you would never have been able to recognise any of them. And the thing that really annoyed me was when he said, "When they're burning buses, at least they're not burning property." If it happened now I'd say a lot more, but I said to him,"You don't think a lot of the passengers if that's the way you feel, or the driver." I suppose they had seen it so often that they were hardened to it. I suppose he was right in a way, they weren't burning property. So, I made my statement and they said they would get back to me if they heard anything more. But that was the last I heard about it.

There were nights later on, when the incident would come back into my mind, perhaps in my sleep but thankfully I have been able to put it behind me. Nobody was hurt. A bus can be replaced but if somebody had been hurt it would have put a whole different complexion on the thing.

There was one wee woman, Ruth, a dear friend of mine who was on the bus that night. She worked in Belfast and would have travelled home on that bus. A couple of months after the attack, my wife and I were in Ballymena when we bumped into Ruth, and she said, "Oh, Dessie, I've been looking out for you." And I says, "What's wrong, what's wrong? How are you?" "Oh," she says, "I'm ok but I just want to thank you from the bottom of my heart for what you did that night." I says, "Do you really mean that?" "I do,"she says. "You kept calm and it was because you kept calm that we all got out and nobody was hurt. So I just want to thank you for how you handled the situation."

Something like that coming from a friend means more than anything to me. You don't want praise, but at least I can think that I did everything that I could. I could do no more.

*A burnt-out Daimler CVG6 smoulders away on the Glen Road, having been used as a barricade*

# Kevin Maguire, BCT/Citybus conductor and driver

**KM**   The first big thing I recall was when the IRA came in, took over Falls depot and burned, I think, about 30 new buses which were stored at the back. We had to stay to about three o'clock in the morning and shift buses from all over the place to have a service operating the next day.

**MC**   *What was going on that they picked on the depot?*

**KM**   I think it was just economic. Just to the destroy the property so that the British would have to pay compensation.

I remember when one of the hunger strikers died, all the lampposts on the road were bent over blocking the road. But, we had to drive down the road and dodge around them.

What used to really annoy me, too, was, when the buses were forced off the road, the taxis were still allowed to operate.

**MC**   *Do you think there was any collusion between the IRA and the taximen or was it just the taximen taking advantage of the absence of buses?*

**KM**   I don't really know the answer to that. The first two men to start the Falls taxi operation, were ex-busmen and at the start they used their own cars. Then they later got old black taxis from London. That was the time the Corporation would pull the buses off for weeks at a time. In fact, they took them off the Whiterock for two years. The longest I remember the buses off the Falls was for five weeks and that gave the taxis the opportunity to get a foothold. The

*Kevin Maguire with Citybus Bristol RE No 2112, which itself became a victim when it was destroyed on the Falls Road on 7 October 1989.*   Mark O'Neill

Corporation was more likely to pull the buses off than was Citybus. In fact, Heubeck would get on the buses and take off the bombs himself. When the buses were taken off we had to go over to a yard in Duncrue Street for a couple of periods and to the Naval Air Yard at Sydenham. When things started to quieten down, we worked the buses from there back on to Ladybrooks for a few days and then, if things stayed quiet, Glen Roads.

One time, at the start of the Troubles, when I was conducting, a soldier got on the bus on Finaghy Road North and said he wanted to go down the road a few stops. I wouldn't let him and put him off. He was on his own. He had his rifle and wanted to join the rest of his group who must have been further up the road. But he had a gun and I wouldn't let him on my bus with a loaded gun. He wouldn't get off at first, but he did get off when my driver wouldn't move the bus.

I worked in the Falls depot for most of the Troubles. It was pretty dangerous during the 1970s when things were really bad. You were driving up and down empty roads which were blacked out. One time I was on the accommodation bus going home and we were going through Turf Lodge. We were stopped by a crowd of fellows. They let us go but a second crowd took the bus off us and we had to walk home.

I remember the Sellafield buses. Everyone said they were contaminated and glowed in the dark. But what I do know was that they were heaps. They probably got them for a few thousand, but they filled the gap. The boys used to love going over to collect those English buses. They were well looked after, well fed and so on. There was a driver called Joe Magrath and he was given one of the English buses for his shift. It was painted green with a white stripe and it had orange indicators. He was driving it up the Shankill Road and he was told to get the bus off the road and not bring it back again because it was painted green, white and orange!

Although you didn't have much trouble with people wanting to know your religion or where you lived, I remember doing a special up to Kells and the first question they asked was, "What are you?" I said, "I'm here to drive you to Portstewart." But they kept on at me so eventually I said, "I'm from the Falls, so what?" And they said, "What are they doing sending Catholics out here?" I said, "Do you want go on your trip?" And that was the end of it. But I got them blacked after that.

You could never refuse to drive. You had to go wherever you were sent. You were a bus driver first. At the minute they are trying to bring more Protestants into the Falls depot, but it doesn't work that way. We have a new fellow, a nice fellow he is too, but he lives in Ballyclare, so has to travel in to work, past Newtownabbey depot, to get to the Falls depot. That doesn't make sense to me.

## Sammy Jeffers, Citybus inspector

SJ    When I joined the Corporation in 1964 as a conductor, it was a good job. It was run partly on military lines and I think that was because a lot of the inspectors were ex-servicemen. One of the managers out of Falls depot, Willie Hamilton, who was one of the four area inspectors, you just knew he was an ex-military man, the peak of the cap was slashed and came down over his forehead like a guardsman's.

In those days pre the Troubles, it was a pleasure to go to work. The craic was unbelievable. When I joined I was allocated to the Haymarket depot and it was great. I had never experienced anything like it. Before the buses I had worked in the Sirroco Works and it wasn't the same. When I went on the buses I met these men and they were so different to anything I had ever worked with before. They made work more like a fun camp than anything else. Whenever you went in to work you never knew what was going to happen.

For example, there were about six accommodation buses used to come from the Short Strand over to the Haymarket about half twelve and everybody would have got on. In those days very few people had cars and by the time they got to the Haymarket you wouldn't have got a seat until someone got off. In those days I only had to go as far as Albert Street, but there were a lot of fellows who lived around Short Strand, Mountpottinger and lower Castlereagh Road. They could have walked home but they used to get on the bus and stayed on, travelling right round the route and back to the depot and then walked home. They did that because they were afraid of missing something!

The other thing was the number of people using the buses. I remember a three-minute trolleybus service on the Cregagh Road and a peak service on the Falls Road of 1½ minutes. On one occasion I was driving a trolley along the Shore Road and about Mount Vernon, she stopped dead. I phoned in and they sent out an engineer. But when he got there he told me that the reason the bus had stopped was because there were so many buses on the wires that the system became overloaded and collapsed.

**MC**     *How did the Troubles change the world that you remember?*

**SJ**     Oh, terrible. I remember the start of the Troubles and there was a fellow, Eddie Jordan, who lived on the Glen Road. We were standing outside the Falls depot and Eddie and his conductor came walking up and I said, as a joke, "Have you lost your bus or something?" And he answered, "It wasn't bloody funny, so it wasn't. We got hijacked down there." The bus had been hijacked around the top of the Donegall Road and they had had to walk up to the depot. At that time, we all just fell about laughing. Things like that hadn't happened before.

There was a driver called Hughie McClune. He was a union man and, like me, an old trolleybus driver and he just loved his pipe. One night we were both on Ligoniels. He had just got a new pipe, a present. We were sitting chatting at the terminus, I was the bus behind him, and he says to me, "I know why you're talking to me. You're trying to keep me late." I hadn't thought of that at all. But he gets the oul' pipe going and heads back down the road. I gets into town behind him and there's the pipe lying broken. I says, "What happened your pipe, Hughie?" He says, "If you hadn't talked me late I'd have seen them." What had happened was that the army had come out and put ramps across the road at the chapel at Ardoyne. They weren't there on the way out, so on the way in Hughie had hit them full tilt and had bit through the stem of his pipe. And what was worse, he couldn't get another smoke until he got home.

At the start nobody could see really what was happening. But as the time went on, it began to dawn on everybody that this wasn't a game. It was a serious business. When they did away with the crew buses, and we went all one-man, the biggest fear the lads had, outside getting robbed, was that of someone getting on and putting a parcel on the bus. I know Jimmy Maguire got one and he had to leave his bus outside the old C&A's and that one went off and blew the bus to pieces. Another one went off in Donegall Square East. There was an inspector and me, I was still a driver at the time, and we were crouching down to see what was going on and, when it went off, it really rattled my ears. The way the blast came, it blew three fellows down the canteen steps in Donegall Square East. The first fellow caught the blast and blew him back into the two fellows coming up the steps behind him and they all ended up in a heap at the bottom. One of them was taken to hospital. That's when the reality of it started to hit home.

I remember Heubeck phoning up one night. He was down in Milewater Road. There was a bomb planted in the timber yard opposite Head Office and he wanted someone to firewatch while the firemen dealt with the fire. Sammy Corbet, another inspector, and I went down. The military had the area all sealed off and they wouldn't let us in. Heubeck came over and said, "I don't care what he says. You come with me." The soldier just looked at him. Heubeck was in his shorts and trainers. He took us into his Jag and went back with him to the offices and went up on to the roof. He said, "Keep an eye out. No-one can tell me that the wind won't change and sparks won't blow on to my property." Everything was his property. We stayed there the rest of the night. Later he brought us down into his office and he made tea. "My secretary has biscuits and she thinks I don't know where they are, but I do," he said. He went and got them and we helped ourselves. Then he said, "We cannot take too many for she might notice." And put them away again.

There was a bomb scare in one of our buses in Wellington Place and I was turning the buses at the 'Black Man' [a statue of Rev Henry Cooke, a Moderator of the General Assembly of the Presbyterian Church in Ireland, erected at College Square East in 1876]. Heubeck came up to me and said, "What is it, Sammy?" And I said, "There's one round the corner, Mr Heubeck." "Right, come with me," he said, "and never mind these buses." We went to the corner and I stood there. A soldier tried to stop Heubeck, but he just pushed him out of the road and walked on down to the bus. He got in, had a look at it and then came back up to where I was standing. "It is a real one; let's go," he said. End of conversation!

Heubeck knew when it was the real thing and when it wasn't. One day I was in his company and he said to me, "Do you know, the British army have blown up more of my buses than the IRA." The one thing about Heubeck was he didn't mince his words.

He was very, very funny at times. Although he was a businessman, he never tried to do away with overtime. He realised that if you keep the overtime flowing you'll get the best out of your men, especially around holiday time. One day, after he retired, I was standing in Donegall Square North and Heubeck came up behind me and he said, "Well Sammy, how's things going?" I was surprised he even remembered me. I said, "How are you? Would you not come back?" He said, "I have not got the time." And that just said it all. He was a one-off.

Another night I was in Donegall Square West and there was a bomb scare. I had just got the Dundonalds and Gilnahirks sorted out and on the move. I then went up to deal with the City Expresses and Holywood Roads and got them moving. The next one then was the Antrim Roads and Shore Roads and I could see the crowds of people and all the heads going. So I walked up the middle of the road and stopped in front of them and said, "Now see, before anyone says anything, just remember one thing, the only person, who is allowed to shout at me or give me grief, is at home making my dinner and I hope to be home in about three quarters of an hour. Now what's your problem?" Although I didn't see them, Frankie Clegg and Chris Childs, the Chief Inspector, were standing there. They just shook their heads and walked away. At that a bus came in. I told him to do a Roughfort. He filled up and left and more buses came round. Within ten minutes I had both the Antrim and Shore Roads stops cleared. I always found that if you tried to defuse a difficult situation, people will respond to it positively.

Another difference between the pre-Troubles period and the Troubles period was the attitude of people. Before the Troubles, regular passengers used to give you little gifts, say a piece of fruit or something for your break. At Christmas you would get some cigarettes or a couple of cans of beer. Once my bus broke down on the Cavehill Road and a wee woman from one of the big houses opposite the fire station came over to the bus and asked me if I would like a cup of tea. I said yes and the next thing she appeared with a teapot, jug, cup, sandwiches and biscuits on a tray. But all that sort of thing has gone now.

| MC | *Do you think the Troubles were a cause of that or would it have happened anyway?* |
|----|----|
| SJ | I don't think it would have happened as quick. It probably would have changed, but more slowly. |
| MC | *So, as a Corporation man you had to deal with the change in your working environment because of the Troubles and then not too long after that the change over to Citybus. When you heard that was going to happen how did you feel?* |
| SJ | When we heard that this was going to happen and that Ulsterbus was going to take us over, a lot of the men were resentful. We knew that Heubeck was very much an Ulsterbus man. The men were very suspicious of the whole thing. And to make it worse, our place was rife with rumours. If you could start a good rumour, and could get someone gullible enough to take it up, you could get great mileage out of it. However, once we got into the working of it and could see how things were going, the worries died away. |

When the pre-paid tickets came in there was a lot of fiddling by passengers who just kept over-stamping the ticket. However, some of the buses had a wee switch which allowed you to switch the stamping machine off. One night these two guys got on and I could see that their tickets were black with over-stampings. So just as the first one was about to frank his ticket, I flicked the switch and the machine wouldn't stamp. I said, "It's okay, I'll sign it for you." "No, it's alright", he said. "I'll get the next bus." And off he got. So I flicked the switch on and the machine was working again. Some passengers got on and stamped their tickets. These two saw that and got on a second time. I flicked the switch off again. "I'll sign it off," I said again. "No, no. We'll get the next bus." And they wouldn't get on and pay their fares. One of them says, "He's doing something to that. Everyone else is getting theirs stamped." "It only works for good tickets," I told them. "That's a new machine. It detects all the bad tickets. We've all got them now." And yer man said, "I'm not standing here." So he paid his fare and sat down. But the next night he got on and said, "You're right and funny, aren't you? That machine and all. It didn't stop me this morning."

| MC | *You said earlier that one of the things you feared most was someone getting on to your bus with a bomb. Did that ever happen to you or were you ever robbed?* |
|----|----|
| SJ | I was fortunate in that I never had a bomb, but I remember one unpleasant incident. I was late into the depot one night and I just grabbed my bus, filled in my numbers and out I went. The first run was up to the Glen Road, back to the City Hall and back up to the Glen Road again. When I got there I had a minute |

or two to spare and I was leaning on my box filling in my numbers when I felt a tap on the head. I thought to myself, "This is one ignorant pig." And I looked up and there was a 'Saturday Night Special' stuck in my nose! And he says to me, "Give me your money." And I says, "Listen lad, I've just started. It's my first journey and there's what I have." There was about six or seven pounds. The two of them scooped it out and away they went. What had happened was that had I bought two new rolls in the depot just before I had started, so I had only my float. Otherwise they would have got over £100. I drove out of the terminus

*Daimler CVG6 No 368 on fire on Grosvenor Road, 3 July 1970. At times, no regard was shown for the safety of adjacent properties, as can be witnessed here with No 368 wedged between the church railings and the houses opposite.*

and the inspectors' car was just coming up the road. I stopped it and said to the inspector, "Those two there have just robbed me." You could still see the two boys clearly. What the inspector didn't know was that a woman on the bus had seen the whole thing and had given me her name and address. When I got to the depot and went in and told the depot inspector that I had been robbed. The next thing was that the inspector who had been in the taxi came in behind me. I said, "Did you see them?" "I never seen anybody there," he said. And I said, "You what?" And he said, "I never seen anybody there." I said, "You're a liar. I could see them at the top of the steps as you went round in the car. You couldn't have missed but see them. They were counting the money. Furthermore, there's a woman's name and address that I've got as a witness." Whenever I showed him that, you should have seen the look on his face! So I wrote out my report describing exactly what had happened. I put it in but was sent for the next morning and asked to rewrite the report but not to mention the inspector's comments. I asked why I should change my report and I was told that if he said he didn't see anything, you can't say that he did. So that was that.

Another incident was at the top of the Donegall Road. Again I was filling in the numbers and this girl got on. It was a summer's night and I was just about to ask her what she wanted when she says, "Irish Republican Army." Then I hears the windows coming in on the bus. She shouts to this fellow, "In there!" The next thing was I was splashed with petrol from the left shoulder down my side to my shoes. I opened the door but my foot was still on the platform when the bus went up. Now there was another chap, Felix McIlstocker, a few months previous to this, who had been parked on the other side of the road. Although the two buses were sitting on the hill, the petrol on mine ran to the back of the bus but the petrol on his ran to the front of the bus. When his went up, Felix got badly burned and he was off for quite some time. But I was fortunate, when they threw the match in and the bus went up, I was just off the bus. I walked up to the depot and told them what happened. The inspector said, "You'll have to get another bus out of the park and finish your duty." But I said, "I'm going home to have a shower and get these clothes off me. Anyone comes near me with a light and I could go up." I was reeking of petrol.

Another time I was hit was during one of the loyalist strikes. I was coming down the Crumlin Road and I got hijacked at Century Street. We were still using the tokens and this young lad says to me, "Have you any donations to the UDA?" And I said, "Take it out of the tokens." When I think of it now, talking back to these fellows.

The first time I was hijacked was at the Alverno Hotel at the top of the Whiterock. I was coming along and the next thing a fellow walks out and puts his hand up. I could see another fellow standing as if he had a rifle. But it was actually a blackthorn stick!

**MC**   *But you weren't going to take any chances.*

**SJ**   No. Whenever it's dark and you see somebody standing like that you don't take chances. So I stopped and this young fellow jumps on. "Out of the bus," he shouts, "we're taking it over." Then these other fellows came over and I says, "Where do you want the bus?" "What do you mean?" they said. "Well," I said, "It's better me parking it than somebody who doesn't know anything about it trying to park it." "Good thinking," he says,"just pull it across the road there at the hotel." So I drove up and parked it. So I thought, "My box is going to go here." And the fellow comes up and says, "What depot are you out of?" And I says Falls. I lifted the box and there was nothing said about lifting the box. He called two fellows over and he said to me, "Just look in front of you, don't turn around. Walk down the Monagh Road alongside the houses. These two fellows will make sure you get down okay, but don't be looking back." I walked down to where the chapel is and then turned left on to the Glen Road where the private houses are and I was listening but I couldn't hear anything behind me, no footsteps. I took a quick look around, but they had gone. They were still with me as far as the chapel, but once I got in amongst the private houses, they left me. So I walked into the depot and one of the inspectors said, "Where were you? We were out looking for you." So I told him and said, "Here's my box, still intact." But whenever anything like that happened they had to do a box check. So they did the check but everything was okay. Wesley Snodden was the depot manager and he said to go home and not worry about putting in a report till the next morning. But I did feel such a fool when I thought about yer man with the blackthorn. But the thing was, although he had a blackthorn, the rest of them, and there were about three of four of them, were all carrying guns.

Another time, I was coming down the Crumlin Road in an oul' Bristol. I used to think there was nothing like the Bristols. I loved driving them. I was coming down and I heard this thump, thump, thump behind me. When I got to Flax Street Mill the army stopped me. The officer, a captain or a major, got a knife out and dug a bullet out of the side of the bus. "Just as I thought men, a low velocity bullet," he says. I says, "Oh great!" "What do you mean, oh great?" He says. "A low velocity bullet. Does that mean it wouldn't have killed me?" I asked. "Cheeky bastard, aren't you?" he says. "I may be a cheeky bastard, but I'm not a stupid one," I said. "What did you come down that way for anyhow?" he says. "Well nobody at the top told me not to," I said. "And this is my route." And I drove on.

There was another one stopped me one night and he says to me, "Are you the driver of this bus?" I says, "No. I'm a pilot on Concorde and I'm just doing this as a hobby." And the look he gave me!

When you got stopped by some of those officers, the questions that they asked you, the obvious questions, where you only had to look to see the answer. There you are with a busload of people and they ask, "Are you the driver of this bus?" You would not believe the number of times I was asked that question. In the end I would just sit and look at them. These are supposed to be intelligent people, in charge of a group of men, men whose lives may depend on a decision taken by them and he gets on my bus and asks me if I'm the driver of the bus. Or it's stuck up on the front, 'City Hall', and he asks, "Where are you going?" At the time when so many men were getting robbed, so that the hoods wouldn't be able to find out our addresses easily, the management made an agreement with the police that we wouldn't carry PSVs or licences, just staff passes. If need be we would go and hand them in within twenty-four hours. But I was stopped one day by a military patrol. They asked for identification and I handed over my staff pass and he looks at the photo and says, "Is that you?" I took it off him, looked at it, handed it back and said, "Oh yes. That's definitely me."

**MC**   *As if you're going to say, "No, it's not me, it's my brother."*

**SJ**   Do you remember when they used to put the barbed wire cradles out at checkpoints?

**MC**   *Yes.*

**SJ**   Well there was this driver and he used to pull a stunt at these. You remember the set up in the old CVGs and Guys with the half cab and to the left there was a wee sidelight sticking out. Well he used to open the window at checkpoints and get one of the soldiers talking. They used to carry their rifles resting the butt on their hip and the strap came round on to their wrist. Well he would get them to come over

142

to talk to him and then he would have taken off and the wee light would catch in the strap forcing the soldier to run alongside the bus until he got it freed.

I also recall when they had the NAAFI in Falls depot. They had it in an old converted London bus. They had a bar upstairs in it and downstairs you could buy things like crisps, sweets, toothpaste, and so on. But in the true tradition of busmen, they took over the bar upstairs. The major had to go and tell Willie Hamilton to get his men out of there because his men couldn't get in for a drink!

**MC**   *Sounds like heaven on earth; a bar in the depot!*

**SJ**   It was like manna from heaven!

Another time the soldiers were drilling with their rifles and presenting arms. But one of them had a bullet up the spout and when he thumped his rifle on the ground, it went off. The bullet ricocheted all around the rafters. It came off one girder and bounced off the next. We were in fits laughing at the reaction it caused. They were all lying on the ground and we were all standing! I think that's what really needled them. In fact there could have been a confrontation that day in the depot between the drivers and the army, but one of the officers and the inspector came along and defused the situation.

So there could be difficult times. On one occasion there was a funeral of an IRA man (who had blown himself up with a bomb) going into the cemetery across the road. Some of the soldiers started signing that song, "I'm in pieces, bits and pieces." One of the drivers lost the rag and said something to one of the soldiers. Holding up his fist, a soldier said to him, "Watch it or you'll get some of this." And the driver said, "You make the first move and I'll finish it." He was big fellow, well over six foot and broad with it. It went no further.

**MC**   *I remember the old BCT buses were always very clean and tidy.*

**SJ**   If your bus wasn't clean coming out of the depot, and any councillor had seen it, he could have got on the phone and that bus would have been changed right away. But once the Troubles started and we started to lose so may buses all that stopped. Later we had to go over to England for replacement buses. We had our breakfast in the morning, and then went to the depot and you picked a bus. Then we drove in convoy from London to Carlisle. We stopped off somewhere on the motorway for lunch and then stayed overnight in Carlisle. The next morning we headed for the docks. There was always a manager and a shop steward with the group.

**MC**   *I hear there were some adventures on those trips.*

**SJ**   Yes, you're right there. On one trip I was driving up past Blackpool and I spotted Geordie Lesley lying on the bank at the side of the road. It was a summer's day and he was stretched out on this bank with his broken down bus beside him. He had to wait for the last bus in the convoy. Frankie Clegg was in the last bus. From the motorway to Blackpool was fourteen miles and Frankie had to go to Blackpool, see someone in Blackpool Corporation. They came out and towed the bus in, fixed it and then got it sent up to Stranraer. We then got it brought over to Larne. The next morning I set off and Geordie said that he would come with me. We driving along this straight stretch of road in Scotland and Geordie said, "I'll give you a break." And I says, "Okay," and stepped out of the cab. You want to have seen Geordie getting into that cab. The bus was still doing about 40 mph when I stepped out of it! He says, "You bloody well might have stopped!" And I said, "Well, I wanted to save time."

**MC**   *Frank Clegg was saying that it was a nightmare for him because London Transport was just palming him off with all their junk. He said that while the Merlins were bad, the Swifts were worse.*

**SJ**   I never liked the Swifts. They were very light in the front. If it was a bad day and raining, and you hit the brakes she was all over the place. They were noted for that. The best buses that I ever drove were the Bristols.

The Troubles killed all the fun in the job, not the camaraderie, but the fun and enjoyment. There was still a bit, but nothing like what there had been when I joined in the 1960s. The job became more dangerous. Jimmy Rutherford was shot at the first stop after Agnes Street on the Crumlin Road. Harry Bradshaw was killed at the same stop. Then there was Alec Millar, an inspector in Ardoyne. Alec had his views and was an ex-'B' Special and all that, but I remember Alec phoning me up one night at half ten to ask me to do a special to Antrim. I didn't want to do it but he pleaded with me for about fifteen minutes and in the end he says, "If you do it I'll see you're all right for overtime from now on." So I did the special for him and he was as good as his word on the overtime. He was based in May Street and I never wanted for overtime out of May Street while he was there. But he was transferred to Ardoyne. He didn't want to go. He said that if he was moved there, it would be the death of him. But he was moved and he was right. He was shot dead in Ardoyne depot.

## Jim Lambert, driver with both Ulsterbus and Citybus

I joined the Belfast Corporation in early 1970 as a driver and was with the BCT and then Citybus until 1980. At that time due to changes in my wife's employment we moved to Derry and I transferred over to Ulsterbus. I retired from Ulsterbus in 2000 due to health problems. As well as my role as a driver, I was also involved at a senior level in the union and played a part in various union teams negotiating with Werner Heubeck. When with the BCT and Citybus I was mostly based in Ardoyne and Falls depots.

The first incident I remember associated with the Troubles was early on in the unrest. I had gone into Falls depot to collect my wages. When I walked into the room the inspector was there and some other men. Someone closed the door behind me and then I saw a man with a gun. Myself and three others were forced into a toilet while the gang raided the office. We were crammed into a cubicle with only enough room for one person, but four of us were squeezed into it and it was very claustrophobic and unpleasant. When we were in there a while we heard a lot of shouting and shots being fired and eventually the door was opened and we were let out. When we got out we saw that the police and army had the gang lined up. I was asked if I recognised any of them as the man who had held us up. I said no, that they were wearing masks. The police said that they couldn't find any masks, but we stuck to our story. We had to continue working there you see – no point in making a target of yourself. Years later I met one of the gunmen in a shop in town. He had done his time and left the IRA. We chatted about the incident and there were no hard feelings on either side after all that time.

The second incident which sticks in my mind didn't happen to me but to another driver, a mate of mine. Now, some blokes on the buses and elsewhere too, I suppose, *think* they are hard men, but this mate of mine *was* a hard man. Now, don't get me wrong, he wasn't a trouble maker. In fact, he was one of the nicest guys you could meet and a good pal, but, he really knew how to look after himself. Well, anyway, he was driving a Fleetline up the Donegall Road this night and when the bus got to a certain stop, anyone going beyond was going into the Catholic area at the top of the road. There were two young lads sitting in the back seat, about 14–15 year old and it was clear they were going on up to the top of the road. At this point a group of men with hatchets jumped on the bus and made for the lads in the back seat. Another thug positioned himself outside at the emergency door to stop the lads getting out that way. My mate yelled at them asking what the hell were they playing at. They told him to keep his nose out of it; it was none of his business. That was their big mistake. He got out of his cab and waded in to them. One of the young fellows had been hit with the hatchet on the shoulder but that was all the damage they suffered. My mate got a hatchet off one of them and laid into them with it. He hospitalised the ones that had got on his bus. He was brought to court, but the judge threw the case out saying what would have happened to the lads would have been worse if he hadn't done what he did. After this incident he received threats from one of the loyalist paramilitary groups. Again, the wrong man to threaten. He knew who the paramilitary bosses were in the Village area and he went and banged on their doors. He asked them what sort of defenders of Ulster they were, backing up hoods trying to kill a couple of wee lads with hatchets. He made his point and had no more threats after that.

The same driver saved the life of one of our inspectors. He pulled into High Street one night and saw three fellows giving the inspector a kicking. He jumped off the bus and gave the three of them a hammering. In fact, he put one through Robb's window. Again, he ended up in court but got off because the judge said the inspector would have probably been killed if the attack had gone on. As it was, he was seriously injured. Robb's tried to claim off the BCT for the cost of a broken window!

One night I was coming down the Falls when, about Clonard Street, a crowd of masked lads stopped the bus and ordered me and the passengers off. I had a crowd of women going to bingo on board but these lads shouted, "We are the IRA. Get off, we're taking the bus!" So, off they went in the bus and headed down Lesson Street. A shopkeeper came out of his shop at the bottom of Clonard Street, obviously upset by what had happened and when the bus drove off this guy disappeared back into his shop. A couple of minutes later a car screeched to a stop beside us. "Are you the driver?," a guy in the car shouted. "Yes," I replied. "Who took your bus?" he shouted again. "The IRA; they're away down Lesson Street with it," I answered. "It wasn't the f***ing IRA!," he shouted, "we're the IRA!" They must have been phoned by the shopkeeper. At that the car raced off down Lesson Street. A couple of minutes later my bus reappeared out of Lesson Street with one of the real IRA men at the wheel. The other guys who had been in the car were in the bus knocking the lights out of the lads who hijacked us! They were kicked off the bus and I got back on with my bingo ladies and headed on into town. But that wasn't the end of it. Because I was so late, I missed my next run and the inspector in the city centre wouldn't believe my story. I was put on a charge and had a job convincing the boss of what had happened. What they couldn't believe was that I had been hijacked but had got my bus back! In the end I convinced him and got off, but he was still very sceptical about my story.

I was hijacked a number of times over the years, six times in Belfast and twice in Derry as I recall, but one of the first times was by these two guys with a 50lb bomb. They got on to my bus with this box and told me to drive to the City Hall via the Donegall Road. They stayed on the bus, one of them holding the bomb on his knees. "You drive carefully!," he said, "this is the real thing, and mind how you go over any ramps if you don't want to go up in smoke!" I drove very carefully down the Donegall Road, but as we got near the bottom, I could smell this sweet smell, like marzipan. One of the guys said, "This is supposed to have a two hour fuse, but I think they've got it wrong, I can smell explosives. Driver, stop the bus and run for it!" I pulled the bus onto a piece of waste ground, near Utility Street and the three of us baled out. The two Provies disappeared and I got the police. The bomb didn't go off right away, but it did go off eventually and wrecked my bus.

On another occasion my bus was boarded by a crowd of men on the Lower Falls. I thought I was going to get my bus taken, but they made no moves to take it. However, when I got up the Falls a bit, a crowd of masked youths came out of a side street and waved down the bus. I knew I was going to lose her then. However, some of the crowd on the bus pulled scarves over their faces and waved the ones outside away. They let the bus through, thinking these guys had already hijacked me. But all the guys on board wanted was to get home. They didn't want the bus!

*Ulsterbus AEC Reliance No 268, new in 1962, was destroyed in the parking area at Oxford Street bus depot on 13 April 1980. In 2006, this area has changed out of all recognition. Oxford Street bus station has been replaced by Laganside BusCentre close by and this site is now occupied the Waterfront Hall and a Hilton hotel.*

**Will Hughes**

Something similar happened when I was driving in Derry. It was 1985, I think. There was a lot of trouble in the Bogside this particular day. I was heading to the Creggan and when I got into William Street a crowd, some of them masked, piled on my bus. I thought I was going to lose the bus but the first thing that was odd was that most of this crowd paid their fares! I said, "I thought you were going to take the bus." "No," this guy answered, "it's hard work cloding stones at the Brits and we're going home for our tea. We'll go back later on and have another go at them." The Brits saw these masked guys getting on my bus on their cameras and when I wasn't hijacked they wanted to know what had happened. I just played innocent and said it was a crowd of fellows going home. I never noticed any masks.

On another occasion my bus was hijacked and another driver and me were taken prisoner. We were put into a car and the other driver began to have a fit. "What's wrong with him?" one of the Provies asked. "He's afraid of being shot," I answered. "Who's going to shoot him, for God's sake?," he said. "Well you've got a gun pointed at him!," I said. At that they chucked him out of the car. I was taken to a house in Beechmount and held prisoner. They left me sitting there with a wee lassie pointing a gun at me. After a couple of hours they came back and I was let go. However, I had only gone up the street a bit when I had a thought and I turned and went back to the house. "What do you want now?," said the guy who answered the door. "What's going to happen to me if any of you are lifted?," I asked. "He looked at me and said, "Well you have the guts to come back here and ask that. You've nothing to worry about." My bus had a bomb on and it was left outside Andersonstown police station. It blew up and the blast ripped the roofs off all the houses beside the police station, but never broke a window. It was used afterwards in a video to show the effects of a bomb going off.

Bombs used to be left in boxes on buses, but not all boxes left on board buses were bombs! Sometimes boxes were left as hoaxes and sometimes not, but if you got the army in, their 'controlled' explosion inevitably wrecked the bus. So, more often than not, if you found something which you didn't think was a bomb, you just bucked it out of the bus. These next two stories relate to two incidents where parcels were left on my bus.

On the first occasion, I was heading up the Malone Road when a passenger said there was an unattended box lying on one of the seats. I stopped the bus and went and had a look at it but decided it was safe enough. I bucked the box out of the bus and over a hedge somewhere about Sans Souci Gardens. When I got back into town the inspector came over and asked me if I had seen a parcel in the bus. I said I had and told him what I'd done with it. He was raging. "That was a pair of shoes that a passenger had left behind," he said. "Well, "I answered, "he'll find his shoes in a garden up around Sans Souci if he goes and looks."

The second occasion involved a bus taking kids up the Antrim Road to school. Sometimes kids would try the fake bomb routine to try and avoid having to go to school. But more often than not it was an obvious hoax and you took no notice of it. But this morning the kids came down the stairs and said there was a bomb upstairs and there was smoke coming out of it. I stopped the bus, cleared it and ran upstairs to have a look. Right enough, there was this box sitting on a seat with wires coming out of it and smoke too. I wasn't taking any chances so I drove the bus down a side street near Alexandra Park. When I jumped out, I saw this fellow mowing the lawn at the front of his house. I shouted for him to get out of the way, that there was a bomb on the bus. However, instead of legging it, he started to shout back, "Get that damn bus away from here. What the hell are you playing at? You'll break all my windows." He was very well spoken, and very cross. I shouted back for him to get out of the way and at that point he did take himself off. When I got back up to the corner at the Antrim Road, the police had arrived, but for some reason so had Werner Heubeck. He took me to one side and asked me what exactly had happened. When I told him he said, "It's a hoax. The IRA would not put a bomb on a bus full of schoolchildren." "But there is smoke coming out of it," I replied. "I will go and have look," he said. The police wouldn't let him go near the bus without formally warning him that if suffered any injuries, they weren't liable. He listened and then off he went. While he was at the bus, the bomb squad arrived. A few minutes later, Heubeck came out of the bus carrying the box with the smoke still coming out of it. "Look," he shouted grinning, "I told you it was a hoax. The smoke is coming from a hand warmer!" The military were having none of this. Being soldiers, they didn't know who this nutter carrying the 'bomb' was. "Put it down, right now!" one of them shouted. "But it's only a hoax," shouted Heubeck. "Put it down immediately or we'll shoot." Heubeck put the bomb down on the road and walked away from it. The bomb disposal people took over and after a while declared that it was, in fact, a hoax and I was able to get my bus back.

There was another occasion when Werner was nearly shot. You know how he was a fitness fanatic. Well, he used to practice his climbing skills on a wall in Ardoyne depot. On one occasion, new troops were brought into the depot during the night and so didn't know who he was. Next day, Werner was scaling a wall and the squaddies thought he was a terrorist. He was saved only because their sergeant was careful and asked one of the boys who the guy climbing the wall was!

Mind you the army could get it wrong too! I recall on one occasion in Derry during a period of trouble when they re-routed my bus down into the middle of a riot. She was just out of PSV, gleaming clean, newly painted but ended up a total loss.

Bombs and hijacking weren't the only problems you had to deal with. There were the problems of fare dodging and pure thuggery against drivers. One night I was going up to Glencairn, in North Belfast, and there was a crowd of hoods, none of whom had paid their fares, shouting and roaring upstairs. An inspector got on and I warned him not to go upstairs to check the tickets. If he had he would have kicked to death. But someone from Head Office was on board and reported that the man hadn't checked the bus properly. The inspector was demoted. I know who squealed on him and I had the pleasure of telling him exactly what I thought of him at a management/union meeting some time later.

I also remember being attacked and robbed by a group of men in broad daylight at Glengormley. I ended up on the floor under the steering wheel trying to protect myself. I was lucky and was only slightly injured. However, the police came on the scene and grabbed them. I think they might have been waiting for them. The leader of that gang, and I can see him yet with his blonde hair, later did time but was shot dead shortly after he got out.

It did get to the men sometimes. At the start of it all, when we still under the control of the Corporation, I was sitting outside the Water Office in a new Fleetline when a CVG6 drove slowly past. I waved to the driver and then watched as the bus slowly mounted the kerb and crashed into a shop window. I jumped out of my bus and rushed around to help the driver out of his cab. He was holding his head. It seems his conductor thought he was going to pass a stop and give the bell rope a good tug. The bell came away from the ceiling and on to the poor driver's head. In his shock he lost control of his bus and it mounted the kerb. "I thought I'd been shot," he told me when he had recovered a bit.

*Citybus Bristol RE No 2343 was burned at Ligoniel on 9 May 1987. Not much remains of the aluminium body.* **Will Hughes collection**

147

# Personal recollections: *Routes* Project interviews by Ruth Graham

## *Frank Murphy, BCT/Citybus driver, later shunter*

**RG**     *If you want to start by telling me when you started working in the bus industry and what attracted you to it. How you came into it.*

**FM**     I was working in London, and I just decided to come back home again. It was 1971. So I applied to the Corporation, which it was then, and got an interview in Utility Street, which was the offices on Donegall Road. Well, that was it. I went out, and did the test for the driving. Well, that was me in really. It wasn't so much an attraction as the fact that it was a job. It got you off the street, if you like. Well, that was it, really.

**RG**     *Did you start as a driver, then?*

**FM**     I started as a driver, yes. It was good. But then 1971–1972, that was really the sort of height of the Troubles. So there were people leaving the job and they were finding it difficult to keep people in. People just getting out because it was too dangerous.

**RG**     *What sort of routes were you driving on?*

**FM**     I did, well, all of them, really. You were on say, Falls Road, Ladybrook, Whiterock, Shaw's Road, that type of thing – although Shaw's Road didn't come into it till wee bit later on. That was sort of an extension, and the same as the Glen Road. It only went to St Teresa's at first but then they extended it out to Glencolin there.

**RG**     *Were you on the double-deckers initially?*

**FM**     On the double-deckers, open backs, so you were. More or less every day you came in, there was something new, not just new routes or on different roads. There was always something happening, which sort of made it – I don't know – maybe to my mind, it was a bit of excitement, really, because you didn't know what was going to happen when you went in. You went out on normal duties, but it didn't stay that way for very long. You were probably diverted, like one day I was going back down the Falls. I came up the road and knew there was something happening as I was going up again. The RUC diverted us down Balaclava Street. So if you went off the main road with a double-decker bus, you were heading into wee side streets which were never meant for horses and carts, never mind double-decker buses. But I would have just gone out and went round to the back and told them there's a bomb scare. We're going to have to go such and such a way. If anyone wants to get off here, get off because I'm going down . . . So nobody would get off, because, I have a sneaking suspicion the passengers thought it was great too. They would have went. So I would take them down, say, Balaclava Street, into Raglan Street, Bosnia Street. These are streets that don't exist anymore. And if it was the Grosvenor Road, you would have went down the Grosvenor and say, cut into Abyssinia Street, which was a wee narrow street.

There was one day I went down Abyssinia Street on a double-decker bus and all the people on it, they thought it was great, because no buses ever went down there, to cut through into Albert Street, which was your 77. And there was an old lady, Mrs Hart, she was very ill. She was in her 80s then. And she was in a house on her own upstairs. But she couldn't believe that she'd seen this bus go past her window, her wee house. She thought, "My God, what is this?" So when her daughter, Brigid, came in, she said to her, "A bus has went past our window this morning." She thought she was not too good. But she was there half an hour, and the next thing she saw a bus coming past. She said, "Ma, you were right, there is a bus going past our house," she says, "and Frank Murphy is driving it." Things like that.

**RG**     *Did that happen quite regularly?*

**FM**     It happened quite a few times, but not everybody would have went off the route. But I always thought to myself, what the hell. It's a bit of craic, you know, you get them there. So people were getting on, say at the Lower Falls when you were coming out again, coming back up the road again and I would have said to them, "There's a bomb scare up the road, we're going to have to go beside Turleys." "Ah that's great." So, I was dropping them off at their doors, like a taxi service, dropping them off at their doors. And they said, "Will you be coming back this way again?' I said, "It depends. If the bomb's away, and it's

148

*Citybus No 2930 was one of the Daimler Fleetline single-deckers acquired second-hand from Potteries Motor Traction, Stoke-on-Trent. Note the large windows which were a feature of the Alexander W-type bodywork carried by these buses. No 2930 was destroyed in an attack on Ardoyne depot on 29 February 1980.*

okay, we'll go back down the Falls Road again. If not, we'll come back . . ." Things like that would have happened. I think the people enjoyed it too. It's a distraction. Things like that were a distraction. It may sound daft but it was a distraction. It was different. And it got them away from the danger, if you like, and they were still getting home, that sort of thing.

**RG**   *You never felt sort of scared or anything, at any time?*

**FM**   No, no, no. Even the one a Saturday morning, I think it was. I think it was Saturday morning, maybe a Sunday morning. This depot here [Falls] is closed on a Sunday now, but it used to be open on a Sunday for services. All the services operate from the Short Strand. But when it did operate, I think it was a Sunday morning. It was a nice morning and these tourists, a couple of Italians, a man and a woman. They had a wee standard eight cine camera. It was 1972, or something like that and there had been riots round Ardoyne all night. I mean, the place was destroyed. Ardoyne depot was attacked and the buses were burnt all over the place, and Ardoyne Road was full of buses. But with it being quiet, they decided to send the service up. This was the sort of thing, you know. So these two people were standing and they were the only two that got on the bus and they come up and say to me, "Could you take us to where the trouble is?" "Trouble?" "Trouble. Last night plenty of trouble. Could you take us to it?" I said, "Yeah, sure, get on, I'll take you up". So I took them up to the middle of Ardoyne and I said, "Get off here. You can get all the trouble you want around here." And the two of them just walked away, they just walked away with their wee standard eight cine camera, taking photographs. There was no trouble then, it was all over. But they wanted to go to the trouble. It's amazing, really, people trying to get away from it, and these people wanted to get in to see it. It sounds silly like now, but I don't know. It was a bit of craic, or something.

**RG**   *It never put you off?*

**FM**   No, no, I never missed a day, I never missed a day. I don't know if it was bravado, or just out and out stupidity, but if they said there's trouble, well, I'll go up anyway. So we went up, and if you got that far, well, you were lucky, and if you got back again, you were even luckier. But there were very few ever refused to take the bus out or say, " I'm not going up there." They went but now, I think it's different. I don't know what it is. I think it's different now. But then, everybody seemed to be involved in it, or something.

| RG | *How is it different now?* |
|---|---|
| FM | I don't know. I think it's, maybe it sounds daft, but to me it seems more serious now. It's more sinister. Then it was sort of new and everybody was out. It's hard to explain. |
| RG | *People got used to it or it was part of the . . .* |
| FM | No, no, not getting used to it. It sounds daft. It's more sinister now. Then they would have attacked a bus, or whatever; it didn't seem to be that they were attacking you personally. It was the bus. You were trying to get yourself out of it, obviously. But you were trying to save the bus and get it out of the road. But I think now they're going for you. You know what I mean? They're not interested – you know, just get somebody – that sort of thing. I don't know. I could be wrong, but that's my opinion. But you just didn't think about it then. You just got on the bus and went. |

It's like one day I was driving down the Falls here, and there was always something happening. But this particular day I got this open back. She was just through PSV so she was gleaming, lovely red and cream paint, all well done up. And I had about maybe eight or nine people on the bus, elderly people, funny enough. And the boys were shouting, "Won't be long till you're back!" I said, "Aye, I know. I'll be back in a couple of minutes," and all this, and drove on past. And as I got to the bottom of Whiterock, these boys came out from St James', and one of them pulled a submachine gun out of his coat and he held it up to the front of me and he says, "I'm hijacking this bus. Get out." I said, "Well, hold on a minute. I've got old people on the bus here. You've got to let them get off. You can't take this." So he says, "Right, go on and get them off." So I helped these people off.

But in the meantime I'd stopped the bus and put the hand brake on when I got out. The buses then were what you call a pre-selector. You were in second, but you were in first. You were in third, but you were in second. You were in fourth, but you were in third. It sounds daft, but you put the arm into third while you were still in second. And it didn't change gear till you depressed the pedal, pulled out, and then you were in third, and then you put it into top gear – that sort of thing. But anyway, I got them all off, and like I said, stopped it. I went back down the bus again and there's a big fella sitting up in the driver's seat with, it looked like a shop coat he had on. He was frittering about anyway, and your man with the gun says to me, "Do you know how to start this?' "I says, "Of course I do, I'm the driver. Do you not know?" He says, "No, he doesn't know." I says, "Well, I'm not going to tell you." So he turned around to say something and your big man with the coat says, "You press a button down here." So right enough, your man, he must have seen it start. He pressed the button and she started.

So he took it away up the Whiterock to what used to be Jim's café. There used to be a wee café up the Whiterock there. If you go up the Whiterock from the Falls, there used to be an ice cream shop which is now Sean Graham's. Sorry, it wasn't an ice cream shop, it was an ice cream factory. And then it was a typical wee 1960s café, and it was called Jim's. But anyway, they brought the bus up there and just put it across the road and put a match to it. and I was standing looking up at it blazing. So I was coming walking back up the Falls and they're all standing there. And I says, "I told you it wouldn't be long till I was back, didn't I?" So that was the end of the bus. It was burnt out. So things like that. I took all the old dears down to the next stop.

What actually did happen that day was that there was a bar at the top of the Whiterock, and somebody had been shot from Springmartin from the roof. There was a guy fixing the roof and he'd been shot off the roof, and the bar, well, it went on fire, or something like that. So this is what brought all this about. So they started hijacking the buses on the road to build barricades. They had some weird ways of thinking. Some of these guys wanted to be wee generals and all this nonsense. Everybody wanted to be a leader. You could see that they were sort of moronic. But that's what happened anyway. I was back about ten minutes after I passed the door and they said, "Where's the bus?" "See that smoke up there? That's her burning." So that was it. A whole dose of different things.

| RG | *Was that sort of thing laughed at, then? It wasn't really taken too seriously?* |
|---|---|
| FM | Nobody was hurt, and you can replace an old bus, same as with an old car. If somebody steals your car – my car was broken into the other night and was busted – they broke into it and they done £400 of damage, but that can be replaced. There's nobody been hurt. It's just your property's been damaged. But same with the old bus. That can be replaced. |

They brought back the old buses we call Stogie buses, and they had big shop windows. See the bus there [pointing to a picture of a bus]. There's five, and probably another five or six on the top there – ten, eleven windows on one side. These had only got three windows, and we called them big shop windows, and they tried to get rid of them here. They hijacked the three of them the same day. The boss here, Billy Hamilton, he put these three Stogie buses out on the road at the at the height of the Troubles, with his fingers crossed that they'd take them. We'll get rid of them . . .

So these people walking up the road seen all this heavy smoke and this boss was standing out at the front gate and I was standing beside him. And he says, "There's a big smoke there, Frank." I says, "Aye, what do you think it is?" He says, "It might be them Stogies." He was hoping it was them Stogies. As it turned out, it was the Stogie buses. So there was one, I think, about the Whiterock, one at the Donegall Road and one at Broadway. So they mangled them. Every window – well, all three windows – six big windows, windscreens, you name it. They smashed every thing they could smash. So he thought, "We're rid of them."

And about five minutes after it, he sees these three vehicles up the road with smoke and all coming out of them. And he's staring, looking and he looked at me and he said, "Is that our Stogies?" I says, "It is, Billy." And three RUC men drove them up, and as soon as the RUC man brought the first one to the gate, he said, "We saved your buses, Mr Hamilton." He cursed them up and down. He thought the rioters had done a good job. He wanted rid of them. So that was that. It was brilliant.

But like I say, we had drivers shot dead, and they were innocent guys. They were just out doing a day's work. There was one wee man shot dead, and all he was ever interested in was he backed the horses. That's all he was interested in – horses, a smoke, and he had the odd wee drink. He didn't drink that much, but he was dead keen on backing horses, and the dogs. And he was sitting there, and he had a full revolver put into his head, and for what? A wee Englishman he was. A nicer wee man you never met. And yes, things like that – that was bad. Couldn't be replaced. You can get a driver, yes, but you couldn't replace him. Very cruel, wicked things. But the bus actually that man was shot in, nobody would drive it. They got it in service, but as soon as they got it, they had to change the bus straight away. They'd find something wrong and they said they wouldn't drive it. They didn't want to be in it. So they took that bus away and modified it. They took the top off and made it into an open top bus and made it for tours in Portrush. And the guys up there didn't know any better. They didn't know about the bus. But it was the bus that this man was shot in – his whole head was down the side of the window – all gruesome. Things like that.

And then another man, another driver, he was. These two men rang Ardoyne depot asking about this particular driver. And they said they were friends of his up from the country, and they were going back that evening and they didn't want to miss him because it was a couple of years since they were up, and they might not be back for some time. So the dispatcher at the depot, he didn't know. He took it as gospel that was who they said they were. So he gave them a point on the road where he would be. So it just happened to be the first stop around Woodvale, before you go onto the Shankill there. And these two boys waited. The bus came round, they got on and the way they were going to pay a fare. He opened the box and they shot him dead. So things like that there . . . Terrible, really terrible.

But when it comes to buses getting burnt, you can replace it. But things like that were sad

**RG**  *Did you enjoy the job?*

**FM**  Oh, I enjoyed it, yeah. The money wasn't great, but the craic was good. But like I say, there's a few guys here – like Noel McGarry. He was on the trolleys and obviously he was on the open-backers and then I think he left for a while and then he came back on. Noel could tell you a few things that happened to him as well, and other guys. Things happened to a lot of guys who are not here now. Well, obviously some were hurt, others got awful beatings and badly injured and had to get out, and guys who were horribly burnt. There was a guy who's back at the minute and he was burnt there a couple of years ago on Clifton Street. They got on the bus. They set him on fire. They set his cab on fire with him in it. That's what I'm saying to you about now. It's more brutal or something. It probably was just as much then, but it was the vehicles they wanted. Now it's get him.

# *Fire In The Depot*, Dundas Keating's interview with *Frank Murphy*

After twenty-five years of the most terrible 'Troubles,' bringing death, destruction, economic blight and ruined lives, it is difficult to talk lightly about terrorist acts, especially, after the Oxford Street bus depot atrocity. But sometimes, in the midst of surrounding chaos, the most bizarre of situations arise. Here Frank Murphy, from the Short Strand bus depot, recalls one occasion when that depot was bombed.

**FM** Everyone in the depot got along well and there was great craic. Sometimes, in the mornings, it was a hell of a job getting the busworkers out. Not because they didn't want to go and work, but because the craic was that good in the depot.

Today, the Short Strand bus depot is vastly different, better than it was before it was bombed. The Short Strand depot boasts a splendid and impressive ticket office which cost £15,000 to build after the original office was destroyed in the bombing. Frank recalls one bombing, early on in the 'Troubles,' when there were five bombs placed throughout the depot, "Different places. Up the shop, down the yard and on the buses," recalls Frank. At that time, one of the bombers who had hidden the bombs throughout the depot, announced a ten minute warning until the bombs exploded. The depot was quickly evacuated with the public being moved away to safety, and kept there. But after the explosions many of the

busworkers went back to the depot to offer whatever assistance they could. "They (the bombs) went off. The place was blazing and the burning roofs came off," recounts Frank.

As the bus sheds started blazing on fire, Frank and a colleague decided to get the depot's fire hoses and start combating the blaze until the fire brigade arrived, and after. Frank and his colleague got the fire hoses, big bulky things, and set about dampening down the blaze. "They were very difficult to hold and the place was just black with smoke," said Frank.

Meantime, the army is coming up to the depot and the fire brigade are coming up to the depot. The army entered the depot building dressed in outfits aimed at protecting them, as they looked for more bombs. The soldiers shouted to Frank and his colleague, "You have to get out of here! You shouldn't be in here. There's bombs!" Frank shouted back, "There's no more bombs, there was five but they've all gone off."

Reflecting back on that night Frank recalls that amidst the chaos of burning buildings and buses his colleague had asked Frank if he wanted a cup of tea. As Frank pondered about the bizarreness of having a cup of tea in the middle of a bombed and still burning bus depot, he replied, "Yeah, go on then." The Fire Brigade arrived as Frank's colleague was boiling the kettle to make tea. "You could hardly see in front of yourself because of all the smoke, and we're making tea. I was stood holding a fire hose, whilst drinking a mug of tea, honest to God," reveals Frank.

*The scene of destruction at Short Strand depot following a fire bomb attack on 10 August 1976. The single-decker is believed to be Alexander-bodied Daimler Fleetline No 2795.*

It was only later that Frank and his colleague realised that they had been using a gas canister to boil the water for the tea and that when the fire brigade officers had seen them and asked, "What are you doing?" Frank and his colleague had simply replied, "Making a cup of tea," before asking the firemen, "Would you like a cup?" Stuck in the middle of a bombed and burning building, using fire hoses to try and combat the blaze and drinking tea, made using gas cylinder, with the media and camera crews everywhere.

"I don't know what it was we thought we were doing. It wasn't bravado. Maybe it was stupidity, or maybe we just weren't thinking," contemplates fireman (for a night) Frank.

## Denis O'Neill, Citybus driver

**DO'N**  I started on the buses in April 1983. Before, I was driving lorries for the fruit and vegetable market in Belfast. Before that, I was a driving instructor. I started on the buses – main interest at that time – the money seemed a lot better than what it was on the lorries. And whenever I started here, I was driving the old double-deckers. They went out of service about a year or two after I had started. I always remember in the training school, you were taken round the bus routes. You spent a month in the training school. They took you for two weeks around the test routes, and then you did a lot of theory and practical work getting ready for your test. But immediately after you passed your test, you were back on the bus again. You hadn't a clue where you were going. Everything just went blank out of your mind – what road you had to go up. What you generally did was to ask the first person coming on the bus, "You going to terminus?" "No, mister." Next one, "You going to terminus?" "Yes." "Would you sit there and tell me where I'm going?" "What?" So, you would get there. But after you did the run the first time, it sticks in your mind.

As I say, there were double-deckers. I was mainly on the 17 to Dundonald, and you had some scary incidents in them. Even though the main Troubles were just over, you were still in the wake of them. And at night time there, you were going up the roads – something similar like today. You'd have gone up, and you're watching up every street corner. You loved the summer time because you could actually see where the people were, but in the dark, early nights, you didn't know who was up these street corners.

And I always remember one incident just up at the Short Strand. I was coming along with a double-decker and there were old houses to the left side of the road. This is before all the new roads were there. And these guys were up in this derelict house, and they threw a brick through the top window of the double-decker. How they missed people, I don't know. But the brick went through the side window on the near side of the bus, right through and out the other window. Now, there were only two seats that there was nobody sitting in, on either side of the upper deck. So whether they had very good aim, or else it was just pot luck. It was amazing. Whenever I got the bus stopped further up the road, everybody told me that they were okay.

**RG**  *Did you have any other incidents that were serious?*

**DO'N**  That was serious, but that was the first time. And as I said, it's always stuck in my mind. Other incidents . . . A comical one, in a sense, but there was a serious background to it. It was, must have been 1985 or 1986. It was whenever the loyalists had called for a day of action on a Monday. That Saturday night, I had been up doing a Glencairn. And as I was going up to do Glencairn, these kids came out near St Andrew's church and threw everything at the bus, and I mean everything. Practically the kitchen sink and everything was thrown. You name it, it was thrown. But actually no windows were broken. And I got up past them, and this man on the bus, a reasonably elderly man, says, "Driver, that's desperate, that there going on. That's ridiculous." I said, "I know. And I've got to back down the road again." He says, "Don't you worry. I'll make sure you get down the road." I thought, this man has some drink in him here. He says, "I'll make sure you get down the road okay." I thought, "What's with him? I thought he must be joking. I said, "That's okay"and he stayed and talked to me, and whenever we got up to the terminus, the whole terminus was lined with paramilitaries. Who they were or what, I don't know, but they all had the combat gear and everything.

**RG**  *Where was this?*

| DO'N | Glencairn terminus. And my heart was just beating faster . . . The bus is going to get hijacked here, it's a cert. And as I pulled into the terminus, the men just stood there. And whenever I opened the door, this oldish man got out on the platform, and he started shouted orders. Now, you can just imagine my face. Like, I just looked at him. And then they all stood to attention for him. And one of them came over and he said something to him, and that man got on the bus. He says, "Driver, wait for a couple of minutes. We're going to make a phone call here, and get that road cleared for you." And your mind starts doing overtime, "What do you mean, get the road cleared?" "Are they going to burn the bus, or are they going to do something to me", or whatever. You don't know. So I waited a couple of minutes because I wasn't going to move. If I had made a quick move to get away, God knows what would have happened. So I waited and the man came back out again. And he says, "Right, driver. They're clearing the road for you. And this guy's going to go down with you to the bottom of the road." Here's me, "Right." So I drove round the terminus . . . |
|---|---|
| RG | *The same guy was coming down with you?* |
| DO'N | No, the oldish man got off the bus. But this was one of the ones who was in paramilitary uniform standing in front of me. So he got on the bus and came down with me. And outside St. Andrew's church, there was a club away on the right-hand side of the road as you're coming down Glencairn. Men then came out of this club and they cleared the place, and they chased the kids, and let me get through. And whenever I got down to the bottom of the road, the man jumped off the bus. He says, "Right, driver. Have a safe journey home and a safe night home. The police will see you . . . " Because the police wouldn't go up in the Glencairn. He says, "The police will see you down the rest of the road." My heart was going like a dinger, as the saying goes here in Belfast. My face had turned forty shades of white. When I got into the City Hall area, I said to the inspector, "Don't send anymore buses up to Glencairn." My last run was the last bus – the 11.00pm 33 to Ormeau. Now, amazingly, not one window was broken despite what was thrown at me. And the inspector says to me, "Do you want to do it?" I says, "Aye, might as well." The east end of the city's quiet. So I took the last 33 up, thinking – ah well, I can relax a wee bit now. And didn't I go up the Cregagh Road, as you never get any bother there. And didn't somebody throw a beer bottle right into the front windscreen of the bus. So after surviving all that, I go up a quiet road and I get the window put in. But that was amazing, that night. |
| RG | *Was that just happening that one night at Glencairn?* |
| DO'N | Just the one night. Well, the following Monday was the day of action, and I think a lot of things all stopped. I think the whole of the North was actually brought to a halt that particular day. But as I say, they were all the young ones who had psyched themselves up beforehand. |
| RG | *It's incredible. Did you ever wonder why or who that person was?* |
| DO'N | No, but there was one thing he told me, and I'm surprised it's coming from the loyalist part of it. This oldish man had said to me, "Driver, that's desperate." He said to me, "Driver, no matter where you go, whether it be on the Falls, or the Shankill, and if anybody asks you for money, they're only wee hoodlums. Don't give it to them." He said, "See the paramilitary organisations, whether it be on the Falls or the Shankill," he said, "they're not interested in the money you carry. It's big money they're after, not your money. So if anybody ever asks you for money, you know they're only hoodlums." So that always stuck in my mind. And it must have been a lot of months after that, I was doing a duty on the Sunday on the Springfield Road. They had the old, what we call the Sellafield buses on that route. I had gone up the Springfield Road through Turf Lodge. The terminus was outside St Teresa's church on the Glen Road,so I stopped there and checked the bus. There was absolutely nothing left on the bus.

So I'm driving back down the same way again, and went in through Turf Lodge, and these young people got on at a social club in the area. They had tickets, punched tickets etc. In those days, they punched their own tickets. If you argued with them, you were going to get a hiding. But they just punched their own tickets, and got on. As we went up the Monagh Road, one of them came up, stuck something into my side, and threw the mirror up so I couldn't see his face. And I just caught a glimpse of one standing at the back of the bus, where the emergency door was. And he says to me, "Driver, don't even look at me. Now, we want you to take this bus to Springfield Road barracks. There's a bomb on this bus, and you're going to drive it to Springfield Road barracks, and do everything that we say." I says, "Right." He says, "Look, take it very easy over these roads" because at that time, a lot of vehicles had been burned out before and the surface of the road was bad. |

154

So as I was crawling the bus over the uneven road, I was thinking, "Where did they bring the bomb on?" because I had searched the bus. They didn't bring a bag on, not that I had seen. So this was all going through my mind. And it came back in my mind again what your man had said to me at Glencairn. If they ask you for money, they are hoodlums. But these guys hadn't asked for money. Here's me thinking, is this a genuine thing? And again, your mind starts playing tricks on you. This was going through my mind. Why is he wanting me to go to Springfield barracks whenever you had the Henry Taggart Barracks there at the time and you had another police station about Cupar Street? They had another one at Springfield Avenue, and then you had the Springfield barracks. Why am I passing these other ones to go to another? And the mind's running riot trying to think of this here. And I turned my head slightly, and your man pushed it back. He said, "I told you not to look." So we came up towards the Henry Taggart, and he says, "Right, driver, pull in here and stop. Remember what to do. Get the people off. Drive this bus to Springfield Road barracks, and you'll have plenty of time before the bomb goes off to do it." And the next thing he says, "And give us your money!" See once he said money, here's me, off like a rocket. And the two of them bolted off the bus and they ran away up the fields laughing their heads off. Then I looked around the bus and I said, "Those lads are only after telling me there's supposed to be a bomb on this bus. There's not. There's nothing here. But I'm going to take you all into the town." And this wee woman says, "Driver, they done this to me last week. They had a wee girl with them. And that's why I got this earlier bus, in case they would do it again."

Then the other incident was on a football special. It was a final was being played down at Seaview, that's Crusaders ground, and it was between Glentoran and Portadown. And a lot of buses had taken the Glentoran supporters, and I was the last bus in the queue. And after the match had finished, the supporters got on, and there was a couple of them giving abuse, shouting at the police and the other supporters. And the Portadown ones came out to try and get them. But the riot police were there, and they'd pulled two of the supporters off the bus. Of course, the rest of the ones on the bus said, "You've got the wrong ones, you've got the wrong ones." The ones who had organised the bus wouldn't let me move. The police were trying to get me to move, but we're staying still till we get these ones back. So the police finally let them back on again and as we were about to move off – the police had been watching the bus – the two guys who had caused the trouble started up again. The police stormed onto the bus, and it was the riot police. Now, they had just the batons. They didn't carry any guns. It was just the batons. And the back door of the bus– the emergency door – had opened. And the Portadown supporters were trying to get at these ones. So like a mini riot, in a sense, was starting at the back of the bus.

And while this is going on, this policeman – he must have been only out of training school – he came walking onto the bus, and he had a submachine gun. And as he started to walk down the bus with a submachine gun (SMG), towards the back, this other police officer come on and shouts at him, "See you with the SMG, will you get off the bus! You with the SMG, will you get off the bus!" And the riot squad looked around, and they said, "Get him off the bus!" Somebody said, "There's no catch on it." And everybody started diving to the floor. And even the miniature riot at the back of the bus stopped because everybody just dived. If anybody had bumped into your man, the machine gun would have went off. I had a side window. I couldn't get out the door, because the police were blocking the door and I just tried to get out that window, and the police were ready to grab me at the other end. But they finally got the policeman off, and quickly enough they put him into a Jeep and got the Jeep away as quick as anything, so nobody could actually see his number. The next thing was the riot squad got off. They took the two fellas with them and they said, "Get this bus away." There were some hairy moments. I used to have brown hair when I started this job, believe it or not.

RG     *You're lucky you still have hair! Did you find the police supportive over the years, helping you on the routes?*

DO'N   Yes, I generally did. I cannot complain about them. The police have genuinely stuck their necks out. And I always remember an incident with a policeman. One time there was a desperate situation. I said to him, "Well, you get danger money, and you get there whenever a riot has already started, whenever you are called into action." He says, "Yeah." Here's me, "Whenever you first go to that riot, what's the first thing you see?" He says, "There's a bus burning." Here's me, "The bus drivers get it first." The police and the army come next. It's always the bus drivers are on the front line. And overall, we might get the odd letter of support, but overall, there's no real back-up.

RG     *Do you feel the company provided support?*

| DO'N | Well, they would go round and say, we thank you for keeping things going, and everything else. But, as I say, we're there in the thick of it, and a lot of people have actually been pensioned out because of incidents. You hear different stories about incidents. A bus has been hijacked, and the hijackers tell the driver could he get off the bus. As the driver's walking down the road away from it, the hijackers come running down, "Here driver, would you come up? We can't drive that bus. Would you drive it and put it across the road for us?" You know, to block the roads. But any time a riot's on, it's always the buses. They go for a bus first, and that's before the police, army, or anything is called in. So up on the front line it's the bus drivers. |
|---|---|
| RG | *Did it never put you off, at all?* |
| DO'N | Not really. It would put a lot of people off and if you were to sit down and think hard about it, I suppose it would. But again, there's getting the buzz, getting the adrenaline pumping. You just have to switch off, and just thank God that you're alive at the end of it, just be thankful for small mercies. |
| RG | *Have you found the job has changed, as the Troubles have abated a bit?* |
| DO'N | It has. It has quietened down a whole lot. You can actually foretell now what months there will be trouble. Lately, the incidents that have happening in North Belfast. Thankfully, I haven't been on those roads, so I can't give any details or make any comments about them. But you do overhear other drivers on the radio saying, "Oh, they're stoning here. They're stoning there, and they're trying to take this, that and the other thing." But you can put the kettle on for July, August – June, July, and August were the main ones. And then the funniest thing is – you may notice it – everybody is at one another's throats during those months. And then whenever it comes to Christmas, you'll find them all in the town, you'll find them all in the bars, you'll find them all out having their Christmas dinner, probably two or three parties booked from all sectors of the community in the one place and they'll all have a good time at Christmas. And then all of a sudden, once the New Year passes, you come up to Easter, the start of the marching season again. And I noticed lately that both sides, their marches are starting earlier, because one is trying to outdo the other, to see who can get the first march in first. I don't know if you've noticed that, or not? |
| RG | *That marches are getting earlier? Yeah.* |
| DO'N | One side is trying to say, we'll get our one in first – marches, that is. We'll get this one. But December, Christmas time. . . as I say, they're at one another's throats probably in summer, but they're sitting there having their drink, having their Christmas dinner. You can go into a hotel, and you can have a crowd from some workplace, say, on the Shankill, some workplace on the Falls. They'll probably pick some place in the city centre, and they're all in having their Christmas dinner, and they're having parties and everybody meets everybody. |
| RG | *They need Christmas in July.* |
| DO'N | Christmas all year round, if they can afford it. |

## John Ferguson, BCT driver

| RG | *If you want to begin by telling me how you got into the Belfast Corporation – when, and what capacity you were working here.* |
|---|---|
| JF | It was in 1968; I came out of the forces in 1967. I worked in Michelin – took a job there, but couldn't stand being closed up. So I left the Michelin and went to Mackie's, and was doing overhead cranes there. I had applied to the buses in the meantime. I got word to go, so I just took the opportunity and went, and have been here ever since. |
| RG | *Do you remember anything from the crew days? Did you enjoy that?* |
| JF | Oh, aye, I enjoyed the crew days. The old Gasworks–Waterworks route. I drove on that route. Well, there wouldn't be a lot of stories on that route because you hadn't time. It was just a racetrack in and out. In those days it was all conductors anyway. |

| | |
|---|---|
| **RG** | *Did you ever have any bad experiences over the years?* |
| **JF** | Oh aye, back in the early days. I think I lost about nine buses during the Troubles. |
| **RG** | *Bricks coming in, or burnt?* |
| **JF** | Oh no, taken off you – hijacks and that. Guns put to your head and things like that. They talk about Troubles nowadays on the buses but you go back to the like of the 1970s . . . that was real trouble. |
| **RG** | *Did it never put you off, or make you afraid, or not want to come to work, or anything like that?* |
| **JF** | No, never put me off. And I lost a good friend called Harry Bradshaw. He was actually shot at the wheel, and that particular day that he was shot, I was behind him. |
| **RG** | *Right. Did you see what happened?* |
| **JF** | No, I didn't see what happened – just the ambulance. The like of the hijackings . . . I remember going to Portrush on a special private, and say around 12:30 coming back, I got to the depot gates at the Strand, and the bus was taken off me there. Now, the boys that took it off me – they didn't throw me around or anything like that. Actually, they asked me would I reverse it to block the street. So, I reversed it into this wee street anyway, and that was it. Then it was getting home because they were shooting over the top of the bridge – things like that. It was really rough in those early days of the Troubles. The job was really bad in those days. |
| **RG** | *Did you feel that the company could have done anything for drivers?* |
| **JF** | No, I don't think the company could have done anything more. Now, they've tried everything, to be quite honest. They tried putting grills over the windscreen. You couldn't see then. Your eyes sort of went funny with the old wire grills that the army boys used. That wasn't a success. They tried everything. They tried unbreakable glass in the windscreen and all that. The company, in those days too, I suppose, they did their best. They just kept them going as best they could. They did a good job, to be quite honest. I can't remember the services being at a standstill for any length of time, you know? A few roads – they would have had to take them off – things like that. Normally the company would always try to keep them going no matter what. |
| **RG** | *Did you feel drivers were appreciated for keeping the service going, either by the company or by the public?* |
| **JF** | Well, you can put things like that down on paper, can't you? You can actually say, you know, we appreciate what you've done for us. But as far as, the driver himself getting to know about things like that, no. You were actually paid to do the job anyway. There wasn't really a lot you could do. |

## Kate McMahon, Citybus driver

| | |
|---|---|
| **RG** | *So roughly when did you start?* |
| **KMcM** | I think it was 1978. You lose track of time, you know. |
| **RG** | *And was there like a big thing going to get women onto the buses at that time?* |
| **KMcM** | I just saw it advertised in a shop in Wellington Place that used to advertise jobs and it just said, "Bus Drivers – male or female," and I thought I'd go for it because I fitted into the age bracket. The driving experience put me off because I'd only been driving a year and a half. I was a late starter, but I went down anyway and they said it was no problem, that I'd be getting training and everything and by the time I had finished all the training I'd have the two years up. I didn't quite have the two years but I got through it anyway after doing their driving test and then the official driving test at Boucher Road. There was a bit of a hullabaloo about it you know – picture in the paper and all that. I don't know where they got their information from. |
| **RG** | *Some of these late shifts must have been a bit scary, especially during the Troubles.* |
| **KMcM** | Oh yeah, I remember being out at Springmartin; it wasn't too long before I was put off the buses with |

the arthritis. I was sitting there – it wasn't really winter time – it must have been coming into autumn. And I was sitting there – it wasn't time to go – and these two guys came along, nice looking guy, one of them, he had a long trench coat on. So I just opened the door and turned my head a fraction and when I looked – I didn't know where the other fellow had gone, the one with the long trench coat – so the fellow paid his fare and got on. I was sitting there listening to the tape playing music and I saw the other chap coming again. But this time he had a jerry can. It never connected, just shows you how stupid you can be, it never connected. And as soon as he put his foot on the platform he said, "Right! Get off!" And with the other one who had got on and actually paid his fare, they were pouring the petrol from one length to the other – and while they were doing that I hardly had time to gather everything but I managed to get my coat and the money and jumped off the bus. And I ran over to where the footpath was and stood there. I don't know where they went because I was no sooner off that bus when the whole thing went up, the windows went out like bullets and the black smoke was unbelievable. They really burned that bus out; the only thing left was the chassis. And then these people came along and they thought the driver was trapped in the bus – they didn't know I was the driver – and they were trying to get the door open and one of them actually burned his hand. I was shouting, "I'm over here," but they couldn't hear me with all the noise. A woman ran over and said, "It's a lady bus driver and she's alright." She said, "Come on in and have a cup of tea." But much as I would have liked to I said, "No, they're bound to have got word of it and probably the inspectors will be up shortly." But as luck would have it there was one of the guys who worked on the buses that lived there and a friend of his was just leaving so they gave me a lift down to Tennant Street barracks so I didn't get home till half past two in the morning, sitting waiting for the detectives, giving my statement and everything.

RG      *Yes the bus drivers are very vulnerable.*

KMcM    Yes, the broken windows, some of the drivers assaulted, some of them were badly beaten up and all that. I was lucky, I only had it happen once. Some guy – he was a flasher – he lived in one of these places off the Antrim Road. Everybody knew him, but I didn't and he got on my bus and that was when they used to have the machine at the drivers end, you know you put your ticket in whereas the driver takes it off you now. It was a bit of a playing card and it was black as black and I said, "I'm sorry but you can't use that." Should have said nothing. He started giving me vile abuse and then he took a swing at me and I went back like that and banged my head off the side window and he jumped off the bus. There was a man who came down to see if I was alright. I was more frightened than anything. It wasn't till I got back and I got a journey off – you know you can get relieved after a thing like that, someone else would do your next run for you. I was describing him and a couple of fellows from one of the other depots – Ardoyne – they knew him because a lot of the Ardoyne men did the Antrim Road services. They knew him. They said, "He's a flasher, Kate. He's not quite all there and he lives in one of those homes off the Antrim Road." That was really the only time I think. Now verbally abused, yes, you got that all the time you know, more from the women than the men for some reason.

## Willie Elliman, *Citybus driver*

RG      *If you just want to start by saying how you got into the Belfast Corporation.*

WE      Well, I came here in May 1967 and I started off as a conductor for a year. Then I decided I wanted to go to driving. So I went to driving for another year with a conductor. Then they introduced a one-man bus, so I went to it. And you're talking about 31 years on a one-man bus, and it's been great. I've enjoyed every minute of it.

It actually started off as the Belfast Corporation. The City Hall ran us. Then, Translink took over, and they were more or less a semi-private company. They've been good to us at times. I enjoyed being with the Corporation. I thought that being with the City Hall the people were running us. I thought that was better with the ratepayers of Belfast running our bus service. I thought we were closer to the people than we are now.

RG      *When did it get taken over, do you know?*

**WE**

It was in the mid 1970s, anyhow. Then the Troubles started. And they started burning our depots, the buses in the depots. We had to bring our buses down to the Airport Road, where the City Airport is. And all buses stopped at nine o'clock because they were rioting all over Belfast, all over Northern Ireland. And the accommodation bus could only leave us after the last journey, nine o'clock, to Short Strand junction there, and we all had to make our own way home. I had to walk from there across the Queen's Bridge, through the city centre, to where I lived on the Oldpark. And when I was walking up one night in the dark, I looked across over the Crumlin Road, and I could see the Falls Road burning. They were burning all the factories on the Falls Road, and that went on for a good while.

There was one night when the buses were coming off at nine o'clock. I just can't remember what journey I was doing – from Dundonald Hospital or Stormont Parliament Buildings. I came down the Newtownards Road and they'd just begun to riot down at the chapel, St Matthew's chapel. And if I had known that, I could have gone down the Albert Bridge, but by the time you were down into the Newtownards Road, there was nowhere to go to the depot. So, just a bit down on the Newtownards Road, actually facing Dee Street, there were a few streets there in the dark. And I was passing the first or the second one, this soldier came out with a gun across his head – you know, holding it up with two hands. And he'd still got – they'd still got the old World War Two helmets. All the British had them. They've new ones now; somebody told me they're made in Germany. I don't know.

But I stopped the bus and he came round to me and I said, "What's wrong with you, fella?" He said, "Ah, our pig left us stranded here." Pig, that's short for the personnel carrier. I said, "What do you mean 'us'?" He said, "I have three of my mates down there in the dark in this wee street and we're panicking. We don't know what we'll do." I said, "Well, fella, you know there's trouble down here?" I said, "Aye, that's the way I'm going." He said, "You're joking." I said, "I can't do nothing here because the streets are all lined with people. I couldn't reverse the bus or nothing." I said, "Well, get them on anyway." So there's four of them, not one.

So these other three came with a big long box with ropes at each end, full of bullets. And they threw the box of bullets down the bus, and they threw their guns down and the four of them lay flat. And they said to me, "Right, wee man, go to your depot. Where is it?" I said, "It's away down there and round into the Short Strand. Just down the bottom." He said, "Well, do your best for us." So that was the night before they started bringing the guns out, and people were dying on the railings of that chapel both sides. This night there were stones and whatever. But these are flying everywhere over my bus. So I went into the Short Strand depot with the four fellas. And we got out; my hand must have been red for an hour after, with them shaking my hand.

And I always think to myself, I wonder if them four men, wherever they are now, ever think of being on my bus and me saving them. Because, I'm not bumming about that, I did save them four fellas. I don't care. People say to me, "Sure." Sure, nothing. I mean, the way things were then, this was all just happening to people in Belfast, and we didn't know what was going to happen. Nobody knew. They thought it was only going to last months or weeks. What did it last? Thirty years.

Now, could I say another thing about a man predicting something? Now, I spoke about the thirty years there. I was on the Castlereagh Road one night coming down in a double-decker bus, and it was raining. And this man in his 60s, which I am now, this big man in his 60s got on. He got his fare off me. And the Troubles might have been on just below a year, nine months. I remarked to myself what he said to me. He says, "Can I talk to you?" I said, "Go ahead. No problem. There's nobody on the bus. It's just you and me." Because, as I said it was a bad night and there was nobody about and with the Troubles, nobody went into the town, you know. He says, "Look, it's not much, but son, you mark my words, these Troubles are just on a while but see by the time they're over, which is going to be years and years and years, this trouble will have touched everyone in Northern Ireland and maybe in England before this is over, because there'll be a lot of causalities here. They mightn't be just your people but you'll have known them and it'll have touched everyone." And I thought that man wasn't right, but now I know he was. Now how did he know that? Because this had never happened to us before. This whole generation of ours and it's lasted thirty years now. How did he know that? When I had to go into the police station for broken windows, I used to tell the old cops that story. And they're all looking at me with that man with that happening to him, the way he set that out. How do I know? Maybe he was a Nostradamus, I don't know.

| RG | *You never felt put off by what was going on?* |
|---|---|
| WE | No. There was another time I left the City Hall and came onto Chichester Street, doing the 6:35pm to Cregagh. And I think I saved another wee woman's life that night, because when I got onto the Woodstock Road, a man got on and took the bus off me. And I said, "Can I have my money?" The money was in my machine, because it was a wee grey machine you put your tickets in. It wasn't the machine they have now – you know, this one is computerised – the ordinary one. He said, "We don't want your money or your machine. We want the bus." So this wee woman was coming on. She was ready to have a heart attack. I said, "Love, you take that machine off for me. The wee grey machine. Would you take that machine off for me?" I said, "And just stand against the wall, because they want me to put this bus across the road because they're going to burn it." Now the whole time, that woman cradled that machine in her breast like a child. Now, when I was putting that bus across the road, there was a side door on the bus. They had already the bus burning while I was driving it. I could feel the heat in the back of my neck. So I put the bus right across the road and blocked the road. And I jumped out of the bus and the flames were just like the flames of what's happening in America now. I was just watching that this lot of weeks – seen that happening. I was lucky. I'm not saying I was lucky to get out of the bus because I had plenty of time. I'm not saying that. But I looked back, and there's the back of the bus burning. Because they probably got on and threw what they had in the side window – the side door down the right hand, down the back of the bus, but eventually it came up. Fire needs oxygen, it needs air to breathe. And it was coming up, you get more. That's the way fire is, it just feeds itself, just like them poor people in New York. |
| RG | *Did you not ever feel scared over the years or not wanted to go to work?* |
| WE | Now, you're saying that about being scared – no. You see once that fella said to me, "We don't want your money. We don't want your machine or anything to do with you. We want your bus." That settled me. I just walked off that bus as if I was walking off to go home as in any other duty. I felt nothing. |
| RG | *Over the years, did you ever not want to go to work?* |
| WE | No. There was another time, on the Antrim Road, I was going up and the bus was packed going up to Fortwilliam. I see this wee lad, a first year, with his big heavy school bag, his hockey stick back swinging in the middle of the road. Now, the wee lad was only out of primary into secondary. He went to BRA school at the bottom of the Cliftonville Road. He was a Protestant, right – I have to say that. And these guys from the school up the road, they were the Catholics. So, he's trying to fight them off. So I put the handbrake on and I got out and I grabbed the wee lad and I shouted at them. I said, "You want to try that with me? Go on and try it with me." The two of them just shook their heads and walked down the road. So I got the wee lad on the bus, and I said to him – it was packed, people were standing up – "Why are you walking up past that school?" He said, "Mister, I've no money for the bus." I said, "Well, come you on this bus with me," I said. And I looked down the bus and I said to people, with two hands up in the air, "If anyone on this bus says that this lad hasn't to get on this bus, I'll pay his fare." And a man down the bus said, "Let any 'b' say anything to you. I watched you. You were great." You see up in Glengormley everybody getting off, nodding to me, thanking me for that wee lad. Maybe again I saved that wee lad's life. I don't know. I saved him maybe getting into hospital – his mummy having to come to hospital to see the wee lad. Again, I hope that wee lad remembers me – wee nipper, first year BRA.

One time, we called it Robb's in High Street – it's where Dixon's is now and HMV, the record place. It used to be called Robb's. Two stories if you can get it on here – two stories. I was sitting at Robb's and I was ready to go. I decided just to wait a minute because I hadn't many on the bus. And it was the time cars and everything could have went through Cornmarket. Now it's a pedestrian thing in Cornmarket. See if I had have left three seconds earlier, the front of Woolworth's would have been on top of my bus. The bombers blew out the front of Woolworth's. I seen it – on my mother's and father's graves, I seen the whole front of Woolworth's. And I always say to myself, Willie, if you hadn't waited that three or so minutes, or seconds, or whatever it was – I can't remember, it was so long ago – that building would have been on top of us. There were four, five people on the bus, just. And the cop ran up to me and he said, "Right, driver, into Cornmarket." I went in there, I went in there, right round to Chichester Street, Victoria Street and away up the Antrim Road. |

# THE MEMORIAL PANEL AT LAGANSIDE BUS CENTRE

*The ceramic memorial panel at Laganside Bus Centre. The names of the men who died are shown on the buses enclosing the lower section of the design.*

Will Hughes

### Introduction

This ceramic panel is a memorial to the twelve staff of the Belfast Corporation, Ulsterbus and Citybus who were killed in the course of their duty during the Troubles. The piece was designed and crafted by Diane McCormick and formally unveiled by Neville Whiteside (former Chairperson of Citybus, Ulsterbus and Northern Ireland Railways) on 1 May 1996.

This panel is the only existing public artwork that commemorates these men, although a double-decker bus was presented to the Ulster Folk and Transport Museum as a memorial and is on display in the transport gallery at Cultra.

The twelve men listed below were killed one way or another, in the course of their duty. The first victim was killed to prevent him from giving evidence in a trial relating to the hijacking and destruction of his bus. Four were killed in the bomb attack on Oxford Street bus station on 'Bloody Friday'. One man was killed in crossfire between paramilitaries and the army. An inspector was singled out and killed because he was a member of a paramilitary group. Five others were killed while driving their buses.

The names of the busmen, and the dates they lost their lives, are listed in the table below:

| | | |
|---|---|---|
| Sydney Agnew | 18 January 1972 | Belfast Corporation Transport |
| Thomas Callaghan | 16 February 1972 | Ulsterbus |
| Robert Gibson | 21 July 1972 | Ulsterbus |
| William Crothers | 21 July 1972 | Ulsterbus |
| William Irvine | 21 July 1972 | Ulsterbus |
| Thomas Killops | 21 July 1972 | Ulsterbus |
| Patrick Crossan | 2 March 1973 | Belfast Corporation Transport |
| Samuel Rush* | 10 June 1973 | Ulsterbus |
| Alexander Millar | 2 May 1975 | Citybus |
| David McDowell | 25 January 1976 | Ulsterbus |
| Harold Bradshaw | 10 May 1977 | Citybus |
| James Gibson | 2 December 1982 | Ulsterbus |

Below is a summary of the events surrounding the deaths of each of these men.

**Sydney Agnew**

Sydney Agnew, a 40-year-old married man with three children and a Protestant, was a bus driver with the Belfast Corporation Transport Department. On the evening of the 18 January 1972 he was at home with family when two youths appeared at his front door. They asked his six-year-old son who answered the door if his father was a bus driver. At this point Mr Agnew came to the door whereupon one of the youths produced a gun. Mr Agnew pushed his son and his 10-year-old daughter into the living room but he was shot several times by one of the youths. His 82-year-old mother-in-law was also slightly wounded in the attack.

It is believed that the reason for his murder was that as principal witness he was due to give evidence the following day against three men from the Short Strand district who were charged with having ordered him off his bus at gunpoint before setting it on fire.

Mr Agnew's killing was given as a reason for abolishing the use of juries in Troubles-related trials and the establishment of the so-called 'Diplock courts' where cases were heard by a single judge.

No organisation ever claimed responsibility for Sydney Agnew's killing, but given the circumstances, it is believed that republicans were behind the attack.

**Thomas Callaghan**

Thomas Callaghan, a 47-year old married man and a Catholic from Limavady, was a private in the UDR. On the 16 February 1972 he was driving his bus in the Creggan in Derry when he was dragged from his bus by members of the IRA and bundled into a car. Three hours later his body was found dumped by the side of the road. He had been hooded, gagged and shot in the back of the head.

Ulsterbus services in Derry were suspended for some time after Mr Callaghan's killing and his death was widely condemned, amongst others, by nationalist politicians and Catholic religious spokesmen.

Thomas Callaghan was the second Catholic member of the UDR to be killed by the IRA.

**Robert Gibson, William Crothers, William Irvine, Thomas Killops**

These four men, all Ulsterbus employees, were killed in the bomb attack on Oxford Street bus station on 'Bloody Friday' 21 July 1972. A car bomb, one of 20 bombs detonated within an hour in Belfast, exploded at the busy Oxford Street bus station and killed the four Ulsterbus employees and two soldiers.

Robert Gibson was a 45-year-old Protestant married man with five children from Crossgar in Co Down. He was a bus driver and a part-time police reservist with the RUC. A bus draped in black cloth carried Ulsterbus employees to Crossgar for his funeral where the mourners included the former Prime Minister of Northern Ireland, Brian Faulkner.

William Crothers was a 15-year-old single man and a Protestant from the Newtownards Road in Belfast. He had left school only three weeks earlier to take up a job as a parcels boy with Ulsterbus.

William Irvine was an 18-year-old single man and a Protestant from East Belfast. He worked as a clerk in the parcels office.

Thomas Killops was a 39-year-old married man and a Protestant from Newtownbreda on the outskirts of Belfast. He also worked in the parcels office as a clerk.

### Patrick Crossan

Patrick Crossan was a 30-year-old married man with two children, a Catholic from Ardoyne in Belfast. He was shot on 2 March 1973 by the UVF on the Woodvale Road when he stopped his Corporation bus to let passengers board. He was talking to a colleague when shot, the other driver receiving minor wounds.

Mr Crossan was the third Catholic to be shot during the previous 24 hours and his death was followed by a three-day strike of busmen in Belfast. About 2000 colleagues attended Mr Crossan's funeral and eight of them, four Catholics and four Protestants, formed a guard of honour at his funeral.

### Samuel Rush

Samuel Rush was a 50-year-old Protestant from South Belfast and a driver with Ulsterbus. On the night of the 10 June 1973, his bus was caught in crossfire between loyalist paramilitaries and the army on the Albertbridge Road in Belfast. He was hit in the head and his bus, out of control, crashed into a military armoured car. There were about a dozen passengers on the bus and they were badly shocked.

A number of years later a man from East Belfast was arrested in England and charged with Mr Rush's murder.

### Alexander Millar

Alexander Millar was a 54-year-old married man with four children, a Protestant and a Citybus inspector. He was shot in Ardoyne bus depot on the afternoon of May 2 1975. Two men entered the depot and asked the security man where they could find Mr Millar. They confronted him in an office and then shot him three times. He died later in hospital of his injuries. Mr Millar was described as a 'captain' in the UDA in newspaper death notices.

### David McDowell

David McDowell was a 26-year-old married man and a Protestant from Co Armagh. An Ulsterbus driver and member of the UDR, he was shot dead by accident on 25 January 1976 at an army observation post at Middletown near the Armagh/Monaghan border. Mr McDowell had stopped his bus at the army post and was talking to soldiers, when a young soldier accidentally discharged his gun, killing the busman.

Mr McDowell had survived an IRA ambush three years previously as well as an earlier attack on a bus he was driving.

### Harold Bradshaw

Harry Bradshaw was a 46-year-old married man with five children, a Protestant and a driver with Citybus. On 10 May 1977, Mr Bradshaw was shot by the UDA on the Crumlin Road when he had stopped his bus to pick up passengers. He was killed during the loyalist strike. When this strike failed to attract sufficient support, the UDA turned to violence and intimidation. Harry Bradshaw was one of its victims because he had refused to stop working.

All bus services were stopped for three days after Harry Bradshaw's killing. In 1979 a member of the UDA was convicted of his murder.

### James Gibson

James Gibson was a 50-year-old widower with seven children, a Protestant and Ulsterbus driver from Dungannon, Co Tyrone. On 2 December 1982, Mr Gibson, a former member of the UDR, was shot by the IRA at Annaghmore Crossroads, Co Tyrone, as he stopped to let schoolchildren off his bus. Two masked men approached the bus as it came to a stop. One climbed aboard and opened fire. However, because the bus had not completely stopped, it rolled on and ended up in a ditch. The hysterical children passengers made their escape through the emergency door.

In 1984, a member of the IRA was imprisoned for his involvement in the murder.

In addition to the men commemorated in the panel, two other Ulsterbus employees lost their lives, though not during the course of their duties. Also, three CIÉ employees were killed in the course of their duties. Brief accounts of these deaths are set out overleaf:

### Robert Jameson

Robert Jameson was a 22-year old, Protestant, single man who worked as a fitter in the Ulsterbus depot in Omagh, Co Tyrone. He was also a part-time member of the UDR. He was shot by the IRA shortly after he had stepped off a bus near his home near Trillick at 5.45pm on 17 January 1974. He was returning home from work and the IRA unit that shot him seemed to have been aware of his routine where he was collected from that bus stop each evening by a relative who took him the rest of the way home. The evening of his death, his mother was collecting him and she found him dying from his wounds at the bus stop.

### Stanley Arthurs

Stanley Arthurs was a 45-year old, Protestant, married man who worked in Dungannon Ulsterbus depot. He was fatally wounded in an IRA attack which took place on 29 April 1976. He died of his wounds on 3 May. The IRA attack was aimed at Mr Arthurs' brother-in-law, Edward Stewart, who was a member of the UDR. Gunmen knocked on the door saying that cattle had got loose. When the two men went outside, the IRA shot them, killing Mr Stewart right away. Bus services in the Dungannon area were suspended as a mark of respect during his funeral.

### George Bradshaw and Thomas Duffy

George Bradshaw was a married man and a bus driver with CIÉ. Thomas Duffy was also a married man and worked for CIÉ as a bus conductor. They were killed when the UVF exploded a large bomb in Dublin city centre on the 1 December 1972. The device exploded at 8.19pm in Sackville Place, off O'Connell Street and was the second bomb to explode that night. The two bombs injured 127 people. On the day of the bombing, George Bradshaw was on duty only because he had swapped duties with a colleague. The President and Taoiseach were represented at both funerals, which were attended by hundreds of CIÉ employees. Flags flew at half mast on all CIÉ premises.

### Thomas Douglas

Thomas Douglas was a 25-year old single man, originally from Stirling, Scotland who worked for CIÉ as a bus driver. He was killed when a no-warning bomb, thought to have been planted by the UVF, exploded in Sackville Place in Dublin city centre on a busy Saturday afternoon. More than a dozen other people were injured in the attack. Thomas Douglas's bus had just reached its terminus and he had got off to buy a paper when he was caught up in the blast. He died on the way to hospital.

# AND IN CONCLUSION, THE LEGACY . . .

Northern Ireland's travelling public owes a great debt of gratitude to the hundreds of men and women who crewed the buses over the thirty years of the Troubles; twelve of their number were murdered, and scores more injured, physically and mentally. Busworkers were shot at, petrol-bombed, stoned, robbed and faced personal attacks from thugs with weapons such as guns, knives, hatchets, iron bars and catapults firing ball bearings. More than 1500 buses were completely destroyed during the period, hundreds more damaged and virtually every depot that Ulsterbus and BCT/Citybus owned was damaged, sometimes more than once, and in several cases suffered complete destruction. Following on from the devastation that was a feature of the darkest days of the Troubles, in recent years bus drivers have had to face a growth in thuggery and relentless low level violence targeted at them; this, too, has taken its toll on health. So, even though the worst years of the Troubles are, we hope, behind us, bus drivers are still facing violence on an almost daily basis, violence which in many ways is now more common than during the Troubles-hit 1970s.

It is therefore now worth recalling the words of a man who, along with Werner Heubeck, was one of the key players during those difficult years, former TGWU officer, Eugene O'Callaghan:

> It's difficult to find the words to praise these men and women. We should be eternally grateful to them, yet, sadly, their magnificent contribution in maintaining a service for the public has largely been ignored.

The author and everyone at Colourpoint Books hope that this volume has gone some way towards addressing Eugene's concern.

# THE TOLL OF DESTRUCTION

## Belfast Corporation Transport Department

| Date | Depot | Fleet No | Type | Location | Notes |
|---|---|---|---|---|---|
| 01/10/64 | F | 174 | Guy BTX trolleybus | Divis Street | |
| | | | | *Total number of vehicles lost in this year* **1** | |
| 15/08/69 | AD | 410 | Daimler CVG6 | Location unknown | |
| 15/08/69 | AD | 517 | Daimler CWA6 | Location unknown | |
| 15/08/69 | AD | 518 | Daimler CWA6 | Herbert Street, Ardoyne | |
| 15/08/69 | SS | 621 | Daimler Fleetline DD | Location unknown | |
| 15/08/69 | F | 662 | Daimler Fleetline DD | Location unknown | |
| 15/08/69 | F | 668 | Daimler Fleetline DD | Location unknown | |
| | | | | *Total number of vehicles lost in this year* **6** | |
| 28/06/70 | F | 359 | Daimler CVG6 | Milltown Cemetery, Falls Road | |
| 28/06/70 | F | 417 | Daimler CVG6 | Whiterock Rd/Springfield Rd jctn | |
| 28/06/70 | AD | 506 | Daimler CWA6 | Ardoyne | |
| 28/06/70 | AD | 671 | Daimler Fleetline DD | Whiterock Road | |
| 28/06/70 | AD | 717 | Daimler Fleetline DD | Hooker Street, Ardoyne | |
| 30/06/70 | F | 657 | Daimler Fleetline DD | Whiterock Rd/Springfield Rd jctn | |
| 03/07/70 | MP | 342 | Guy Arab III | Albert Street/Cullingtree Road | |
| 03/07/70 | F | 368 | Daimler CVG6 | Raglan Street | |
| 03/07/70 | AD | 405 | Daimler CVG6 | Grosvenor Road/Cullingtree Road | |
| 21/08/70 | MP | 468 | Daimler CWA6 | Mountpottinger depot | 1 |
| 21/08/70 | AD | 498 | Daimler CWA6 | Mountpottinger depot | 1 |
| 21/08/70 | AD | 501 | Daimler CWA6 | Mountpottinger depot | 1 |
| 21/08/70 | MP | 525 | Daimler CWA6 | Mountpottinger depot | 1 |
| 21/08/70 | SS | 544 | Daimler CWA6 | Mountpottinger depot | 1 |
| | | | | *Total number of vehicles lost in this year* **14** | |
| 03/02/71 | F | 680 | Daimler Fleetline DD | Clonard Gardens, Falls Road | |
| 06/02/71 | F | 743 | Daimler Roadliner | North Queen Street | |
| 06/02/71 | AD | 715 | Daimler Fleetline DD | Cromac Square | |
| 05/03/71 | F | 362 | Daimler CVG6 | Leeson Street | |
| 06/03/71 | AD | 697 | Daimler Fleetline DD | Leeson Street | |
| 21/07/71 | F | 354 | Daimler CVG6 | Location unknown | |
| 22/07/71 | F | 374 | Daimler CVG6 | Location unknown | |
| 09/08/71 | AD | 404 | Daimler CVG6 | Short Strand | |
| 09/08/71 | SS | 629 | Daimler Fleetline DD | Ardoyne depot | |
| 09/08/71 | AD | 702 | Daimler Fleetline DD | Crumlin Road | |
| 09/08/71 | SS | 802 | Daimler Fleetline SD | Short Strand | |
| 23/09/71 | F | 659 | Daimler Fleetline DD | Slemish Way, Andersonstown | |
| 30/09/71 | F | 371 | Daimler CVG6 | Location unknown | |
| 04/10/71 | F | 373 | Daimler CVG6 | Glen Road | |
| 04/10/71 | AD | 429 | Daimler CVG6 | Springfield Road | |
| 04/10/71 | SS | 820 | Daimler Fleetline DD | Oldpark Road | 9 |
| 05/10/71 | F | 666 | Daimler Fleetline DD | Ligoniel | 5 |
| 05/10/71 | SS | 834 | Daimler Fleetline DD | Oldpark | |
| 09/10/71 | F | 669 | Daimler Fleetline DD | Ballysillan Rd/Crumlin Rd jctn | 2 |
| 14/10/71 | AD | 414 | Daimler CVG6 | Location unknown | |
| 14/10/71 | SS | 560 | Daimler Fleetline DD | Location unknown | 4 |
| 14/10/71 | SS | 814 | Daimler Fleetline DD | Cregagh Park | 6 |
| 14/10/71 | SS | 817 | Daimler Fleetline DD | Antrim Road/New Lodge Road | 7 |
| 16/10/71 | SS | 830 | Daimler Fleetline DD | Jamaica St/Alliance Ave | 8 |
| 16/10/71 | SS | 845 | Daimler Fleetline DD | Cliftonville Circus | 10 |
| 21/10/71 | F | 356 | Daimler CVG6 | Location unknown | |
| 23/10/71 | F | 365 | Daimler CVG6 | Location unknown | |
| 23/10/71 | F | 370 | Daimler CVG6 | Whiterock Road | |
| 23/10/71 | F | 383 | Daimler CVG6 | Location unknown | |
| 27/10/71 | SS | 637 | Daimler Fleetline DD | Donegall Rd/Falls Rd jctn | 5 |
| 01/11/71 | F | 369 | Daimler CVG6 | Slievegallion Drive, Andersonstown | |
| 08/11/71 | F | 681 | Daimler Fleetline DD | Location unknown | 3 |
| | | | | *Total number of vehicles lost in this year* **32** | |
| 30/01/72 | SS | 388 | Daimler CVG6 | Norfolk Parade | |
| 01/02/72 | SS | 387 | Daimler CVG6 | Location unknown | |
| 01/02/72 | F | 627 | Daimler Fleetline DD | Mountpottinger Road | 12 |
| 01/02/72 | SS | 824 | Daimler Fleetline DD | Location unknown | 14 |
| 02/02/72 | F | 651 | Daimler Fleetline DD | Short Strand | 12 |
| 02/02/72 | AD | 774 | Daimler Fleetline SD | Location unknown | 15 |
| 02/02/72 | SS | 829 | Daimler Fleetline DD | Carr's Glen | 17 |
| 25/03/72 | – | 814 | Daimler Fleetline DD | Alexanders Coachworks, Dunmore Park | |
| 15/04/72 | AD | 396 | Daimler CVG6 | Glen Road/Shaw's Road | |
| 15/04/72 | F | 416 | Daimler CVG6 | Glen Road/Shaw's Road | |
| 30/04/72 | SS | 384 | Daimler CVG6 | Falls Road (outside depot) | |
| 11/05/72 | SS | 349 | Guy Arab III | Falls Road/Whiterock Road jctn | |
| 11/05/72 | F | 358 | Daimler CVG6 | Location unknown | |
| 13/05/72 | AD | 400 | Daimler CVG6 | McCrory Park, Whiterock Road | |
| 21/05/72 | AD | 686 | Daimler Fleetline DD | Location unknown | |
| 21/05/72 | AD | 696 | Daimler Fleetline DD | Location unknown | |
| 13/06/72 | SS | 385 | Daimler CVG6 | Roden Street/Grosvenor Road | |
| 13/06/72 | F | 667 | Daimler Fleetline DD | Ligoniel | |
| 13/06/72 | AD | 716 | Daimler Fleetline DD | Longlands Rd, Newtownabbey | 13 |
| 13/06/72 | SS | 827 | Daimler Fleetline DD | Mountpottinger Rd/Sherriff St | 16 |
| 13/06/72 | SS | 841 | Daimler Fleetline DD | Jamaica Street/Hooker Street | |
| 16/06/72 | F | 361 | Daimler CVG6 | Shaw's Road | |
| 30/06/72 | F | 357 | Daimler CVG6 | Location unknown | |
| 21/07/72 | AD | 714 | Daimler Fleetline DD | New Lodge Rd/North Queen St | |
| 25/07/72 | SS | 561 | Daimler Fleetline DD | Lepper Street | |
| 26/07/72 | SS | 582 | Daimler Fleetline DD | New Lodge Road/Antrim Road | |
| 09/08/72 | F | 660 | Daimler Fleetline DD | Location unknown | |
| 09/08/72 | SS | 828 | Daimler Fleetline DD | Location unknown | |
| 17/08/72 | F | 407 | Daimler CVG6 | Location unknown | |
| 18/08/72 | F | 449 | Daimler CVG6 | Location unknown | |
| 25/08/72 | AD | 433 | Daimler CVG6 | Location unknown | |
| 05/09/72 | SS | 595 | Daimler Fleetline DD | Location unknown | 11 |
| 29/09/72 | F | 382 | Daimler CVG6 | Grosvenor Road/Falls Road/ Springfield Road jctn | |
| 29/09/72 | AD | 441 | Daimler CVG6 | Grosvenor Road/Falls Road/ Springfield Road jctn | |
| 11/10/72 | F | 646 | Daimler Fleetline DD | Boucher Road/Tates Avenue | |
| 17/10/72 | F | 654 | Daimler Fleetline DD | Milner Street, Donegall Road | |
| | | | | *Total number of vehicles lost in this year* **36** | |
| 24/01/73 | AD | 438 | Daimler CVG6 | Location unknown | |
| 31/01/73 | SS | 345 | Guy Arab III | Location unknown | |
| 31/01/73 | SS | 559 | Daimler Fleetline DD | Location unknown | |
| 31/01/73 | SS | 820 | Daimler Fleetline DD | Location unknown | |
| 15/02/73 | AD | 793 | Daimler Fleetline SD | Location unknown | |
| 10/03/73 | AD | 810 | Daimler Fleetline DD | Location unknown | 18 |
| | | | | *Total number of vehicles lost in this year* **6** | |
| | | | | **TOTAL FOR BCT – 95** | |

## Citybus

| Date | Depot | Fleet No | Type | Location | Notes |
|---|---|---|---|---|---|
| 24/04/73 | F | 2411 | Daimler CVG6 | Iveagh Parade, Belfast | |
| 04/07/73 | F | 2352 | Daimler CVG6 | Dunville Park | |
| 04/07/73 | F | 2376 | Daimler CVG6 | Springfield Rd/Whiterock Rd jctn | |
| 04/07/73 | F | 2745 | Daimler Roadliner | Limestone Road | |
| 04/07/73 | SS | 2863 | Daimler Fleetline DD | Cliftonville Road | 19 |
| 06/07/73 | F | 2364 | Daimler CVG6 | Glen Road | |
| 09/07/73 | F | 2380 | Daimler CVG6 | Ladybrook | |
| 09/07/73 | SS | 2575 | Daimler Fleetline DD | Mill Road, Whitehouse | |
| 09/07/73 | SS | 2614 | Daimler Fleetline DD | Donegall Road/Falls Road jctn | |
| 09/07/73 | AD | 2641 | Daimler Fleetline DD | Divis Street | |
| 09/07/73 | F | 2663 | Daimler Fleetline DD | Oliver Plunkett School, Glen Road | |
| 28/11/73 | F | 2393 | Daimler CVG6 | Falls Road/Percy Street | 20 |

| Date | Depot | Fleet No | Type | Location | Notes |
|------|-------|----------|------|----------|-------|
| 28/11/73 | F | 2644 | Daimler Fleetline DD | location unknown | |
| 28/11/73 | F | 2664 | Daimler Fleetline DD | location unknown | |
| 13/12/73 | F | 2390 | Daimler CVG6 | Donegall Place | |

*Total number of vehicles lost in this year* **15**

| Date | Depot | Fleet No | Type | Location | Notes |
|------|-------|----------|------|----------|-------|
| 19/01/74 | SS | 2341 | Guy Arab III | Albertbridge Road | |
| 19/01/74 | SS | 2602 | Daimler Fleetline DD | Newtownards Rd/Templemore Ave | |
| 19/01/74 | SS | 2759 | AEC Swift | Newtownards Rd/Templemore Ave | |
| 19/01/74 | SS | 2857 | Daimler Fleetline DD | Newtownards Road | 21 |
| 24/01/74 | F | 2332 | Guy Arab III | Turf Lodge | |
| 24/01/74 | AD | 2448 | Daimler CVG6 | Turf Lodge | |
| 04/02/74 | F | 2822 | Daimler Fleetline DD | location unknown | |
| 25/02/74 | SS | 2337 | Guy Arab III | Newtownards Road | |
| 25/02/74 | SS | 2853 | Daimler Fleetline DD | Newtownards Road | |
| 26/02/74 | AD | 2708 | Daimler Fleetline DD | location unknown | |
| 27/02/74 | F | 2784 | Daimler Fleetline SD | Falls | |
| 03/03/74 | F | 2649 | Daimler Fleetline DD | location unknown | |
| 09/04/74 | F | 2329 | Guy Arab III | location unknown | |
| 09/04/74 | F | 2377 | Daimler CVG6 | location unknown | |
| 09/04/74 | F | 2392 | Daimler CVG6 | location unknown | |
| 09/04/74 | F | 2420 | Daimler CVG6 | location unknown | |
| 14/04/74 | AD | 2673 | Daimler Fleetline DD | location unknown | |
| 14/04/74 | AD | 2736 | Daimler Fleetline DD | Ardoyne | |
| 12/05/74 | F | 2684 | Daimler Fleetline DD | Falls Road | |
| 20/05/74 | SS | 2588 | Daimler Fleetline DD | location unknown | |
| 20/05/74 | AD | 2809 | Daimler Fleetline DD | location unknown | |
| 18/06/74 | SS | 2604 | Daimler Fleetline DD | Short Strand | |
| 05/07/74 | AD | 2630 | Daimler Fleetline DD | Ardoyne | |
| 05/07/74 | F | 2655 | Daimler Fleetline DD | Falls Road | |
| 08/08/74 | F | 2643 | Daimler Fleetline DD | Broadway | |
| 08/08/74 | F | 2823 | Daimler Fleetline DD | Glen Road | |
| 16/10/74 | SS | 2599 | Daimler Fleetline DD | Oldpark Avenue | |
| 16/10/74 | F | 2635 | Daimler Fleetline DD | Waterworks, Antrim Road | |
| 16/10/74 | F | 2640 | Daimler Fleetline DD | Casement Park | |
| 17/10/74 | F | 2645 | Daimler Fleetline DD | Ligoniel | |
| 17/10/74 | F | 2652 | Daimler Fleetline DD | Brompton Park, Crumlin Road | |
| 17/10/74 | F | 2831 | Daimler Fleetline DD | Ligoniel | |
| 06/11/74 | SS | 2307 | Guy Arab III | Thompson Street | |
| 06/11/74 | F | 2829 | Daimler Fleetline DD | location unknown | 21 |

*Total number of vehicles lost in this year* **34**

| Date | Depot | Fleet No | Type | Location | Notes |
|------|-------|----------|------|----------|-------|
| 10/06/75 | AD | 2693 | Daimler Fleetline DD | Tennent Street | 22 |
| 15/07/75 | AD | 2700 | Daimler Fleetline DD | location unknown | |
| 11/08/75 | F | 2824 | Daimler Fleetline DD | Agnes Street/Shankill Road jctn | |
| 28/12/75 | SS | 2560 | Daimler Fleetline DD | Short Strand depot | |
| 28/12/75 | SS | 2570 | Daimler Fleetline DD | Short Strand depot | |
| 28/12/75 | SS | 2608 | Daimler Fleetline DD | Short Strand depot | |
| 28/12/75 | SS | 2618 | Daimler Fleetline DD | Short Strand depot | |

*Total number of vehicles lost in this year* **7**

| Date | Depot | Fleet No | Type | Location | Notes |
|------|-------|----------|------|----------|-------|
| 27/01/76 | F | 2740 | Daimler Roadliner | Whiterock Road | |
| 27/01/76 | F | 2801 | Daimler Fleetline SD | Whiterock Road | |
| 28/01/76 | F | 2636 | Daimler Fleetline DD | Glen Road/Monagh Road jctn | 23 |
| 12/02/76 | SS | 2613 | Daimler Fleetline DD | Thompson Street | |
| 14/02/76 | SS | 2870 | Daimler Fleetline DD | Shankill Road | |
| 27/02/76 | SS | 2553 | Daimler Fleetline DD | Glen Road, Braniel | |
| 27/02/76 | SS | 2864 | Daimler Fleetline DD | John Longs Corner, Castlereagh Rd | |
| 27/02/76 | AD | 2908 | Leyland Atlantean | York Road Railway Station | |
| 09/08/76 | AD | 2724 | Daimler Fleetline DD | Kennedy Way | |
| 10/08/76 | SS | 2556 | Daimler Fleetline DD | Short Strand depot | |
| 10/08/76 | SS | 2631 | Daimler Fleetline DD | Short Strand depot | |
| 10/08/76 | F | 2691 | Daimler Fleetline DD | Short Strand depot | |
| 10/08/76 | F | 2692 | Daimler Fleetline DD | Short Strand depot | |
| 10/08/76 | F | 2795 | Daimler Fleetline SD | Short Strand depot | |
| 10/08/76 | F | 2807 | Daimler Fleetline DD | Short Strand depot | |
| 10/08/76 | F | 2818 | Daimler Fleetline DD | Short Strand depot | |
| 10/08/76 | SS | 2860 | Daimler Fleetline DD | Short Strand depot | |
| 10/08/76 | SS | 2871 | Daimler Fleetline DD | Short Strand depot | |
| 13/09/76 | F | 2688 | Daimler Fleetline DD | Crumlin Road | |
| 13/09/76 | AD | 2710 | Daimler Fleetline DD | Shankill Road | |
| 13/09/76 | AD | 2731 | Daimler Fleetline DD | Shankill Road | |
| 13/09/76 | AD | 2734 | Daimler Fleetline DD | Shankill Road | |
| 14/09/76 | F | 2653 | Daimler Fleetline DD | Donegall Road | 24 |
| 14/09/76 | AD | 2909 | Leyland Atlantean | location unknown | |
| 15/09/76 | F | 2687 | Daimler Fleetline DD | Donegall Road | |
| 15/09/76 | SS | 2776 | Daimler Fleetline SD | Carr's Glen | |
| 15/09/76 | SS | 2837 | Daimler Fleetline DD | Carr's Glen | |
| 17/09/76 | F | 2656 | Daimler Fleetline DD | Sicily Park | |
| 17/09/76 | AD | 2777 | Daimler Fleetline SD | Woodstock Road | |
| 17/09/76 | AD | 2890 | Leyland Atlantean | Skegoniel Avenue | |
| 20/09/76 | SS | 2594 | Daimler Fleetline DD | Sydenham Road | |
| 24/09/76 | F | 2676 | Daimler Fleetline DD | Springfield Road | |
| 30/09/76 | F | 2658 | Daimler Fleetline DD | location unknown | |
| 02/11/76 | F | 2813 | Daimler Fleetline DD | Falls Road | |
| 13/12/76 | F | 2632 | Daimler Fleetline DD | location unknown | |
| 13/12/76 | F | 2679 | Daimler Fleetline DD | location unknown | |
| 13/12/76 | AD | 2791 | Daimler Fleetline SD | location unknown | |
| 14/12/76 | F | 2683 | Daimler Fleetline DD | Glen Road | |
| 14/12/76 | F | 2817 | Daimler Fleetline DD | Glen Road | |

*Total number of vehicles lost in this year* **39**

| Date | Depot | Fleet No | Type | Location | Notes |
|------|-------|----------|------|----------|-------|
| 05/01/77 | F | 2650 | Daimler Fleetline DD | location unknown | |
| 05/01/77 | F | 2812 | Daimler Fleetline DD | location unknown | |
| 06/01/77 | SS | 2563 | Daimler Fleetline DD | Monagh Road | |
| 06/01/77 | F | 2624 | Daimler Fleetline DD | Falls Park depot | |
| 06/01/77 | F | 2639 | Daimler Fleetline DD | Falls Park depot | |
| 06/01/77 | F | 2675 | Daimler Fleetline DD | Falls Park depot | |
| 06/01/77 | F | 2748 | Daimler Roadliner | Falls Park depot | |
| 21/01/77 | SS | 2049 | Bristol RE | location unknown | |
| 21/01/77 | F | 2628 | Daimler Fleetline DD | location unknown | |
| 21/01/77 | F | 2665 | Daimler Fleetline DD | location unknown | |
| 21/01/77 | F | 2674 | Daimler Fleetline DD | location unknown | |
| 21/01/77 | F | 2678 | Daimler Fleetline DD | location unknown | |
| 21/01/77 | AD | 2732 | Daimler Fleetline DD | location unknown | |
| 21/01/77 | F | 2806 | Daimler Fleetline DD | location unknown | |
| 22/01/77 | F | 2637 | Daimler Fleetline DD | location unknown | |
| 22/01/77 | F | 2811 | Daimler Fleetline DD | location unknown | |
| 17/02/77 | F | 2681 | Daimler Fleetline DD | location unknown | |
| 18/02/77 | AD | 2555 | Daimler Fleetline DD | Glen Road terminus | |
| 18/02/77 | AD | 2565 | Daimler Fleetline DD | Glen Road terminus | |
| 18/02/77 | AD | 2711 | Daimler Fleetline DD | Monagh Road | |
| 18/02/77 | AD | 2779 | Daimler Fleetline SD | Monagh Road | |
| 19/02/77 | SS | 2574 | Daimler Fleetline DD | Short Strand depot | |
| 19/02/77 | SS | 2595 | Daimler Fleetline DD | Short Strand depot | |
| 19/02/77 | SS | 2612 | Daimler Fleetline DD | Short Strand depot | |
| 19/02/77 | F | 2651 | Daimler Fleetline DD | Donegall Road | |
| 19/02/77 | F | 2682 | Daimler Fleetline DD | Donegall Road | |
| 19/02/77 | SS | 2836 | Daimler Fleetline DD | Short Strand depot | |
| 19/02/77 | SS | 2840 | Daimler Fleetline DD | Short Strand depot | |
| 19/02/77 | SS | 2867 | Daimler Fleetline DD | Short Strand depot | |
| 24/02/77 | AD | 2557 | Daimler Fleetline DD | Mill Road, Newtownabbey | |
| 24/02/77 | SS | 2591 | Daimler Fleetline DD | York Street | |
| 24/02/77 | AD | 2701 | Daimler Fleetline DD | Cliftonville Circus | |
| 24/02/77 | AD | 2799 | Daimler Fleetline SD | Limestone Road | |
| 19/03/77 | F | 2666 | Daimler Fleetline DD | location unknown | |
| 19/03/77 | F | 2808 | Daimler Fleetline DD | location unknown | |
| 20/03/77 | F | 2749 | Daimler Roadliner | location unknown | |
| 21/03/77 | F | 2669 | Daimler Fleetline DD | location unknown | |
| 22/03/77 | F | 2577 | Daimler Fleetline DD | location unknown | 27 |
| 08/04/77 | F | 2606 | Daimler Fleetline DD | location unknown | 25 |
| 08/04/77 | F | 2611 | Daimler Fleetline DD | location unknown | |
| 08/04/77 | F | 2627 | Daimler Fleetline DD | location unknown | |
| 08/04/77 | F | 2672 | Daimler Fleetline DD | location unknown | |
| 08/05/77 | SS | 2583 | Daimler Fleetline DD | West Circular Rd/Springfield Rd jctn | |
| 29/06/77 | AD | 2928 | Daimler Fleetline SD | Glencairn | |
| 30/06/77 | AD | 2524 | AEC Merlin | Springmartin | |
| 04/07/77 | SS | 2077 | Bristol RE | location unknown | |
| 08/07/77 | F | 2647 | Daimler Fleetline DD | Glen Road | |
| 13/07/77 | F | 2816 | Daimler Fleetline DD | Monagh Road | |
| 14/07/77 | AD | 2525 | AEC Merlin | Springfield Road | |
| 15/07/77 | F | 2642 | Daimler Fleetline DD | Glen Road | |
| 15/07/77 | F | 2685 | Daimler Fleetline DD | Glen Road | |
| 08/08/77 | F | 2661 | Daimler Fleetline DD | Shaw's Road | 26 |
| 14/08/77 | F | 2648 | Daimler Fleetline DD | Glen Road/Ramoan Gardens | 26, 28 |
| 21/08/77 | F | 2782 | Daimler Fleetline SD | Falls Park depot | 26 |
| 22/08/77 | F | 2773 | Daimler Fleetline SD | Glen Road | 26 |
| 27/08/77 | F | 2633 | Daimler Fleetline DD | Donegall Road/Falls Road jctn | 2 |
| 04/09/77 | F | 2805 | Daimler Fleetline DD | Springmartin terminus | |
| 07/09/77 | F | 2622 | Daimler Fleetline DD | Glen Road | |
| 09/09/77 | AD | 2721 | Daimler Fleetline DD | location unknown | |
| 14/09/77 | F | 2619 | Daimler Fleetline DD | Glen Road | |
| 14/09/77 | F | 2623 | Daimler Fleetline DD | Ladybrook | |
| 17/09/77 | AD | 2527 | AEC Merlin | location unknown | |
| 19/09/77 | AD | 2526 | AEC Merlin | location unknown | |
| 19/09/77 | F | 2669 | Daimler Fleetline DD | location unknown | |
| 19/09/77 | F | 2694 | Daimler Fleetline DD | location unknown | |
| 19/09/77 | SS | 2765 | AEC Swift | location unknown | |
| 24/09/77 | F | 2605 | Daimler Fleetline DD | location unknown | |

| Date | Depot | Fleet No | Type | Location | Notes |
|---|---|---|---|---|---|
| 27/09/77 | F | 2720 | Daimler Fleetline DD | Cliftonville Circus | |
| 05/10/77 | AD | 2530 | AEC Merlin | Monagh Roundabout | |
| 11/10/77 | F | 2558 | Daimler Fleetline DD | Cliftonville Road | |
| 19/10/77 | AD | 2770 | AEC Swift | Monagh Road | |
| 19/10/77 | F | 2774 | Daimler Fleetline SD | Monagh Road | |
| 24/10/77 | AD | 2755 | AEC Swift | Springfield Road | |
| 24/10/77 | SS | 2868 | Daimler Fleetline DD | Cliftonville Road/Oldpark Avenue | |
| 10/11/77 | AD | 2772 | AEC Swift | Monagh Roundabout | |
| 12/11/77 | SS | 2569 | Daimler Fleetline DD | Glen Road | |
| 26/11/77 | F | 2554 | Daimler Fleetline DD | Glen Road | |
| 26/11/77 | F | 2638 | Daimler Fleetline DD | Shaw's Road | |

*Total number of vehicles lost in this year* **78**

| Date | Depot | Fleet No | Type | Location | Notes |
|---|---|---|---|---|---|
| 29/01/78 | F | 2757 | AEC Swift | Monagh Road | |
| 29/01/78 | F | 2781 | Daimler Fleetline SD | Donegall Road/Falls Road jctn | |
| 29/01/78 | F | 2788 | Daimler Fleetline SD | Whiterock Road | |
| 18/02/78 | F | 2610 | Daimler Fleetline DD | location unknown | |
| 25/04/78 | F | 2500 | AEC Merlin | Springfield Rd/Whiterock Rd jctn | |
| 27/04/78 | AD | 2108 | Bristol RE | Ardoyne depot | |
| 27/04/78 | AD | 2111 | Bristol RE | Ardoyne depot | 32 |
| 27/04/78 | AD | 2163 | Bristol RE | Ardoyne depot | 33 |
| 27/04/78 | AD | 2214 | Bristol RE | Ardoyne depot | 32 |
| 27/04/78 | AD | 2225 | Bristol RE | Ardoyne depot | |
| 27/04/78 | AD | 2885 | Leyland Atlantean | Ardoyne depot | |
| 27/04/78 | AD | 2900 | Leyland Atlantean | Ardoyne depot | |
| 27/04/78 | AD | 2910 | Leyland Atlantean | Ardoyne depot | |
| 27/04/78 | AD | 2912 | Leyland Atlantean | Ardoyne depot | |
| 28/04/78 | AD | 2901 | Leyland Atlantean | Ardoyne depot | |
| 28/04/78 | AD | 2926 | Daimler Fleetline SD | Ardoyne depot | |
| 10/05/78 | F | 2501 | AEC Merlin | location unknown | 29 |
| 11/05/78 | AD | 2882 | Leyland Atlantean | Duncairn Gardens, Hillman Street | 3 |
| 11/05/78 | AD | 2939 | Daimler Fleetline SD | Springfield Road | 29 |
| 12/05/78 | F | 2634 | Daimler Fleetline DD | Glen Road | 29 |
| 12/05/78 | SS | 2119 | Bristol RE | Short Strand | 29, 32 |
| 12/05/78 | F | 2505 | AEC Merlin | Monagh Road | 29 |
| 24/06/78 | F | 2934 | Daimler Fleetline SD | Monagh Road/Springfield Road jctn | |
| 27/06/78 | F | 2504 | AEC Merlin | New Barnsley Police Station, Springfield Road | |
| 09/08/78 | F | 2609 | Daimler Fleetline DD | Andersonstown | |
| 10/08/78 | F | 2797 | Daimler Fleetline SD | Andersonstown | |
| 21/08/78 | F | 16 | AEC Swift | Springfield Road | |
| 23/09/78 | SS | 2531 | AEC Merlin | Springfield Road | |
| 02/10/78 | AD | 2689 | Daimler Fleetline DD | Falls Road | 30 |
| 10/10/78 | F | 2607 | Daimler Fleetline DD | location unknown | 31 |
| 02/11/78 | F | 2626 | Daimler Fleetline DD | Andersonstown Police Station | |
| 08/11/78 | F | 2792 | Daimler Fleetline SD | Springfield Road | |
| 29/11/78 | F | 2568 | Daimler Fleetline DD | St Theresas School, Glen Road | |
| 04/12/78 | F | 2564 | Daimler Fleetline DD | Finaghy Road North. | |

*Total number of vehicles lost in this year* **34**

| Date | Depot | Fleet No | Type | Location | Notes |
|---|---|---|---|---|---|
| 18/01/79 | F | 3 | AEC Swift | Falls Park depot | |
| 18/01/79 | F | 11 | AEC Swift | Falls Park depot | |
| 18/01/79 | F | 19 | AEC Swift | Falls Park depot | |
| 18/01/79 | F | 27 | AEC Swift | Falls Park depot | |
| 18/01/79 | F | 33 | AEC Swift | Falls Park depot | |
| 18/01/79 | F | 2091 | Bristol RE | Falls Park depot | |
| 18/01/79 | F | 2098 | Bristol RE | Falls Park depot | |
| 18/01/79 | AD | 2503 | AEC Merlin | Falls Park depot | |
| 18/01/79 | SS | 2544 | AEC Merlin | Falls Park depot | |
| 18/01/79 | F | 2567 | Daimler Fleetline DD | Falls Park depot | |
| 18/01/79 | F | 2572 | Daimler Fleetline DD | Falls Park depot | |
| 18/01/79 | F | 2603 | Daimler Fleetline DD | Falls Park depot | |
| 18/01/79 | F | 2616 | Daimler Fleetline DD | Falls Park depot | |
| 18/01/79 | F | 2617 | Daimler Fleetline DD | Falls Park depot | |
| 18/01/79 | F | 2625 | Daimler Fleetline DD | Falls Park depot | |
| 18/01/79 | F | 2798 | Daimler Fleetline SD | Falls Park depot | |
| 18/01/79 | F | 2810 | Daimler Fleetline DD | Falls Park depot | |
| 18/01/79 | F | 2826 | Daimler Fleetline DD | Falls Park depot | |
| 18/01/79 | F | 2827 | Daimler Fleetline DD | Falls Park depot | |
| 18/01/79 | F | 2829 | Daimler Fleetline DD | Falls Park depot | |
| 18/01/79 | AD | 2874 | Leyland Atlantean | Falls Park depot | |
| 18/01/79 | F | 2936 | Daimler Fleetline SD | Falls Park depot | |
| 18/01/79 | F | 2941 | Daimler Fleetline SD | Falls Park depot | |
| 18/01/79 | F | 2946 | Daimler Fleetline SD | Falls Park depot | |
| 25/01/79 | F | 51 | AEC Swift | location unknown | |
| 02/05/79 | F | 55 | AEC Swift | Andersonstown | |
| 27/05/79 | AD | 2165 | Bristol RE | Ardoyne depot | |
| 27/05/79 | AD | 2166 | Bristol RE | Ardoyne depot | |
| 27/05/79 | AD | 2168 | Bristol RE | Ardoyne depot | |
| 27/05/79 | AD | 2170 | Bristol RE | Ardoyne depot | |
| 27/05/79 | AD | 2213 | Bristol RE | Ardoyne depot | |
| 27/05/79 | AD | 2215 | Bristol RE | Ardoyne depot | |
| 27/05/79 | AD | 2226 | Bristol RE | Ardoyne depot | |
| 27/05/79 | AD | 2230 | Bristol RE | Ardoyne depot | |
| 27/05/79 | AD | 2735 | Daimler Fleetline DD | Ardoyne depot | |
| 27/05/79 | AD | 2833 | Daimler Fleetline DD | Ardoyne depot | |
| 27/05/79 | AD | 2927 | Daimler Fleetline SD | Ardoyne depot | |
| 27/05/79 | AD | 2933 | Daimler Fleetline SD | Ardoyne depot | |
| 04/07/79 | F | 2096 | Bristol RE | Springfield | |
| 04/07/79 | AD | 2118 | Bristol RE | Glencairn | |
| 04/07/79 | AD | 2886 | Leyland Atlantean | Berlin Street | |
| 13/08/79 | AD | 2495 | AEC Merlin | location unknown | |
| 13/08/79 | F | 2794 | Daimler Fleetline SD | Andersonstown Road | |
| 13/08/79 | F | 2940 | Daimler Fleetline SD | Finaghy Road North | |
| 21/09/79 | AD | 2228 | Bristol RE | Glencairn | |
| 24/09/79 | AD | 2217 | Bristol RE | Springmartin | |
| 26/09/79 | F | 2615 | Daimler Fleetline DD | location unknown | 34 |
| 16/10/79 | AD | 2110 | Bristol RE | Berlin Street | |
| 18/11/79 | F | 30 | AEC Swift | Falls Park depot | |
| 18/11/79 | F | 31 | AEC Swift | Falls Park depot | |
| 18/11/79 | F | 639 | AEC Merlin | Falls Park depot | |
| 18/11/79 | SS | 2925 | AEC Merlin | Falls Park depot | |
| 18/11/79 | F | 2944 | Daimler Fleetline SD | Falls Park depot | |
| 18/11/79 | F | 2949 | Daimler Fleetline SD | Falls Park depot | |

*Total number of vehicles lost in this year* **54**

| Date | Depot | Fleet No | Type | Location | Notes |
|---|---|---|---|---|---|
| 01/02/80 | F | 20 | AEC Swift | Falls Park depot | |
| 01/02/80 | F | 36 | AEC Swift | Falls Park depot | |
| 01/02/80 | R | 72 | AEC Swift | Falls Park depot | |
| 01/02/80 | F | 77 | AEC Swift | Falls Park depot | |
| 01/02/80 | F | 625 | AEC Merlin | Falls Park depot | |
| 01/02/80 | F | 631 | AEC Merlin | Falls Park depot | |
| 01/02/80 | F | 2076 | Bristol RE | Falls Park depot | |
| 01/02/80 | F | 2079 | Bristol RE | Falls Park depot | |
| 01/02/80 | F | 2084 | Bristol RE | Falls Park depot | |
| 01/02/80 | F | 2093 | Bristol RE | Falls Park depot | |
| 01/02/80 | F | 2094 | Bristol RE | Falls Park depot | |
| 01/02/80 | F | 2562 | Daimler Fleetline DD | Falls Park depot | |
| 01/02/80 | F | 2620 | Daimler Fleetline DD | Falls Park depot | |
| 01/02/80 | F | 2775 | Daimler Fleetline SD | Falls Park depot | |
| 01/02/80 | F | 2787 | Daimler Fleetline SD | Falls Park depot | |
| 01/02/80 | F | 2790 | Daimler Fleetline SD | Falls Park depot | |
| 01/02/80 | F | 2796 | Daimler Fleetline SD | Falls Park depot | |
| 01/02/80 | F | 2804 | Daimler Fleetline DD | Falls Park depot | |
| 01/02/80 | F | 2821 | Daimler Fleetline DD | Falls Park depot | |
| 29/02/80 | AD | 2 | AEC Swift | Ardoyne depot | |
| 29/02/80 | AD | 24 | AEC Swift | Ardoyne depot | |
| 29/02/80 | AD | 29 | AEC Swift | Ardoyne depot | |
| 29/02/80 | AD | 74 | AEC Swift | Ardoyne depot | |
| 29/02/80 | AD | 80 | AEC Swift | Ardoyne depot | |
| 29/02/80 | AD | 2105 | Bristol RE | Ardoyne depot | |
| 29/02/80 | AD | 2106 | Bristol RE | Ardoyne depot | |
| 29/02/80 | AD | 2111 | Bristol RE | Ardoyne depot | |
| 29/02/80 | AD | 2220 | Bristol RE | Ardoyne depot | |
| 29/02/80 | AD | 2552 | AEC Merlin | Ardoyne depot | |
| 29/02/80 | AD | 2553 | AEC Merlin | Ardoyne depot | |
| 29/02/80 | DS | 2586 | Daimler Fleetline DD | Ardoyne depot | |
| 29/02/80 | AD | 2699 | Daimler Fleetline DD | Ardoyne depot | |
| 29/02/80 | AD | 2703 | Daimler Fleetline DD | Ardoyne depot | |
| 29/02/80 | AD | 2876 | Leyland Atlantean | Ardoyne depot | |
| 29/02/80 | AD | 2878 | Leyland Atlantean | Ardoyne depot | |
| 29/02/80 | AD | 2880 | Leyland Atlantean | Ardoyne depot | |
| 29/02/80 | AD | 2884 | Leyland Atlantean | Ardoyne depot | |
| 29/02/80 | AD | 2889 | Leyland Atlantean | Ardoyne depot | |
| 29/02/80 | AD | 2902 | Leyland Atlantean | Ardoyne depot | |
| 29/02/80 | AD | 2930 | Daimler Fleetline SD | Ardoyne depot | |
| 09/05/80 | F | 2789 | Daimler Fleetline SD | City Hall | |
| 10/05/80 | F | 2778 | Daimler Fleetline SD | location unknown | |
| 07/07/80 | AD | 25 | AEC Swift | Ardoyne depot | |
| 07/07/80 | AD | 1218 | Bedford VAM | Ardoyne depot | |
| 07/07/80 | AD | 2042 | Bristol RE | Ardoyne depot | |
| 07/07/80 | AD | 2576 | Daimler Fleetline DD | Ardoyne depot | |
| 07/07/80 | F | 2815 | Daimler Fleetline DD | Ardoyne depot | |
| 07/07/80 | AD | 2888 | Leyland Atlantean | Ardoyne depot | |
| 07/07/80 | AD | 2897 | Leyland Atlantean | Ardoyne depot | |
| 07/07/80 | AD | 2903 | Leyland Atlantean | Ardoyne depot | |
| 10/07/80 | AD | 2115 | Bristol RE | Springmartin | |
| 22/07/80 | AD | 2048 | Bristol RE | Ligoniel Road | |

| Date | Depot | Fleet No | Type | Location | Notes |
|---|---|---|---|---|---|
| 22/07/80 | SS | 2579 | Daimler Fleetline DD | Short Strand | |
| 03/10/80 | F | 624 | AEC Merlin | Finaghy Road North. | |
| 03/10/80 | F | 2088 | Bristol RE | Grosvenor Road | |
| 16/12/80 | AD | 2114 | Bristol RE | Ardoyne depot | |
| 16/12/80 | AD | 2490 | AEC Merlin | Ardoyne depot | |
| 16/12/80 | AD | 2499 | AEC Merlin | Ardoyne depot | |

*Total number of vehicles lost in this year* **58**

| Date | Depot | Fleet No | Type | Location | Notes |
|---|---|---|---|---|---|
| 11/04/81 | F | 2064 | Bristol RE | Broadway | |
| 11/04/81 | F | 2074 | Bristol RE | Broadway/Falls Road jctn | |
| 16/04/81 | F | 719 | Bristol RE | Finaghy Road North | |
| 20/04/81 | F | 2945 | Daimler Fleetline SD | Beechmount | |
| 24/04/81 | AD | 2911 | Leyland Atlantean | Flax Street | |
| 26/04/81 | SS | 2152 | Bristol RE | Madrid Street/Woodstock Road | |
| 27/04/81 | F | 2529 | AEC Merlin | Beechmount | |
| 05/05/81 | F | 652 | AEC Merlin | Limestone Road | |
| 05/05/81 | AD | 2843 | Daimler Fleetline DD | Crumlin Road | |
| 19/05/81 | F | 2543 | AEC Merlin | Falls Road | |
| 20/05/81 | AD | 2218 | Bristol RE | Crumlin Road/Kerrera Street | |
| 22/05/81 | F | 2092 | Bristol RE | Etna Drive | |
| 22/05/81 | F | 2937 | Daimler Fleetline SD | Clonard | |
| 25/05/81 | SS | 2921 | Daimler Fleetline SD | Kennedy Way | |
| 29/05/81 | F | 721 | Bristol RE | Beechmount | |
| 29/05/81 | AD | 2518 | AEC Merlin | Monagh Road | |
| 29/05/81 | F | 2540 | AEC Merlin | Glen Road | |
| 29/05/81 | F | 2942 | Daimler Fleetline SD | Beechmount | |
| 01/06/81 | F | 2537 | AEC Merlin | Whiterock Road | |
| 06/06/81 | AD | 2211 | Bristol RE | Ardoyne depot | |
| 06/06/81 | AD | 2838 | Daimler Fleetline DD | Ardoyne depot | |
| 06/06/81 | AD | 2875 | Leyland Atlantean | Ardoyne depot | |
| 29/06/81 | AD | 2229 | Bristol RE | Glencairn | |
| 08/07/81 | F | 726 | Bristol RE | Andersonstown Leisure Centre | |
| 08/07/81 | F | 2063 | Bristol RE | Kennedy Way | |
| 12/07/81 | F | 643 | AEC Merlin | Monagh Road | |
| 13/07/81 | F | 720 | Bristol RE | Andersonstown | |
| 17/07/81 | F | 2550 | AEC Merlin | Glen Road | |
| 19/07/81 | SS | 635 | AEC Merlin | Glen Road | |
| 20/07/81 | F | 2541 | AEC Merlin | Glen Road | |
| 31/07/81 | AD | 2116 | Bristol RE | Ardoyne depot | |
| 08/08/81 | AD | 2532 | AEC Merlin | Ardoyne depot | |
| 08/08/81 | AD | 2780 | Daimler Fleetline SD | Ardoyne depot | |
| 18/08/81 | AD | 2522 | AEC Merlin | Beechmount | |
| 19/08/81 | F | 2072 | Bristol RE | Etna Drive | |
| 19/08/81 | AD | 2513 | AEC Merlin | Etna Drive | |
| 21/08/81 | F | 724 | Bristol RE | Etna Drive | |
| 21/08/81 | F | 728 | Bristol RE | Flax Street | |
| 30/08/81 | F | 2800 | Daimler Fleetline SD | Glen Road | |

*Total number of vehicles lost in this year* **39**

| Date | Depot | Fleet No | Type | Location | Notes |
|---|---|---|---|---|---|
| 27/01/82 | F | 712 | Bristol RE | Beechmount | |
| 31/01/82 | AD | 2146 | Bristol RE | Tennent Street/Crumlin Road | |
| 18/03/82 | AD | 674 | AEC Merlin | location unknown | |
| 12/05/82 | F | 717 | Bristol RE | Glen Road/Shaw's Road terminus | |
| 12/05/82 | F | 2104 | Bristol RE | Whiterock Road | |
| 13/05/82 | F | 718 | Bristol RE | Glen Road | |
| 21/05/82 | F | 713 | Bristol RE | Beechmount | |
| 10/06/82 | F | 741 | Bristol RE | Ladybrook | |
| 14/09/82 | AD | 2892 | Leyland Atlantean | Crumlin Road | |
| 31/10/82 | AD | 2899 | Leyland Atlantean | Ligoniel terminus | |
| 03/11/82 | F | 715 | Bristol RE | Butler Street, Crumlin Road | |
| 04/11/82 | F | 2068 | Bristol RE | Snugville Street, Shankill Road | |

*Total number of vehicles lost in this year* **12**

| Date | Depot | Fleet No | Type | Location | Notes |
|---|---|---|---|---|---|
| 09/08/83 | F | 722 | Bristol RE | Springfield Road | |
| 09/08/83 | F | 2136 | Bristol RE | Celtic Park, Donegall Road | |
| 11/08/83 | F | 2081 | Bristol RE | Ardoyne | |
| 13/08/83 | F | 739 | Bristol RE | Andersonstown | |
| 14/08/83 | F | 716 | Bristol RE | Andersonstown | |
| 26/08/83 | SS | 2475 | Bristol RE | Rodney Parade/Donegall Road | |
| 17/09/83 | F | 2061 | Bristol RE | Hooker Street, Crumlin Road | |
| 24/09/83 | F | 727 | Bristol RE | Monagh Road | |
| 04/10/83 | F | 731 | Bristol RE | Falls Park depot | |
| 04/10/83 | F | 736 | Bristol RE | Falls Park depot | |
| 04/10/83 | F | 2057 | Bristol RE | Falls Park depot | |
| 04/10/83 | F | 2102 | Bristol RE | Falls Park depot | |
| 04/10/83 | F | 2119 | Bristol RE | Falls Park depot | |
| 04/10/83 | F | 2138 | Bristol RE | Falls Park depot | |

*Total number of vehicles lost in this year* **14**

| Date | Depot | Fleet No | Type | Location | Notes |
|---|---|---|---|---|---|
| 14/03/84 | F | 2078 | Bristol RE | Slemish Way, Andersonstown Road | |
| 04/05/84 | F | 2051 | Bristol RE | Glen Road | |
| 05/05/84 | F | 2143 | Bristol RE | Donegall Road/Falls Road jctn | |
| 05/05/84 | AD | 2339 | Bristol RE | Crumlin Road | |
| 05/05/84 | SS | 2427 | Bristol RE | Turf Lodge | |
| 06/05/84 | F | 748 | Bristol RE | Donegall Road/Falls Road jctn | |
| 06/05/84 | F | 2109 | Bristol RE | Butler Street, Crumlin Road | |
| 07/05/84 | F | 2056 | Bristol RE | Donegall Road/Falls Road jctn | |
| 09/05/84 | F | 759 | Bristol RE | Turf Lodge | |
| 12/05/84 | F | 2050 | Bristol RE | Andersonstown Leisure Centre | |
| 13/05/84 | F | 750 | Bristol RE | Suffolk Road | |
| 21/05/84 | F | 743 | Bristol RE | Glen Road | |
| 21/05/84 | AD | 764 | Bristol RE | Monagh Road | |
| 15/06/84 | F | 2070 | Bristol RE | Glen Road terminus | |
| 08/08/84 | AD | 707 | Bristol RE | Ardoyne depot | |
| 08/08/84 | F | 2113 | Bristol RE | Glen Road terminus | |
| 08/08/84 | F | 2117 | Bristol RE | Casement Park | |
| 09/08/84 | F | 746 | Bristol RE | Whiterock Road | |
| 11/08/84 | F | 2071 | Bristol RE | Glen Road terminus | |
| 13/08/84 | F | 711 | Bristol RE | Whiterock | |
| 13/08/84 | F | 747 | Bristol RE | Etna Drive | |
| 13/08/84 | F | 751 | Bristol RE | Monagh Road | |
| 13/08/84 | SS | 2501 | Bristol RE | Oldpark | 35 |
| 13/08/84 | SS | 2859 | Daimler Fleetline DD | Shaw's Road | |
| 14/08/84 | F | 742 | Bristol RE | Alliance Avenue | |
| 14/08/84 | F | 2069 | Bristol RE | Donegall Road/Falls Road jctn | |
| 16/08/84 | F | 2053 | Bristol RE | Donegall Road/Falls Road jctn | |
| 16/08/84 | AD | 2167 | Bristol RE | Turf Lodge | |
| 17/08/84 | F | 710 | Bristol RE | Glen Road terminus | |
| 18/08/84 | F | 700 | Bristol RE | Suffolk Road | |
| 18/08/84 | AD | 709 | Bristol RE | Shaw's Road | |

*Total number of vehicles lost in this year* **31**

| Date | Depot | Fleet No | Type | Location | Notes |
|---|---|---|---|---|---|
| 30/01/85 | F | 2082 | Bristol RE | White Horse Inn, Andersonstown Rd | |
| 26/02/85 | F | 2065 | Bristol RE | Donegall Road/Falls Road jctn | |
| 26/02/85 | F | 2099 | Bristol RE | Andersonstown Leisure Centre | |
| 05/03/85 | F | 2086 | Bristol RE | Slemish Way, Andersonstown Road | |
| 08/03/85 | F | 2095 | Bristol RE | Donegall Road/Falls Road jctn | |
| 05/05/85 | F | 768 | Bristol RE | Falls Road/Whiterock Road jctn | |
| 01/08/85 | F | 776 | Bristol RE | Donegall Road/Falls Road jctn | |
| 07/08/85 | F | 771 | Bristol RE | Finaghy Road North. | |
| 08/08/85 | F | 774 | Bristol RE | Ladybrook | |
| 10/08/85 | F | 770 | Bristol RE | Glen Road terminus | |
| 10/08/85 | F | 779 | Bristol RE | Andersonstown Leisure Centre | |
| 12/08/85 | F | 704 | Bristol RE | Clonard | |
| 14/08/85 | F | 760 | Bristol RE | Falls Road/Whiterock Road jctn | |
| 20/12/85 | F | 744 | Bristol RE | Clonard Street/Falls Road jctn | |

*Total number of vehicles lost in this year* **14**

| Date | Depot | Fleet No | Type | Location | Notes |
|---|---|---|---|---|---|
| 08/02/86 | F | 714 | Bristol RE | Monagh Road | |
| 02/04/86 | AD | 2224 | Bristol RE | Ballysillan Park (also Ardoyne) | |
| 06/05/86 | SS | 2430 | Bristol RE | New Lodge Road | |
| 12/05/86 | F | 2157 | Bristol RE | Holy Cross, Crumlin Road | |
| 17/06/86 | F | 2140 | Bristol RE | North Queen St/Limestone Rd jctn | |
| 25/06/86 | AD | 2407 | Bristol RE | Berlin Street, Shankill Road | |
| 12/07/86 | AD | 2346 | Bristol RE | Oldpark Road | |
| 14/07/86 | F | 757 | Bristol RE | Springfield Rd/Whiterock Rd jctn | |
| 16/07/86 | F | 2041 | Bristol RE | Ligoniel | |
| 09/08/86 | AD | 708 | Bristol RE | Monagh Road | |
| 10/08/86 | F | 2100 | Bristol RE | Donegall Road/Falls Road jctn | |

*Total number of vehicles lost in this year* **11**

| Date | Depot | Fleet No | Type | Location | Notes |
|---|---|---|---|---|---|
| 27/02/87 | SS | 2504 | Bristol RE | Glencairn | |
| 28/02/87 | AD | 2419 | Bristol RE | Ballygomartin | |
| 03/03/87 | AD | 2401 | Bristol RE | Shankill Road | |
| 31/03/87 | F | 778 | Bristol RE | Andersonstown Leisure Centre | |
| 06/04/87 | AD | 2341 | Bristol RE | Paisley Park | |
| 07/04/87 | F | 703 | Bristol RE | Clonard Street | |
| 07/04/87 | AD | 738 | Bristol RE | Dunville Park | |
| 07/04/87 | F | 785 | Bristol RE | Donegall Road/Falls Road jctn | |
| 07/04/87 | F | 2054 | Bristol RE | Leeson Street | |
| 07/04/87 | F | 2101 | Bristol RE | Falls Road/Donegall Road jctn | |

| Date | Depot | Fleet No | Type | Location | Notes |
|---|---|---|---|---|---|
| 08/04/87 | F | 784 | Bristol RE | Glen Road terminus | |
| 08/04/87 | AD | 797 | Bristol RE | Springfield Parade/Springfield Road | |
| 08/04/87 | AD | 2312 | Bristol RE | Oldpark Road | |
| 09/04/87 | F | 2085 | Bristol RE | Whiterock/Ballymurphy | |
| 05/05/87 | F | 769 | Bristol RE | Shaw's Road | |
| 05/05/87 | F | 794 | Bristol RE | Andersonstown Leisure Centre | |
| 06/05/87 | F | 749 | Bristol RE | Falls Road/Whiterock Road jctn | |
| 06/05/87 | F | 2107 | Bristol RE | Springfield Rd/Whiterock Rd jctn | |
| 07/05/87 | F | 2080 | Bristol RE | Springfield Rd/Whiterock Rd jctn | |
| 07/05/87 | F | 2090 | Bristol RE | Springfield Rd/Whiterock Rd jctn | |
| 07/05/87 | F | 2221 | Bristol RE | Brompton Park, Ardoyne | |
| 07/05/87 | AD | 2422 | Bristol RE | Antrim Road/New Lodge Road jctn | |
| 09/05/87 | F | 2083 | Bristol RE | Falls Road/Whiterock Road jctn | |
| 09/05/87 | AD | 2343 | Bristol RE | Ligoniel | |
| 13/05/87 | F | 714(2) | Bristol RE | Crumlin Road (lasted two days) | |
| 17/06/87 | AD | 2227 | Bristol RE | Ardoyne depot | |
| 17/06/87 | AD | 2325 | Bristol RE | Ardoyne depot | |
| 17/06/87 | AD | 2342 | Bristol RE | Ardoyne depot | |
| 08/08/87 | F | 2150 | Bristol RE | Whiterock Road | |
| 10/08/87 | F | 799 | Bristol RE | Clonard | |
| 22/09/87 | F | 798 | Bristol RE | Monagh Road | |
| 31/10/87 | AD | 2855 | Daimler Fleetline DD | Ardoyne depot | 36 |
| 02/11/87 | F | 800 | Bristol RE | Clonard Street/Falls Road | |
| 25/11/87 | AD | 737 | Bristol RE | Ardoyne depot | |
| 25/11/87 | F | 2141 | Bristol RE | Lanark Way | |
| 25/11/87 | F | 2158 | Bristol RE | Antrim Road | |
| 25/11/87 | F | 2164 | Bristol RE | Posnett Street, Donegall Pass | |

*Total number of vehicles lost in this year 37*

| Date | Depot | Fleet No | Type | Location | Notes |
|---|---|---|---|---|---|
| 19/01/88 | F | 712(2) | Bristol RE | Antrim Road | |
| 24/02/88 | F | 780 | Bristol RE | Springfield Rd/Whiterock Rd jctn | |
| 24/02/88 | F | 790 | Bristol RE | Springfield Rd/Whiterock Rd jctn | |
| 25/02/88 | F | 791 | Bristol RE | Springfield Rd/Whiterock Rd jctn | |
| 25/02/88 | F | 2055 | Bristol RE | Springfield Rd/Whiterock Rd jctn | |
| 06/03/88 | AD | 725 | Bristol RE | Springfield Rd/Whiterock Rd jctn | |
| 07/03/88 | F | 701 | Bristol RE | Shaw's Road | |
| 07/03/88 | F | 2162 | Bristol RE | Flax Street, Oldpark | |
| 09/03/88 | F | 777 | Bristol RE | Springfield Rd/Whiterock Rd jctn | |
| 11/03/88 | F | 715(2) | Bristol RE | Springhill Avenue, Springfield Road | |
| 11/03/88 | F | 781 | Bristol RE | Springhill Avenue, Springfield Road | |
| 14/03/88 | F | 2089 | Bristol RE | Springhill Avenue, Whiterock Road | |
| 16/03/88 | F | 773 | Bristol RE | Flax Street | |
| 16/03/88 | F | 2139 | Bristol RE | Springfield Rd/Whiterock Rd jctn | |
| 16/03/88 | F | 2212 | Bristol RE | Falls Road/Whiterock Road jctn | |
| 16/03/88 | SS | 2487 | Bristol RE | Mountpottinger Link | |
| 17/03/88 | F | 2137 | Bristol RE | Whiterock Leisure Centre | |
| 28/07/88 | SS | 2555 | Bristol RE | East Bridge Street | |
| 27/08/88 | F | 710(2) | Bristol RE | St Theresa's, Glen Road | |
| 27/08/88 | F | 729(2) | Bristol RE | Donegall Road/Falls Road jctn | |
| 27/08/88 | F | 730(2) | Bristol RE | Falls Road/Whiterock Road jctn | |
| 27/08/88 | F | 745 | Bristol RE | Falls Road/Whiterock Road jctn | |
| 27/08/88 | F | 792 | Bristol RE | Broadway/Falls Road jctn | |
| 27/08/88 | F | 2120 | Bristol RE | Broadway/Falls Road jctn | |
| 27/08/88 | AD | 2357 | Bristol RE | Springfield Road/Monagh Road jctn | |
| 27/08/88 | AD | 2461 | Bristol RE | Lanark Way/Springfield Road | |
| 27/08/88 | AD | 2464 | Bristol RE | Falls Road/Whiterock Road jctn | |
| 29/08/88 | F | 2073 | Bristol RE | Ardoyne Shops | |
| 30/08/88 | F | 707(2) | Bristol RE | Monagh Road | |
| 30/08/88 | F | 742(2) | Bristol RE | Monagh Road/Glen Road | |
| 31/08/88 | F | 2222 | Bristol RE | Millfield/Divis Street | |
| 31/08/88 | SS | 2518 | Bristol RE | Short Strand | |

*Total number of vehicles lost in this year 32*

| Date | Depot | Fleet No | Type | Location | Notes |
|---|---|---|---|---|---|
| 17/05/89 | AD | 716(2) | Bristol RE | Ardoyne depot | |
| 17/05/89 | AD | 734 | Bristol RE | Ardoyne depot | |
| 02/07/89 | AD | 704(2) | Bristol RE | Ardoyne depot | |
| 02/07/89 | AD | 708(2) | Bristol RE | Ardoyne depot | |
| 02/07/89 | AD | 713(2) | Bristol RE | Ardoyne depot | |
| 02/07/89 | AD | 750(2) | Bristol RE | Ardoyne depot | |
| 08/08/89 | F | 2043 | Bristol RE | Shaw's Road | |
| 12/08/89 | F | 793 | Bristol RE | Glen Road | |
| 14/08/89 | F | 726 | Bristol RE | Springfield Road | |
| 14/08/89 | F | 2247 | Bristol RE | Andersonstown Road | |
| 14/08/89 | SS | 2529 | Bristol RE | Mountpottinger Road | |
| 16/08/89 | F | 739 | Bristol RE | Falls Park depot | |
| 16/08/89 | AD | 2412 | Bristol RE | Falls Park depot | |
| 19/08/89 | F | 2066 | Bristol RE | Falls Road | |
| 23/08/89 | F | 736(2) | Bristol RE | Glen Road | |
| 07/10/89 | F | 702(2) | Bristol RE | Glen Road | |
| 07/10/89 | F | 711(2) | Bristol RE | Donegall Road/Falls Road jctn | |
| 07/10/89 | F | 718(2) | Bristol RE | Falls Road | |
| 07/10/89 | F | 743(2) | Bristol RE | Falls Road | |
| 07/10/89 | F | 752(2) | Bristol RE | Glen Road | |
| 07/10/89 | F | 2112 | Bristol RE | Falls Road | |
| 07/10/89 | F | 2296 | Bristol RE | Falls Road/Whiterock Road juction | |

*Total number of vehicles lost in this year 22*

| Date | Depot | Fleet No | Type | Location | Notes |
|---|---|---|---|---|---|
| 13/01/90 | F | 2148 | Bristol RE | Casement Park | |
| 11/02/90 | AD | 2404 | Bristol RE | Ballygomartin Road | |
| 13/02/90 | F | 2159 | Bristol RE | Peters Hill | |
| 17/02/90 | F | 709(2) | Bristol RE | Falls Road/Donegall Road jctn | |
| 17/02/90 | F | 2044 | Bristol RE | Falls Road/Donegall Road jctn | |
| 11/03/90 | AD | 2394 | Bristol RE | Unity Flats | |
| 15/05/90 | AD | 2356 | Bristol RE | Ballygomartin Road | |
| 19/05/90 | AD | 2423 | Bristol RE | Shankill Road | |
| 21/05/90 | SS | 2632 | Leyland Tiger | Forthriver Road | |
| 31/05/90 | F | 2195 | Bristol RE | Falls Road/Beechmount Avenue | |
| 02/06/90 | F | 2103 | Bristol RE | Glen Road | |
| 07/07/90 | F | 2223 | Bristol RE | Wellington Place | |
| 09/10/90 | F | 2145 | Bristol RE | Springfield Rd/Whiterock Rd jctn | |
| 10/11/90 | F | 2147 | Bristol RE | Laganbank Road | |
| 24/11/90 | F | 2144 | Bristol RE | Falls Park depot | |
| 24/11/90 | F | 2163 | Bristol RE | Falls Park depot | |
| 24/11/90 | F | 2219 | Bristol RE | Falls Park depot | |
| 24/11/90 | F | 2323 | Bristol RE | Falls Park depot | |
| 24/11/90 | F | 2335 | Bristol RE | Falls Park depot | |

*Total number of vehicles lost in this year 19*

| Date | Depot | Fleet No | Type | Location | Notes |
|---|---|---|---|---|---|
| 17/01/91 | SS | 2574 | Bristol RE | Short Strand depot | 37 |
| 17/01/91 | SS | 2578 | Bristol RE | Short Strand depot | |
| 23/02/91 | F | 2241 | Bristol RE | Falls Park depot | |
| 23/02/91 | F | 2289 | Bristol RE | Falls Park depot | |
| 04/06/91 | F | 2327 | Bristol RE | Falls Road | |
| 04/06/91 | F | 2359 | Bristol RE | Falls Road | |
| 05/06/91 | F | 2360 | Bristol RE | Falls Road | |
| 15/07/91 | F | 2153 | Bristol RE | Springmartin | |
| 15/07/91 | SS | 2637 | Leyland Tiger | Century Street, Oldpark Road | |
| 09/08/91 | F | 2331 | Bristol RE | Falls Road/Beechmount Avenue | |
| 15/08/91 | F | 2347 | Bristol RE | location unknown | |
| 15/08/91 | F | 2351 | Bristol RE | Donegall Square East | |
| 15/08/91 | SS | 2558 | Bristol RE | North Queen Street | |

*Total number of vehicles lost in this year 13*

| Date | Depot | Fleet No | Type | Location | Notes |
|---|---|---|---|---|---|
| 17/02/92 | F | 2261 | Bristol RE | North Queen Street/Spamount Street | |
| 17/02/92 | AD | 2488 | Bristol RE | Antrim Road/New Lodge Road jctn | |
| 17/02/92 | SS | 2566 | Bristol RE | Antrim Road/New Lodge Road jctn | |
| 21/02/92 | F | 2309 | Bristol RE | Clifton Street | |
| 07/09/92 | SS | 2549 | Bristol RE | Antrim Road/New Lodge Road jctn | |
| 16/09/92 | AD | 2617 | Leyland Tiger | Ardoyne depot | |
| 02/12/92 | F | 2409 | Bristol RE | Woodbourne Police Station | |

*Total number of vehicles lost in this year 7*

| Date | Depot | Fleet No | Type | Location | Notes |
|---|---|---|---|---|---|
| 02/07/93 | F | 2411 | Bristol RE | Limestone Road | |
| 02/07/93 | F | 2417 | Bristol RE | Donegall Road | |

*Total number of vehicles lost in this year 2*

| Date | Depot | Fleet No | Type | Location | Notes |
|---|---|---|---|---|---|
| 22/03/94 | NB | 2513 | Bristol RE | location unknown | |
| 19/08/94 | F | 2445 | Bristol RE | Shankill Road | |
| 13/09/94 | SS | 2622 | Leyland Tiger | North Queen Street | |

*Total number of vehicles lost in this year 3*

| Date | Depot | Fleet No | Type | Location | Notes |
|---|---|---|---|---|---|
| 03/07/95 | SS | 625 | Dennis Dart | Andersonstown Road | |

*Total number of vehicles lost in this year 1*

| Date | Depot | Fleet No | Type | Location | Notes |
|---|---|---|---|---|---|
| 18/03/96 | SS | 638 | Dennis Dart | Ballygomartin | |
| 18/03/96 | SS | 2553 | Bristol RE | Forthriver | |
| 08/07/96 | V | 2507 | Bristol RE | Crumlin Road | |
| 12/07/96 | R | 2332 | Bristol RE | Short Strand depot | |

| Date | Depot | Fleet No | Type | Location | Notes |
|---|---|---|---|---|---|
| 12/07/96 | SS | 2633 | Leyland Tiger | Short Strand depot | |

*Total number of vehicles lost in this year* **5**

| Date | Depot | Fleet No | Type | Location | Notes |
|---|---|---|---|---|---|
| 07/07/97 | F | 2496 | Bristol RE | Andersonstown Road | |
| 07/07/97 | F | 2508 | Bristol RE | Whiterock Road | |
| 07/07/97 | F | 2546 | Bristol RE | Whiterock Road | |
| 07/07/97 | NB | 2652 | Leyland Tiger | Dawson Street, Antrim Road | |
| 07/07/97 | F | 2736 | Volvo B10L | Andersonstown Road | |
| 08/07/97 | F | 2503 | Bristol RE | Falls Park depot | |
| 08/07/97 | F | 2536 | Bristol RE | Falls Park depot | |

*Total number of vehicles lost in this year* **7**

| Date | Depot | Fleet No | Type | Location | Notes |
|---|---|---|---|---|---|
| 07/07/98 | F | 2515 | Bristol RE | Donegall Road | |

*Total number of vehicles lost in this year* **1**

| Date | Depot | Fleet No | Type | Location | Notes |
|---|---|---|---|---|---|
| 15/03/99 | F | 2735 | Volvo B10L | Whiterock Road | |

*Total number of vehicles lost in this year* **1**

| Date | Depot | Fleet No | Type | Location | Notes |
|---|---|---|---|---|---|
| 07/07/00 | F | 2713 | Volvo B10L | Ligoniel | 38 |

*Total number of vehicles lost in this year* **1**

| Date | Depot | Fleet No | Type | Location | Notes |
|---|---|---|---|---|---|
| 28/07/01 | V | 2779 | Volvo B10BLE | Ardoyne Road | |
| 26/09/01 | F | 2728 | Volvo B10L | Cambrai Street | |

*Total number of vehicles lost in this year* **2**

| Date | Depot | Fleet No | Type | Location | Notes |
|---|---|---|---|---|---|
| 04/08/05 | SS | 2927 | Volvo B7TL | Enfield Street | |
| 10/09/05 | SS | 2669 | Leyland Tiger | North Queen Street | |
| 12/09/05 | F | 803 | Scania L94 | Cambrai Street | |

*Total number of vehicles lost in this year* **3**

**TOTAL FOR CITYBUS – 596**

Notes:-

| | |
|---|---|
| 1 | date is a 'by' date; vehicles detaxed 30/06/70. |
| 2 | rebodied with Alexander (Belfast) H44/31F body 9/73. |
| 3 | rebodied with Alexander (Belfast) H44/31F body 10/73. |
| 4 | rebodied with Alexander (Belfast) H44/31F body 11/73. |
| 5 | rebodied with Alexander (Belfast) H44/31F body 12/73. |
| 6 | destroyed in explosion at Alexander (Belfast) factory 26/03/72 whilst receiving new H46/31D body. |
| 7 | rebodied with Alexander (Belfast) H46/31D body 7/72. |
| 8 | rebodied with Alexander (Belfast) H46/31D body 8/72. |
| 9 | rebodied with Alexander (Belfast) H46/31D body 9/72. |
| 10 | rebodied with Alexander (Belfast) H46/31D body 10/72. |
| 11 | rebodied with Alexander (Belfast) H44/31F body 10/73. |
| 12 | rebodied with Alexander (Belfast) H44/31F body 1/74. |
| 13 | rebodied with Alexander (Belfast) H44/31F body 2/74. |
| 14 | rebodied with Alexander (Belfast) H46/31D body 10/72. |
| 15 | rebodied with Alexander (Belfast) B32D body 11/74. |
| 16 | rebodied with Alexander (Belfast) H46/31D body 6/73. |
| 17 | rebodied with Alexander (Belfast) H46/31D body 6/72. |
| 18 | rebodied with Alexander (Belfast) H46/31D body 3/74. |
| 19 | rebodied with Alexander (Belfast) H46/31D body 5/74. |
| 20 | lso recorded as 28/11/73. |
| 21 | rebodied with Alexander (Belfast) H49/37F body 4/76. |
| 22 | detaxed 30/06/75 with fire damage. |
| 23 | also reported as Falls Road, Monagh Road. |
| 24 | also reported as Shankill Road/Tennent Street jctn. |
| 25 | Detaxed 30/04/77 with malicious damage; withdrawn 16/05/77. |
| 26 | Detaxed 31/08/77; all destroyed. |
| 27 | also reported as 2677 (normal withdrawal) |
| 28 | damaged 08/04/77; withdrawn 31/08/77. |
| 29 | Detaxed 31/05/78; maliciously destroyed. |
| 30 | Written off 13/11/78. |
| 31 | Written off 31/01/79 after damage. |
| 32 | rebodied with Alexander (Belfast) B43D body 7/79. |
| 33 | rebodied with Alexander (Belfast) B43D body 9/79. |
| 34 | Written off 09/10/79 following damage. |

| | |
|---|---|
| 35 | Maliciously damaged 13/08/84; written off 02/01/85. |
| 36 | detaxed with malicious damage. |
| 37 | maliciously damaged 17/01/91; written off 01/02/91. |
| 38 | detaxed 31/07/00 with malicious damage; written off 15/11/00. |

## Ulster Transport Authority

| Date | Depot | Fleet Nr | Type | Location |
|---|---|---|---|---|
| 1957? | Ballymena | A495 | Leyland PS1 | Culnafay |
| 1957? | Ballymena | A666 | Leyland PS1 | Culnafay |
| 29/03/57 | Dungiven | Z773? | Leyland PS1 | Dungiven depot |
| 29/03/57 | Dungiven | Z774 | Leyland PS1 | Dungiven depot |
| 29/03/57 | Dungiven | A8587 | Leyland PS1 | Dungiven depot |
| 29/03/57 | Dungiven | B8675 | Leyland PS1 | Dungiven depot |
| 29/03/57 | Dungiven | C8851 | Leyland PS2/1 | Dungiven depot |
| 30/04/58 | Ballymena | B865 | Leyland PD1A | Toomebridge station yard |
| 30/04/58 | Ballymena | Z907 | Leyland PD1 | Toomebridge station yard |
| 12/05/58 | Cookstown | G8983 | Leyland PSU1/9 | Coagh |
| 08/11/58 | Larne | B8668 | Leyland PS1 | Feystown Parochial Hall, Glenarm |

*Total number of vehicles lost* **11**

## Ulsterbus

| Date | Depot | Fleet No | Type | Location | Notes |
|---|---|---|---|---|---|
| 24/04/69 | OM | 9106 | Leyland Olympic | Newtownstewart | 39 |
| 14/06/69 | NY | 32 | Bedford SB5 | Kilkeel depot | 40 |
| 14/06/69 | NY | 64 | Albion Aberdonian | Kilkeel depot | 40 |
| 14/06/69 | NY | 471 | Leyland Tiger Cub | Kilkeel depot | 40 |
| 14/06/69 | NY | 477 | Leyland Tiger Cub | Kilkeel depot | 40 |
| 14/06/69 | NY | 1234 | Bedford VAM | Kilkeel depot | 40 |
| 14/06/69 | NY | 8972 | Leyland Royal Tiger | Kilkeel depot | 40 |
| 14/06/69 | NY | 9002 | Leyland Royal Tiger | Kilkeel depot | 40 |
| 14/06/69 | NY | 9031 | Leyland Royal Tiger | Kilkeel depot | 40 |
| 15/06/69 | LD | 83 | Albion Aberdonian | Strabane depot | |
| 14/08/69 | DG | 52 | Bedford SB5 | Dungannon | |
| 14/08/69 | DG | 109 | Albion Aberdonian | Dungannon | |
| 15/08/69 | DG | 391 | Leyland Tiger Cub | Pomeroy | |
| 10/09/69 | S | 255 | AEC Reliance | Carrickfergus | |

*Total number of vehicles lost in this year* **13**

| Date | Depot | Fleet No | Type | Location | Notes |
|---|---|---|---|---|---|
| 11/06/70 | NC | 8960 | Leyland Royal Tiger | (may not be malicious) | 41 |
| 06/08/70 | LD | 231 | AEC Reliance | Foyle Rd bus pk, Londonderry | 42 |
| 06/08/70 | LD | 297 | AEC Reliance | Foyle Rd bus pk, Londonderry | 42 |

*Total number of vehicles lost in this year* **3**

| Date | Depot | Fleet No | Type | Location | Notes |
|---|---|---|---|---|---|
| 06/02/71 | V | 988 | Leyland Titan PD3 | Shaw's Road, Belfast | |
| 08/03/71 | V | 696 | Leyland Titan PD2 | Leeson Street, Falls Road, Belfast | |
| 15/06/71 | LD | 274 | AEC Reliance | Foyle Road bus park, Londonderry | |
| 17/06/71 | LD | 232 | AEC Reliance | Londonderry | |
| 08/07/71 | LD | 901 | Leyland Titan PD3 | Londonderry | |
| 11/07/71 | LD | 1069 | Bristol RE | Northland Road, Londonderry | |
| 24/07/71 | P | 452 | Leyland Tiger Cub | Lurgan depot | |
| 24/07/71 | LG | 475 | Leyland Tiger Cub | Lurgan depot | |
| 24/07/71 | LG | 489 | Leyland Leopard | Lurgan depot | |
| 24/07/71 | LD | 900 | Leyland Titan PD3 | Location unknown | |
| 26/07/71 | V | 1104 | Bristol LH | Shaw's Road, Belfast | |
| 09/08/71 | E | 307 | Leyland Tiger Cub | Belcoo | |
| 09/08/71 | NY | 314 | Leyland Tiger Cub | Derrybeg, Newry | |
| 09/08/71 | V | 848 | Leyland Titan PD3 | Glen Road, Belfast | |
| 10/08/71 | DG | 336 | Leyland Tiger Cub | Dungannon | |
| 13/08/71 | E | 100 | Albion Aberdonian | Newtownbutler | |
| 13/08/71 | E | 313 | Leyland Tiger Cub | Newtownbutler | |
| 20/08/71 | DG | 450 | Leyland Tiger Cub | Ardboe | |
| 11/09/71 | BM | 261 | AEC Reliance | Brandywell, Londonderry | |
| 18/09/71 | NY | 463 | Leyland Tiger Cub | Kilcoo, Newry | |
| 30/09/71 | C | 371 | Leyland Tiger Cub | Kilrea | |
| 04/10/71 | V | 904 | Leyland Titan PD3 | Shaw's Road/Glen Road, Belfast | |
| 05/10/71 | V | 249 | AEC Reliance | Ramoan Gardens, Belfast | |
| 15/10/71 | M | 479 | Leyland Tiger Cub | Drumany, Coagh | |
| 19/10/71 | NY | 1398 | Leyland Leopard | Newry | 49 |
| 23/10/71 | NC | 9000 | Leyland Royal Tiger | Attical, Kilkeel | 44 |

| Date | Depot | Fleet No | Type | Location | Notes |
|---|---|---|---|---|---|
| 26/10/71 | NY | 35 | Bedford SB5 | Rostrevor | |
| 26/10/71 | LD | 528 | Leyland Leopard | Claudy | |
| 07/11/71 | DG | 90 | Albion Aberdonian | Dungannon | |
| 07/11/71 | NY | 435 | Leyland Tiger Cub | Drumintee, Newry | |
| 13/11/71 | M | 1394 | Leyland Leopard | Bellaghy, Portglenone | 48 |
| 17/11/71 | LD | 1222 | Bedford VAM | Strabane depot | |
| 17/11/71 | LD | 1419 | Leyland Leopard | Strabane depot | 47 |
| 17/11/71 | LD | 1441 | Leyland Leopard | Strabane depot | 46 |
| 20/11/71 | LD | 278 | AEC Reliance | Location unknown | |
| 23/11/71 | OM | 457 | Leyland Tiger Cub | Strabane | |
| 27/11/71 | NY | 58 | Bedford SB5 | McKeogh's Corner, Crossmaglen | |
| 27/11/71 | M | 389 | Leyland Tiger Cub | Coagh | |
| 27/11/71 | LD | 488 | Leyland Leopard | Strabane | |
| 27/11/71 | M | 1047 | Leyland Tiger Cub | Coagh | |
| 27/11/71 | DG | 968 | Leyland Titan PD3 | Dungannon | |
| 29/11/71 | E | 419 | Leyland Tiger Cub | Aghalane | |
| 01/12/71 | DG | 430 | Leyland Tiger Cub | Washing Bay | |
| 07/12/71 | LD | 1229 | Bedford VAM | Limavady | |
| 08/12/71 | E | 315 | Leyland Tiger Cub | Pettigo | |
| 08/12/71 | E | 470 | Leyland Tiger Cub | between Enniskillen and Clones | 45 |
| 14/12/71 | NY | 53 | Bedford SB5 | Jonesborough | |
| 15/12/71 | DG | 1207 | Bedford VAM | Coalisland | |
| 16/12/71 | NY | 42 | Bedford SB5 | Crossmaglen | |
| 17/12/71 | NY | 59 | Bedford SB5 | Jonesborough | |
| 21/12/71 | NY | 247 | AEC Reliance | Belleeks, Newry | |
| 22/12/71 | NY | 21 | Bedford SB5 | Location unknown | 43 |
| 22/12/71 | M | 48 | Bedford SB5 | Location unknown | |
| 22/12/71 | NY | 123 | Bedford SB5 | Newry | |
| 22/12/71 | M | 316 | Leyland Tiger Cub | Coagh | |
| 22/12/71 | M | 380 | Leyland Tiger Cub | Location unknown | |
| 23/12/71 | E | 99 | Albion Aberdonian | Enniskillen | |
| 23/12/71 | E | 461 | Leyland Tiger Cub | Kilturk | |

*Total number of vehicles lost in this year* **58**

| Date | Depot | Fleet No | Type | Location | Notes |
|---|---|---|---|---|---|
| 04/01/72 | LG | 364 | Leyland Tiger Cub | Lurgan | |
| 07/01/72 | OM | 464 | Leyland Tiger Cub | Castlederg | |
| 15/01/72 | LD | 288 | AEC Reliance | Ballyarnett, Londonderry | |
| 23/01/72 | LD | 1237 | Bedford VAM | Claudy | |
| 29/01/72 | E | 107 | Albion Aberdonian | Teemore Crossroads, Enniskillen | |
| 30/01/72 | LD | 8 | Bedford VAS | Claudy depot | |
| 30/01/72 | LD | 57 | Bedford SB5 | Claudy depot | |
| 30/01/72 | NY | 135 | Bedford SB5 | Derrybeg Estate, Newry | |
| 30/01/72 | LD | 144 | Bedford VAS | Claudy depot | |
| 30/01/72 | LD | 283 | AEC Reliance | Claudy depot | |
| 30/01/72 | LD | 993 | Leyland Titan PD3 | Claudy depot | |
| 31/01/72 | NY | 417 | Leyland Tiger Cub | Bessbrook | |
| 31/01/72 | M | 651 | Leyland Titan PD2 | Magherafelt depot | |
| 31/01/72 | V | 1107 | Bristol LH | Glen Road, Belfast | |
| 31/01/72 | AM | 1400 | Leyland Leopard | Lurgan | 51 |
| 31/01/72 | OM | 1423 | Leyland Leopard | Cookstown (also recorded as Carrickmore) | 51 |
| 31/01/72 | M | 1428 | Leyland Leopard | Magherafelt depot | 52 |
| 31/01/72 | M | 1429 | Leyland Leopard | Magherafelt depot | 52 |
| 01/02/72 | OM | 1225 | Bedford VAM | Carrickmore | |
| 02/02/72 | M | 1215 | Bedford VAM | Toomebridge | |
| 04/02/72 | E | 469 | Leyland Tiger Cub | Aghalane | |
| 09/02/72 | LD | 75 | Albion Aberdonian | Claudy | |
| 22/02/72 | LD | 104 | Albion Aberdonian | Strabane | |
| 22/02/72 | NY | 8971 | Leyland Royal Tiger | Newcastle | |
| 24/02/72 | BM | 264 | AEC Reliance | Antrim depot | |
| 24/02/72 | BM | 360 | Leyland Tiger Cub | Antrim depot | |
| 27/02/72 | LB | 362 | Leyland Tiger Cub | Dromara depot | |
| 27/02/72 | LB | 363 | Leyland Tiger Cub | Dromara depot | |
| 27/02/72 | LB | 397 | Leyland Tiger Cub | Dromara depot | |
| 27/02/72 | LB | 398 | Leyland Tiger Cub | Dromara depot | |
| 07/03/72 | V | 600 | Leyland Titan PD2 | Location unknown | |
| 11/03/72 | NY | 1380 | Leyland Leopard | Hilltown | 53 |
| 25/03/72 | C | 516 | Leyland Leopard | Alexanders Coachworks, Belfast | 54 |
| 02/04/72 | C | 403 | Leyland Tiger Cub | Kilrea depot | |
| 02/04/72 | C | 831 | Leyland Titan PD3 | Kilrea depot | |
| 02/04/72 | C | 832 | Leyland Titan PD3 | Kilrea depot | |
| 13/04/72 | S | 155 | Bedford SB5 | Smithfield depot | |
| 13/04/72 | S | 254 | AEC Reliance | Smithfield depot | |
| 13/04/72 | S | 633 | Leyland Titan PD2 | Smithfield depot | |
| 13/04/72 | S | 636 | Leyland Titan PD2 | Smithfield depot | |
| 13/04/72 | S | 640 | Leyland Titan PD2 | Smithfield depot | |
| 13/04/72 | S | 689 | Leyland Titan PD2 | Smithfield depot | |
| 13/04/72 | S | 751 | Leyland Titan PD2 | Smithfield depot | |
| 13/04/72 | S | 814 | Leyland Titan PD3 | Smithfield depot | |
| 13/04/72 | S | 915 | Leyland Atlantean | Smithfield depot | |
| 13/04/72 | S | 971 | Leyland Titan PD3 | Smithfield depot | |
| 13/04/72 | S | 986 | Leyland Titan PD3 | Smithfield depot | |
| 14/04/72 | DG | 431 | Leyland Tiger Cub | Dungannon | |
| 15/04/72 | LB | 532 | Leyland Leopard | Glen Road, Belfast | |
| 15/04/72 | V | 725 | Leyland Titan PD2 | Falls Road, Belfast (also recorded as Glen Road) | |
| 28/04/72 | LD | 7 | Bedford VAS | Claudy depot | |
| 28/04/72 | LD | 26 | Bedford SB5 | Claudy depot | |
| 28/04/72 | LD | 275 | AEC Reliance | Claudy depot | |
| 28/04/72 | LD | 973 | Leyland Titan PD3 | Claudy depot | |
| 28/04/72 | LD | 1373 | Leyland Leopard | Claudy depot | 55 |
| 11/05/72 | M | 17 | Bedford SB5 | Swatragh | |
| 11/05/72 | M | 43 | Bedford SB5 | Swatragh | |
| 11/05/72 | C | 361 | Leyland Tiger Cub | Swatragh | |
| 13/05/72 | M | 22 | Bedford SB5 | Maghera | |
| 21/05/72 | S | 875 | Leyland Titan PD3 | Greenisland/Carrickfergus | |
| 23/06/72 | NY | 45 | Bedford SB5 | Forkhill | |
| 24/06/72 | NC | 1525 | Leyland Leopard | Drumaness | 56 |
| 30/06/72 | M | 1016 | Leyland Tiger Cub | Location unknown | 50 |
| 16/07/72 | OM | 1477 | Leyland Leopard | Strabane | 57 |
| 21/07/72 | S | 62 | Albion Aberdonian | Smithfield depot | |
| 21/07/72 | GS | 149 | Bedford SB5 | Great Victoria Street depot | |
| 21/07/72 | V | 239 | AEC Reliance | Great Victoria Street depot | |
| 21/07/72 | V | 621 | Leyland Titan PD2 | Smithfield depot | |
| 21/07/72 | S | 730 | Leyland Titan PD2 | Smithfield depot | |
| 21/07/72 | S | 738 | Leyland Titan PD2 | Smithfield depot | |
| 21/07/72 | S | 755 | Leyland Titan PD2 | Smithfield depot | |
| 21/07/72 | S | 850 | Leyland Titan PD3 | Smithfield depot | |
| 21/07/72 | S | 880 | Leyland Titan PD3 | Smithfield depot | |
| 21/07/72 | S | 978 | Leyland Titan PD3 | Smithfield depot | |
| 21/07/72 | S | 1036 | Leyland Tiger Cub | Smithfield depot | |
| 21/07/72 | V | 1108 | Bristol LH | Great Victoria Street depot | |
| 21/07/72 | V | 1109 | Bristol LH | Great Victoria Street depot | |
| 21/07/72 | LG | 1231 | Bedford VAM | Great Victoria Street depot | |
| 25/07/72 | NC | 420 | Leyland Tiger Cub | Ballynahinch depot | |
| 25/07/72 | NC | 1324 | Leyland Leopard | Ballynahinch depot | 58 |
| 25/07/72 | NC | 1455 | Leyland Leopard | Ballynahinch depot | 51 |
| 31/07/72 | DG | 1336 | Leyland Leopard | Eglish | 57 |
| 04/08/72 | NY | 258 | AEC Reliance | Carrickagavna | |
| 09/08/72 | NY | 56 | Bedford SB5 | Derrybeg Estate, Newry | |
| 09/08/72 | NY | 137 | Bedford SB5 | Derrybeg Estate, Newry | |
| 12/09/72 | LY | 1053 | Bristol RE | Creggan Estate, Londonderry | |
| 12/09/72 | LD | 1555 | Leyland Leopard | Eglinton | 59 |
| 25/09/72 | AM | 484 | Leyland Leopard | Drumarg Estate, Armagh | |
| 29/09/72 | V | 844 | Leyland Titan PD3 | Grosvenor Road, Belfast | |
| 29/09/72 | LB | 1243 | Bedford VAM | Grosvenor Road, Belfast | |
| 19/10/72 | DG | 310 | Leyland Tiger Cub | Dungannon depot | |
| 23/10/72 | LY | 276 | AEC Reliance | Donemana | |
| 23/10/72 | LD | 539 | Leyland Leopard | Donemana | |
| 31/10/72 | AM | 1512 | Leyland Leopard | Tullymore | 60 |
| 02/11/72 | NC | 1202 | Bedford VAM | Newcastle depot | |
| 02/11/72 | NC | 9025 | Leyland Royal Tiger | Newcastle depot | |
| 09/11/72 | LD | 19 | Bedford SB5 | Drumahoe | |
| 27/11/72 | M | 389 | Leyland Tiger Cub | Coagh | |
| 20/12/72 | DG | 1504 | Leyland Leopard | Meenagh Park, Coalisland | 59 |

*Total number of vehicles lost in this year* **99**

| Date | Depot | Fleet No | Type | Location | Notes |
|---|---|---|---|---|---|
| 11/01/73 | P | 400 | Leyland Tiger Cub | Obins Street, Portadown | |
| 31/01/73 | DG | 1303 | Leyland Leopard | Bridge Street, Strabane | 62 |
| 01/02/73 | OX | 1438 | Leyland Leopard | Tullycarnet, Belfast | 63 |
| 02/02/73 | OX | 1371 | Leyland Leopard | Castlereagh Road, Belfast | 64 |
| 02/02/73 | OX | 1474 | Leyland Leopard | Castlereagh Road, Belfast | 65 |
| 08/03/73 | NY | 141 | Bedford SB5 | Newry | |
| 22/05/73 | LY | 1070 | Bristol RE | Creggan, Londonderry | |
| 04/07/73 | LY | 1060 | Bristol RE | Shantallow, Londonderry | |
| 12/07/73 | NY | 125 | Bedford SB5 | Location unknown | |
| 21/07/73 | SF | 806 | Leyland Titan PD3 | Smithfield depot | |
| 13/08/73 | LY | 1063 | Bristol RE | Creggan, Londonderry | |
| 01/09/73 | LG | 883 | Leyland Titan PD3 | Lurgan depot | |
| 01/09/73 | LG | 889 | Leyland Titan PD3 | Lurgan depot | |
| 01/09/73 | LG | 941 | Leyland Atlantean | Lurgan depot | |
| 01/09/73 | LG | 942 | Leyland Atlantean | Lurgan depot | |
| 01/09/73 | LG | 943 | Leyland Atlantean | Lurgan depot | |
| 10/10/73 | OX | 896 | Leyland Titan PD3 | Location unknown | |
| 26/10/73 | AM | 112 | Albion Aberdonian | Armagh | |
| 26/10/73 | M | 1213 | Bedford VAM | Glenshane Pass | |
| 07/11/73 | SF | 857 | Leyland Titan PD3 | Monkstown Estate, Newtownabbey | 61 |
| 27/11/73 | OM | 118 | Bedford VAL | Strabane | 61 |
| 27/11/73 | M | 355 | Leyland Tiger Cub | Coagh | 61 |

| Date | Depot | Fleet No | Type | Location | Notes |
|------|-------|----------|------|----------|-------|
| 27/11/73 | LG | 1383 | Leyland Leopard | Lurgan | **61, 66** |
| 27/11/73 | NY | 1432 | Leyland Leopard | Egyptian Arch, Newry | **61, 62** |
| 29/12/73 | R | 723 | Leyland Titan PD2 | Lisburn depot | |
| 29/12/73 | R | 728 | Leyland Titan PD2 | Lisburn depot | |
| 29/12/73 | R | 776 | Leyland Titan PD2 | Lisburn depot | |
| 29/12/73 | wtn | 820 | Leyland Titan PD3 | Lisburn depot | |
| 29/12/73 | wtn | 1100 | Ford R192 | Lisburn depot | |

*Total number of vehicles lost in this year* **30**

| Date | Depot | Fleet No | Type | Location | Notes |
|------|-------|----------|------|----------|-------|
| 06/01/74 | AM | 61 | Albion Aberdonian | Middleton | **68** |
| 13/01/74 | LR | 293 | AEC Reliance | Carnlough depot | **69** |
| 13/01/74 | LR | 1488 | Leyland Leopard | Carnlough depot | **69, 70** |
| 13/01/74 | LR | 1547 | Leyland Leopard | Carnlough depot | **69, 71** |
| 19/01/74 | NA | 803 | Leyland Titan PD3 | Ballybeen, Dundonald | |
| 19/01/74 | OX | 1525 | Leyland Leopard | Newtownards Road, Belfast | |
| 24/01/74 | V | 1529 | Leyland Leopard | Norglen Parade, Belfast | |
| 31/01/74 | E | 79 | Albion Aberdonian | Location unknown | **77** |
| 31/01/74 | C | 808 | Leyland Titan PD3 | Location unknown | **67, 77** |
| 17/02/74 | LD | 1420 | Leyland Leopard | Strabane | **74** |
| 18/02/74 | DG | 1410 | Leyland Leopard | Dungannon | **72** |
| 28/02/74 | NA | 827 | Leyland Titan PD3 | Location unknown | **77** |
| 25/06/74 | LD | 1418 | Leyland Leopard | Strabane | **67** |
| 09/08/74 | LB | 526 | Leyland Leopard | Alma Street, Belfast | |
| 09/08/74 | NY | 1613 | Bristol LH | Warrenpoint Road, Newry | |
| 08/09/74 | LY | 280 | AEC Reliance | Location unknown | |
| 08/09/74 | LD | 290 | AEC Reliance | Location unknown | |
| 29/09/74 | LD | 298 | AEC Reliance | Londonderry | |
| 10/10/74 | LD | 299 | AEC Reliance | Londonderry | |
| 12/10/74 | LY | 233 | AEC Reliance | Londonderry | |
| 16/10/74 | SF | 816 | Leyland Titan PD3 | Shore Road, Belfast | |
| 16/10/74 | V | 1347 | Leyland Leopard | Twinbrook | **73** |
| 17/10/74 | C | 787 | Leyland Titan PD3 | Ballymoney depot | |
| 17/10/74 | C | 800 | Leyland Titan PD3 | Ballymoney depot | |
| 17/10/74 | C | 882 | Leyland Titan PD3 | Ballymoney depot | |
| 17/10/74 | SF | 1325 | Leyland Leopard | Antrim Road, Belfast | |
| 17/10/74 | C | 1562 | Leyland Leopard | Ballymoney depot | |
| 17/10/74 | C | 1664 | Bristol LH | Ballymoney depot | **75** |
| 17/10/74 | C | 1690 | Bristol LH | Ballymoney depot | |
| 22/10/74 | LD | 485 | Leyland Leopard | Strabane | |
| 24/10/74 | LY | 1068 | Bristol RE | Shantallow, Londonderry | |
| 25/10/74 | C | 1692 | Bristol LH | Kilrea | **76** |
| 06/11/74 | AM | 84 | Albion Aberdonian | Armagh | |
| 06/11/74 | LD | 270 | AEC Reliance | Dungiven depot | |
| 06/11/74 | LD | 273 | AEC Reliance | Dungiven depot | |
| 06/11/74 | M | 429 | Leyland Tiger Cub | Campbells Corner, Bellaghy | |
| 06/11/74 | LD | 1240 | Bedford VAM | Dungiven depot | |
| 06/11/74 | M | 1449 | Leyland Leopard | Hillhead/Bellaghy | |
| 06/11/74 | LD | 1656 | Bristol LH | Dungiven depot | |
| 07/11/74 | DG | 426 | Leyland Tiger Cub | Pomeroy | |
| 07/11/74 | DG | 1729 | Bedford YRQ | Cappagh | |
| 09/11/74 | LG | 881 | Leyland Titan PD3 | Lurgan depot | |
| 09/11/74 | LG | 979 | Leyland Titan PD3 | Lurgan depot | |
| 20/12/74 | M | 1339 | Leyland Leopard | Bellaghy | |

*Total number of vehicles lost in this year* **44**

| Date | Depot | Fleet No | Type | Location | Notes |
|------|-------|----------|------|----------|-------|
| 19/01/75 | AM | 423 | Leyland Tiger Cub | Darkley, Keady | |
| 26/05/75 | LR | 797 | Leyland Titan PD3 | Main Street, Ballycraigy | |
| 08/08/75 | V | 1930 | Leyland Leopard | Dunville Park | **67** |

*Total number of vehicles lost in this year* **3**

| Date | Depot | Fleet No | Type | Location | Notes |
|------|-------|----------|------|----------|-------|
| 13/01/76 | DG | 436 | Leyland Tiger Cub | Dungannon depot | |
| 13/01/76 | DG | 449 | Leyland Tiger Cub | Dungannon depot | |
| 13/01/76 | DG | 456 | Leyland Tiger Cub | Dungannon depot | |
| 13/01/76 | DG | 460 | Leyland Tiger Cub | Dungannon depot | |
| 13/01/76 | DG | 472 | Leyland Tiger Cub | Dungannon depot | |
| 13/01/76 | DG | 503 | Leyland Leopard | Dungannon depot | |
| 23/01/76 | V | 1929 | Leyland Leopard | Whiterock Road | |
| 12/02/76 | LB | 1504 | Leyland Leopard | The Cutts, Derriaghy | |
| 13/02/76 | C | 335 | Leyland Tiger Cub | Ballycastle depot | |
| 13/02/76 | LD | 505 | Leyland Leopard | Strabane | |
| 13/02/76 | LY | 2009 | Bristol RE | Gobnascale | |
| 25/05/76 | SF | 1210 | Bedford VAM | Carrickfergus depot | |
| 25/05/76 | SF | 1261 | Bedford VAM | Carrickfergus depot | |
| 25/05/76 | SF | 1309 | Leyland Leopard | Carrickfergus depot | |
| 27/07/76 | LY | 1065 | Bristol RE | Location unknown | |
| 08/08/76 | LB | 1709 | Bedford YRQ | Location unknown | |
| 08/08/76 | V | 1931 | Leyland Leopard | Location unknown | |
| 08/08/76 | SF | 1953 | Leyland Leopard | Location unknown | |
| 14/08/76 | OX | 269 | AEC Reliance | Oxford Street depot | |
| 16/08/76 | NY | 1326 | Leyland Leopard | Clontygora, Newry | |
| 05/09/76 | LD | 487 | Leyland Leopard | Pennyburn depot, Londonderry | |
| 05/09/76 | LD | 501 | Leyland Leopard | Pennyburn depot, Londonderry | |
| 05/09/76 | LD | 1372 | Leyland Leopard | Pennyburn depot, Londonderry | |
| 05/09/76 | LY | 2010 | Bristol RE | Pennyburn depot, Londonderry | |
| 13/09/76 | SF | 1331 | Leyland Leopard | Newtownabbey | |
| 15/09/76 | OX | 267 | AEC Reliance | Great Victoria Street depot | |
| 15/09/76 | GS | 586 | Leyland Leopard | Great Victoria Street depot | |
| 15/09/76 | V | 1531 | Leyland Leopard | Great Victoria Street depot | |
| 15/09/76 | OX | 2030 | Bristol RE | Great Victoria Street depot | |
| 15/09/76 | BG | 2040 | Bristol RE | Bangor depot | |
| 16/09/76 | M | 1809 | Bedford YRT | Magherafelt depot | |
| 16/10/76 | C | 352 | Leyland Tiger Cub | Ballycastle depot | |
| 16/10/76 | C | 374 | Leyland Tiger Cub | Ballycastle depot | |
| 16/10/76 | BM | 409 | Leyland Tiger Cub | Ballycastle depot | |
| 16/10/76 | C | 1563 | Leyland Leopard | Ballycastle depot | |
| 16/10/76 | C | 1564 | Leyland Leopard | Ballycastle depot | |
| 16/10/76 | C | 1839 | Bedford YLQ | Ballycastle depot | |
| 28/10/76 | DG | 347 | Leyland Tiger Cub | Dungannon depot | |
| 28/10/76 | DG | 366 | Leyland Tiger Cub | Dungannon depot | |
| 28/10/76 | DG | 401 | Leyland Tiger Cub | Dungannon depot | |
| 28/10/76 | DG | 418 | Leyland Tiger Cub | Dungannon depot | |
| 28/10/76 | DG | 445 | Leyland Tiger Cub | Dungannon depot | |
| 28/10/76 | DG | 447 | Leyland Tiger Cub | Dungannon depot | |
| 28/10/76 | NY | 448 | Leyland Tiger Cub | Dungannon depot | |
| 28/10/76 | DG | 455 | Leyland Tiger Cub | Dungannon depot | |
| 28/10/76 | DG | 496 | Leyland Tiger Cub | Dungannon depot | |
| 28/10/76 | DG | 504 | Leyland Leopard | Dungannon depot | |
| 28/10/76 | DG | 508 | Leyland Leopard | Dungannon depot | |
| 28/10/76 | DG | 1711 | Bedford YRQ | Dungannon depot | |
| 28/10/76 | DG | 1772 | Bedford YRQ | Dungannon depot | |
| 28/10/76 | DG | 1776 | Bedford YRQ | Dungannon depot | |
| 28/10/76 | DG | 1805 | Bedford YRT | Dungannon depot | |
| 28/10/76 | DG | 1906 | Leyland Leopard | Dungannon depot | |
| 07/11/76 | OX | 263 | AEC Reliance | Oxford Street depot | |
| 07/11/76 | OX | 1358 | Leyland Leopard | Oxford Street depot | |
| 13/12/76 | MF | 390 | Leyland Tiger Cub | Location unknown | |
| 13/12/76 | LG | 1204 | Bedford VAM | Location unknown | |

*Total number of vehicles lost in this year* **58**

| Date | Depot | Fleet No | Type | Location | Notes |
|------|-------|----------|------|----------|-------|
| 28/01/77 | OX | 1415 | Leyland Leopard | Comber | |
| 10/02/77 | DG | 411 | Leyland Leopard | Dungannon depot | |
| 10/02/77 | NY | 1430 | Leyland Leopard | Forkhill Road, Newry | |
| 28/02/77 | M | 927 | Leyland Atlantean | Ballymena depot | |
| 28/02/77 | BM | 1667 | Bristol LH | Ballymena depot | |
| 28/02/77 | BM | 1682 | Bristol LH | Ballymena depot | |
| 28/02/77 | BM | 1693 | Bristol LH | Ballymena depot | |
| 28/02/77 | BM | 1914 | Leyland Leopard | Ballymena depot | |
| 21/03/77 | V | 1509 | Leyland Leopard | Monagh By-Pass, Belfast | |
| 29/04/77 | DS | 330 | Leyland Tiger Cub | Oxford Street depot | |
| 07/07/77 | SB | 308 | Leyland Tiger Cub | Whiterock, Belfast | |
| 13/07/77 | C | 1404 | Leyland Leopard | Ballycastle depot | |
| 13/07/77 | C | 1848 | Bedford YLQ | Ballycastle depot | |
| 13/07/77 | C | 1851 | Bedford YLQ | Ballycastle depot | |
| 22/07/77 | LG | 1223 | Bedford VAM | Location unknown | **79** |
| 11/08/77 | LD | 1785 | Bedford YRQ | Claudy | |
| 15/10/77 | C | 465 | Leyland Tiger Cub | Ballycastle depot | |
| 15/10/77 | C | 1258 | Bedford VAM | Ballycastle depot | |
| 15/10/77 | C | 1844 | Bedford YLQ | Ballycastle depot | |
| 25/10/77 | NY | 2521 | AEC Merlin | Meigh. | |
| 10/11/77 | V | 1455 | Leyland Leopard | Twinbrook, Belfast | |
| 30/11/77 | V | 1532 | Leyland Leopard | Twinbrook, Belfast | |
| 17/12/77 | OX | 259 | AEC Reliance | Great Victoria Street depot | |
| 17/12/77 | OX | 1461 | Leyland Leopard | Great Victoria Street depot | |
| 17/12/77 | GS | 1702 | Bedford YRQ | Great Victoria Street depot | |

*Total number of vehicles lost in this year* **24**

| Date | Depot | Fleet No | Type | Location | Notes |
|------|-------|----------|------|----------|-------|
| 29/01/78 | LD | 1946 | Leyland Leopard | Twinbrook, Belfast | |
| 19/02/78 | LD | 277 | AEC Reliance | Pennyburn depot, Londonderry | |
| 19/02/78 | LY | 282 | AEC Reliance | Pennyburn depot, Londonderry | |
| 19/02/78 | LY | 285 | AEC Reliance | Pennyburn depot, Londonderry | |
| 19/02/78 | LY | 289 | AEC Reliance | Pennyburn depot, Londonderry | |
| 19/02/78 | LY | 294 | AEC Reliance | Pennyburn depot, Londonderry | |

| Date | Depot | Fleet No | Type | Location | Notes |
|---|---|---|---|---|---|
| 19/02/78 | LD | 578 | Leyland Leopard | Pennyburn depot, Londonderry | |
| 19/02/78 | LY | 1056 | Bristol RE | Pennyburn depot, Londonderry | |
| 19/02/78 | LY | 1057 | Bristol RE | Pennyburn depot, Londonderry | |
| 19/02/78 | LY | 1061 | Bristol RE | Pennyburn depot, Londonderry | |
| 19/02/78 | LY | 1064 | Bristol RE | Pennyburn depot, Londonderry | |
| 19/02/78 | LD | 1557 | Leyland Leopard | Pennyburn depot, Londonderry | |
| 19/02/78 | LD | 1947 | Leyland Leopard | Pennyburn depot, Londonderry | |
| 19/02/78 | LD | 1949 | Leyland Leopard | Pennyburn depot, Londonderry | |
| 19/02/78 | LY | 2001 | Bristol RE | Pennyburn depot, Londonderry | |
| 19/02/78 | LY | 2002 | Bristol RE | Pennyburn depot, Londonderry | |
| 19/02/78 | LY | 2013 | Bristol RE | Pennyburn depot, Londonderry | |
| 19/02/78 | LD | 2206 | Bristol RE | Pennyburn depot, Londonderry | |
| 19/02/78 | LD | 2207 | Bristol RE | Pennyburn depot, Londonderry | |
| 19/02/78 | LD | 2209 | Bristol RE | Pennyburn depot, Londonderry | |
| 29/04/78 | V | 238 | AEC Reliance | Twinbrook, Belfast | |
| 07/05/78 | DG | 490 | Leyland Leopard | Dungannon depot | |
| 07/05/78 | DG | 2510 | AEC Merlin | Dungannon depot | |
| 07/05/78 | DG | 2514 | AEC Merlin | Dungannon depot | |
| 29/05/78 | V | 1933 | Leyland Leopard | Location unknown | |
| 04/06/78 | CL | 1857 | Bedford YLQ | Ballycastle depot | |
| 10/06/78 | NY | 530 | Leyland Leopard | Newry depot | |
| 10/06/78 | NY | 1486 | Leyland Leopard | Newry depot | |
| 12/06/78 | SF | 912 | Leyland Atlantean | Smithfield depot | |
| 12/06/78 | SF | 936 | Leyland Atlantean | Smithfield depot | |
| 12/06/78 | SF | 937 | Leyland Atlantean | Smithfield depot | |
| 12/06/78 | SF | 938 | Leyland Atlantean | Smithfield depot | |
| 12/06/78 | SF | 1308 | Leyland Leopard | Smithfield depot | |
| 12/06/78 | SF | 1310 | Leyland Leopard | Smithfield depot | |
| 12/06/78 | SF | 1315 | Leyland Leopard | Smithfield depot | |
| 12/06/78 | SF | 1316 | Leyland Leopard | Smithfield depot | |
| 12/06/78 | SF | 1319 | Leyland Leopard | Smithfield depot | |
| 12/06/78 | SF | 1324 | Leyland Leopard | Smithfield depot | |
| 12/06/78 | SF | 1332 | Leyland Leopard | Smithfield depot | |
| 12/06/78 | SF | 1438 | Leyland Leopard | Smithfield depot | |
| 12/06/78 | SF | 1477 | Leyland Leopard | Smithfield depot | |
| 12/06/78 | SF | 1517 | Leyland Leopard | Smithfield depot | |
| 12/06/78 | SF | 1518 | Leyland Leopard | Smithfield depot | |
| 12/06/78 | SF | 1760 | Bedford YRQ | Smithfield depot | |
| 12/06/78 | SF | 1761 | Bedford YRQ | Smithfield depot | |
| 12/06/78 | SF | 1762 | Bedford YRQ | Smithfield depot | |
| 12/06/78 | SF | 1795 | Bedford YRQ | Smithfield depot | |
| 12/06/78 | SF | 1952 | Leyland Leopard | Smithfield depot | |
| 12/06/78 | SF | 2121 | Bristol RE | Smithfield depot | |
| 18/08/78 | NY | 1328 | Leyland Leopard | Newry depot | |
| 18/08/78 | NY | 1329 | Leyland Leopard | Newry depot | |
| 18/08/78 | NY | 1407 | Leyland Leopard | Newry depot | |
| 18/08/78 | NY | 1408 | Leyland Leopard | Newry depot | |
| 18/08/78 | NY | 1618 | Bristol LH | Newry depot | |
| 18/08/78 | NY | 1871 | Bedford YLQ | Newry depot | |
| 18/08/78 | NY | 1872 | Bedford YLQ | Newry depot | |
| 23/08/78 | LY | 1054 | Bristol RE | Rosemount, Londonderry | |
| 24/08/78 | LD | 1679 | Bristol LH | Location unknown | |
| 01/10/78 | V | 1344 | Leyland Leopard | Twinbrook, Belfast | |
| 15/10/78 | LY | 2494 | AEC Merlin | Location unknown | |
| 09/12/78 | wtn | 287 | AEC Reliance | Pennyburn depot, Londonderry | |
| 09/12/78 | LD | 292 | AEC Reliance | Pennyburn depot, Londonderry | |
| 09/12/78 | wtn | 985 | Leyland Titan PD3 | Pennyburn depot, Londonderry | |
| 09/12/78 | LD | 1214 | Bedford VAM | Pennyburn depot, Londonderry | |
| 09/12/78 | LY | 1221 | Bedford VAM | Pennyburn depot, Londonderry | |
| 09/12/78 | LD | 1233 | Bedford VAM | Pennyburn depot, Londonderry | |
| 09/12/78 | LY | 1244 | Bedford VAM | Pennyburn depot, Londonderry | |
| 09/12/78 | R | 2496 | AEC Merlin | Pennyburn depot, Londonderry | |
| 09/12/78 | LD | 2707 | Daimler Fleetline DD | Pennyburn depot, Londonderry | |
| 09/12/78 | LD | 2709 | Daimler Fleetline DD | Pennyburn depot, Londonderry | |
| 09/12/78 | LD | 2728 | Daimler Fleetline DD | Pennyburn depot, Londonderry | |
| 31/12/78 | R | 319 | Leyland Tiger Cub | Ballycastle depot | |
| 31/12/78 | R | 406 | Leyland Tiger Cub | Ballycastle depot | |

*Total number of vehicles lost in this year* **73**

| Date | Depot | Fleet No | Type | Location | Notes |
|---|---|---|---|---|---|
| 21/01/79 | V | 1426 | Leyland Leopard | Twinbrook, Belfast | |
| 04/02/79 | LD | 115 | Leyland Leopard | Dungannon depot | |
| 04/02/79 | DG | 516 | Leyland Leopard | Dungannon depot | |
| 04/02/79 | DG | 1410 | Leyland Leopard | Dungannon depot | |
| 04/02/79 | DG | 1901 | Leyland Leopard | Dungannon depot | |
| 04/02/79 | DG | 1907 | Leyland Leopard | Dungannon depot | |
| 04/02/79 | DG | 1976 | Leyland Leopard | Dungannon depot | |
| 04/02/79 | DG | 1988 | Leyland Leopard | Dungannon depot | |
| 04/02/79 | DG | 1989 | Leyland Leopard | Dungannon depot | |
| 03/03/79 | NY | 2520 | AEC Merlin | Meigh | |
| 01/05/79 | V | 1346 | Leyland Leopard | Twinbrook, Belfast | |
| 04/06/79 | DG | 2516 | AEC Merlin | Location unknown | 80 |
| 08/06/79 | OX | 1460 | Leyland Leopard | Saintfield | |
| 08/08/79 | CL | 1950 | Leyland Leopard | North Queen Street, Belfast | |
| 08/08/79 | NA | 1956 | Leyland Leopard | North Queen Street, Belfast | |
| 09/08/79 | LY | 1062 | Bristol RE | Location unknown | |
| 11/08/79 | OM | 154 | Leyland Leopard | Aughnacloy | |
| 01/12/79 | NY | 1612 | Bristol LH | Rathfriland depot | |
| 01/12/79 | NY | 1616 | Bristol LH | Rathfriland depot | |
| 01/12/79 | NY | 1617 | Bristol LH | Rathfriland depot | |
| 01/12/79 | NY | 1619 | Bristol LH | Rathfriland depot | |
| 01/12/79 | NY | 1625 | Bristol LH | Rathfriland depot | |
| 01/12/79 | NY | 1626 | Bristol LH | Rathfriland depot | |
| 01/12/79 | NY | 1627 | Bristol LH | Rathfriland depot | |
| 01/12/79 | NY | 1628 | Bristol LH | Rathfriland depot | |
| 01/12/79 | NY | 1873 | Bedford YLQ | Rathfriland depot | |

*Total number of vehicles lost in this year* **26**

| Date | Depot | Fleet No | Type | Location | Notes |
|---|---|---|---|---|---|
| 02/02/80 | SF | 14 | AEC Swift (on loan from Citybus) | Oxford Street depot | |
| 29/02/80 | NY | 160 | Leyland Leopard | Newry depot | |
| 29/02/80 | NY | 1330 | Leyland Leopard | Newry depot | |
| 29/02/80 | NY | 1359 | Leyland Leopard | Newry depot | |
| 29/02/80 | NY | 1533 | Leyland Leopard | Newry depot | |
| 29/02/80 | NY | 1870 | Bedford YLQ | Newry depot | |
| 29/02/80 | NY | 1879 | Bedford YLQ | Newry depot | |
| 29/02/80 | NY | 2243 | Bristol RE | Newry depot | |
| 29/02/80 | NY | 2248 | Bristol RE | Newry depot | |
| 29/02/80 | NY | 2370 | Bristol RE | Newry depot | |
| 29/02/80 | NY | 2372 | Bristol RE | Newry depot | |
| 29/02/80 | NY | 2507 | AEC Merlin | Newry depot | |
| 13/04/80 | OX | 268 | AEC Reliance | Oxford Street depot | |
| 12/06/80 | CL | 1833 | Bedford YLQ | Kilrea depot | |
| 12/06/80 | CL | 1835 | Bedford YLQ | Kilrea depot | |
| 06/07/80 | R | 1218 | Bedford VAM | Ardoyne depot (on loan to Citybus) | |
| 09/08/80 | LY | 1059 | Bristol RE | Westland Street or Iniscain Road, Creggan | |
| 12/08/80 | LY | 1052 | Bristol RE | William Street, Londonderry | |
| 14/08/80 | LY | 1055 | Bristol RE | Creggan, Londonderry | |
| 16/08/80 | NA | 1355 | Leyland Leopard | Donaghadee depot | |
| 16/08/80 | NA | 1365 | Leyland Leopard | Donaghadee depot | |
| 16/08/80 | NA | 1411 | Leyland Leopard | Donaghadee depot | |
| 16/08/80 | OX | 1414 | Leyland Leopard | Donaghadee depot | |
| 16/08/80 | NA | 1715 | Bedford YRQ | Donaghadee depot | |
| 12/12/80 | LB | 1429 | Leyland Leopard | Lisburn depot | |
| 12/12/80 | LY | 2020 | Bristol RE | Shantallow, Londonderry | |

*Total number of vehicles lost in this year* **26**

| Date | Depot | Fleet No | Type | Location | Notes |
|---|---|---|---|---|---|
| 01/02/81 | LY | 2011 | Bristol RE | William Street, Londonderry | |
| 17/03/81 | LR | 1791 | Bedford YRQ | Carnlough depot | |
| 23/04/81 | DG | 1774 | Bedford YRQ | The Square, Coalisland | |
| 25/04/81 | NY | 1783 | Bedford YRQ | Jonesborough | |
| 27/04/81 | M | 110 | Leyland Leopard | Toomebridge | |
| 05/05/81 | AT | 1485 | Leyland Leopard | Staffordstown Road, Toomebridge | |
| 05/05/81 | LD | 1650 | Bristol LH | Shantallow, Londonderry | |
| 05/05/81 | AM | 1712 | Bedford YRQ | Monaghan | |
| 05/05/81 | CL | 1846 | Bedford YLQ | Swatragh | |
| 05/05/81 | CL | 1942 | Leyland Leopard | Swatragh | |
| 05/05/81 | M | 2303 | Bristol RE | Swatragh | |
| 16/05/81 | R | 1196 | Leyland Leopard | Ballycastle depot | |
| 16/05/81 | CL | 1850 | Bedford YLQ | Ballycastle depot | |
| 16/05/81 | CL | 1854 | Bedford YLQ | Ballycastle depot | |
| 19/05/81 | E | 234 | Leyland Leopard | Belleek | |
| 19/05/81 | LY | 1067 | Bristol RE | Rosemount, Londonderry | |
| 21/05/81 | BM | 1688 | Bristol LH | Glarryford | |
| 22/05/81 | NY | 1817 | Bedford YRT | Derrybeg Estate, Newry | |
| 26/05/81 | LY | 2122 | Bristol RE | Creggan, Londonderry | |
| 03/06/81 | LY | 1144 | Leyland Leopard | Shantallow, Londonderry | |
| 05/06/81 | CL | 512 | Leyland Leopard | Ballymoney depot | |
| 05/06/81 | CL | 920 | Leyland Atlantean | Ballymoney depot | |
| 05/06/81 | CL | 1176 | Leyland Leopard | Ballymoney depot | |
| 05/06/81 | CL | 1567 | Leyland Leopard | Ballymoney depot | |
| 05/06/81 | CL | 1799 | Bedford YRQ | Ballymoney depot | |
| 05/06/81 | CL | 1849 | Bedford YLQ | Ballymoney depot | |
| 05/06/81 | CL | 1853 | Bedford YLQ | Ballymoney depot | |
| 05/06/81 | LY | 2023 | Bristol RE | Creggan, Londonderry | |
| 05/06/81 | CL | 2278 | Bristol RE | Ballymoney depot | |
| 05/06/81 | CL | 2396 | Bristol RE | Ballymoney depot | |
| 11/06/81 | NY | 1814 | Bedford YRT | Derrybeg Estate, Newry | |

*The last Bristol RE built for service in Northern Ireland, although not the last to enter service, was No 2600, a Coleraine-allocated bus. It spent much of its life based at the Ballycastle sub-depot.* **Jonathan Miller collection**

**Left and opposite top:**
*What would surely have been a worthy preservation candidate, No 2600's life was brought to a premature end on 13 July 1996 when it was destroyed in an arson attack on Ballycastle depot.*
**Jonathan Miller collection**

*Another Coleraine sub-depot, Portrush, was attacked on 5 May 2004 with the loss of a number of buses, including Leopard No 284. Leyland Tigers Nos 1220 and 1442 were also destroyed in this incident. The remains of No 1442 can be glimpsed just to the left of No 284.*
**Jonathan Miller**

| Date | Depot | Fleet No | Type | Location | Notes |
|---|---|---|---|---|---|
| 06/07/81 | LY | 2008 | Bristol RE | Creggan, Londonderry | |
| 15/07/81 | DG | 1544 | Leyland Leopard | Washing Bay, Coalisland | |
| 17/07/81 | LY | 1148 | Leyland Leopard | Creggan, Londonderry | |
| 17/07/81 | LY | 1183 | Leyland Leopard | Creggan, Londonderry | |
| 17/07/81 | LY | 1199 | Leyland Leopard | Slievemore, Shantallow, Londonderry | |
| 22/07/81 | M | 1353 | Leyland Leopard | Moneynick | |
| 01/08/81 | DG | 1458 | Leyland Leopard | Dungannon | |
| 01/08/81 | LD | 1572 | Leyland Leopard | Feeny | |
| 05/08/81 | LY | 1066 | Bristol RE | Spencer Road, Londonderry | |
| 11/10/81 | LY | 1135 | Leyland Leopard | Rosemount, Londonderry | |

*Total number of vehicles lost in this year* **41**

| Date | Depot | Fleet No | Type | Location | Notes |
|---|---|---|---|---|---|
| 21/03/82 | LY | 2004 | Bristol RE | Rossville Flats, Londonderry | |
| 22/03/82 | LY | 1134 | Leyland Leopard | Rossville Flats, Londonderry | |
| 23/03/82 | LY | 1145 | Leyland Leopard | Rossville Flats/William Street, Londonderry | |
| 29/03/82 | LY | 1137 | Leyland Leopard | Rossville Flats, Londonderry | |
| 31/03/82 | LY | 1136 | Leyland Leopard | Location unknown | 67 |
| 17/04/82 | LY | 1147 | Leyland Leopard | Racecourse Road, Londonderry | |
| 17/04/82 | LD | 1697 | Bristol LH | Rossville Flats, Londonderry | |
| 21/04/82 | LY | 1150 | Leyland Leopard | Lone Moor, Londonderry | |
| 21/04/82 | LY | 2016 | Bristol RE | Shantallow, Londonderry | |
| 23/04/82 | LD | 1658 | Bristol LH | Creggan, Londonderry | |
| 27/04/82 | AM | 101 | Leyland Leopard | Armagh depot | |
| 27/04/82 | AM | 143 | Leyland Leopard | Armagh depot | |
| 27/04/82 | AM | 156 | Leyland Leopard | Armagh depot | |
| 27/04/82 | AM | 191 | Leyland Leopard | Armagh depot | |
| 27/04/82 | AM | 216 | Leyland Leopard | Armagh depot | |
| 27/04/82 | AM | 486 | Leyland Leopard | Armagh depot | |
| 27/04/82 | AM | 513 | Leyland Leopard | Armagh depot | |
| 27/04/82 | AM | 514 | Leyland Leopard | Armagh depot | |
| 27/04/82 | AM | 515 | Leyland Leopard | Armagh depot | |
| 27/04/82 | AM | 1543 | Leyland Leopard | Armagh depot | |
| 27/04/82 | AM | 1545 | Leyland Leopard | Armagh depot | |
| 27/04/82 | AM | 1703 | Bedford YRQ | Armagh depot | |
| 27/04/82 | AM | 1704 | Bedford YRQ | Armagh depot | |
| 27/04/82 | AM | 1707 | Bedford YRQ | Armagh depot | |
| 27/04/82 | AM | 1720 | Bedford YRQ | Armagh depot | |
| 27/04/82 | AM | 1721 | Bedford YRQ | Armagh depot | |
| 27/04/82 | AM | 1737 | Bedford YRQ | Armagh depot | |
| 27/04/82 | AM | 1738 | Bedford YRQ | Armagh depot | |
| 27/04/82 | AM | 1768 | Bedford YRQ | Armagh depot | |
| 27/04/82 | AM | 1770 | Bedford YRQ | Armagh depot | |
| 27/04/82 | AM | 1771 | Bedford YRQ | Armagh depot | |
| 27/04/82 | AM | 1798 | Bedford YRQ | Armagh depot | |
| 27/04/82 | R | 1803 | Bedford YRT | Armagh depot | |
| 27/04/82 | R | 1806 | Bedford YRT | Armagh depot | |
| 27/04/82 | AM | 1908 | Leyland Leopard | Armagh depot | |
| 27/04/82 | AM | 1977 | Leyland Leopard | Armagh depot | |
| 09/05/82 | OX | 1592 | Leyland Leopard | Oxford Street depot | |
| 09/05/82 | OX | 2262 | Bristol RE | Oxford Street depot | 83 |
| 05/06/82 | LR | 1754 | Bedford YRQ | Carnlough depot | |
| 05/06/82 | LR | 1756 | Bedford YRQ | Carnlough depot | |
| 05/06/82 | LR | 1789 | Bedford YRQ | Carnlough depot | |
| 25/06/82 | BM | 1490 | Leyland Leopard | Portglenone depot | 82 |
| 25/06/82 | BM | 1498 | Leyland Leopard | Portglenone depot | 82 |
| 25/06/82 | BM | 1668 | Bristol LH | Portglenone depot | |
| 25/06/82 | BM | 1669 | Bristol LH | Portglenone depot | |
| 25/06/82 | BM | 1937 | Leyland Leopard | Portglenone depot | |
| 12/07/82 | BM | 106 | Leyland Leopard | Pennyburn depot | |
| 12/07/82 | LD | 916 | Leyland Atlantean | Pennyburn depot | 81 |
| 12/07/82 | LD | 949 | Leyland Atlantean | Pennyburn depot | |
| 12/07/82 | LD | 950 | Leyland Atlantean | Pennyburn depot | |
| 12/07/82 | LD | 1349 | Leyland Leopard | Pennyburn depot | |
| 12/07/82 | LD | 1481 | Leyland Leopard | Pennyburn depot | |
| 12/07/82 | LD | 1570 | Leyland Leopard | Pennyburn depot | |
| 12/07/82 | LY | 2024 | Bristol RE | Pennyburn depot | |
| 12/07/82 | LD | 2210 | Bristol RE | Pennyburn depot | |
| 12/07/82 | LD | 2448 | Bristol RE | Pennyburn depot | |
| 16/07/82 | OM | 929 | Leyland Atlantean | Omagh depot | |
| 16/07/82 | OM | 944 | Leyland Atlantean | Omagh depot | |
| 16/07/82 | R | 952 | Leyland Atlantean | Omagh depot | 81 |
| 26/07/82 | LD | 1574 | Leyland Leopard | Dungiven depot | |
| 04/08/82 | OX | 2261 | Bristol RE | Oxford Street depot | 84 |
| 21/08/82 | CL | 1838 | Bedford YLQ | Ballymoney depot | |
| 03/09/82 | LD | 1670 | Bristol LH | Creggan, Londonderry | |
| 14/09/82 | R | 1678 | Bristol LH | Pennyburn depot | |

*Total number of vehicles lost in this year* **64**

| Date | Depot | Fleet No | Type | Location | Notes |
|---|---|---|---|---|---|
| 25/01/83 | LY | 2018 | Bristol RE | Shantallow, Londonderry | |
| 29/01/83 | LD | 1700 | Bristol LH | Bogside, Londonderry | |
| 29/01/83 | LY | 2125 | Bristol RE | Shantallow, Londonderry | |
| 31/01/83 | LD | 1676 | Bristol LH | Shantallow, Londonderry | |
| 03/02/83 | LY | 1140 | Leyland Leopard | Longmoor Road, Bogside, Londonderry | |
| 03/02/83 | LY | 2021 | Bristol RE | Creggan, Londonderry | |
| 05/02/83 | LY | 1133 | Leyland Leopard | Shantallow, Londonderry | |
| 16/02/83 | LY | 1051 | Bristol RE | Creggan, Londonderry | |
| 02/03/83 | OM | 534 | Leyland Leopard | Omagh depot | |
| 02/03/83 | OM | 581 | Leyland Leopard | Omagh depot | |
| 02/03/83 | R | 951 | Leyland Atlantean | Omagh depot | |
| 02/03/83 | OM | 970 | Leyland Atlantean | Omagh depot | |
| 21/04/83 | LY | 2019 | Bristol RE | Shantallow, Londonderry | |
| 21/05/83 | LD | 1661 | Bristol LH | Shantallow, Londonderry | |
| 09/06/83 | LD | 1680 | Bristol LH | Shantallow, Londonderry | |
| 02/07/83 | LD | 1314 | Leyland Leopard | Shantallow, Londonderry | |
| 02/07/83 | LY | 2028 | Bristol RE | Shantallow, Londonderry | |
| 15/07/83 | LY | 753 | Bristol RE | Creggan, Londonderry | |
| 04/08/83 | LY | 2014 | Bristol RE | Shantallow, Londonderry | |
| 08/08/83 | DG | 1384 | Leyland Leopard | Coalisland | |
| 10/08/83 | V | 310 | Leyland Leopard | Broadway, Belfast | |
| 13/08/83 | LY | 1130 | Leyland Leopard | Shantallow, Londonderry | |
| 27/08/83 | LD | 1684 | Bristol LH | Shantallow, Londonderry | |

*Total number of vehicles lost in this year* **23**

| Date | Depot | Fleet No | Type | Location | Notes |
|---|---|---|---|---|---|
| 01/03/84 | NY | 2371 | Bristol RE | Derrybeg Estate, Newry | |
| 10/03/84 | LY | 1644 | Bristol LH | Shantallow, Londonderry | |
| 13/03/84 | LY | 767 | Bristol RE | Shantallow, Londonderry | |
| 14/03/84 | V | 1378 | Leyland Leopard | Slemish Way, Andersonstown Road, Belfast | |
| 21/03/84 | LY | 752 | Bristol RE | Shantallow, Londonderry | |
| 25/04/84 | LY | 2124 | Bristol RE | Gobnascale, Londonderry | |
| 08/05/84 | V | 1451 | Leyland Leopard | Donegall Road/Falls Road jctn, Belfast | |
| 07/08/84 | V | 1387 | Leyland Leopard | Location unknown | |
| 09/08/84 | LY | 754 | Bristol RE | Lecky Road Flyover, Brandywell Road, Londonderry | |
| 12/08/84 | NY | 255 | Leyland Leopard | Derrybeg Estate, Newry | |
| 12/08/84 | V | 1581 | Leyland Leopard | Stewartstown Road, Belfast | |
| 13/08/84 | LY | 2017 | Bristol RE | Lecky Road Flyover, Brandywell Road, Londonderry | |
| 02/12/84 | LY | 2005 | Bristol RE | Shantallow, Londonderry | |
| 07/12/84 | LY | 756 | Bristol RE | Beechwood Avenue, Londonderry | |
| 09/12/84 | LY | 766 | Bristol RE | Belmont, Shantallow, Londonderry | |
| 17/12/84 | NY | 2369 | Bristol RE | Derrybeg Estate, Newry | |

*Total number of vehicles lost in this year* **16**

| Date | Depot | Fleet No | Type | Location | Notes |
|---|---|---|---|---|---|
| 28/02/85 | LD | 1677 | Bristol LH | Shantallow, Londonderry | |
| 16/04/85 | AM | 292 | Leyland Leopard | Armagh depot | |
| 16/04/85 | AM | 1493 | Leyland Leopard | Armagh depot | |
| 16/04/85 | AM | 1775 | Bedford YRQ | Armagh depot | |
| 05/05/85 | V | 1519 | Leyland Leopard | Falls Road, Belfast | |
| 20/05/85 | LY | 787 | Bristol RE | Shantallow, Londonderry | |
| 22/05/85 | V | 2240 | Bristol RE | Great Victoria Street, Belfast | |
| 28/05/05 | LY | 765 | Bristol RE | Shantallow, Londonderry | 85 |
| 26/07/85 | V | 1343 | Leyland Leopard | Casement Park, Andersonstown Road, Belfast | |
| 27/07/85 | LY | 2025 | Bristol RE | William Street, Londonderry | |
| 29/07/85 | LY | 2130 | Bristol RE | Rossville Flats, Londonderry | |
| 09/08/85 | DG | 269 | Leyland Leopard | Dungannon | |
| 09/08/85 | V | 1402 | Leyland Leopard | Monagh Road, Belfast | |
| 14/08/85 | LY | 1320 | Leyland Leopard | Rossville Flats, Londonderry | |
| 14/08/85 | LD | 1422 | Leyland Leopard | Rossville Flats, Londonderry | |

*Total number of vehicles lost in this year* **15**

| Date | Depot | Fleet No | Type | Location | Notes |
|---|---|---|---|---|---|
| 02/02/86 | LY | 1417 | Leyland Leopard | Shantallow, Londonderry | |
| 16/02/86 | OX | 2191 | Bristol RE | Oxford Street depot | |
| 16/02/86 | OX | 2265 | Bristol RE | Oxford Street depot | |
| 16/02/86 | OX | 2295 | Bristol RE | Oxford Street depot | |
| 22/02/86 | LY | 788 | Bristol RE | Rossville Flats, Londonderry | |
| 26/02/86 | LD | 1695 | Bristol LH | Shantallow, Londonderry | |
| 01/04/86 | V | 197 | Leyland Leopard | Longstone Street, Lisburn | |
| 11/04/86 | LB | 246 | Leyland Leopard | Milewater Road yard, Belfast | |
| 11/04/86 | AT | 264 | Leyland Leopard | Milewater Road yard, Belfast | |

| Date | Depot | Fleet No | Type | Location | Notes |
|---|---|---|---|---|---|
| 11/04/86 | OM | 266 | Leyland Leopard | Milewater Road yard, Belfast | |
| 11/04/86 | OX | 2253 | Bristol RE | Milewater Road yard, Belfast | |
| 11/04/86 | OX | 2582 | Bristol RE | Milewater Road yard, Belfast | |
| 09/05/86 | OX | 2585 | Bristol RE | Monkstown | |
| 12/08/86 | LY | 782 | Bristol RE | Rossville Flats, Londonderry | |
| 12/08/86 | V | 1528 | Leyland Leopard | Donegall Rd/Falls Rd jctn, Belfast | |
| 14/08/86 | LY | 796 | Bristol RE | Shantallow, Londonderry | |
| 08/11/86 | LD | 445 | Leyland Tiger | Curryneirin, Londonderry | 86 |
| 14/11/86 | OX | 2586 | Bristol RE | Doagh Road, Newtownabbey | |

*Total number of vehicles lost in this year* **18**

| Date | Depot | Fleet No | Type | Location | Notes |
|---|---|---|---|---|---|
| 24/03/87 | LD | 412 | Leyland Tiger | Strabane | |
| 30/03/87 | V | 1514 | Leyland Leopard | Casement Park, Belfast | |
| 07/04/87 | V | 196 | Leyland Leopard | Falls Rd/Whiterock Rd jctn, Belfast | |
| 07/04/87 | LY | 2039 | Bristol RE | Lecky Road, Londonderry | |
| 07/04/87 | OX | 2252 | Bristol RE | Oxford Street depot | |
| 07/04/87 | OX | 2364 | Bristol RE | Oxford Street depot | |
| 09/05/87 | DP | 471 | Leyland Tiger | Flying Horse Estate, Downpatrick | |
| 09/05/87 | DP | 472 | Leyland Tiger | Flying Horse Estate, Downpatrick | |
| 09/05/87 | LY | 2026 | Bristol RE | Shantallow, Londonderry | |
| 09/05/87 | LY | 2032 | Bristol RE | Shantallow, Londonderry | |
| 09/05/87 | NY | 2244 | Bristol RE | Derrybeg Estate, Newry | |
| 11/05/87 | DG | 329 | Leyland Leopard | Coalisland | |
| 11/05/87 | LY | 786 | Bristol RE | Creggan, Londonderry | |
| 14/05/87 | LY | 720 | Bristol RE | Belmont, Shantallow, Londonderry | |
| 09/08/87 | V | 1448 | Leyland Leopard | Poleglass, Belfast | |
| 15/08/87 | LY | 783 | Bristol RE | Rossville Flats, Londonderry | |
| 31/10/87 | NY | 332 | Leyland Leopard | Derrybeg Estate, Newry | |
| 03/11/87 | LY | 719 | Bristol RE | Rossville Flats, Londonderry | |

*Total number of vehicles lost in this year* **18**

| Date | Depot | Fleet No | Type | Location | Notes |
|---|---|---|---|---|---|
| 23/02/88 | LD | 114 | Leyland Leopard | Strabane | |
| 01/03/88 | BM | 1062 | Leyland Tiger | Antrim Rd/New Lodge Rd jctn, Belfast | |
| 02/03/88 | CG | 2236 | Bristol RE | Parkmore Estate, Craigavon | |
| 07/03/88 | V | 2274 | Bristol RE | Stewartstown Road, Belfast | |
| 08/03/88 | NY | 2036 | Bristol RE | Barcroft Park, Newry | |
| 09/03/88 | LY | 795 | Bristol RE | Creggan, Londonderry | |
| 09/03/88 | LD | 1787 | Bedford YRQ | Shantallow, Londonderry | |
| 11/03/88 | AM | 453 | Leyland Tiger | Derrybeg Estate, Newry | |
| 17/03/88 | NY | 1986 | Leyland Leopard | Warrenpoint | |
| 25/03/88 | V | 359 | Leyland Tiger | Springfield Road, Belfast | |
| 03/08/88 | V | 2263 | Bristol RE | Springfield Road, Belfast | |
| 20/08/88 | R | 103 | Leyland Leopard | Braghagh | |
| 27/08/88 | NY | 202 | Leyland Leopard | Patrick Street, Newry | |
| 27/08/88 | LY | 2003 | Bristol RE | Racecourse Road, Londonderry | |
| 27/08/88 | V | 2245 | Bristol RE | Falls Rd/Whiterock Rd jctn, Belfast | |
| 27/08/88 | LB | 2365 | Bristol RE | Springfield Road, Belfast | |
| 30/08/88 | LY | 755 | Bristol RE | Shantallow, Londonderry | |

*Total number of vehicles lost in this year* **17**

| Date | Depot | Fleet No | Type | Location | Notes |
|---|---|---|---|---|---|
| 07/04/89 | LD | 362 | Leyland Tiger | Strabane | |
| 13/04/89 | V | 1187 | Leyland Tiger | Whiterock Road, Belfast | |
| 14/04/89 | NY | 1219 | Leyland Tiger | Newry | |
| 27/06/89 | LY | 2131 | Bristol RE | Foyle Bridge, Londonderry | |
| 09/08/89 | CG | 2188 | Bristol RE | Taghnevin, Lurgan | |
| 11/08/89 | LY | 857 | Mercedes Benz minibus | Creggan, Londonderry | |
| 12/08/89 | DG | 293 | Leyland Leopard | Coalisland | |
| 12/08/89 | LY | 2560 | Bristol RE (on loan from Citybus) | Creggan, Londonderry | |
| 13/08/89 | LY | 2127 | Bristol RE | Shantallow, Londonderry | |
| 13/08/89 | LY | 2132 | Bristol RE | Lecky Road Flyover, Londonderry | |
| 14/08/89 | LD | 231 | Leyland Leopard | Strabane | |
| 14/08/89 | NY | 811 | Mercedes Benz minibus | Location unknown | |
| 16/08/89 | LY | 837 | Mercedes Benz minibus | Creggan, Londonderry | |
| 16/08/89 | R | 1506 | Leyland Leopard | Falls Park depot | |
| 14/10/89 | V | 164 | Leyland Leopard | Casement Park, Belfast | |

*Total number of vehicles lost in this year* **15**

| Date | Depot | Fleet No | Type | Location | Notes |
|---|---|---|---|---|---|
| 10/02/90 | V | 1959 | Leyland Leopard | Location unknown | |
| 17/02/90 | AM | 1132 | Leyland Tiger | Armagh depot | |
| 17/02/90 | AM | 1230 | Leyland Tiger | Armagh depot | |
| 17/02/90 | AM | 1231 | Leyland Tiger | Armagh depot | |
| 30/05/90 | V | 360 | Leyland Tiger | Beechmount, Falls Road, Belfast | |

| Date | Depot | Fleet No | Type | Location | Notes |
|---|---|---|---|---|---|
| 07/08/90 | LR | 121 | Leyland Leopard | Killyglen, Larne | |
| 14/10/90 | AT | 1159 | Leyland Tiger | Antrim depot | |
| 14/10/90 | AT | 1998 | Leyland Leopard | Antrim depot | |
| 14/10/90 | AT | 2597 | Bristol RE | Antrim depot | |
| 10/11/90 | V | 358 | Leyland Tiger | Springfield Rd/Whiterock Rd jctn, Belfast | |
| 14/11/90 | LY | 2135 | Bristol RE | Westland Road, Londonderry | |
| 15/11/90 | LY | 2282 | Bristol RE | Gobnascale, Londonderry | |

*Total number of vehicles lost in this year* **12**

| Date | Depot | Fleet No | Type | Location | Notes |
|---|---|---|---|---|---|
| 02/03/91 | V | 481 | Leyland Tiger | Stewartstown Road, Belfast | |
| 04/03/91 | DG | 491 | Leyland Tiger | Coalisland | |

*Total number of vehicles lost in this year* **2**

| Date | Depot | Fleet No | Type | Location | Notes |
|---|---|---|---|---|---|
| 23/01/92 | LY | 2123 | Bristol RE | Pennyburn depot, Londonderry | |
| 23/01/92 | LY | 2128 | Bristol RE | Pennyburn depot, Londonderry | 87 |
| 23/01/92 | LY | 2133 | Bristol RE | Pennyburn depot, Londonderry | |
| 20/02/92 | DP | 1240 | Leyland Tiger | Flying Horse Estate, Downpatrick | |
| 27/02/92 | DG | 1170 | Leyland Tiger | Coalisland | |
| 10/07/92 | OX | 1378 | Leyland Tiger | Ballybeen, Dundonald | |
| 15/08/92 | LY | 840 | Mercedes Benz minibus | Creggan | 92 |
| 31/12/92 | LD | 1997 | Leyland Leopard | Pennyburn depot, Londonderry | 88 |
| 31/12/92 | LY | 2183 | Bristol RE | Pennyburn depot, Londonderry | 89 |

*Total number of vehicles lost in this year* **9**

| Date | Depot | Fleet No | Type | Location | Notes |
|---|---|---|---|---|---|
| 02/07/93 | NB | 1289 | Leyland Tiger | Rathcoole, Newtownabbey | |
| 02/07/93 | NB | 1329 | Leyland Tiger | Mount Vernon, Shore Road, Belfast | |
| 03/07/93 | OX | 809 | Mercedes Benz minibus | Comber depot | |
| 03/07/93 | OX | 1045 | Leyland Tiger | Comber depot | |
| 03/07/93 | BG | 1059 | Leyland Tiger | Kilcooley Estate, Bangor | |
| 30/10/93 | LY | 841 | Mercedes Benz minibus | Creggan, Londonderry | |
| 01/11/93 | LY | 819 | Mercedes Benz minibus | Creggan, Londonderry | |

*Total number of vehicles lost in this year* **7**

| Date | Depot | Fleet No | Type | Location | Notes |
|---|---|---|---|---|---|
| 23/05/94 | LY | 858 | Mercedes Benz minibus | Creggan, Londonderry | |
| 27/06/94 | NC | 300 | Leyland Leopard | Ballynahinch depot | |
| 27/06/94 | NC | 377 | Leyland Tiger | Ballynahinch depot | |
| 27/06/94 | NC | 416 | Leyland Tiger | Ballynahinch depot | |
| 02/07/94 | NC | 375 | Leyland Tiger | Derryvolgie Avenue, Belfast | 90 |
| 29/07/94 | NC | 353 | Leyland Tiger | Ballynahinch depot | |
| 29/07/94 | NC | 1152 | Leyland Tiger | Ballynahinch depot | |
| 20/08/94 | NB | 1266 | Leyland Tiger | Doagh Road, Newtownabbey | |
| 18/09/94 | LB | 138 | Leyland Leopard | Dromore depot | |

*Total number of vehicles lost in this year* **9**

| Date | Depot | Fleet No | Type | Location | Notes |
|---|---|---|---|---|---|
| 03/07/95 | NY | 394 | Leyland Tiger | Crossmaglen | |
| 03/07/95 | LD | 849 | Mercedes Benz minibus | Strabane | |
| 04/07/95 | NY | 1264 | Leyland Tiger | Silverbridge | |
| 04/07/95 | AM | 1581 | Volvo B10M | Cullaville | |
| 05/07/95 | LY | 838 | Mercedes Benz minibus | Creggan, Londonderry | |
| 06/07/95 | CG | 1543 | Volvo B10M | Old Portadown Road, Taghnevin, Lurgan | |
| 07/07/95 | NC | 1077 | Leyland Tiger | Rostrevor | |
| 07/07/95 | CG | 1097 | Leyland Tiger | Drumnamoe Estate, Lurgan | |
| 20/07/95 | LR | 1083 | Leyland Tiger | Carnlough depot | |
| 20/07/95 | LR | 1084 | Leyland Tiger | Carnlough depot | |
| 29/07/95 | OX | 335 | Leyland Leopard | Oxford Street depot | |
| 08/08/95 | BM | 1222 | Leyland Tiger | Ballymena depot | |
| 08/08/95 | BM | 1564 | Volvo B10M | Ballymena depot | |
| 10/08/95 | OM | 1020 | Leyland Tiger | Castlederg | |
| 10/08/95 | OM | 1134 | Leyland Tiger | Castlederg | |
| 12/08/95 | AM | 364 | Leyland Tiger | Armagh depot | |
| 12/08/95 | AM | 1423 | Leyland Tiger | Armagh depot | |
| 12/08/95 | AM | 1513 | Volvo B10M | Armagh depot | |
| 19/08/95 | CL | 1092 | Leyland Tiger | Cookstown | |

*Total number of vehicles lost in this year* **19**

| Date | Depot | Fleet No | Type | Location | Notes |
|---|---|---|---|---|---|
| 15/01/96 | CL | 2392 | Bristol RE | Coleraine depot | |
| 25/02/96 | LR | 20 | Renault minibus | Larne depot | |
| 08/07/96 | NB | 2373 | Bristol RE | Carrickfergus | |

| Date | Depot | Fleet No | Type | Location | Notes |
|------|-------|----------|------|----------|-------|
| 10/07/96 | LR | 456 | Leyland Tiger | Cloughfern, Newtownabbey | |
| 10/07/96 | OX | 486 | Leyland Tiger | Ballygowan | |
| 10/07/96 | OX | 1095 | Leyland Tiger | Ballygowan | |
| 11/07/96 | CG | 252 | Leyland Leopard | Lurgan | |
| 11/07/96 | AM | 346 | Leyland Tiger | Armagh depot | |
| 11/07/96 | DG | 435 | Leyland Tiger | Coalisland | |
| 11/07/96 | AM | 452 | Leyland Tiger | Armagh depot | |
| 11/07/96 | AM | 487 | Leyland Tiger | Armagh depot | |
| 11/07/96 | AM | 1070 | Leyland Tiger | Armagh depot | |
| 11/07/96 | AM | 1071 | Leyland Tiger | Armagh depot | |
| 11/07/96 | AM | 1104 | Leyland Tiger | Armagh depot | |
| 11/07/96 | DG | 1129 | Leyland Tiger | Armagh depot | |
| 11/07/96 | AM | 1136 | Leyland Tiger | Armagh depot | |
| 11/07/96 | AM | 1283 | Leyland Tiger | Armagh depot | |
| 11/07/96 | AM | 1284 | Leyland Tiger | Armagh depot | |
| 11/07/96 | AM | 1305 | Leyland Tiger | Armagh depot | |
| 11/07/96 | AM | 1307 | Leyland Tiger | Armagh depot | |
| 11/07/96 | AM | 1308 | Leyland Tiger | Armagh depot | |
| 11/07/96 | BM | 1314 | Leyland Tiger | Cushendall | |
| 11/07/96 | AM | 1618 | Volvo B10M | Armagh depot | |
| 12/07/96 | LD | 215 | Leyland Leopard | Dungiven depot | |
| 12/07/96 | LD | 327 | Leyland Leopard | Dungiven depot | |
| 12/07/96 | LD | 389 | Leyland Tiger | Dungiven depot | |
| 12/07/96 | GS | 539 | Leyland Tiger | Short Strand depot | |
| 12/07/96 | LY | 835 | Mercedes Benz minibus | Creggan, Londonderry | |
| 12/07/96 | DP | 1008 | Leyland Tiger | Ardglass | |
| 12/07/96 | DP | 1127 | Leyland Tiger | Ardglass | |
| 12/07/96 | LD | 1137 | Leyland Tiger | Dungiven depot | |
| 12/07/96 | LD | 1554 | Volvo B10M | Dungiven | |
| 12/07/96 | LD | 2239 | Bristol RE | Dungiven depot | |
| 13/07/96 | CL | 2600 | Bristol RE | Ballycastle depot | |
| 14/07/96 | NY | 868 | Mercedes Benz minibus | Courtney Hill, Newry | |
| 15/07/96 | OM | 427 | Leyland Tiger | Sixmilecross | |
| 10/08/96 | LY | 836 | Mercedes Benz minibus | Central Drive, Londonderry | |
| 30/11/96 | CL | 1577 | Volvo B10M | Harryville, Ballymena | |

*Total number of vehicles lost in this year* **38**

| Date | Depot | Fleet No | Type | Location | Notes |
|------|-------|----------|------|----------|-------|
| 13/06/97 | AM | 157 | Leyland Leopard | Armagh depot | |
| 13/06/97 | AM | 521 | Leyland Tiger | Armagh depot | |
| 13/06/97 | AM | 1076 | Leyland Tiger | Armagh depot | |
| 13/06/97 | AM | 1416 | Leyland Tiger | Armagh depot | |
| 06/07/97 | NY | 479 | Leyland Tiger | Bridge Street, Newry | |
| 06/07/97 | LD | 1361 | Leyland Tiger | Dungiven | |
| 06/07/97 | LD | 2286 | Bristol RE | Bogside, Londonderry | |
| 07/07/97 | V | 165 | Leyland Leopard | Andersonstown Road, Belfast | |
| 07/07/97 | LY | 911 | Mercedes Benz minibus | Bogside, Londonderry | |
| 07/07/97 | CG | 2587 | Bristol RE | Tullygalley Road Estate, Lurgan | |
| 18/11/97 | CG | 2237 | Bristol RE | Lake Street, Lurgan | |
| 13/12/97 | LY | 910 | Mercedes Benz minibus | Foyle Street, Londonderry | |
| 13/12/97 | LY | 913 | Mercedes Benz minibus | Queens Quay, Londonderry | |
| 13/12/97 | LY | 2308 | Bristol RE | Custom House Street, Londonderry | |
| 27/12/97 | LR | 430 | Leyland Tiger | Harryville, Ballymena | |

*Total number of vehicles lost in this year* **15**

| Date | Depot | Fleet No | Type | Location | Notes |
|------|-------|----------|------|----------|-------|
| 23/05/98 | NY | 1334 | Leyland Tiger | Newry Courthouse. | 91 |
| 06/07/98 | CG | 1039 | Leyland Tiger | Parkmore Estate, Craigavon | |
| 10/07/98 | OX | 483 | Leyland Tiger | Ballybeen, Dundonald | |

*Total number of vehicles lost in this year* **3**

| Date | Depot | Fleet No | Type | Location | Notes |
|------|-------|----------|------|----------|-------|
| 18/03/99 | DG | 1396 | Leyland Tiger | Garvaghy Road, Portadown | |
| 19/03/99 | CG | 1191 | Leyland Tiger | Taghnevin, Lurgan | |
| 20/03/99 | CG | 144 | Leyland Leopard | Lake Street Lurgan | |
| 07/09/99 | NB | 1114 | Leyland Tiger | Rathcoole, Newtownabbey | |

*Total number of vehicles lost in this year* **4**

| Date | Depot | Fleet No | Type | Location | Notes |
|------|-------|----------|------|----------|-------|
| 07/05/00 | CL | 263 | Leyland Leopard | Coleraine depot | |
| 07/05/00 | CL | 1518 | Volvo B10M | Coleraine depot | |

*Total number of vehicles lost in this year* **2**

| Date | Depot | Fleet No | Type | Location | Notes |
|------|-------|----------|------|----------|-------|
| 12/01/02 | BM | 228 | Leyland Leopard | Cushendall | |

*Total number of vehicles lost in this year* **1**

| Date | Depot | Fleet No | Type | Location | Notes |
|------|-------|----------|------|----------|-------|
| 06/05/04 | CL | 284 | Leyland Leopard | Portrush depot | |
| 06/05/04 | CL | 1220 | Leyland Tiger | Portrush depot | |
| 06/05/04 | CL | 1442 | Leyland Tiger | Portrush depot | |

*Total number of vehicles lost in this year* **3**

| Date | Depot | Fleet No | Type | Location | Notes |
|------|-------|----------|------|----------|-------|
| 11/09/05 | BG | 1350 | Leyland Tiger | Conlig, Bangor | |

*Total number of vehicles lost in this year* **1**

**TOTAL FOR ULSTERBUS – 810**

Notes:-

| | |
|---|---|
| **39** | detaxed with damage 30/04/69. |
| **40** | date recorded as 13–14/06/69. |
| **41** | detaxed 30/06/70; may not be malicious. |
| **42** | detaxed 31/08/70; reported as lost 4–5/8/70. |
| **43** | damaged Derrybeg 26/10/71; destroyed 22/12/71. |
| **44** | police report states 24–25/10/71. |
| **45** | card states 08/12/71; detaxed 31/12/71. |
| **46** | rebodied Alexander (Belfast) B53F body 2/73. |
| **47** | rebodied Alexander (Belfast) B53F body 3/73. |
| **48** | rebodied Alexander (Belfast) B53F body 2/74. |
| **49** | rebodied Alexander (Belfast) DP49F body 5/73 |
| **50** | detaxed 30/6/72 with malicious damage. |
| **51** | rebodied Alexander (Belfast) DP49F body 4/73. |
| **52** | rebodied Alexander (Belfast) DP49F body 2/73. |
| **53** | rebodied Alexander (Belfast) DP49F body 7/73. |
| **54** | rebodied Alexander (Belfast) DP49F body 6/76. |
| **55** | rebodied Alexander (Belfast) DP49F body 8/73. |
| **56** | rebodied Alexander (Belfast) B53F body 3/73. |
| **57** | rebodied Alexander (Belfast) B53F body 2/74. |
| **58** | rebodied Alexander (Belfast) DP49F body 3/73. |
| **59** | rebodied Alexander (Belfast) B53F body 7/74. |
| **60** | rebodied Alexander (Belfast) B53F body 5/76. |
| **61** | date detaxed following damage. |
| **62** | rebodied Alexander (Belfast) B53F body 1/75. |
| **63** | rebodied Alexander (Belfast) B53F body 6/76. |
| **64** | rebodied Alexander (Belfast) B53F body 2/74. |
| **65** | rebodied Alexander (Belfast) B53F body 6/76. |
| **66** | rebodied Alexander (Belfast) B53F body 5/76. |
| **67** | detaxed with malicious damage. |
| **68** | recorded as 13–14/01/74. |
| **69** | record card states 13—14/01/74 |
| **70** | rebodied Alexander (Belfast) B53F body 6/76. |
| **71** | rebodied Alexander (Belfast) B53F body 9/78. |
| **72** | rebodied Alexander (Belfast) B53F body 7/76. |
| **73** | rebuilt and rebodied with Alexander (Belfast) B53F body 9/78 as 1591 (SOI 3591) |
| **74** | rebuilt and rebodied with Alexander (Belfast) B53F body 9/79 as 1592 (TOI 3592) |
| **75** | rebuilt and rebodied with Alexander (Belfast) B45F body 2/79 as 1664 (SOI 6664) |
| **76** | rebodied Alexander (Belfast) B45F body 12/78. |
| **77** | dates are 'by' dates; exact date not known |
| **78** | detaxed with malicious damage; written off 28/02/77. |
| **79** | detaxed with malicious damage; written off 19/10/77; damage suffered 22/07/77. |
| **80** | detaxed 31/05/79 awaiting engine; withdrawn 31/08/79. |
| **81** | withdrawn 27/07/82 after suffering malicious damage. |
| **82** | reported as 24–25/06/82 |
| **83** | rebodied Alexander (Belfast) B52F body 3/83. |
| **84** | rebodied Alexander (Belfast) B52F body 5/83. |
| **85** | detaxed 30/06/85 with malicious damage |
| **86** | detaxed 30/11/86 with malicious damage. |
| **87** | maliciously damaged 23/01/92; detaxed 31/01/92; written off 11/03/92. |
| **88** | detaxed 31/12/92 with malicious damage; written off 12/03/93. |
| **89** | detaxed 31/12/92 with malicious damage; written off 08/03/93. |
| **90** | detaxed 31/07/94 with malicious damage. |
| **91** | detaxed 31/05/98 with malicious damage; written off 26/06/98. |
| **92** | rebuilt by Ulsterbus Engineering as a replica charabanc 11/94 and re-registered CZ 1988 3/96 |

## Flexibus

| Date | Depot | Fleet No | Type | Location | Notes |
|------|-------|----------|------|----------|-------|
| 07/07/95 | B | 43 | Mercedes Benz minibus | Coalisland | |

*Total number of vehicles lost* **1**

## Londonderry & Lough Swilly Railway Company

| Date | Fleet No | Type | Location |
|------|----------|------|----------|
| 12/02/76 | 117 (7001 UI) | Bristol LHL/Plaxton | Londonderry |
| 12/02/76 | 133 (AZD 186) | Leyland Leopard/CIE | Location unknown |
| 12/02/76 | 135 (NZE 584) | Leyland Leopard/CIE | Location unknown |
| 02/11/80 | 145 (NZO 18) | Leyland Leopard/Plaxton | Pennyburn depot |
| 02/11/80 | 178 (BUI 1495, *209 CCH*) | Leyland Leopard/Willowbrook | Pennyburn depot |
| 20/04/81 | 146 (NZO 19) | Leyland Leopard/Plaxton | Foyle Street |
| 28/04/81 | 162 (AUI 7660, *UCK 540*) | Leyland Leopard/Marshall | Foyle Street |
| 17/08/91 | 299 (72 DL 42, *DOI 1583*) | Leyland Leopard/Alexander | Location unknown |
| ??/07/92 | 211 (211 CZO, *EUG 462K*) | Leyland Leopard/Plaxton | Location unknown |

*Total number of vehicles lost* **9**

## Sureline, Lurgan

| Date | Reg No | Type | Location |
|------|--------|------|----------|
| 09/08/71 | 921 FVD | AEC Reliance/Willowbrook | Shankill Estate, Lurgan |
| 19/10/71 | JBO 53 | Leyland Tiger Cub/Weymann | Aghagallon |
| 19/10/71 | 922 FVD | AEC Reliance/Willowbrook | Aghagallon |
| 20/04/73 | NPM 307F | Ford R192/Strachan | Lurgan |
| ??/05/85 | FIB 6799 (*MWA 844P*) | Bedford YRT/Duple | North Belfast |

*Total number of vehicles lost* **5**

## The toll of destruction (summary)

**By operator:**

| | |
|------|------|
| Belfast Corporation Transport Department | 95 |
| Citybus | 596 |
| Ulster Transport Authority | 11 |
| Ulsterbus | 810 |
| Flexibus | 1 |
| Lough Swilly | 9 |
| Sureline | 5 |
| *Total* | *1527* |

| By year: | | By type: | |
|----------|-----|----------|-----|
| 1957 | 7 | AEC Merlin | 43 |
| 1958 | 4 | AEC Reliance | 41 |
| | | AEC Swift | 27 |
| 1964 | 1 | Albion Aberdonian | 14 |
| | | Bedford SB5 | 24 |
| 1969 | 20 | Bedford VAL | 1 |
| 1970 | 17 | Bedford VAM | 23 |
| 1971 | 93 | Bedford VAS | 3 |
| 1972 | 135 | Bedford YLQ | 18 |
| 1973 | 52 | Bedford YRQ | 33 |
| 1974 | 78 | Bedford YRT | 7 |
| 1975 | 10 | Bristol LH/L | 39 |
| 1976 | 100 | Bristol RE | 390 |
| 1977 | 102 | Daimler CVG6 | 45 |
| 1978 | 107 | Daimler CWA6 | 8 |
| 1979 | 80 | Daimler Fleetline DD | 209 |
| 1980 | 86 | Daimler Fleetline SD | 45 |
| 1981 | 82 | Daimler Roadliner | 5 |
| 1982 | 76 | Dennis Dart | 2 |
| 1983 | 37 | Ford R192 | 2 |
| 1984 | 47 | Guy Arab III | 8 |
| 1985 | 30 | Guy BTX trolleybus | 1 |
| 1986 | 29 | Leyland Atlantean | 42 |
| 1987 | 55 | Leyland Leopard | 232 |
| 1988 | 49 | Leyland Olympic | 1 |
| 1989 | 37 | Leyland PD1/A | 2 |
| 1990 | 31 | Leyland PD2 | 16 |
| 1991 | 16 | Leyland PD3 | 35 |
| 1992 | 17 | Leyland PS1 | 7 |
| 1993 | 9 | Leyland PS2 | 1 |
| 1994 | 12 | Leyland Royal Tiger | 8 |
| 1995 | 21 | Leyland Tiger | 89 |
| 1996 | 43 | Leyland Tiger Cub | 73 |
| 1997 | 22 | Mercedes Benz minibus | 17 |
| 1998 | 4 | Renault minibus | 1 |
| 1999 | 5 | Scania L94 | 1 |
| 2000 | 3 | Volvo B7TL | 1 |
| 2001 | 2 | Volvo B10BLE | 1 |
| 2002 | 1 | Volvo B10L | 4 |
| 2003 | 0 | Volvo B10M | 8 |
| 2004 | 3 | | |
| 2005 | 4 | | |

Between 1964 and 1998, the main period covered by this volume, BCT, Citybus, Ulsterbus and Flexibus had 1484 vehicles maliciously destroyed. The combined Metro (Citybus)/Ulsterbus/Flexibus fleet at 1 June 2006 totalled 1492 vehicles, so effectively a whole fleet of buses was lost during that thirty-five year period!

Vehicles belonging to Córas Iompair Éireann (CIÉ), private operators, education boards, voluntary groups, etc, were also destroyed during the Troubles. Unfortunately, detailed records of these losses are not so readily available.

## Citybus/Ulsterbus/Flexibus depot allocation codes

| Code | Depot | Code | Depot | Code | Depot |
|------|-------|------|-------|------|-------|
| AD | Ardoyne | F | Falls Park | NY | Newry |
| AM | Armagh | GS | Glengall Street (Tour Pool) | OM | Omagh |
| AT | Antrim | LB | Lisburn | OX | Oxford Street |
| B | Belfast (Flexibus) | LD | Londonderry (Country) | P | Portadown |
| BG | Bangor | LG | Lurgan | R | Reserve fleet |
| BM | Ballymena | LR | Larne | S or SF | Smithfield |
| C or CL | Coleraine | LY | Londonderry (City) | SS | Short Strand |
| CG | Craigavon | M or MF | Magherafelt | V | Great Victoria Street |
| DG | Dungannon | MP | Mountpottinger | wtn | withdrawn vehicle |
| DP | Downpatrick | NA | Newtownards | | |
| E | Enniskillen | NC | Newcastle | | |

# THE END OF THE ROAD

*At the time of writing, the last Ulsterbus vehicle to be hijacked and destroyed was Leyland Tiger No 1350, which was allocated to Bangor depot. This vehicle, which was returning worshippers from a church service in Belfast, was hijacked on the outskirts of Bangor on 11 September 2005. The driver was forced to take the vehicle to Conlig, where it was burned. What remained was recovered and is seen here at a Co Down scrapyard, awaiting breaking up.*

**Raymond Bell**

# BIBLIOGRAPHY

Books
Bardon, J, *A History of Ulster*, Appletree Press
Boyle, BC, *Buses in Ulster Vol 1: The Northern Ireland Road Transport Board 1935–1948*, Colourpoint
Boyle, BC, *Buses in Ulster Vol 2: The Ulster Transport Authority 1948–1967*, Colourpoint
Montgomery, WH, *Buses in Ulster Vol 3: Belfast Corporation Buses 1926–1973*, Colourpoint
Millar, GI, *Buses in Ulster Vol 4: Ulsterbus 1967–1988, The Heubeck Years*, Colourpoint
Hughes, W, *Buses in Ulster Vol 5: Citybus: Belfast's buses 1973–1988*, Colourpoint 2005
Jenkinson, KA, *Exiles in Ulster*, Autobus Review Publications Ltd
McKitterick, D, Kelters, S, Feeny, B, Thornton, C, and McVea, D, *Lost Lives*, Mainstream Publishing, 2004
McKittrick, D and McVea, D, *Making Sense of the Troubles*, Blackstaff Press
Deutsch, R and Magowan, V, *Northern Ireland: A Chronology of Events*
Elliot, S and Flackes, WD, *Northern Ireland: A Political Directory 1968-1999*, Blackstaff Press
Barzilay, D, *The British Army in Ulster Vols 1 and 2*, Century Services Ltd
Corcoran, M, *Through Streets Broad and Narrow*, Midland Publishing
McKitterick, D, *Through the Minefield*, Blackstaff Press


Newspapers
*Belfast Telegraph*
*Derry Journal*
*Irish News*
*Irish Times*
*News Letter*
*The Busworker*            AT&GWU
*The Times*


Magazines & Periodicals
*Belfast Corporation Transport: Fleet History PI 4*, PSV Circle/Omnibus Soc.
*Fortnight* (various issues)
*NIRTB/UTA/Ulsterbus: Fleet History PI 5*, PSV Circle/Omnibus Soc.
Wall, T, Railways and Telecommunicatons 4, *Journal of the Irish Railway Record Society, Vol 21*, February 2002
*The Troubles* (various issues), Glenravel Publications


Other Sources
Annual Reports and Accounts for Ulsterbus and Citybus
NIO Cuttings Files-Parades, Northern Ireland Office
NIO Cuttings Files-Riot Damage, Northern Ireland Office
The *Routes* project, AT&GWU
The Urban Motorway Plan, February 1967, Travers Morgan & Partners, Prepared for Belfast Corporation
The Transportation Plan, June 1969, Travers Morgan & Partners, Prepared for Belfast Corporation
The Belfast Area Plan, June 1969, Travers Morgan & Partners, Prepared for Belfast Corporation


Websites
Across Borders, Brian Gill, www.law:gonzaga.edu/borders/irish
Fintan O'Toole's Irish Times Century, F O'Toole, www..ireland.com/special/times2000/century
BBC History website, War and Conflict Series, www.bbc.co.uk\history
Cain: Sutton Index of Deaths, Malcolm Sutton, http://cain.ulst.ac.uk/issues/violence/deaths.htm

# INDEX

'B' Specials   6, 8, 10, 11

Adams, Gerry   14, 16

Adams, Robert   39, 53, 76, 81

AEC Reliance   44, 71, 110, 126–27, 145

Agnew, Sydney   25, 92, 121, 162

Air Yard   82–4, 87, 91, 138

Andersonstown   7, 8, 34, 62, 97, 108, 112–4, 124, 146

Ardoyne   10, 27–8, 30, 34, 36, 39, 41, 52, 60, 63, 67, 70–1, 83, 87, 93, 100, 103, 114, 116, 139, 143–4, 147, 149, 151, 158, 163

Ardoyne Depot   52, 60, 67, 71, 144, 147, 149, 151

Armagh   9–10, 13, 19, 22, 25, 27–8, 30, 132, 163

Arthurs, Stanley   164

Assault Pay   95

Atlantean   53

Baird, Ernest   44

Baldwin, Victor   125

Ballygomartin   46, 51

Ballymena   134–6

Ballymurphy   25, 40, 109, 118

Bangor   16, 34, 45–6, 49, 54, 116, 119, 122

Belfast Agreement   5, 6, 12, 17, 43

Belfast Corporation Transport (BCT)

  4, 5, 10, 12, 18, 23–6, 34–6, 39, 46–8, 51–5, 61, 76, 81–2, 84, 86–7, 89, 91, 114, 121, 137, 143–4, 148, 156, 162, 164

Bell, Raymond   122

Black taxis   36, 50, 52, 59, 65–6, 77, 85–6, 92, 102, 121, 137

Blair, Tony   17

Bloody Friday   12, 32–3, 101–2, 123, 161–2

Bloody Sunday   11

Bradshaw, George   164

Bradshaw, Harry (Harold)   27–8, 45, 55, 92, 101, 121, 143, 157, 162–3

Breen, George   37

Bristol   42, 44, 60, 70, 72, 74–6, 89, 90, 96, 106, 124–5, 128, 131, 133, 137, 142–3, 147

Buick, Fred   127, 130

Burntollet   9, 61, 70

Callaghan, Thomas   10, 25, 53, 64, 66, 100, 104, 126, 162, 164

Campbell, Jack   32, 72, 76, 101

Campbell, Tom   72, 76

Canavan, Frank   28

Carr's Glen   25, 51

Carrickmore   18, 28, 34

Central bus station   34, 50–1, 78

CIÉ   26, 35, 40, 43, 46, 79, 123, 129, 163–4

Citybus   2, 4, 5, 12, 16–18, 26–30, 36–38, 40–63, 68, 71–2, 75–81, 86–7, 90–94, 96–99, 110–114, 119, 122, 124, 125, 134, 137–8, 140, 144, 147–9, 153, 157–8, 161–164

Citylink   55, 89–90

Clegg, Frank   5, 57, 61, 81–2, 90, 140, 143

Clinton, President Bill   17

Clones   22

Coagh   19, 21–2, 39

Coalisland   10

Coleraine   7, 16, 49

Collins, Jim   2, 112

Collins, Michael   109, 112, 129

Conductors   39, 51, 53, 57, 83, 85–6, 91, 103–7, 119, 156

Conlig   17

Cooper, Bob   14, 32

Craig, William   8, 9

Creggan   25, 36, 128–9, 132, 146, 162

Crossan, Patrick   26, 121, 162–3

Crossmaglen   22

Crothers, William   32, 162

CVG   10, 23, 35, 39, 52, 82, 84, 86, 112, 137, 141–2, 147

| | | | |
|---|---|---|---|
| Derry | 6, 8–15, 18–20, 23, 25, 29, 34–46, 49, 56–7, 61–65, 69–71, 76, 79, 92, 104, 106, 125–133, 144–147, 162 | Glencairn | 41, 46, 51, 109, 120, 147, 153–5 |
| | | Glengall Street | 7, 80, 125 |
| DeValera | 6 | GNR | 18–20, 70 |
| Dillon, ? | 101 | Goulding, Cathal | 8 |
| Disruption Day | 35 | Graham, Ruth | 5, 61, 148 |
| Divis Street | 6–8, 10, 18, 22–3, 110, 120 | Graham, Willie | 121 |
| Divis Street riots | 6, 18, 22 | Great Victoria Street | 12, 31–4, 49–51, 56, 65, 80, 108, 114, 120, 122–3, 126, 135 |
| Dixon, Dessie | 134, 160 | Hale, Max | 38, 41, 76, 79, 81, 91, 121–2 |
| Doherty, Eddie | 127, 132 | Harold's Cross, Dublin | 5 |
| Doherty, John | 127, 132 | Heath, Edward | 11–2 |
| Donegall Road | 23, 36, 46, 82, 124–5, 139, 141, 144–5, 148, 151 | Hesketh, Ted | 67, 75, 78, 87, 97, 121 |
| Douglas, Thomas | 164 | Heubeck, Werner | 2, 36–38, 41, 45–8, 51–8, 61, 64, 68, 72, 75, 77–81, 87, 91–2, 94, 96–102, 105–6, 110–11, 117, 122, 123, 128, 138, 139, 140, 144, 146, 164 |
| Drivers | 5, 28, 36–7, 40, 42, 45, 50–3, 57–9, 63–7, 76, 80–4, 88, 91–106, 113, 121, 126, 129, 130, 132, 143, 147, 151, 155–8, 164 | | |
| | | Heuston, James | 70, 128 |
| Duffy, Thomas | 164 | HMS *Maidstone* | 39 |
| Dungannon | 7, 10, 18, 33–4, 39, 56, 78, 100, 104–6, 130, 132, 163–4 | Howden, George | 46 |
| | | Hughes, Liam | 100, 104 |
| Dungiven | 10, 18–9, 35, 130 | IRA | 5–20, 22, 25–6, 28, 32, 35–6, 39, 42, 44, 51, 54, 56, 63–4, 67–8, 79, 91, 98, 108, 112, 115–8, 125, 130, 134, 137, 139, 143–6, 16–4 |
| Edinburgh | 59, 68, 80, 87, 130 | | |
| Elliman, Willie | 158 | | |
| Enniskillen | 6–7, 14–5, 26, 34, 78 | Irish Transport Trust | 5, 73–4 |
| Falls | 7, 10–1, 22–3, 29–32, 35–9, 42–3, 46, 55, 62–7, 70–1, 75–8, 82–8, 91, 93, 96–102, 107, 110–25, 137–9, 142–5, 148–50, 15–6, 159 | Irvine, William | 32, 42, 61, 68, 101–2, 162–3 |
| | | Jameson, Robert | 164 |
| | | Jeffers, Sammy | 138 |
| | | Johnston, Ruby | 25 |
| Falls Curfew | 11, 107 | Kelly, Joseph | 25–6 |
| Fares increases | 42, 51 | Kilfedder, Jim | 7, 33 |
| Faulkner, Brian | 9, 11–2, 43, 52, 162 | Killops, Thomas | 32, 101, 103, 162–3 |
| Ferguson, John | 156 | Lambert, Jim | 144 |
| Ferris, Bill | 37–8 | Leeson Street | 170 |
| Feystown | 21–2 | Lemass, Sean | 6 |
| Finaghy | 36, 108, 138 | Leopard | 30, 44, 72–4, 78–9, 87, 94, 109, 124, 131 |
| Fitt, Gerry | 12, 14, 77 | | |
| FitzGerald, Garrett | 14 | Ligoniel | 27, 40–1, 45, 139, 147 |
| Fleetline | 23, 26, 29, 3–9, 52, 84–5, 93, 107, 112, 120, 144, 147, 149, 152 | Lisburn | 5, 34, 41, 62, 124, 126 |
| | | London | 6–19, 29, 44, 48–9, 56, 58, 61–72, 81, 87–91, 97, 102, 131–3, 137, 143, 148 |
| Frazer, Alex | 124 | | |
| Gallagher, George | 127, 130 | London Country | 88–90 |
| Gibson, James | 104, 162–3 | London Transport | 29, 56, 58, 68, 71–2, 81, 87, 89–91, 132, 143 |
| Gibson, Robert | 32, 162 | | |
| Glen Road | 25, 34, 36–7, 41, 43, 62, 75, 86, 108–13, 137–42, 148, 154 | Londonderry | 6, 9, 15, 18–9, 44, 61, 63–5, 69, 71, 131, 133 |

Lough Swilly 18, 20, 56, 12–9
Lurgan 16, 36, 57–8
Maguire, Kevin 137, 139
Markets 8, 11, 39, 50, 52
McClune, Hugh 55, 139
McCracken, David 68, 80
McCrory, Brian 37, 119
McDaid, Tony 127
McDowell, David 27–8, 162–3
McGinley, John 129
McGreevy, Eddie 135
McGrogan, Frank 86, 95
McHenry, Frank 114, 119, 122
McMahon, Kate 53, 157
McMonagle, Roy 128–9
Meehan, Brendan 27–8
Merlin 58, 71–2, 87, 89–90, 132, 143
Millar, Alexander 27, 162–3
Millar, Irvine 42, 61, 68
Millisle 45
Mitchell, George 17
Monkstown 44, 59, 108–9
Mountbatten, Earl 13, 28, 123
Mowlam, Mo 17
Murphy, Frank 25, 40, 109, 118, 148, 152
Murray, Michael 33, 80, 127, 129
Narrow Water 28, 123
Newcastle 37, 71
Newry 6, 10, 15, 19–20, 32, 34–5, 46, 76, 125
Newtownabbey 41, 44, 58, 138
Newtownbutler 35
North, Robert 27
Northern Ireland Civil Rights Association 8, 23
O'Callaghan, Eugene 53, 64, 66, 100, 104, 164
O'Neill, Captain Terence 6, 8, 11
O'Neill, Denis 5, 153
Oldpark Road 28, 40–1
Oliver, Richard 25
Operation *Harvest* 6
Operation *Motorman* 132
Paisley, Rev Ian 6–13, 22, 28, 44, 65, 101
Papal Visit 56

Pennyburn 44, 70, 127–33
People's taxis 36, 52, 98
PD3 (Leyland) 59, 93, 108–10, 113–4, 128
Pomeroy 18, 39
Rostrevor 19–21
*Routes* project 5, 61, 100, 107, 148, 181
Rush, Samuel 26, 162–3
Sackville Street, Dublin 5
Saor Uladh 6
Shankill Road 7–10, 16, 23, 28, 35, 41–5, 60, 85, 98–9, 109–11, 120, 138, 151, 154, 156
Shore Road 35–6, 85, 98–9, 110–1, 115, 134, 139–40
Short Strand 24, 32, 39, 45, 63, 81, 83, 87, 89, 96, 109, 114–9, 138, 149, 152–3, 159, 162
'Skippy' 126
Smithfield 59, 78, 108
Springmartin 40, 45–6, 51, 150, 157
Stitt, Gerard 27–8
Strabane 10, 15, 127, 130–1
Strikes 13, 57, 101, 103, 123, 125, 141
Swift 29, 72, 82, 84, 89–91, 111, 143
Tall Ships Race 57
Thatcher, Margaret 13–4
Tiger Cub 31, 59, 71, 87, 130
Tokens 51–5, 141
Toomebridge 20–1
Translink 5, 48–9, 61, 158
Turf Lodge 10, 25, 28, 36, 39, 109, 120, 138, 154
Twinbrook 40, 123–7
Ulster Defence Association (UDA) 11, 13, 17, 27, 43–5, 64–8, 98, 102–3, 109, 111–5, 123, 126, 141, 163
Ulster Defence Regiment 10, 63, 129
Ulster Transport Authority (UTA) 2, 5, 18–22, 43, 46–8, 61, 68–9, 100, 108, 113, 129, 151
Ulster Workers Council Strike 97
Ulster Workers' Council (UWC) 12,–3, 43, 86, 111
Ulsterbus 5, 12, 18, 23–88, 93–4, 98, 100, 104, 107–0, 112–3, 122–6, 131–4, 140, 144, 161–4
Wallace Arnold 40
Wilson, Harold 7–9, 12, 43